BEST-EVER 300
POTATO
RECIPES

Delicious recipes
featuring the
world's best-loved
vegetable, in over
300 photographs

BEST-EVER 300
POTATO
RECIPES

ELIZABETH WOODLAND

southwater

This edition is published by Southwater, an imprint of Anness Publishing Ltd, Hermes House, 88–89 Blackfriars Road, London SE1 8HA; tel. 020 7401 2077; fax 020 7633 9499 www.southwaterbooks.com; www.annesspublishing.com

If you like the images in this book and would like to investigate using them for publishing, promotions or advertising, please visit our website www.practicalpictures.com for more information.

UK agent/distributor: Book Trade Services; tel. 0116 2759086; fax 0116 2759090; uksales@booktradeservices.com; exportsales@booktradeservices.com
North American distributor: National Book Network; tel. 301 459 3366; fax 301 429 5746; www.nbnbooks.com
Australian distributor: Pan Macmillan Australia; tel. 1300 135 113; fax 1300 135 103; customer.service@macmillan.com.au
New Zealand distributor: David Bateman Ltd; tel. (09) 415 7664; fax (09) 415 8892

Publisher: Joanna Lorenz
Project Editor: Daniel Hurst
Jacket Design: Adelle Morris
Proofreading Manager: Lindsay Zamponi
Production Controller: Christine Ni

ETHICAL TRADING POLICY
At Anness Publishing we believe that business should be conducted in an ethical and ecologically sustainable way, with respect for the environment and a proper regard to the replacement of the natural resources we employ. As a publisher, we use a lot of wood pulp to make high-quality paper for printing, and that wood commonly comes from spruce trees. We are therefore currently growing more than 750,000 trees in three Scottish forest plantations: Berrymoss (130 hectares/320 acres), West Touxhill (125 hectares/305 acres) and Deveron Forest (75 hectares/185 acres). The forests we manage contain more than 3.5 times the number of trees employed each year in making paper for the books we manufacture. Because of this ongoing ecological investment programme, you, as our customer, can have the pleasure and reassurance of knowing that a tree is being cultivated on your behalf to naturally replace the materials used to make the book you are holding. Our forestry programme is run in accordance with the UK Woodland Assurance Scheme (UKWAS) and will be certified by the internationally recognized Forest Stewardship Council (FSC). The FSC is a non-government organization dedicated to promoting responsible management of the world's forests. Certification ensures forests are managed in an environmentally sustainable and socially responsible way.
For further information about this scheme, go to www.annesspublishing.com/trees

Previously published as part of a larger volume, *500 Potato Recipes*

PUBLISHER'S NOTE
Although the advice and information in this book are believed to be accurate and true at the time of going to press, neither the authors nor the publisher can accept any legal responsibility or liability for any errors or omissions that may have been made nor for any inaccuracies nor for any loss, harm or injury that comes about from following instructions or advice in this book.

Notes

Bracketed terms are intended for American readers.

For all recipes, quantities are given in both metric and imperial measures and, where appropriate, in standard cups and spoons. Follow one set of measures, but not a mixture, because they are not interchangeable.

Standard spoon and cup measures are level. 1 tsp = 5ml, 1 tbsp = 15ml, 1 cup = 250ml/8fl oz. Australian standard tablespoons are 20ml. Australian readers should use 3 tsp in place of 1 tbsp for measuring small quantities.

American pints are 16fl oz/2 cups. American readers should use 20fl oz/2.5 cups in place of 1 pint when measuring liquids. Electric oven temperatures in this book are for conventional ovens. When using a fan oven, the temperature will probably need to be reduced by about 10–20°C/20–40°F. Since ovens vary, you should check with your manufacturer's instruction book for guidance. The nutritional analysis given for each recipe is calculated per portion (i.e. serving or item), unless otherwise stated. If the recipe gives a range, such as Serves 4–6, then the nutritional analysis will be for the smaller portion size, i.e. 6 servings. Measurements for sodium do not include salt added to taste. Medium (US large) eggs are used unless otherwise stated.

Main front cover image shows Baked Jacket Potatoes – for recipe see page 136.

Contents

Introduction

There are few more important foods in the world than the potato. Its history goes back to the early days of man and it has long played a vital role as one of the best all-round sources of nutrition for mankind.

The potato was discovered by pre-Inca inhabitants in the foothills of the Andes Mountains in South America. Archaeological remains have been found dating from 400BC on the shores of Lake Titicaca, in ruins near Bolivia, and on the coast of Peru.

The first recorded information about the potato was written in 1553 by the Spanish conquistador Pedro Cieza de Leon, and soon potatoes joined the treasures carried away by Spanish invaders. Its cultivation spread quickly throughout Europe via explorers such as Sir Francis Drake, who is reputed to have brought potatoes back to Britain. During Charles II's reign, the Royal Society recognized the potato as being nutritional and inexpensive and tried to persuade their farmers to start growing this valuable crop in abundance.

The United States, one of the world's largest producers of potatoes, was introduced to the potato by early European immigrants, but it was not until the Irish took the potato to Londonderry, New Hampshire, in 1719, that it began to be grown in any quantity.

Today the potato is the staple food for two-thirds of the world's population and our third most important food crop. Its high carbohydrate content makes it an excellent source of energy and growing potatoes is the world's most efficient means of converting land, water and labour into an edible product – a field of potatoes can produce more energy per acre per day than a field of any other crop.

This book explores the infinite adaptability of the potato and is the ultimate resource for the potato-loving cook. As you'd expect, it includes all the classic potato dishes, such as Rosemary Potato Wedges, Shepherd's Pie and Irish Potato Soup, but we've also investigated every conceivable way of introducing our favourite ingredient into some familiar and much-loved dishes. There are delicious and deceptively healthy Thai Potato Samosas, a rich and luxurious Fish Pie with Saffron Mash, an exotic and delicately spiced Beef Tagine with Sweet Potatoes and an unusual, and truly decadent, Chocolate Potato Cake.

Other tempting and surprising recipes include a flavoursome Aubergine and Sweet Potato Stew, an impressive Spicy Potato Strudel, and a delightfully piquant Devil's Chicken and Potato Curry. There are countless distinctive variations of classic and mouthwatering potato dishes as well as a seemingly endless array of new and exciting recipes that will be sure to broaden your potato repertoire and have you cooking delectable potato dishes every day of the week.

The recipes are neatly split into eight easy-to-use sections which divide the book between Soups; Appetizers and Snacks; Salads; Fish and Shellfish; Meat and Poultry; Vegetable Dishes; Side Dishes; and finally Desserts, Bakes and Breads, making it easy to find the ideal potato dish, whatever the occasion. Whether you are looking for a sensational potato recipe for an elaborate formal dinner party, a simple and nutritious dish for a mid-week family meal, or a light and tasty snack to keep you going through the afternoon, the plethora of wonderful potato recipes on display here will be sure to deliver the perfect dish time and time again.

This book is the ultimate celebration of an underrated staple of the vegetable kingdom and clearly illustrates the many delicious uses of the potato, whatever the variety – whether you are using large maincrop potatoes, small new potatoes or candied sweet potatoes. So go on – expand your culinary horizons and unlock the potential of the nutritional powerhouse of the vegetable world, the humble potato, today.

Irish Potato Soup

This most Irish of all soups is not only excellent as it is, but versatile too, as it can be used as an ideal base for numerous other delicious soups.

Serves 6–8
50g/2oz/¼ cup butter
2 large onions, peeled and finely chopped

675g/1½lb floury potatoes, diced
about 1.75 litres/3 pints/7½ cups hot chicken stock
sea salt and ground black pepper
a little milk, if necessary
chopped fresh chives, to garnish

1 Melt the butter in a large heavy pan and add the onions, turning them in the butter until well coated. Cover and leave to sweat over a very low heat for about 10 minutes.

2 Add the potatoes to the pan, and mix well with the butter and onions. Season with salt and pepper, cover and cook without browning over a gentle heat for about 10 minutes.

3 Add the stock, bring to the boil and simmer for 25 minutes, or until the vegetables are tender.

4 Remove the pan from the heat and allow the soup to cool slightly. Press the soup through a sieve (strainer) or pass it through a food mill, and return to the rinsed-out pan.

5 Reheat the soup over a low heat and adjust the seasoning. If the soup seems too thick, add a little extra stock or milk to achieve the right consistency.

6 Ladle the soup into warmed bowls. Sprinkle each serving with chopped chives and serve immediately.

> **Cook's Tip**
> *The best potatoes to use in soups are the floury ones, because they cook more quickly and disintegrate easily. Choose varieties such as Golden Wonder, Estima and King Edward.*

Leek and Potato with Heart of Palm Soup

This delicate soup has a luxurious, creamy, almost velvety texture. The subtle yet distinctive flavour of the hearts of palm complements the delicate traditional tastes of leek and potato. Serve with fresh bread for a really satisfying lunch.

Serves 4
25g/1oz/2 tbsp butter
10ml/2 tsp olive oil
1 onion, finely chopped
1 large leek, finely sliced

15ml/1 tbsp plain (all-purpose) flour
1 litre/1¾ pints/4 cups well-flavoured chicken stock
350g/12oz potatoes, peeled and cubed
2 x 400g/14oz cans hearts of palm, drained and sliced
250ml/8fl oz/1 cup double (heavy) cream
salt and ground black pepper
cayenne pepper and chopped fresh chives, to garnish

1 Heat the butter and oil in a large pan over a low heat. Add the onion and leek and stir well until coated in butter. Cover and cook for 5 minutes until softened and translucent.

2 Sprinkle the flour into the pan over the vegetables. Stir and cook, still stirring, for 1 minute.

3 Pour in the stock and add the potatoes. Bring to the boil, stirring, then lower the heat and simmer for 10 minutes. Stir in the hearts of palm and the cream, and simmer gently for a further 10 minutes.

4 Process the soup in a food processor or blender until smooth. Pour it back into the rinsed-out pan and heat gently, adding a little water if necessary. The consistency should be thick but not too heavy. Do not allow to boil. Season with salt and ground black pepper.

5 Ladle the soup into warm bowls and garnish each portion with a pinch of cayenne pepper and a sprinkling of fresh chives. Serve immediately.

Irish Potato Soup Energy 167kcal/699kJ; Protein 2.9g; Carbohydrate 23.5g, of which sugars 5.3g; Fat 7.5g, of which saturates 4.5g; Cholesterol 18mg; Calcium 26mg; Fibre 2.1g; Sodium 201mg.
Leek and Potato Energy 486kcal/2013kJ; Protein 5.2g; Carbohydrate 25.1g, of which sugars 7.9g; Fat 41.2g, of which saturates 24.5g; Cholesterol 99mg; Calcium 147mg; Fibre 4.9g; Sodium 184mg.

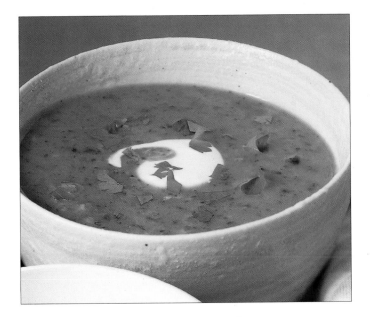

Cabbage and Potato Soup with Caraway

Earthy floury potatoes are essential to the texture of this soup, so it is best not to use waxy salad potatoes. Caraway seeds come from a plant in the parsley family. They are aromatic and nutty, with a delicate anise flavour, adding a subtle accent to this smooth and satisfying dish.

Serves 4
30ml/2 tbsp olive oil
2 small onions, sliced
6 garlic cloves, halved
350g/12oz green
  cabbage, shredded
4 potatoes, unpeeled
5ml/1 tsp caraway seeds
5ml/1 tsp sea salt
1.2 litres/2 pints/5 cups
  boiling water

1 Pour the olive oil into a large pan and add the onions. Cook, stirring occasionally, for 10 minutes, until the onions are softened, but not browned.

2 Add the garlic and the cabbage and continue to cook over a low heat for 10 minutes, stirring occasionally to prevent the cabbage from sticking.

3 Add the potatoes, caraway seeds, sea salt and water. Bring to the boil. Reduce the heat and cover the pan, then simmer until all the vegetables are cooked through, about 20–30 minutes.

4 Remove the pan from the heat and allow the soup to cool slightly before mashing it into a purée or processing in a food processor. Pass the soup through a sieve (strainer), if you like.

5 Return the soup to the rinsed-out pan and reheat gently, stirring, until almost boiling before serving.

Cook's Tip
Use floury potatoes to achieve the correct texture for this soup. King Edward or Maris Piper (US russet or Idaho) are excellent choices. Peel the potatoes if preferred or if they are old.

Potato and Mushroom Soup

Using a mixture of mushrooms in this soup adds character and the flavour mingles well with the earthy potatoes. Serve with fresh crusty bread.

Serves 4–6 as a light meal or 6–8 as a soup course
20g/¾oz/1½ tbsp butter
15ml/1 tbsp oil
1 onion, roughly chopped
4 potatoes, about 250–350g/
  9–12oz, roughly chopped

350g/12oz mixed mushrooms,
  such as brown cap (cremini),
  field (portabello) and button
  (white), roughly chopped
1 or 2 garlic cloves, crushed
150ml/¼ pint/⅔ cup white wine
  or dry (hard) cider
1.2 litres/2 pints/5 cups
  vegetable stock
bunch of fresh parsley, chopped
salt and ground black pepper
whipped or sour cream, to garnish

1 Heat the butter and oil in a large pan, over medium heat. Add the onion and potatoes. Cover and sweat over a low heat for 5–10 minutes until softened but not browned.

2 Add the mushrooms, garlic and white wine or cider and stock. Season, bring to the boil and cook for 15 minutes, until all the ingredients are tender.

3 Put the mixture through a food mill, using the coarse blade, or purée in a food processor or blender.

4 Return the soup to the rinsed-out pan, and add three-quarters of the parsley. Reheat and taste for seasoning, adding more salt or pepper if necessary. Serve garnished with cream and the remaining parsley.

Variation
Mustard and tarragon are a delicious combination together with mushrooms: try adding 15ml/1 tbsp wholegrain mustard to the onions and potatoes before stirring in the stock. For a hint of sweetness, use a medium sherry instead of the wine or cider, and add the leaves from a large sprig of fresh tarragon.

Mushroom Soup Energy 155kcal/648kJ; Protein 3.3g; Carbohydrate 13.6g, of which sugars 3.4g; Fat 7.6g, of which saturates 3.1g; Cholesterol 11mg; Calcium 23mg; Fibre 2.1g; Sodium 117mg.
Cabbage and Potato Energy 144kcal/601kJ; Protein 3.1g; Carbohydrate 20.4g, of which sugars 8.1g; Fat 6g, of which saturates 0.9g; Cholesterol 0mg; Calcium 60mg; Fibre 3.3g; Sodium 507mg.

Country Vegetable Soup

Soup-making is a good way to make the most of seasonal vegetables. It is also a great way of making healthy meals from the best selection of frozen foods – plain frozen vegetables that cook fast and taste terrific. Serve this classic mixed vegetable soup with crusty bread and perhaps a wedge of cheese as a light meal.

Serves 6
15ml/1 tbsp oil
25g/1oz/2 tbsp butter
2 onions, finely chopped

4 carrots, sliced
2 celery sticks, sliced
2 leeks, sliced
1 potato, cut into small cubes
1 small parsnip, cut into small cubes
1 garlic clove, crushed
900ml/1½ pints/3¾ cups vegetable stock
300ml/½ pint/1¼ cups milk
25g/1oz/4 tbsp cornflour (cornstarch)
handful of frozen peas
30ml/2 tbsp chopped fresh parsley
salt and ground black pepper

1 Heat the oil and butter in a large pan and add the onions, carrots and celery. Cook over a medium heat for 5–10 minutes, stirring occasionally, until soft and just beginning to turn golden brown. Stir in the leeks, potato, parsnip and garlic.

2 Add the stock to the pan and stir into the vegetables. Bring the mixture slowly to the boil, reduce the heat if necessary and cover the pan. Simmer gently for 20–30 minutes until all the vegetables are soft.

3 Stir the milk into the cornflour to make a smooth paste. Stir into the vegetables. Add the frozen peas. Bring to the boil and simmer for 5 minutes, season to taste, add the parsley, and serve.

> **Variation**
> For a freezer soup, use onion as the base, with whatever other fresh vegetables you have. From a typical freezer stock, add any of the following: mixed vegetables, broccoli, broad (fava) and runner (green) beans, corn, peas, baby Brussels sprouts and cauliflower.

Creamy Corn, Cannellini Bean and Potato Chowder

This creamy, yet chunky, potato soup is filled with the sweet taste of corn. Punchy Cheddar cheese rounds off the fabulous flavour.

Serves 4
1 onion, chopped
1 garlic clove, crushed
1 baking potato, chopped
2 celery sticks, sliced
1 small green (bell) pepper, seeded, halved and sliced

30ml/2 tbsp sunflower oil
25g/1oz/2 tbsp butter
600ml/1 pint/2½ cups vegetable stock or water
300ml/½ pint/1¼ cups milk
200g/7oz can flageolet (small cannellini) beans
300g/11oz can corn
good pinch of dried sage or a few small fresh sage leaves
salt and ground black pepper
Cheddar cheese or Monterey Jack, grated, to serve

1 Put the onion, garlic, potato, celery and green pepper into a large heavy pan with the oil and butter.

2 Heat until the ingredients are sizzling, then reduce the heat to low. Cover and cook for 10 minutes, shaking the pan occasionally.

3 Pour in the stock or water, season with salt and pepper and bring to the boil. Reduce the heat, cover again and simmer gently for about 15 minutes or until the vegetables are tender.

4 Add the milk, beans and corn, including the liquor from the cans. Stir in the sage. Heat until simmering, then cook gently, uncovered, for 5 minutes. Check the seasoning before ladling the chowder into bowls. Sprinkle with cheese and serve immediately.

> **Variations**
> • Chickpeas are delicious with corn – add a can as well as the flageolet (small cannellini) beans.
> • For refreshingly spicy, zesty flavour, peel and chop a large chunk of fresh root ginger and cook it with the vegetables. Then add the grated rind of one lemon with the sage.

Country Vegetable Energy 160kcal/665kJ; Protein 3.6g; Carbohydrate 11.5g, of which sugars 10g; Fat 11.4g, of which saturates 6.8g; Cholesterol 27mg; Calcium 72mg; Fibre 5.4g; Sodium 106mg.
Corn and Potato Energy 320kcal/1347kJ; Protein 9.4g; Carbohydrate 43.2g, of which sugars 15.7g; Fat 13.5g, of which saturates 5g; Cholesterol 18mg; Calcium 119mg; Fibre 5g; Sodium 500mg.

Jerusalem Artichoke and Potato Soup with Anchovy Bruschetta

Jerusalem artichokes are a nutty and delicious addition to this potato soup.

Serves 6
squeeze of lemon juice
450g/1lb Jerusalem artichokes, peeled and diced
65g/2½oz/5 tbsp butter
175g/6oz potatoes, roughly diced
1 small onion, chopped
1 garlic clove, chopped
1 celery stick, chopped
1 small fennel bulb, chopped
1.2 litres/2 pints/5 cups vegetable stock
300ml/½ pint/1¼ cups double (heavy) cream
pinch of freshly grated nutmeg
salt and ground black pepper
basil leaves, to garnish

For the bruschetta
6 thick slices French bread
1 garlic clove, halved
50g/2oz/¼ cup unsalted (sweet) butter
400g/14oz can artichoke hearts, drained and halved
45ml/3 tbsp tapenade
9 salted anchovy fillets, halved lengthways

1 Prepare a bowl of water with lemon juice. Add the artichokes to the water to prevent discoloration.

2 Melt the butter in a large pan. Drain the artichokes and add to the pan with the potatoes, onion, garlic, celery and fennel. Cook for 10 minutes, stirring occasionally, until softening.

3 Add the stock, bring to the boil, and simmer for around 10–15 minutes, until all the vegetables are soft. Cool slightly, then purée until smooth. Add the cream and nutmeg, and season well.

4 For the bruschetta, lightly toast the French bread on both sides. Rub with the cut side of the garlic. Melt the butter in a small pan. Add the artichoke hearts and cook for 3–4 minutes, turning once.

5 Spread the tapenade on the toast and arrange the artichoke hearts on top. Top with anchovy fillets and garnish with basil.

6 Reheat the soup without boiling, then ladle it into shallow bowls. Serve the bruschetta with the soup.

Celeriac, Potato and Bacon Soup

Versatile, yet often overlooked, celeriac is a winter vegetable that makes excellent soup and is the perfect companion to potatoes.

Serves 4
50g/2oz/¼ cup butter
2 onions, chopped
675g/1½lb celeriac, roughly diced
450g/1lb potatoes, roughly diced
1.2 litres/2 pints/5 cups vegetable stock
150ml/¼ pint/⅔ cup single (light) cream
salt and ground black pepper
sprigs of fresh thyme, to garnish

For the topping
1 small Savoy cabbage
50g/2oz/¼ cup butter
175g/6oz rindless streaky (fatty) bacon, roughly chopped
15ml/1 tbsp roughly chopped fresh thyme
15ml/1 tbsp roughly chopped fresh rosemary

1 Melt the butter in a pan. Add the onions and cook for 4–5 minutes, until softened, then add the celeriac. Put a lid on the pan and cook gently for 10 minutes.

2 Stir in the potatoes and stock. Bring to the boil, reduce the heat and simmer for 20 minutes or until the vegetables are tender. Leave to cool slightly. Using a slotted spoon, remove about half the celeriac and potatoes and set them aside.

3 Purée the soup in a food processor or blender. Return it to the rinsed-out pan with the reserved celeriac and potatoes.

4 Prepare the topping. Discard the tough outer leaves from the cabbage. Roughly tear the remaining leaves, discarding any hard stalks, and blanch them in boiling salted water for 2–3 minutes. Refresh under cold running water and drain.

5 Melt the butter in a large frying pan and cook the bacon for 3–4 minutes. Add the cabbage, thyme and rosemary, and stir-fry for 5–6 minutes, until tender. Season well.

6 Add the cream to the soup and season it well, then reheat gently. Ladle the soup into bowls and pile the cabbage mixture in the middle. Garnish with sprigs of fresh thyme.

Artichoke Soup Energy 533kcal/2212kJ; Protein 7.2g; Carbohydrate 25.9g, of which sugars 4.3g; Fat 45.3g, of which saturates 27.1g; Cholesterol 114mg; Calcium 167mg; Fibre 3.4g; Sodium 787mg.
Celeriac and Potato Energy 462kcal/1919kJ; Protein 12.3g; Carbohydrate 24.3g, of which sugars 7.3g; Fat 35.8g, of which saturates 20.4g; Cholesterol 97mg; Calcium 144mg; Fibre 4.3g; Sodium 954mg.

Vegetable Noodle Soup

Potatoes and noodles are a good soup combination, especially on cold winter days. This tasty and warming soup, served with warm crusty bread, is both substantial and delicious, making it the perfect lunchtime energy boost.

Serves 4

1 large onion, finely sliced
25g/1oz/2 tbsp butter
350g/12oz potatoes, peeled and diced

900ml/1½ pints/3¾ cups vegetable stock
1 bay leaf
salt and ground black pepper

For the drop noodles

75g/3oz/⅔ cup self-raising (self-rising) flour
pinch of salt
15g/½oz/1 tbsp butter
15ml/1 tbsp chopped fresh parsley, plus a little extra to garnish
1 egg, beaten
crusty bread, to serve

1 In a wide, heavy pan, cook the onion in the butter gently for 10 minutes, or until it begins to brown.

2 Add the diced potatoes and cook for 2–3 minutes, then pour in the vegetable stock. Add the bay leaf, salt and pepper. Slowly bring to the boil, then reduce the heat, cover and simmer gently for 10 minutes.

3 Meanwhile, make the noodles. Sift the flour and salt into a bowl and rub in the butter. Stir in the parsley, then add the egg to the flour mixture and mix to a soft dough.

4 Drop half-teaspoonfuls of the noodle dough into the gently simmering soup. Cover the pan and simmer gently for a further 10 minutes.

5 To serve, ladle the soup into warmed deep bowls, sprinkle over a little parsley, and serve immediately with generous chunks of warm crusty bread.

Cook's Tip
Use old potatoes, of a floury texture, such as King Edwards or Maris Pipers, so that they break down slightly in the soup.

Potato, Cabbage, Beetroot and Tomato Borscht

There are numerous versions of this classic soup, which originates in Eastern Europe. Beetroot and sour cream are the traditional ingredients in every borscht, but other ingredients tend to be many and varied. This slow-cooker version featuring potatoes and cabbage has a deliciously sweet and sour taste and can be served piping hot or refreshingly chilled.

Serves 6

1 onion, chopped
1 carrot, chopped

6 raw or vacuum-packed (cooked, not pickled) beetroot (beets), 4 diced and 2 coarsely grated
400g/14oz can chopped tomatoes
6 new potatoes, cut into bitesize pieces
1 small white cabbage, thinly sliced
600ml/1 pint/2½ cups vegetable stock
45ml/3 tbsp sugar
30–45ml/2–3 tbsp white wine vinegar or cider vinegar
45ml/3 tbsp chopped fresh dill
salt and ground black pepper
sour cream and dill, to garnish
buttered rye bread, to serve

1 Put the onion, carrot, diced beetroot, tomatoes, potatoes and cabbage into the ceramic cooking pot of a slow cooker and pour over the vegetable stock. Cover the cooking pot with the lid and cook in the slow cooker on high for about 4 hours, or until the vegetables are just tender.

2 Add the grated beetroot, sugar and vinegar to the slow cooker and stir to combine. Cook for a further hour until the beetroot is cooked through.

3 Taste the soup, checking for a good sweet/sour balance, and add more sugar and/or vinegar if necessary. Season to taste with plenty of salt and ground black pepper.

4 Just before serving, stir the chopped dill into the soup and ladle into warmed soup bowls. Garnish each serving with a generous spoonful of sour cream and plenty more fresh dill, then serve with thick slices of buttered rye bread.

Vegetable Noodle Energy 241kcal/1010kJ; Protein 5.7g; Carbohydrate 33.6g, of which sugars 4.9g; Fat 10.3g, of which saturates 5.7g; Cholesterol 69mg; Calcium 63mg; Fibre 2.5g; Sodium 91mg.
Cabbage Borscht Energy 125kcal/531kJ; Protein 3.5g; Carbohydrate 27.8g, of which sugars 7g; Fat 0.7g, of which saturates 0.1g; Cholesterol 0mg; Calcium 58mg; Fibre 3.2g; Sodium 357mg.

Creamy Cauliflower and Potato Soup

This soup is light in flavour, yet the potatoes add volume and make it silky, thick and satisfying enough for a lunchtime snack.

Serves 6

30ml/2 tbsp olive oil
2 large onions, finely diced
1 garlic clove, crushed
3 large floury potatoes, finely diced
3 celery sticks, finely diced
1.75 litres/3 pints/7½ cups vegetable stock
2 carrots, finely diced
1 medium cauliflower, chopped
15ml/1 tbsp chopped fresh dill
15ml/1 tbsp lemon juice
5ml/1 tsp mustard powder
1.5ml/¼ tsp caraway seeds
300ml/½ pint/1¼ cups single (light) cream
salt and ground black pepper
shredded spring onions (scallions), to garnish

1 Heat the oil in a large heavy pan, add the onions and garlic and fry them for a few minutes until they soften.

2 Add the diced potatoes and celery to the pan. Pour in the stock and simmer for 10 minutes.

3 Stir the carrots into the pan and simmer the vegetables for a further 10 minutes.

4 Mix in the cauliflower, fresh dill, lemon juice, mustard powder and caraway seeds and simmer for 20 minutes.

5 Press the soup through a sieve (strainer) by pressing it with a wooden spoon, or pass it through a food mill, and return the mixture to the rinsed-out pan.

6 Stir in the cream, season to taste and serve, garnished with shredded spring onions.

> **Cook's Tip**
> Fresh vegetable stock can be made simply by simmering vegetables in water for around an hour and then straining. For the best flavour avoid bitter vegetables such as cabbage.

Cauliflower and Potato Soup with Broccoli and Bacon

Creamy cauliflower soup is given real bite by adding garlic, potato and broccoli florets. This is delicious generously topped with melting Cheddar cheese and served with crusty bread.

Serves 4

1 onion, chopped
1 garlic clove, chopped
50g/2oz/¼ cup butter
2 cauliflowers, broken into florets
1 large potato, cut into chunks
900ml/1½ pints/3¾ cups chicken stock
225g/8oz broccoli, cut into florets
150ml/¼ pint/⅔ cup single (light) cream
6 rindless streaky (fatty) bacon rashers (strips)
1 small baguette, cut into 4 pieces
225g/8oz/2 cups medium-mature Cheddar cheese, grated
salt and ground black pepper
chopped fresh parsley, to garnish

1 Cook the onion and garlic in the butter for 4–5 minutes. Add half the cauliflower, all the potato and the stock. Bring to the boil, reduce the heat and simmer for 20 minutes.

2 Boil the remaining cauliflower for about 6 minutes, or until just tender. Use a draining spoon to remove the florets and rinse under cold running water, then drain well. Cook the broccoli in the water for 3–4 minutes, until just tender. Drain, refresh under cold water, then add to the cauliflower.

3 Cool the soup slightly, then purée it until smooth and return it to the rinsed pan. Add the cream and seasoning, then heat gently. Add the cauliflower and broccoli and heat through.

4 Preheat the grill (broiler) to high. Grill (broil) the bacon until crisp, then cool slightly. Ladle the soup into flameproof bowls.

5 Place a piece of baguette in each bowl. Sprinkle grated cheese over the top and grill for 2–3 minutes, until the cheese is melted and bubbling. Take care when serving the hot bowls.

6 Crumble the bacon and sprinkle it over the melted cheese, then scatter the parsley over the top and serve immediately.

Creamy Cauliflower Energy 169kcal/711kJ; Protein 7.4g; Carbohydrate 27.7g, of which sugars 10.8g; Fat 4g, of which saturates 1.1g; Cholesterol 3mg; Calcium 111mg; Fibre 4g; Sodium 55mg.
Cauliflower Soup Energy 737kcal/3071kJ; Protein 34.8g; Carbohydrate 45.5g, of which sugars 9.2g; Fat 46.2g, of which saturates 26.4g; Cholesterol 121mg; Calcium 589mg; Fibre 6.6g; Sodium 1206mg.

Chunky Corn, Pepper and Sweet Potato Soup

The combination of corn kernels and sweet potato gives this soup a flavour that is deep and delicious.

Serves 6
15ml/1 tbsp olive oil
1 onion, finely chopped
2 garlic cloves, crushed
1 small red chilli, seeded and
   finely chopped
1.75 litres/3 pints/7½ cups
   vegetable stock
10ml/2 tsp ground cumin
1 medium sweet potato, diced
½ red (bell) pepper,
   finely chopped
450g/1lb corn kernels
salt and ground black pepper
lime wedges, to serve

1 Heat the oil in a large heavy pan and fry the onion for about 5 minutes until softened. Add the garlic and chilli and fry for a further 2 minutes.

2 In the same pan, add 300ml/½ pint/1¼ cups of the stock, and simmer for 10 minutes.

3 Mix the cumin with a little stock to form a paste and then stir into the soup. Add the diced sweet potato, stir and simmer for 10 minutes. Season to taste with salt and black pepper and stir again.

4 Add the chopped pepper, corn kernels and the remaining stock to the pan and simmer for 10 minutes.

5 Process half of the soup in a blender or food processor until smooth and then stir into the chunky soup. Check the seasoning and serve with lime wedges for squeezing over.

Cook's Tip
You may need to wear rubber gloves when chopping fresh chillies as the oils from the chilli may cause irritation to the skin, or inflammation to the eyes if touched after handling.

Creamy Chicken and Potato Soup

A flavoursome creamy chicken soup thickened with potatoes makes a fabulous lunch served with crispy bread. It is essential to use a really strong, home-made chicken stock for this recipe to give the soup a full flavour.

Serves 6
50g/2oz/¼ cup butter
2 onions, chopped
2 medium potatoes, chopped
1 large carrot, diced
1 celery stick, diced
750ml/1¼ pints/3 cups
   chicken stock
25g/1oz/¼ cup plain
   (all-purpose) flour
150ml/¼ pint/ ⅔ cup milk
175g/6oz cooked chicken
300ml/½ pint/1¼ cups single
   (light) cream
salt and ground black pepper
parsley leaves, to garnish

1 Melt the butter in a large pan and cook the onions, potatoes, carrot and celery gently for 5 minutes. Do not allow the vegetables to brown.

2 Add the stock and simmer gently for 30 minutes. Season with salt and pepper to taste. Purée the soup in a food processor or blender until smooth and then return to the pan. Blend the flour with the milk and stir into the soup. Cook over a low heat, stirring, until the soup thickens.

3 Meanwhile, chop the chicken finely. Add to the soup and heat through for 5 minutes. Add 75ml/2½fl oz/⅓ cup of the cream and simmer for 5 minutes more.

4 Serve in individual bowls topped with a swirl of the remaining cream and garnished with ground black pepper and parsley leaves.

Cook's Tip
Fresh parsley is simple to grow yourself. Buy a plant and keep it on a sunny windowsill in your kitchen. Ensure it is kept moist but don't over-water it and pull off the leaves as and when you need them. They will regrow in a matter of days.

Corn and Sweet Potato Energy 146kcal/618kJ; Protein 2.9g; Carbohydrate 28.9g, of which sugars 10.7g; Fat 2.9g, of which saturates 0.5g; Cholesterol 0mg; Calcium 15mg; Fibre 2.3g; Sodium 217mg.
Creamy Chicken Soup Energy 295kcal/1231kJ; Protein 11g; Carbohydrate 23.6g, of which sugars 8.9g; Fat 18.2g, of which saturates 11.1g; Cholesterol 61mg; Calcium 111mg; Fibre 2.1g; Sodium 137mg.

Chicken, Pork and Sweet Potato Soup with Aubergine Sauce

A garlicky aubergine sauce mingles well with chicken, pork and sweet potatoes.

Serve 6–8

225g/8oz/generous 1 cup chickpeas, soaked overnight
1.3kg/3lb chicken, cut into eight
350g/12oz belly of pork, rind removed or pork fillet, cubed
2 chorizo, thickly sliced
2 onions, chopped
60ml/4 tbsp vegetable oil
2 garlic cloves, crushed
3 large tomatoes, peeled, seeded and chopped
15ml/1 tbsp tomato purée (paste)
1–2 sweet potatoes, cut into 1cm/½in cubes
2 plantains, sliced (optional)
salt and ground black pepper
chives or chopped spring onions (scallions), to garnish
½ head Chinese leaves (Chinese cabbage), shredded, to serve

For the aubergine sauce
1 large aubergine (eggplant), skin pricked in places
3 garlic cloves, crushed
60–90ml/4–6 tbsp wine vinegar or cider vinegar

1 Put the drained chickpeas in a pan with water to cover; boil rapidly for 10 minutes. Reduce the heat and simmer for 30 minutes until the chickpeas are half-tender. Drain.

2 Put the chickpeas, chicken, pork, chorizo and half of the onions in a pan with 2.5 litres/4 pints/10 cups water. Boil, lower the heat, cover and simmer for 1 hour until the meat is tender.

3 Preheat the oven to 200°C/400°F/Gas 6. Bake the aubergine for 30 minutes. Cool, peel and mash with the garlic, seasoning and vinegar to sharpen the sauce.

4 Heat the oil in a pan and fry the remaining onion and garlic for 5 minutes. Add the tomatoes and tomato purée and cook for 2 minutes. Add the sweet potato and plantains, if using. Simmer for 20 minutes until the sweet potato is cooked. Add the Chinese leaves for the last minute or two.

5 Serve the soup and vegetables separately, garnished with chives or spring onions. Serve with the aubergine sauce.

Chicken, Leek and Potato Soup

This chicken and potato soup makes a substantial main course when served with fresh crusty bread.

Serves 4–6

1.4kg/3lb whole chicken
1 small head of celery, trimmed
1 onion, coarsely chopped
1 bouquet garni
3 large leeks
65g/2½oz/5 tbsp butter
2 potatoes, cut into chunks
150ml/¼ pint/⅔ cup dry white wine
30–45ml/2–3 tbsp single (light) cream (optional)
salt and ground black pepper
90g/3½oz pancetta, grilled until crisp, to garnish

1 Cut the breasts from the chicken and set aside. Chop the rest of the chicken carcass into eight or ten pieces and place in a large pan. Chop four or five of the celery sticks and add them to the pan with the onion and bouquet garni. Pour in about 2.4 litres/4 pints/10 cups water to cover and bring to the boil. Reduce the heat and cover the pan, then simmer for 1½ hours.

2 Remove the chicken and cut off and reserve the meat. Strain the stock, then return it to the pan and boil rapidly until it has reduced to about 1.5 litres/2½ pints/6¼ cups.

3 Set about 150g/5oz of the leeks aside. Slice the remaining leeks and the remaining celery, reserving any celery leaves. Melt half the butter in a pan. Add the sliced leeks and celery, cover and cook over a low heat for 10 minutes, until soft but not brown. Add the potatoes, wine and 1.2 litres/2 pints/5 cups of the stock. Season, bring to the boil and reduce the heat. Part-cover and simmer for 15–20 minutes, or until the potatoes are cooked.

4 Dice the reserved uncooked chicken. Melt the remaining butter in a pan and fry the chicken for 5–7 minutes, until cooked. Slice the remaining leeks, add to the chicken and cook, stirring occasionally, for a further 3–4 minutes, until just cooked.

5 Purée the soup and diced chicken from the stock. Season and add more stock if the soup is thick. Stir in the cream and chicken and leek mixture. Reheat gently and serve topped with pancetta and the chopped reserved celery leaves.

Chicken and Pork Energy 290kcal/1219kJ; Protein 46.4g; Carbohydrate 9.8g, of which sugars 8.7g; Fat 7.5g, of which saturates 1.5g; Cholesterol 169mg; Calcium 40mg; Fibre 2.2g; Sodium 150mg.
Chicken and Leek Energy 294kcal/1246kJ; Protein 40.5g; Carbohydrate 22.1g, of which sugars 5.9g; Fat 2.8g, of which saturates 0.7g; Cholesterol 105mg; Calcium 69mg; Fibre 4.8g; Sodium 124mg.

Spicy Chicken and Potato Broth

This colourful South-east Asian chicken and potato soup can be served as an appetizer or as a dish on its own.

Serves 4–6

30ml/2 tbsp palm, groundnut (peanut) or corn oil
25g/1oz fresh root ginger, finely chopped
5ml/1 tsp ground turmeric
1 lemon grass stalk, finely chopped
4–5 kaffir lime leaves, crushed
4 candlenuts, coarsely ground
2 garlic cloves, crushed
5ml/1 tsp coriander seeds
5ml/1 tsp shrimp paste
2 litres/3½ pints chicken stock

corn or vegetable oil, for deep-frying
2 waxy potatoes, finely sliced
350g/12oz skinless chicken breast fillets, thinly sliced widthways
150g/5oz leafy green cabbage, finely sliced
150g/5oz mung beansprouts
3 hard-boiled eggs, thinly sliced
salt and ground black pepper

To serve

1 bunch fresh coriander (cilantro) leaves, roughly chopped
2–3 spring onions (scallions), finely sliced
2–3 hot red or green chillies, seeded and finely sliced
2 limes, cut into wedges
kecap manis (Indonesian soy sauce)

1 Prepare the ingredients for serving by putting the coriander, spring onions, chillies and lime wedges into a serving bowl.

2 Heat the oil in a pan, stir in the ginger, turmeric, lemon grass, kaffir lime leaves, candlenuts, garlic, coriander seeds and shrimp paste. Fry until the mixture darkens and becomes fragrant. Pour in the stock, bring to the boil, then simmer for about 20 minutes.

3 Meanwhile, heat the oil for deep-frying in a wok. Fry the potato slices until crisp. Remove with a slotted spoon, drain on kitchen paper and put aside. Strain the chicken stock and reserve. Pour back into the pan and season. Return to the boil, reduce the heat and add the chicken. Simmer for 2–3 minutes.

4 Sprinkle the finely sliced cabbage and beansprouts into the base of the serving bowls. Ladle over the broth and top with the thinly sliced boiled eggs and potatoes, and serve. Diners help themselves to the ingredients for serving, and drizzle the kecap manis over the top.

Rich Chicken, Bacon and Potato Minestrone Soup

This special minestrone made with succulent chicken and potatoes makes a hearty meal served with crusty bread.

Serves 4–6

15ml/1 tbsp olive oil
2 chicken thighs
3 rindless streaky (fatty) bacon rashers (strips), chopped
1 onion, finely chopped
a few fresh basil leaves, shredded
a few fresh rosemary leaves, finely chopped
15ml/1 tbsp chopped fresh parsley

2 potatoes, cut into 1cm/½in cubes
1 large carrot, cut into 1cm/½in cubes
2 small courgettes (zucchini), cut into 1cm/½in cubes
1–2 celery sticks, cut into 1cm/½in cubes
1 litre/1¾ pints/4 cups chicken stock
200g/7oz/1¾ cups frozen peas
90g/3½oz/scant 1 cup stellette or other dried tiny soup pasta
salt and ground black pepper
coarsely shaved Parmesan cheese
fresh basil leaves, to garnish

1 Heat the oil in a large frying pan, add the chicken and fry for about 5 minutes on each side. Remove and set aside.

2 Lower the heat, add the bacon, onion and herbs to the pan and stir well. Cook gently, stirring constantly, for 5–7 minutes. Add all the vegetables, except the frozen peas, to the pan and cook for 5–7 minutes more, stirring frequently.

3 Return the chicken thighs to the pan, add the stock and bring to the boil. Cover and cook over a low heat for about 35–40 minutes, stirring the soup occasionally.

4 Remove the chicken thighs with a slotted spoon and place them on a board. Stir the peas and pasta into the soup and bring back to the boil. Simmer, stirring frequently until the pasta is al dente: 7–8 minutes or according to the packet instructions.

5 Meanwhile, remove and discard the chicken skin, then cut the meat from the bones and chop into 1cm/½in pieces. Add the chicken to the soup, season with salt and pepper, and heat through. Serve garnished with Parmesan shavings and basil leaves.

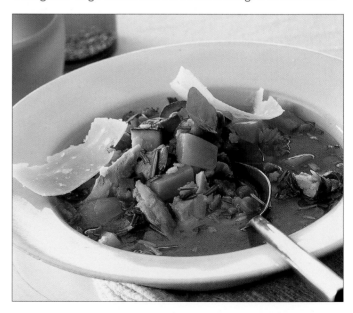

Spicy Broth Energy 296kcal/1238kJ; Protein 21.1g; Carbohydrate 14.8g, of which sugars 3g; Fat 17.5g, of which saturates 2.8g; Cholesterol 136mg; Calcium 63mg; Fibre 2.7g; Sodium 96mg.
Minestrone Energy 226kcal/948kJ; Protein 15.7g; Carbohydrate 25.1g, of which sugars 11.4g; Fat 7.7g, of which saturates 3.2g; Cholesterol 43mg; Calcium 75mg; Fibre 5.2g; Sodium 102mg.

Clear Chickpea and Potato Broth with Sausage

Chickpeas are very versatile and are a terrific addition to soups, providing a boost of flavour and bulk, and transforming a light broth into a substantial meal. Here, the distinctive nutty flavour of the chickpeas is used to enhance the flavours of potato and salami. The flavour can be varied according to the herbs and spices used.

Serves 4–6
500g/1¼lb/3½ cups chickpeas, rinsed and drained
2 litres/3½ pints/8 cups vegetable stock
3 garlic cloves, sliced
3 large waxy potatoes, peeled and cut into bitesize chunks
50ml/2fl oz/¼ cup olive oil
50g/2oz salami, sliced
225g/8oz spinach leaves, washed and drained well
a little freshly grated nutmeg
salt and ground black pepper

1 Place the chickpeas in a large bowl of cold water and leave to soak overnight. The next day, drain them well and place in a large pan with the stock.

2 Bring to the boil, then reduce the heat and cook gently for about 1 hour. Add the garlic, potatoes, olive oil, salami and seasoning and cook for a further 15 minutes, until the potatoes are tender but not broken.

3 Add the spinach leaves to the soup and bring it back to simmering point, then cook for a further 5 minutes, until the spinach has wilted.

4 Season the soup with a little freshly grated nutmeg and taste, adding salt and pepper, if necessary. Ladle into bowls to serve.

> **Variation**
> Instead of salami, slice Polish sausage, ham sausage or garlic sausage to add to the soup with the potatoes. Grilled (broiled) fresh sausages can be sliced and added, if you like.

Kale, Chorizo and Potato Soup

This hearty winter soup with delicious earthy chunks of potato and shredded iron-rich kale is given a spicy kick from the addition of chorizo sausage. The soup becomes more potent if chilled overnight. It is worth buying the best possible chorizo sausage to achieve superior flavour.

Serves 6–8
225g/8oz kale, stems removed
225g/8oz chorizo sausage
675g/1½lb potatoes, cut into chunks
1.75 litres/3 pints/7½ cups vegetable stock
5ml/1 tsp ground black pepper
pinch of cayenne pepper (optional)
12 slices French bread, toasted on both sides
salt and ground black pepper

1 Place the kale in a food processor or blender and process for a few seconds to chop it finely. Alternatively, shred it finely by hand.

2 Prick the sausages and place in a pan with enough water to cover. Bring just to boiling point, then reduce the heat immediately before the water boils too rapidly and simmer for 15 minutes. Drain and cut into thin slices.

3 Boil the potatoes for about 15 minutes or until the slices are just tender. Drain, and place in a bowl, then mash, adding a little of the cooking liquid to form a thick paste.

4 Bring the vegetable stock to the boil and add the kale. Bring back to the boil. Reduce the heat to a simmer and add the chorizo, then cook for 5 minutes. Gradually add the potato paste, stirring it into the soup, then simmer for 20 minutes. Season with black pepper and cayenne pepper.

5 Divide the freshly-made toast among serving bowls. Pour the soup over and serve immediately, sprinkled with black pepper.

> **Cook's Tip**
> Select maincrop, floury potatoes for this soup rather than new potatoes or waxy salad potatoes.

Chickpea Broth Energy 399Kcal/1681kJ; Protein 20.5g; Carbohydrate 58g, of which sugars 4g; Fat 10.9g, of which saturates 1.4g; Cholesterol 0mg; Calcium 203mg; Fibre 10.7g; Sodium 96mg.
Kale and Chorizo Energy 411kcal/1740kJ; Protein 13.2g; Carbohydrate 69.3g, of which sugars 6.2g; Fat 11g, of which saturates 4.1g; Cholesterol 15mg; Calcium 140mg; Fibre 4g; Sodium 812mg.

Tamarind, Pork and Vegetable Soup

This sweet-and-sour soup, flavoured with tamarind, has its roots in South-east Asian cooking. The punchy combination of sweet potato, fish sauce and ginger gives this robust lunchtime dish a delightful piquancy, but despite the exotic sounding ingredients this impressive soup is quick and easy to make.

Serves 4–6

2 litres/3½ pints/8 cups pork or chicken stock, or a mixture of stock and water

15–30ml/1–2 tbsp tamarind paste (see Cook's Tip)
30ml/2 tbsp patis (fish sauce)
25g/1oz fresh root ginger, finely grated
1 sweet potato, cut into bitesize chunks
8–10 snake beans (yard-long beans)
225g/8oz kangkong (water spinach) or ordinary spinach, well rinsed
350g/12oz pork tenderloin, sliced widthways
2–3 spring onions (scallions), white parts only, finely sliced
salt and ground black pepper

1 Bring the stock to the boil in a wok or deep pan. Stir in the tamarind paste, patis and ginger, reduce the heat and simmer for about 20 minutes. Season with salt and lots of pepper.

2 Add the sweet potato and snake beans to the pan and bring back to the boil, then immediately reduce the heat and cook gently for 3–4 minutes, until the sweet potato is tender.

3 Stir in the kangkong or spinach and the sliced pork tenderloin and simmer gently for 2–3 minutes, until the pork is just cooked and turns opaque.

4 Ladle the soup into individual warmed bowls and sprinkle the sliced spring onions over the top.

> **Cook's Tip**
> Fresh tamarind pods, packaged tamarind pulp and pots of tamarind paste are all available in Middle Eastern, Indian, African and South-east Asian food stores.

Hearty Gammon, Potato and Bean Broth

In this hearty soup, the potatoes cook in the gammon stock, absorbing its flavour and saltiness. Take care not to add too much salt and spoil the soup.

Serves 4

450g/1lb gammon (smoked or cured ham), in one piece

2 bay leaves
2 onions, sliced
10ml/2 tsp paprika
675g/1½lb baking potatoes, cut into large chunks
225g/8oz spring greens (collards)
425g/15oz can haricot (navy) or cannellini beans, drained
salt and ground black pepper

1 Soak the gammon overnight in cold water. Drain and put in a large pan with the bay leaves and onions. Pour in 1.5 litres/2½ pints/6¼ cups cold water. Bring to the boil, reduce the heat and simmer very gently for 1½ hours or until the meat is deliciously tender.

2 Remove the meat from the cooking liquid and leave to cool slightly. Discard the skin and any excess fat and cut the meat into small even chunks. Return to the pan with the paprika and potatoes. Bring back to the boil, then reduce the heat, cover and simmer for 20 minutes until the potatoes are cooked through, but not falling apart.

3 Trim the greens. Roll up the leaves and cut into thin shreds. Add to the pan with the beans and simmer, uncovered, for about 10 minutes. Remove the bay leaves. Season with salt and pepper to taste and serve hot.

> **Variations**
> • Bacon knuckle can be used instead of the gammon (smoked or cured ham) – they are economical and the bones will give the stock a delicious flavour. Freeze any stock you don't use.
> • Peel the potatoes if you prefer, but the flavour is best when the skins are left on.

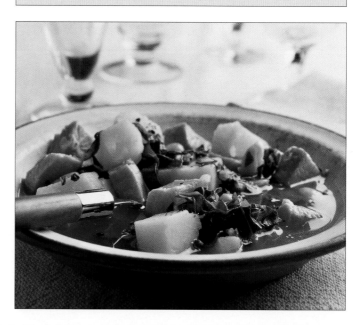

Tamarind Pork Soup Energy 126kcal/532kJ; Protein 14g; Carbohydrate 12.3g, of which sugars 4.1g; Fat 2.7g, of which saturates 0.9g; Cholesterol 37mg; Calcium 31mg; Fibre 2g; Sodium 417mg.
Gammon Broth Energy 405kcal/1703kJ; Protein 31.7g; Carbohydrate 48.8g, of which sugars 8.2g; Fat 10.5g, of which saturates 3.2g; Cholesterol 26mg; Calcium 216mg; Fibre 10g; Sodium 1411mg.

Sweet-and-sour Pork, Prawn and Sweet Potato Soup

This hearty and delicious soup is ideal as a main course, served with crusty bread or even some plain boiled rice. The complex sweet and sour flavours, as well as the stunning appearance of the soup, make it a great centrepiece for a special occasion.

Serves 4–6

350g/12oz lean pork
225g/8oz raw or cooked prawn (shrimp) tails
30ml/2 tbsp tamarind sauce
juice of 2 limes
1 small green guava, peeled, seeded and chopped
1 small, under-ripe mango, peeled, seeded and chopped
1.4 litres/2½ pints/6¼ cups chicken stock
15ml/1 tbsp fish or soy sauce
285g/10oz sweet potato, peeled and cut into even pieces
225g/8oz unripe tomatoes, quartered
115g/4oz green beans, trimmed and halved
1 star fruit (carambola), thickly sliced widthways
85g/3oz green cabbage, shredded
5ml/1 tsp crushed black pepper
salt
2 spring onions (scallions), shredded, to garnish
lime wedges, to serve

1 Trim any fat from the pork and finely dice the meat. Peel the prawns and set aside.

2 Gently heat the tamarind sauce and lime juice in a large heavy pan and add the pork pieces. Add the guava, mango, chicken stock, and fish or soy sauce to the pan and stir until well combined.

3 Bring the mixture to the boil, then reduce the heat and simmer, uncovered, for about 30 minutes, stirring occasionally.

4 Stir the prawns into the pan, then add all the remaining fruit and vegetables. Simmer the soup for a further 10–15 minutes until all the vegetables are tender.

5 Add the black pepper, and salt to taste. Garnish with the spring onions and serve immediately with lime wedges.

Country Lamb and Potato Soup

Traditionally, Irish soda bread would be served with this hearty one-pot meal based on classic Irish lamb and potato stew.

Serves 4

15ml/1 tbsp vegetable oil
675g/1½lb boneless lamb chump chops, trimmed and cut into small cubes
2 small onions, quartered
2 leeks, thickly sliced
1 litre/1¾ pints/4 cups lamb stock or water
2 large potatoes, cut into chunks
2 carrots, thickly sliced
sprig of fresh thyme, plus extra to garnish
15g/½oz/1 tbsp butter
30ml/2 tbsp chopped fresh parsley
salt and ground black pepper
Irish soda bread, to serve

1 Heat the oil in a pan. Add the lamb and brown in batches. Use a slotted spoon to remove the lamb from the pan.

2 Add the onions and cook for 4–5 minutes, until browned. Return the meat to the pan and add the leeks. Pour in the stock or water, then bring to the boil. Reduce the heat, cover and simmer gently for about 1 hour.

3 Add the potatoes, carrots and thyme, and continue cooking for a further 40 minutes, until the lamb is tender. Remove from the heat and leave to stand for 5 minutes to allow the fat to settle on the surface of the soup.

4 Skim off the fat. Pour off the stock from the soup into a clean pan and whisk in the butter. Stir in the parsley and season well, then pour the liquid back over the soup ingredients.

5 Ladle the soup into warmed bowls and garnish with sprigs of fresh thyme. Serve with chunks of brown or Irish soda bread.

> **Variation**
> The vegetables in this rustic soup can be varied according to the season. Swede (rutabaga), turnip, celeriac and even cabbage could be added in place of some of the listed vegetables.

Sweet-and-sour Soup Energy 234kcal/981kJ; Protein 26.2g; Carbohydrate 24.8g, of which sugars 1.6g; Fat 3.3g, of which saturates 1g; Cholesterol 137mg; Calcium 84mg; Fibre 1.1g; Sodium 681mg.
Country Lamb Soup Energy 500kcal/2092kJ; Protein 38.2g; Carbohydrate 30.2g, of which sugars 12.2g; Fat 26g, of which saturates 11.3g; Cholesterol 136mg; Calcium 104mg; Fibre 6.1g; Sodium 197mg.

Lamb Meatball and Vegetable Soup

A variety of vegetables creates a tasty base for meatballs in this substantial soup, which will make a hearty meal served with crusty bread.

Serves 4

1 litre/1¾ pints/4 cups lamb stock
1 onion, finely chopped
2 carrots, finely sliced
½ celeriac, finely diced
75g/3oz/¾ cup frozen peas
50g/2oz green beans, cut into 2.5cm/1in pieces
3 tomatoes, seeded and chopped
1 red (bell) pepper, seeded and diced
1 potato, coarsely diced
2 lemons, sliced
salt and ground black pepper
crusty bread, to serve

For the meatballs

225g/8oz/1 cup very lean minced (ground) lamb
40g/1½oz/¼ cup short grain rice
30ml/2 tbsp chopped fresh parsley
plain (all-purpose) flour, for coating

1 Pour the stock into a large pan and place over medium heat. Stir in the onion, carrot, celeriac and peas.

2 Add the beans, tomatoes, red pepper and potato with the slices of lemon. Stir in a little salt and ground black pepper and bring the mixture to the boil. Reduce the heat, cover the pan and simmer for 15–20 minutes.

3 Meanwhile, prepare the meatballs. Mix the meat, rice and parsley together in a bowl and season well. The best way of mixing meat for meatballs is by hand, squeezing and kneading the mixture so that the meat mixes with the rice.

4 Take out a rounded teaspoon of the meat mixture and roll it into a small ball, roughly the size of a walnut. Toss it in the flour. Repeat with the remaining mixture.

5 Add the meatballs to the soup and simmer gently for 25–30 minutes, stirring occasionally, to prevent the meatballs from sticking. The rice should be plumped up and cooked in the meat. Adjust the seasoning and serve in warm bowls, accompanied by crusty bread.

Lamb and Vegetable Stew with Rice

This is based on a traditional Jewish dish of baked meats, potatoes and beans. A parcel of rice is often added to the broth part way through cooking, to produce pressed, chewy rice.

Serves 8

250g/9oz/1 cup chickpeas, soaked overnight
45ml/3 tbsp olive oil
1 onion, chopped
10 garlic cloves, chopped
1 parsnip, sliced
3 carrots, sliced
5–10ml/1–2 tsp ground cumin
2.5ml/½ tsp ground turmeric
15ml/1 tbsp chopped fresh root ginger
2 litres/3½ pints/8 cups beef stock
1 potato, cut into chunks
½ vegetable marrow, sliced
400g/14oz fresh or canned tomatoes, diced
45–60ml/3–4 tbsp brown or green lentils
2 bay leaves
250g/9oz salted meat such as salt beef
250g/9oz piece of lamb
½ large bunch fresh coriander (cilantro), chopped
200g/7oz/1 cup long grain rice

For serving

chopped fresh chillies
1 lemon, cut into wedges

1 Preheat the oven to 120°C/250°F/Gas ½. Drain the chickpeas. Heat the oil in a deep flameproof casserole, add the onion, garlic, parsnip, carrots, cumin, turmeric and ginger and cook for 2–3 minutes. Add the chickpeas, stock, potato, marrow, tomatoes, lentils, bay leaves, salted meat, lamb and coriander. Cover and cook in the oven for 1 hour.

2 Tie the rice in a double thickness of muslin (cheesecloth), allowing enough room for it to expand while it is cooking. Place the rice parcel in the casserole, anchoring the edge of the muslin parcel under the lid so it is held above the soup and allowed to steam. Return the casserole to the oven and continue cooking for a further 2 hours.

3 Carefully remove the lid and the rice. Skim any fat off the top of the soup. Ladle the soup into bowls. Open the rice parcel and add a scoop to each bowl with one or two pieces of meat. Sprinkle with chopped fresh chillies and serve with lemon.

Lamb Meatball Soup Energy 226kcal/948kJ; Protein 15.7g; Carbohydrate 25.1g, of which sugars 11.4g; Fat 7.7g, of which saturates 3.2g; Cholesterol 43mg; Calcium 75mg; Fibre 5.2g; Sodium 102mg.
Lamb Stew Energy 463kcal/1941kJ; Protein 28.5g; Carbohydrate 60.5g, of which sugars 17g; Fat 12.7g, of which saturates 3.5g; Cholesterol 47mg; Calcium 130mg; Fibre 9.4g; Sodium 409mg.

Fisherman's Potato Stew

This substantial one-pot soup of fish and potatoes makes a rewarding supper after a hard day's fishing.

Serves 6
500g/1¼lb mussels
3 onions
2 garlic cloves, sliced
300ml/½ pint/1¼ cups fish stock
12 scallops, shelled
450g/1lb cod fillet, cut into cubes
30ml/2 tbsp olive oil
1 potato, cut into 1cm/½in slices
few sprigs of fresh thyme, chopped
1 red and 1 green (bell) pepper, seeded and cut into chunks
120ml/4fl oz/½ cup dry white wine
250ml/8fl oz/1 cup crème fraîche
275g/10oz peeled prawns (shrimp)
salt and ground black pepper
fresh thyme sprigs, to garnish
75g/3oz/¾ cup grated mature (sharp) Cheddar cheese, to serve

1 Clean the mussel shells, removing any beards. Discard any that stay open when tapped. Rinse in cold water.

2 Pour water to a depth of 2.5cm/1in into a large, deep frying pan. Chop one onion and add it to the pan, with the garlic. Bring to the boil, then add the mussels and cook, covered, for 5–6 minutes, shaking the pan occasionally. Remove the mussels as they open, discarding any that remain shut. Set aside.

3 Strain the cooking liquid from the mussels through muslin (cheesecloth) to remove any remaining sand. Make up the liquid with fish stock to 300ml/½ pint/1¼ cups.

4 Cut the remaining onions into wedges. Heat the oil in a large pan and fry the wedges for 3 minutes. Add the potato and thyme, cover and cook for 15 minutes, until the potato has softened.

5 Add the peppers to the pan and cook for a few minutes. Stir in the mixed mussel and fish stock, the wine and crème fraîche. Bring to near-boiling point, then add the cod and scallops.

6 Reduce the heat and simmer for 5 minutes, then add the prawns. Simmer for 3–4 minutes more, until the seafood is cooked. Add the mussels for 1–2 minutes. Season if necessary, then spoon into bowls, garnish with thyme sprigs. Serve with the cheese on the side so diners can help themselves.

Hearty Beef and Vegetable Soup

This substantial meat and vegetable soup has a deliciously rustic flavour and is great for using the less expensive cuts of beef.

Serves 6
225g/8oz braising steak, cut into 1.5cm/½in cubes
225g/8oz lean boned pork shoulder, cut into 1.5cm/½in cubes
2 litres/3½ pints/8 cups beef stock
1 bay leaf
350g/12oz tomatoes, skinned, seeded and chopped
1 small red (bell) pepper, seeded and chopped
1 small onion, chopped
2 carrots, chopped
1 large boiling potato, peeled and diced
175g/6oz fresh or thawed frozen corn kernels
15ml/1 tbsp Worcestershire sauce
salt and ground black pepper

1 Put the beef and pork in a large heavy pan and add the stock. Bring to the boil, skimming off all the froth that rises to the surface.

2 When you have removed all of the froth from the liquid, add the bay leaf. Partially cover the pan and gently simmer over a very low heat for about 1 hour.

3 Add the tomatoes, red pepper, onion, carrots and potato. Bring back to the boil, then reduce the heat and continue simmering, partly covered, for about 45 minutes. Stir the soup from time to time.

4 Add the corn and simmer for a further 20–30 minutes or until all the vegetables and meat are tender.

5 Discard the bay leaf. Stir in the Worcestershire sauce. Taste and adjust the seasoning before serving.

Cook's Tip
This soup is ideal to make two or three days before you plan to serve it as the flavours will continue to develop and improve over time.

Hearty Beef Soup Energy 226kcal/948kJ; Protein 15.7g; Carbohydrate 25.1g, of which sugars 11.4g; Fat 7.7g, of which saturates 3.2g; Cholesterol 43mg; Calcium 75mg; Fibre 5.2g; Sodium 102mg.
Fisherman's Stew Energy 450kcal/1880kJ; Protein 42.7g; Carbohydrate 14.9g, of which sugars 5.7g; Fat 23.1g, of which saturates 14.4g; Cholesterol 220mg; Calcium 208mg; Fibre 1.4g; Sodium 408mg.

Mediterranean Potato and Fish Soup

This chunky fish and potato soup makes a robust and wonderfully aromatic dish, perfect for a lingering al fresco summer lunch or a light supper with friends. Serve it with fresh crusty bread dunked in warm olive oil.

Serves 6

2 large thick leeks
15ml/1 tbsp olive oil
5ml/1 tsp crushed coriander seeds
pinch of dried red chilli flakes
300g/11oz small salad potatoes, peeled and thickly sliced
400g/14oz can chopped tomatoes
600ml/1 pint/2½ cups fish stock
150ml/¼ pint/⅔ cup white wine
1 fresh bay leaf
1 star anise
strip of pared orange rind
good pinch of saffron threads
450g/1lb white fish fillets, such as monkfish, sea bass, cod or haddock
450g/1lb small squid, cleaned
250g/9oz fresh raw peeled prawns (shrimp)
30–45ml/2–3 tbsp chopped fresh flat leaf parsley
salt and ground black pepper

1 Slice the leeks, keeping the green and white parts separate. Wash both sets of leek slices thoroughly and drain them well. Set the white slices aside for later.

2 Heat the oil in a heavy pan and add the green leek slices, crushed coriander seeds and dried red chilli flakes. Cook gently, stirring occasionally, for 5 minutes.

3 Add the potatoes and tomatoes, and pour in the stock and wine. Add the bay leaf, star anise, orange rind and saffron. Bring to the boil, then reduce the heat and partially cover the pan. Simmer for 20 minutes, or until the potatoes are tender. Taste and adjust the seasoning.

4 Cut the white fish into chunks. Cut the squid sacs into rectangles and score in a criss-cross pattern. Add the fish to the soup and cook gently for 4 minutes.

5 Add the prawns and cook for 1 minute. Add the squid and the reserved white parts of the leeks and cook for 2 minutes. Finally, stir in the chopped parsley and serve immediately.

Salmon and Potato Chowder

Dill is the perfect partner for salmon in this classic, full-flavoured dish. Use the best possible boneless fish.

Serves 4

20g/¾oz/1½ tbsp butter
1 onion, finely chopped
1 leek, finely chopped
1 small fennel bulb, finely chopped
25g/1oz/¼ cup plain (all-purpose) flour
1.75 litres/3 pints/7½ cups fish stock
2 potatoes, cut into 1cm/½in cubes
450g/1lb boneless, skinless salmon, cut in 2cm/¾in cubes
175ml/6fl oz/¾ cup milk
120ml/4fl oz/½ cup whipping cream
30ml/2 tbsp chopped fresh dill
salt and ground black pepper

1 Melt the butter in a large pan. Add the onion, leek and chopped fennel and cook over a medium heat for 5–8 minutes until softened, stirring from time to time.

2 Stir in the flour. Reduce the heat to low and cook for 3 minutes, stirring occasionally.

3 Add the fish stock and potatoes. Season with salt and ground black pepper. Bring to the boil, then reduce the heat, cover and simmer for about 20 minutes or until the potatoes are just tender.

4 Add the salmon to the pan and simmer gently for about 3–5 minutes until it is just cooked.

5 Stir in the milk, cream, and dill. Cook until just warmed through, but do not boil. Adjust the seasoning and then serve.

Variation
Fresh young mackerel fillets are delicious in soup. They are particularly good in this recipe, which has lots of vegetables. Add a crushed garlic clove, if you like, and use tarragon instead of dill. For a zesty flavour to cut the oily fish, add the grated rind of 1 lemon and season with a hint of cayenne pepper.

Fish Soup Energy 249kcal/1051kJ; Protein 35.2g; Carbohydrate 13.3g, of which sugars 4.5g; Fat 4.7g, of which saturates 0.9g; Cholesterol 285mg; Calcium 90mg; Fibre 3g; Sodium 223mg.
Salmon Chowder Energy 301kcal/1254kJ; Protein 18.3g; Carbohydrate 13g, of which sugars 3.8g; Fat 19.9g, of which saturates 8.6g; Cholesterol 67mg; Calcium 83mg; Fibre 1.5g; Sodium 78mg.

Fish and Sweet Potato Cream Soup

The subtle honeyed taste of sweet potato combines with the stronger flavours of fish and oregano to make this appetizing soup, popular throughout the Caribbean.

Serves 4

175g/6oz white fish fillet, skinned
1/2 onion, chopped
1 sweet potato, about 175g/6oz, peeled and diced
1 small carrot, about 50g/2oz, chopped
5ml/1 tsp chopped fresh oregano or 2.5ml/1/2 tsp dried oregano
2.5ml/1/2 tsp ground cinnamon
1.35 litres/2 1/4 pints/5 1/2 cups fish stock
75ml/5 tbsp single (light) cream
chopped fresh parsley, to garnish

1 Remove any bones from the white fish and put it in a pan. Add the onion, sweet potato, carrot, oregano, cinnamon and half the stock. Bring to the boil, then simmer for around 20 minutes or until the potatoes are cooked through.

2 Leave to cool, then pour into a food processor or blender and blend until smooth. Return the soup to the pan, stir in the remaining fish stock and gently bring to the boil. Reduce the heat.

3 Stir the cream into the soup, then gently heat it through without allowing it to boil. If the soup boils the cream will curdle. Serve hot, garnished with the chopped parsley.

Variations
• Omit the fish and use ham or chicken stock. Serve the soup topped with crisp fried bacon or pancetta.
• Use ordinary potato instead of sweet potato and omit the cinnamon. Add a pinch of ground mace.
• For a chicken and sweet potato soup, use 2 diced, skinless chicken breast fillets instead of the fish, and chicken stock instead of the fish stock.
• For a ham and sweet potato soup, use 1 trimmed, diced gammon steak (cured or smoked ham) instead of the fish, and ham or chicken stock.

Smoked Haddock and Potato Soup

This is a classic Scottish dish, known as Cullen Skink, which uses one of the country's tastiest fish, the haddock. The result is a thick, creamy potato soup with a deliciously rich, smoky fish flavour. Serve with plenty of fresh crusty bread for a substantial meal.

bouquet garni
900ml/1 1/2 pints/3 3/4 cups water
500g/1 1/4lb floury potatoes, quartered
600ml/1 pint/2 1/2 cups milk
40g/1 1/2oz/3 tbsp butter
salt and ground black pepper
chopped chives, to garnish
crusty bread, to serve

Serves 6

350g/12oz smoked haddock fillet
1 onion, chopped

1 Put the haddock, onion, bouquet garni and water into a large heavy pan and bring to the boil. Skim off any foam that rises to the surface, then cover the pan and reduce the heat. Gently poach the fillets for about 10–15 minutes until the haddock flakes easily when tested with a fork.

2 Lift the haddock from the pan and leave to cool slightly, then remove the skin and bones, but do not discard. Flake the fish flesh and put to one side. Return the skin and bones to the pan and simmer for about 30 minutes.

3 Strain the fish stock and return it to the pan, then add the potatoes and simmer for about 25 minutes. Using a slotted spoon, remove the potatoes from the pan. Add the milk to the pan and bring to the boil briefly.

4 Mash the potatoes with the butter, then whisk into the soup. Add the flaked fish and heat through. Season to taste, then ladle into soup bowls, sprinkle with chives and serve with crusty bread.

Cook's Tip
This soup works best if you use naturally smoked fish fillets, which will be off-white, rather than those that are dyed yellow.

Fish and Sweet Potato Energy 119kcal/501kJ; Protein 9.4g; Carbohydrate 11.9g, of which sugars 4.7g; Fat 4.1g, of which saturates 2.4g; Cholesterol 30mg; Calcium 38mg; Fibre 1.6g; Sodium 53mg.
Smoked Haddock Energy 205kcal/864kJ; Protein 16.1g; Carbohydrate 19g, of which sugars 6.4g; Fat 7.8g, of which saturates 4.7g; Cholesterol 41mg; Calcium 142mg; Fibre 1g; Sodium 536mg.

Spiced Mussel and Potato Soup

Chunky and colourful, this Turkish fish and potato soup is like a chowder in its consistency. It is flavoured with harissa sauce, which is a spicy red paste made from dried chillies and garlic.

Serves 6
1.3–1.6kg/3–3½lb fresh mussels
900ml/1½ pints/3¾ cups
  vegetable stock
150ml/¼ pint/⅔ cup white wine
2 bay leaves
30ml/2 tbsp olive oil
1 onion, finely chopped
2 garlic cloves, crushed
2 celery sticks, finely sliced
bunch of spring onions (scallions),
  finely sliced
1 potato, diced
7.5ml/1½ tsp harissa sauce
3 tomatoes, peeled and diced
45ml/3 tbsp chopped
  fresh parsley
ground black pepper
thick natural (plain) yogurt, to
  serve (optional)

1 Scrub the mussels under cold running water and remove their beards. Discard any mussels that are damaged or do not close with a sharp tap of a knife. Leave in a basin of cold water until they are needed.

2 Bring the stock and wine to the boil in a large pan with the bay leaves. Add the mussels and cover with a lid. Cook for 4–5 minutes until the mussels have opened wide. Discard any mussels that remain closed. Drain the mussels, reserving the cooking liquid. Reserve a few mussels in their shells to use as a garnish and shell the rest.

3 Heat the oil in a pan and fry the onion, garlic, celery and spring onions for 5 minutes.

4 Add the reserved liquid from the shelled mussels, along with the potato, harissa sauce and tomatoes. Bring to the boil, reduce the heat and cover. Simmer gently for 25 minutes or until the potatoes are breaking up.

5 Stir in the parsley and pepper and add the shelled mussels. Heat through for 1–2 minutes. Ladle into bowls and garnish with the unshelled mussels. Serve hot with a spoonful of yogurt, if you like.

Clam, Mushroom and Potato Chowder

The delicate, sweet shellfish taste of clams and the soft earthiness of wild mushrooms combine with potatoes to make this a great meal on its own – fit for any occasion.

Serves 4
48 clams, scrubbed
50g/2oz/¼ cup unsalted
  (sweet) butter
1 large onion, chopped
1 celery stick, sliced
1 carrot, sliced
225g/8oz assorted wild
  mushrooms, such as
  chanterelles, ceps, porcini or field
  (portabello) mushrooms, sliced
225g/8oz floury potatoes,
  thickly sliced
1.2 litres/2 pints/5 cups light
  chicken or vegetable stock
1 thyme sprig
4 parsley stalks
salt and ground black pepper
fresh thyme, to garnish

1 Place the clams in a large pan, making sure to discard any that are open. Put 1cm/½in of water in the pan, cover, bring to the boil and steam the clams over a medium heat for between 6–8 minutes until they have opened (be sure to discard any clams that do not open).

2 Drain the clams over a bowl, remove the shells, reserving a few clams in their shells for the garnish. Chop the shelled clams into quarters. Strain the cooking juices into the bowl, add the chopped clams and set aside.

3 Add the butter, onion, celery and carrot to the pan and cook gently for about 10 minutes, until the vegetables are softened but not coloured.

4 Add the mushrooms to the pan and cook for 3–4 minutes until their juices begin to seep out. Add the thickly sliced potatoes, the clams and their juices, the chicken or vegetable stock, thyme and parsley stalks.

5 Bring the soup to the boil, then reduce the heat, cover the pan and simmer for about 25 minutes, stirring occasionally. Check the chowder for seasoning, ladle into bowls and garnish with the reserved clams and fresh thyme.

Spiced Mussel Soup Energy 153kcal/644kJ; Protein 14.5g; Carbohydrate 7.8g, of which sugars 3.2g; Fat 5.6g, of which saturates 0.9g; Cholesterol 30mg; Calcium 178mg; Fibre 1.5g; Sodium 175mg.
Clam Chowder Energy 203kcal/848kJ; Protein 10.8g; Carbohydrate 15.8g, of which sugars 5.2g; Fat 11.2g, of which saturates 6.8g; Cholesterol 60mg; Calcium 66mg; Fibre 2.4g; Sodium 696mg.

Potato, Corn and Scallop Chowder

Fresh corn is ideal for this potato and scallop chowder, although canned corn also works well. This soup makes a perfect lunch dish.

Serves 4–6

2 corn on the cob or 200g/7oz
   frozen or canned corn
600ml/1 pint/2½ cups milk
15g/½oz butter or margarine
1 small leek or onion, chopped
1 small garlic clove, crushed
40g/1½oz smoked lean bacon,
   finely chopped
1 small green (bell) pepper,
   seeded and diced
1 celery stick, chopped
1 medium potato, diced
15ml/1 tbsp plain
   (all-purpose) flour
300ml/½ pint/1¼ cups chicken
   or vegetable stock
4 scallops
115g/4oz cooked fresh mussels
pinch of paprika
150ml/¼ pint/⅔ cup single
   cream (optional)
salt and ground black pepper

1 If using corn on the cob, slice down the corn cobs with a sharp knife to remove the kernels. Place half of the kernels in a food processor or blender and process with a little of the milk.

2 Melt the butter or margarine in a large pan and gently fry the leek or onion, garlic and bacon for 4–5 minutes until the leek is soft but not browned. Add the green pepper, chopped celery and diced potato and cook over low heat for a further 3–4 minutes, stirring frequently.

3 Stir in the flour and cook for 1–2 minutes until the mixture is golden and frothy. Gradually stir in the milk and corn mixture, stock, the remaining milk, reserved corn kernels and seasoning.

4 Bring to the boil, then reduce the heat and simmer, partially covered, for about 15–20 minutes or until the vegetables are tender.

5 Pull the pink corals away from the scallops and carefully slice the white flesh into 5mm/¼in slices. Stir the scallops into the soup, cook for 4 minutes and then stir in the corals, mussels and paprika. Heat through for a few minutes and then stir in the cream, if using. Adjust the seasoning to taste and serve.

Chunky Prawn and Potato Chupe

South American chupes are a substantial meal in themselves. Potatoes are always included, but the other ingredients vary. This chupe uses annatto oil, which is olive oil infused with annatto seeds: if unavailable, use chilli, or olive oil.

Serves 6

500g/1¼lb raw king prawns
   (jumbo shrimp)
750ml/1¼ pints/3 cups fish stock
1 carrot, finely chopped
2 celery sticks, thinly sliced
45ml/3 tbsp annatto (achiote) oil
1 large onion, finely chopped
1 red (bell) pepper, seeded
   and diced
2 garlic cloves, crushed
2 fresh red chillies, seeded
   and chopped
5ml/1 tsp ground turmeric
1 large tomato, peeled
   and chopped
675g/1½lb potatoes, peeled and
   cut into 2.5cm/1in cubes
115g/4oz/1 cup fresh or
   frozen peas
15ml/1 tbsp chopped fresh mint
15ml/1 tbsp chopped fresh
   coriander (cilantro)
salt

1 Peel the prawns and set them aside. Place the shells in a large pan with the fish stock, carrot and celery. Bring to the boil, then simmer over a low heat for 20 minutes. Strain into a bowl or jug (pitcher) and set the stock aside.

2 Heat the oil in a large pan over a low heat. Stir in the onion and red pepper and sauté for 5 minutes. Stir in the garlic, chillies and turmeric and cook for a further 2 minutes.

3 Add the chopped tomato and potatoes to the pan, season to taste with salt and cook for about 10 minutes, allowing the tomato to break down slightly and the potatoes to absorb the flavours of the other ingredients.

4 Pour in the strained stock and bring to the boil. Lower the heat and simmer for 15 minutes, or until the potatoes are cooked through.

5 Stir the prawns and peas into the soup and simmer for 4–5 minutes, or until the prawns become opaque. Finally, stir in the mint and coriander, and serve in warmed bowls.

Corn and Scallop Energy 200kcal/845kJ; Protein 13g; Carbohydrate 23.6g, of which sugars 10.5g; Fat 6.7g, of which saturates 3.2g; Cholesterol 31mg; Calcium 150mg; Fibre 1.9g; Sodium 326mg.
Prawn Chupe Energy 175kcal/742kJ; Protein 18.9g; Carbohydrate 23.2g, of which sugars 4.3g; Fat 1.4g, of which saturates 0.3g; Cholesterol 163mg; Calcium 100mg; Fibre 2.7g; Sodium 175mg.

Mini Baked Potatoes with Blue Cheese

These little oven-baked potatoes are perfect as finger food for a party, especially as you can prepare them in advance.

Makes 20

20 small new or salad potatoes
60ml/4 tbsp vegetable oil
coarse salt
120ml/4fl oz/½ cup sour cream
25g/1oz blue cheese, crumbled
30ml/2 tbsp chopped fresh
   chives, for sprinkling

1 Preheat the oven to 180°C/350°F/Gas 4. Wash and dry the potatoes. Pour the oil into a bowl. Add the potatoes and toss to coat well with oil.

2 Dip the potatoes in the coarse salt to coat lightly. Spread out the potatoes on a baking sheet. Bake in the oven for about 45–50 minutes until tender.

3 In a small bowl, mix together the sour cream and blue cheese until well combined.

4 Cut a cross in the top of each potato. Pinch gently with your fingers to open up the cross.

5 Top each potato with a dollop of the cheese mixture. It will melt down into the potato gently.

6 Sprinkle the potatoes with chives on a serving dish and serve them hot. Alternatively, leave them to cool and serve at room temperature.

> **Cook's Tip**
> *This dish works just as well as a light snack; if you don't want to be bothered with lots of fiddly small potatoes, simply bake an ordinary baking potato.*

Mini Filled Jacket Potatoes

Jacket potatoes are always delicious, and the toppings can easily be varied: choose from luxurious and extravagant ingredients, such as caviar and smoked salmon, to equally satisfying, but more everyday fare, such as grated cheese and baked beans.

Makes 36

36 potatoes, about 4cm/1½in
   in diameter, well scrubbed
250ml/8fl oz/1 cup thick
   sour cream
45–60ml/3–4 tbsp chopped
   fresh chives
coarse salt, for sprinkling

1 Preheat the oven to 180°C/350°F/Gas 4. Place the potatoes on a baking sheet and bake in the oven for 30–35 minutes, or until the potatoes are tender when pierced with the tip of a sharp kitchen knife.

2 Cut a cross in the top of each potato and squeeze the sides gently to open up the cross. Make a small hole in the centre of each potato.

3 Fill each hole with a dollop of sour cream, then sprinkle with a little salt and top with some chopped chives. Serve the filled potatoes immediately.

> **Cook's Tip**
> *For convenience, the potatoes can be baked in advance in the oven, then reheated in a hot oven for 10 minutes, or reheat in the microwave on the highest setting for 3–4 minutes.*

> **Variation**
> *If your guests are likely to be hungry, use larger potatoes and bake at the same temperature until tender. When cooked, cut each one in half, scoop out the flesh, mash with the other ingredients and spoon the mixture back into the potato skins. Serve the potatoes while still hot.*

Mini Baked Potatoes Energy 63kcal/262kJ; Protein 1.1g; Carbohydrate 6.3g, of which sugars 0.7g; Fat 3.9g, of which saturates 1.3g; Cholesterol 5mg; Calcium 14mg; Fibre 0.4g; Sodium 22mg.
Mini Jacket Potatoes Energy 73kcal/309kJ; Protein 1.7g; Carbohydrate 13.7g, of which sugars 1.4g; Fat 1.6g, of which saturates 1g; Cholesterol 4mg; Calcium 14mg; Fibre 0.9g; Sodium 12mg.

Spicy Jacket Potatoes

Potatoes baked in their jackets are the ultimate comfort food and enjoyed by everyone. This twist on the traditional baked potato sees the flesh being scooped out and mixed with a blend of delicate spices before being put back in its shell. The result is a deliciously fragrant, spiced alternative to a traditional classic.

Serves 2–4
2 large baking potatoes
5ml/1 tsp sunflower oil
1 small onion, finely chopped
2.5cm/1in piece fresh root ginger,
*   peeled and grated*
5ml/1 tsp ground cumin
5ml/1 tsp ground coriander
2.5ml/½ tsp ground turmeric
garlic salt
natural (plain) yogurt and fresh
*   coriander (cilantro) sprigs,*
*   to garnish*

1 Preheat the oven to 190°C/375°F/Gas 5. Prick the potatoes all over with a fork. Bake in the oven for about 35–40 minutes, or until tender.

2 Cut the potatoes in half and scoop out the flesh with a spoon. Heat the oil in a non-stick frying pan and cook the onion for a few minutes to soften. Stir in the ginger, cumin, coriander and turmeric.

3 Cook over a low heat for about 2 minutes, stirring frequently until the spices release their fragrances. Add the potato flesh to the pan, and season to taste with garlic salt.

4 Cook the spiced potato mixture for a further 2 minutes, stirring occasionally. Spoon the filling back into the potato shells and top each with a spoonful of natural yogurt and a sprig or two of fresh coriander. Serve immediately.

Cook's Tip
Ensure that the potatoes are completely cooked by inserting a sharp knife or a metal skewer all the way through the potato. You will be able to tell if they need cooking a bit longer because there will be a little resistance.

New Potatoes with Mock Caviar and Cream Cheese

These mini stuffed potatoes are pretty to look at and make an impressive one-bite snack for a party or decadent buffet. They make the most of tender new potatoes with their waxy texture. If you are feeling especially extravagant authentic caviar finishes these treats off perfectly, but they are almost as delicious with Danish black mock caviar.

Makes 30
30 small new potatoes
200g/7oz/scant 1 cup full-fat
*   cream cheese*
15ml/1 tbsp chopped
*   fresh parsley*
1 jar Danish black mock caviar
*   (lumpfish roe)*
1 jar salmon roe
salt and ground black pepper
dill sprigs, to garnish

1 Cook the potatoes in a large pan of boiling water for about 10–15 minutes or until tender. Drain through a colander and then trim off both ends of each potato, creating a flat base so they will stand up on a serving plate.

2 Sit the potatoes on one of their cut ends. Beat the cream cheese and chopped parsley together and season with salt and pepper to taste. Spoon the mixture on to the potatoes and top with a little mock caviar and salmon roe. Garnish with sprigs of dill and serve immediately.

Cook's Tip
Fresh parsley is simple to grow yourself. Buy a plant and keep it on a sunny windowsill in your kitchen. Ensure it is kept moist but don't over-water it, and pull off the leaves as and when you need them. They will regrow in a matter of days.

Variation
If you can't get hold of any mock caviar, then top the new potatoes with thin slices of smoked salmon.

Spicy Jacket Potatoes Energy 85kcal/361kJ; Protein 2g; Carbohydrate 17.6g, of which sugars 2.2g; Fat 1.2g, of which saturates 0.2g; Cholesterol 0mg; Calcium 18mg; Fibre 1.5g; Sodium 17mg.
New Potatoes Energy 83kcal/348kJ; Protein 2.8g; Carbohydrate 10.7g, of which sugars 0.9g; Fat 3.5g, of which saturates 2.1g; Cholesterol 28mg; Calcium 11mg; Fibre 0.7g; Sodium 35mg.

Spiced Sweet Potato Turnovers

The subtle flavour of sweet potato makes a great filling when enhanced with spices.

Serves 4
1 sweet potato, about 225g/8oz
30ml/2 tbsp vegetable oil
2 shallots, finely chopped
10ml/2 tsp coriander seeds, crushed
5ml/1 tsp ground cumin
5ml/1 tsp garam masala
115g/4oz/1 cup frozen peas
15ml/1 tbsp chopped fresh mint
salt and ground black pepper
mint sprigs, to garnish

For the pastry
15ml/1 tbsp olive oil
1 small egg
150ml/¼ pint/⅔ cup natural
   (plain) yogurt
115g/4oz/8 tbsp
   butter, melted
275g/10oz/2½ cups plain
   (all-purpose) flour
1.5ml/¼ tsp bicarbonate of soda
   (baking soda)
10ml/2 tsp paprika
5ml/1 tsp salt
beaten egg, to glaze

1 Cook the sweet potato in boiling salted water for 15–20 minutes, until tender. Drain well and leave to cool. When cool enough to handle, peel the potato and cut into 1cm/½in cubes.

2 Heat the oil in a frying pan, add the shallots and cook until soft. Add the sweet potato cubes and fry until brown at the edges. Mix in the spices and fry for a few seconds. Remove from the heat and add the peas, mint and seasoning. Leave to cool.

3 Preheat the oven to 200°C/400°F/Gas 6. To make the pastry, whisk together the oil and egg, stir in the yogurt, then add the melted butter. Sift the flour, bicarbonate of soda, paprika and salt into a bowl, then stir into the yogurt mixture to form a soft dough. Knead gently, then roll it out and stamp into rounds with a 7.5cm/3in pastry (cookie) cutter.

4 Spoon about 10ml/2 tsp of the filling on to one side of each round, then fold over and seal the edges. Re-roll the trimmings and stamp out more rounds until the filling is used up.

5 Arrange the turnovers on a greased baking sheet and brush the tops with beaten egg. Bake for about 20 minutes until crisp and golden brown. Serve hot, garnished with mint.

Curry-spiced Potato Pakoras

These delicious potato bites make a wonderful snack, drizzled with fragrant chutney.

Makes 25
15ml/1 tbsp sunflower oil
20ml/4 tsp cumin seeds
5ml/1 tsp black mustard seeds
1 small onion, finely chopped
10ml/2 tsp grated fresh
   root ginger
2 fresh green chillies, seeded
   and chopped
600g/1lb 5oz potatoes, cooked
200g/7oz fresh peas
juice of 1 lemon
90ml/6 tbsp chopped fresh
   coriander (cilantro) leaves
115g/4oz/1 cup gram flour

25g/1oz/¼ cup self-raising
   (self-rising) flour
40g/1½oz/⅓ cup rice flour
large pinch of turmeric
10ml/2 tsp coriander seeds,
   finely crushed
350ml/12fl oz/1½ cups water
vegetable oil, for frying
salt and ground black pepper

For the chutney
105ml/7 tbsp coconut cream
200ml/7fl oz/scant 1 cup natural
   (plain) yogurt
50g/2oz mint leaves,
   finely chopped
5ml/1 tsp golden caster
   (superfine) sugar
juice of 1 lime

1 Heat a wok over a medium heat and add the sunflower oil. When hot, fry the cumin and mustard seeds for 1–2 minutes. Add the onion, ginger and chillies and cook for 3–4 minutes more. Add the cooked potatoes and peas and stir-fry for a further 5–6 minutes. Season, then stir in the lemon juice and coriander leaves. Leave the mixture to cool slightly, then divide into 25 portions. Shape each portion into a ball and chill.

2 To make the chutney, place all the ingredients in a blender and process until smooth. Season, then chill.

3 To make the batter, put the gram flour, self-raising flour and rice flour in a bowl. Season and add the turmeric and coriander seeds. Gradually whisk in the water to make a smooth batter.

4 Fill a wok one-third full of oil and heat to 180°C/350°F. Working in batches, dip the chilled balls in the batter, then drop into the oil and fry for 1–2 minutes, or until golden. Drain on kitchen paper, and serve immediately with the chutney.

Spiced Turnovers Energy 660kcal/2760kJ; Protein 13.9g; Carbohydrate 75.8g, of which sugars 9.3g; Fat 35.9g, of which saturates 17g; Cholesterol 105mg; Calcium 216mg; Fibre 5.2g; Sodium 740mg.
Curry-spiced Pakoras Energy 126kcal/525kJ; Protein 4.1g; Carbohydrate 8.3g, of which sugars 2.6g; Fat 8.8g, of which saturates 5.2g; Cholesterol 0mg; Calcium 35mg; Fibre 1.3g; Sodium 16mg.

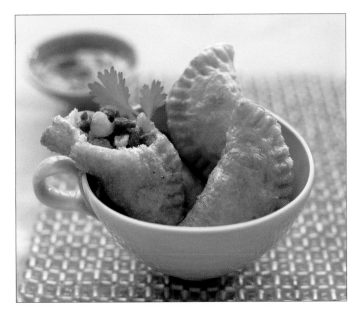

Spiced Beef and Potato Puffs

These crisp, golden pillows of pastry filled with spiced beef and potatoes are delicious served straight from the wok. The light pastry puffs up in the hot oil and contrasts enticingly with the fragrant spiced beef.

Serves 4
15ml/1 tbsp sunflower oil
½ small onion, finely chopped
3 garlic cloves, crushed
5ml/1 tsp fresh root ginger, grated
1 red chilli, seeded and chopped
30ml/2 tbsp hot curry powder
75g/3oz minced (ground) beef
115g/4oz mashed potato
60ml/4 tbsp chopped fresh
  coriander (cilantro)
2 sheets ready-rolled, fresh
  puff pastry
1 egg, lightly beaten
vegetable oil, for frying
salt and ground black pepper
fresh coriander (cilantro) leaves,
  to garnish
tomato ketchup, to serve

1 Heat the oil in a wok, then add the onion, garlic, ginger and chilli. Stir-fry over a medium heat for 2–3 minutes. Add the curry powder and beef and stir-fry over a high heat for a further 4–5 minutes, or until the beef is browned and just cooked through, then remove from the heat.

2 Transfer the beef mixture to a large bowl and add the mashed potato and chopped fresh coriander. Stir well, then season and set aside.

3 Lay the pastry sheets on a clean, dry surface and cut out eight rounds, using a 7.5cm/3in pastry (cookie) cutter. Place a large spoonful of the beef mixture in the centre of each pastry round. Brush the edges of the pastry with the beaten egg and fold each round in half to enclose the filling. Press and crimp the edges with the tines of a fork to seal.

4 Fill a wok one-third full of oil and heat to 180°C/350°F (or until a cube of bread, dropped into the oil, browns in 15 seconds).

5 Deep-fry the puffs, in batches, for about 2–3 minutes until they turn a golden brown colour. Drain on kitchen paper and serve garnished with fresh coriander leaves. Offer tomato ketchup to diners for dipping.

Potato Samosas

Throughout the East, these tasty potato snacks are eaten at any time of day.

Makes about 20
1 packet 25cm/10in square spring
  roll wrappers, thawed if frozen
30ml/2 tbsp plain (all-purpose)
  flour, mixed to a paste
  with water
vegetable oil, for deep frying
coriander (cilantro) leaves,
  to garnish

For the filling
25g/1oz/2 tbsp ghee or
  unsalted (sweet) butter
1 small onion, finely chopped
1cm/½in piece fresh root ginger,
  peeled and chopped
1 garlic glove, crushed
2.5ml/½ tsp chilli powder
1 large potato, about 225g/8oz,
  cooked until just tender and
  finely diced
50g/2oz/½ cup cauliflower
  florets, lightly cooked, chopped
  into small pieces
50g/2oz/½ cup frozen
  peas, thawed
5–10ml/1–2 tsp garam masala
15ml/1 tbsp chopped fresh
  coriander (cilantro) (leaves and
  stems)
squeeze of lemon juice
salt

1 Heat the ghee or butter in a large frying pan and fry the onion, ginger and garlic for 5 minutes until the onion has softened but not browned.

2 Add the chilli powder to the pan and cook for 1 minute, then stir in the potato, cauliflower and peas. Sprinkle with garam masala and set aside to cool. Stir in the chopped coriander, lemon juice and salt.

3 Cut the spring roll wrappers into three strips (or two for larger samosas). Brush the edges with a little of the flour paste. Place a small spoonful of filling about 2cm/¾in in from the edge of one strip. Fold one corner over the filling to make a triangle and continue this folding until the entire strip has been used and a triangular package has been formed. Seal any open edges with more flour and water paste.

4 Heat the oil for deep frying to 190°C/375°F and fry the samosas, a few at a time, until golden and crisp. Drain well on kitchen paper and serve hot, garnished with coriander leaves.

Beef and Potato Puffs Energy 408kcal/1695kJ; Protein 9g; Carbohydrate 24.2g, of which sugars 1.8g; Fat 31.8g, of which saturates 4.2g; Cholesterol 67mg; Calcium 46mg; Fibre 0.5g; Sodium 202mg.
Samosas Energy 56kcal/235kJ; Protein 1.3g; Carbohydrate 10g, of which sugars 0.8g; Fat 1.4g, of which saturates 0.2g; Cholesterol 0mg; Calcium 16mg; Fibre 0.7g; Sodium 8mg.

Thai Potato Samosas

Most samosas are deep-fried, but these are baked, making them a healthier option. They are also perfect for parties as no deep-frying is involved.

Makes 25
I large potato, about 250g/9oz, diced
15ml/1 tbsp groundnut (peanut) oil
2 shallots, finely chopped
I garlic clove, finely chopped
60ml/4 tbsp coconut milk
5ml/1 tsp Thai red or green curry paste
75g/3oz/¾ cup peas
juice of ½ lime
25 samosa wrappers or 10cm/4in x 5cm/2in strips of filo pastry
salt and ground black pepper oil, for brushing

1 Preheat the oven to 220°C/425°F/Gas 7. Bring a small pan of water to the boil, add the diced potato, cover and cook for 10–15 minutes, until tender. Drain and set aside.

2 Meanwhile, heat the groundnut oil in a large frying pan and cook the shallots and garlic over a medium heat, stirring occasionally, for 4–5 minutes, until softened and golden.

3 Add the drained potato, coconut milk, red or green curry paste, peas and lime juice to the frying pan. Mash coarsely with a wooden spoon. Season to taste with salt and pepper and cook over a low heat for 2–3 minutes, then remove the pan from the heat and set aside until the mixture has cooled a little.

4 Lay a samosa wrapper or filo strip flat on the work surface. Brush with a little oil, then place a generous teaspoonful of the mixture in the middle of one end. Turn one corner diagonally over the filling to meet the long edge.

5 Continue folding over the filling, keeping the triangular shape as you work down the strip. Brush with a little more oil if necessary and place on a baking sheet. Prepare all the other samosas in the same way.

6 Bake for 15 minutes, or until the pastry is golden and crisp. Leave to cool slightly before serving.

Rosemary Potato Wedges with Salmon Dip

This creamy dip with spiced herby potato wedges can be served as an appetizer or as part of a buffet lunch.

Serves 4
115g/4oz smoked salmon
250g/9oz/generous 1 cup mascarpone cheese
60ml/4 tbsp chopped fresh chives
grated rind and juice of 1 lemon
I red (bell) pepper, seeded and cut into strips
I yellow (bell) pepper, seeded and cut into strips
sea salt and ground black pepper

For the potato wedges
675g/1½lb large potatoes
60ml/4 tbsp olive oil
30ml/2 tbsp chopped fresh rosemary
I fresh red chilli, seeded and finely chopped

1 Preheat the oven to 200°C/400°F/Gas 6. To make the wedges, cut the potatoes into thick pieces. Pour the oil into a roasting pan and heat it in the oven for 10 minutes. Toss the wedges in the pan, then sprinkle over the rosemary and the chilli.

2 Shake the pan gently to coat the potatoes in the oil, rosemary and chilli. Season with salt and black pepper. Bake for 50–60 minutes or until tender, turning occasionally.

3 Cut the smoked salmon into small pieces, using kitchen scissors or a sharp filleting knife. Put the mascarpone cheese, chives and lemon rind in a bowl and mix with a fork until thoroughly blended.

4 Add the lemon juice, a little at a time, mixing constantly, so that the mixture is thinned and is given a lemony tang, but does not curdle.

5 Add the salmon to the cheese mixture and season with pepper. Place into a serving bowl, cover and chill until required.

6 To serve, arrange the pepper strips and wedges around the edge of a serving platter and place the dip in the centre.

Thai Samosas Energy 42kcal/178kJ; Protein 1.2g; Carbohydrate 8.5g, of which sugars 0.6g; Fat 0.6g, of which saturates 0.1g; Cholesterol 0mg; Calcium 14mg; Fibre 0.5g; Sodium 4mg.
Rosemary Wedges Energy 487kcal/2030kJ; Protein 16.9g; Carbohydrate 33.2g, of which sugars 7.9g; Fat 32.7g, of which saturates 14.2g; Cholesterol 71mg; Calcium 124mg; Fibre 3.9g; Sodium 774mg.

Spicy Potato Wedges with Chilli Dip

For a healthy snack with a superb flavour, try these roasted potato wedges. The crisp spice crust makes them taste irresistible, especially when they are served with a vibrant chilli dip.

Serves 2
2 baking potatoes, about 225g/
  8oz each
30ml/2 tbsp olive oil
2 garlic cloves, crushed
5ml/1 tsp ground allspice
5ml/1 tsp ground coriander
15ml/1 tbsp paprika
salt and ground black pepper

For the chilli dip
15ml/1 tbsp olive oil
1 small onion, finely chopped
1 garlic clove, crushed
200g/7oz can chopped tomatoes
1 fresh red chilli, seeded and
  finely chopped
15ml/1 tbsp balsamic vinegar
15ml/1 tbsp chopped fresh
  coriander (cilantro), plus extra
  to garnish

1 Preheat the oven to 200°C/400°F/Gas 6. Cut the potatoes in half, then cut each half lengthways into eight wedges.

2 Place the wedges in a pan of cold water. Bring to the boil, then lower the heat and simmer gently for 10 minutes or until the potatoes have softened slightly. Drain well and pat dry on kitchen paper.

3 Mix the oil, garlic, allspice, coriander and paprika in a roasting pan and add salt and pepper to taste. Add the potatoes to the pan and shake to coat them thoroughly in the spicy oil. Roast for 20 minutes, turning the potato wedges occasionally, or until they are browned, crisp and fully cooked.

4 Meanwhile, to make the chilli dip, heat the oil in a pan and add the onion and garlic. Cook over a medium heat for 5–10 minutes until softened. Add the tomatoes, with their juice. Stir in the chilli and vinegar.

5 Cook gently for 10 minutes until the mixture has reduced and thickened, then check the seasoning. Stir in the fresh coriander and serve hot, with the potato wedges, garnished with salt and fresh coriander sprigs.

Tangy Potato Wedges with Garlic Tofu Dip

Tofu makes a fabulous dip that is cool and creamy – the perfect foil for these deliciously crispy and piquant potato wedges.

Serves 4
6 potatoes, scrubbed
15ml/1 tbsp cumin seeds, ground
2.5–5ml/½–1 tsp cayenne pepper
grated rind of 2 limes or 1 lemon
45ml/3 tbsp olive oil
sea salt and ground black pepper

For the garlic tofu dip
1 garlic clove, crushed
175g/6oz silken tofu
dash of lemon juice
25ml/1½ tbsp olive oil
10g/¼oz fresh mint, stalks
  removed (optional)

1 Cut the potatoes lengthways in half, then cut each half lengthways into thirds or quarters to make wedges. Place them in a shallow dish and sprinkle over the spices, citrus rind, oil and seasoning. Toss together and leave to marinate for at least 30 minutes. Meanwhile, preheat the oven to 220°C/425°F/Gas 7.

2 Place the potato wedges in a roasting pan and bake for 30–35 minutes, until golden and tender, turning occasionally.

3 Meanwhile, make the garlic tofu dip by placing all the ingredients, except the oil, in a blender or food processor and processing until smooth.

4 With the machine running, gradually add the olive oil in a slow, steady stream until the dip is smooth and thickened. Season with salt and pepper to taste, then pour into a serving bowl. Transfer the potato wedges to a warm dish and serve with the dip.

Cook's Tips
• Garlic tofu dip is good with any roasted root vegetables, such as carrots, swede (rutabaga), celeriac and parsnips.
• If covered, the dip will keep in the refrigerator for up to 1 week.

Spicy Potato Wedges Energy 239kcal/1001kJ; Protein 4g; Carbohydrate 30.8g, of which sugars 4.9g; Fat 11.9g, of which saturates 1.9g; Cholesterol 0mg; Calcium 23mg; Fibre 2.6g; Sodium 28mg.
Tangy Potato Wedges Energy 320kcal/1340kJ; Protein 8.2g; Carbohydrate 38.5g, of which sugars 3.1g; Fat 15.9g, of which saturates 2.3g; Cholesterol 0mg; Calcium 246mg; Fibre 2.3g; Sodium 28mg.

Idaho Potato Slices

This unusual and tasty dish is made from a layered ring of potatoes, cheese and herbs. Cooking the ingredients together gives them a very rich flavour.

Serves 4
3 large potatoes
butter, for greasing

1 small onion, finely sliced
   into rings
200g/7oz/1¾ cups red Leicester
   or mature (sharp) Cheddar
   cheese, grated
fresh thyme sprigs
150ml/¼ pint/⅔ cup single
   (light) cream
salt and ground black pepper
salad leaves, to serve

1 Preheat the oven to 200°C/400°F/Gas 6. Peel the potatoes and cook in boiling water for 10 minutes until they are just starting to soften. Remove from the water and pat dry with kitchen paper.

2 Finely slice the potatoes, using the straight edge of a grater or a mandoline. Grease the base and sides of an 18cm/7in cake tin (pan) with butter and lay some of the potatoes on the base to cover it completely. Season with salt and pepper.

3 Sprinkle some of the onion rings over the potatoes and top with a little of the cheese. Sprinkle over some of the thyme and then continue to layer the ingredients, finishing with a layer of cheese and a little more seasoning.

4 Press the potato layers right down. (The mixture may seem quite high at this point but it will cook down.)

5 Pour over the cream and bake in the oven for between 35–45 minutes. Remove from the oven and cool. Invert on to a plate and cut into wedges. Serve immediately with a few salad leaves.

Variation
If you want to make this dish more substantial, top the potato wedges with slices of crispy bacon, or strips of roasted red or yellow (bell) peppers.

Potato Pizza

This 'pizza' is made with mashed potatoes, and contains a tasty filling of anchovies, capers and tomatoes. It is a speciality from Puglia in northern Italy.

2 garlic cloves, finely chopped
350g/12oz tomatoes, chopped
3 anchovy fillets, chopped
30ml/2 tbsp capers, rinsed
salt and ground black pepper

Serves 4
1kg/2¼lb floury potatoes
120ml/4fl oz/½ cup extra virgin
   olive oil

1 Cook the potatoes in their skins in boiling water until tender. Drain well and leave to cool slightly. When they are cool enough to handle, peel them and mash or pass through a food mill. Beat in 45ml/3 tbsp of the oil and season to taste with salt and pepper. Set aside.

2 Heat another 45ml/3 tbsp of the oil in a medium pan. Add the garlic and the chopped tomatoes and cook over a medium heat for 12–15 minutes, stirring a little to cook evenly, until the tomatoes soften and begin to dry out a little. Meanwhile, preheat the oven to 200°C/400°F/Gas 6.

3 Oil a round, shallow baking dish. Spread half the mashed potatoes in the dish in an even layer. Cover with the chopped tomatoes, and dot with the chopped anchovies and capers.

4 Spread over the rest of the potatoes in an even layer. Brush the top with the remaining oil and bake for 20–25 minutes until the top is golden brown. Sprinkle with black pepper and serve immediately.

Variation
For a vegetarian version of this dish, simply omit the anchovies. A few pitted and chopped olives may be added to the filling instead. Add them in step 3, on top of the tomatoes.

Potato Pancakes

These little potato snacks are popular street food in the Czech Republic, and they are available at roadside stalls and cafés. Quick and easy to make, they are a tasty adaptation of the classic flour-based pancake.

Serves 6–8
6 large waxy potatoes, peeled
2 eggs, beaten
1–2 garlic cloves, crushed
115g/4oz/1 cup plain
   (all-purpose) flour
5ml/1 tsp chopped
   fresh marjoram
50g/2oz/¼ cup butter
60ml/4 tbsp oil
salt and ground black pepper
sour cream, chopped fresh parsley
   and a tomato salad, to serve

1 Grate the potatoes and squeeze thoroughly dry, using a clean dish towel.

2 Put the potatoes in a bowl with the eggs, garlic, flour, marjoram and seasoning and mix well.

3 Heat half the butter and oil together in a large frying pan, then add large spoonfuls of the potato mixture to form rounds. Carefully flatten the 'pancakes' well with the back of a dampened spoon.

4 Fry the pancakes until crisp and golden brown, then turn them over and cook on the other side. Drain on kitchen paper and keep warm while cooking the rest of the pancakes, adding the remaining butter and oil to the frying pan as necessary.

5 Serve the pancakes topped with sour cream, sprinkled with chopped fresh parsley, and accompanied by a fresh, juicy tomato salad.

Cook's Tip
Put the peeled potatoes in water with a few drops of lemon juice, to prevent them turning brown.

Boxty Potato Pancakes

Said to have originated during the Irish famine, these delicious pancakes use blended potatoes in the batter mix and can be made as thin or thick as you like. They are delicious served rolled around a hot savoury filling, such as cooked cabbage and chopped bacon bound together in a light mustard sauce.

Makes 4 pancakes
450g/1lb potatoes, peeled
   and chopped
50–75g/2–3oz/½–⅔ cup plain
   (all-purpose) flour
about 150ml/¼ pint/⅔ cup milk
salt and ground black pepper
knob (pat) of butter

1 Place the peeled and chopped potatoes in a blender or in the bowl of a food processor and process until the potato is thoroughly blended and smooth.

2 Add the flour and enough milk to the processed potato to give a dropping consistency, about the thickness of double (heavy) cream. Season to taste with salt and ground black pepper. The milk and flour can be adjusted, depending on how thin you like your pancake. Heat a little butter on a griddle or cast-iron frying pan.

3 Pour about a quarter of the mixture into the pan – if the consistency is right it will spread evenly over the base. Cook over a medium heat for about 5 minutes on each side, depending on the thickness of the cake. Serve rolled, with the hot filling of your choice.

Cook's Tip
To prepare a mustardy cabbage and bacon filling: Chop half a large Savoy cabbage, discarding the tough veins, and dice 4–6 rashers (strips) of bacon. Fry these together in a large frying pan until the bacon is cooked through and the cabbage has softened and wilted a little. Stir 30ml/2 tbsp of wholegrain mustard into the cabbage and bacon.

Potato Pancakes Energy 291kcal/1221kJ; Protein 6g; Carbohydrate 35.4g, of which sugars 2.9g; Fat 15g, of which saturates 2.2g; Cholesterol 63mg; Calcium 36mg; Fibre 2.1g; Sodium 42mg.
Boxty Pancakes Energy 163kcal/689kJ; Protein 4.8g; Carbohydrate 30.9g, of which sugars 2.7g; Fat 3.1g, of which saturates 1.7g; Cholesterol 8mg; Calcium 69mg; Fibre 1.9g; Sodium 236mg.

Rice and Potato Tortitas

Like miniature tortillas, these little rice and potato pancakes are great served hot, either plain or with tomato sauce for dipping. They make an excellent scoop for any soft vegetable mixture or dip.

Serves 4
30ml/2 tbsp olive oil
115g/4oz/1 cup cooked long
   grain white rice
1 potato, grated
4 spring onions (scallions),
   thinly sliced
1 garlic clove, finely chopped
15ml/1 tbsp chopped
   fresh parsley
3 large (US extra large)
   eggs, beaten
2.5ml/½ tsp paprika
salt and ground black pepper

1 Heat half the olive oil in a large frying pan and stir-fry the rice, with the potato, spring onions and garlic, over a high heat for 3 minutes until golden.

2 Transfer the rice and vegetable mixture into a bowl and stir in the parsley and eggs, with the paprika and plenty of salt and pepper. Mix well.

3 Heat the remaining oil in the frying pan and drop in large spoonfuls of the rice mixture, leaving enough room for the mixture to spread. Cook the tortitas for about 1–2 minutes on each side.

4 Drain the tortitas on kitchen paper and keep hot in a warm oven while cooking the remaining mixture. Pile the cooked tortitas on a large serving platter or on individual plates and serve immediately.

> **Cook's Tip**
> These tortitas can be used as a base for a variety of dishes. Try using them in place of plain boiled rice or mashed potatoes for a change. Children love them just as they are, with a large dollop of tomato ketchup for dipping.

Potato Cakes with Spicy Chickpeas and Green Chillies

These spicy potato cakes and the accompanying chickpeas are typical of tasty Indian cuisine. They make a delicious and substantial appetizer or light lunch.

Makes 10 to 12
30ml/2 tbsp vegetable oil
30ml/2 tbsp ground coriander
30ml/2 tbsp ground cumin
2.5ml/½ tsp ground turmeric
2.5ml/½ tsp salt
2.5ml/½ tsp sugar
30ml/2 tbsp flour paste
450g/1lb cooked
   chickpeas, drained
2 fresh green chillies, chopped
5cm/2in piece fresh root ginger,
   finely crushed
75g/3oz fresh coriander (cilantro)
   leaves, chopped
2 firm tomatoes, chopped

For the potato cakes
450g/1lb potatoes, boiled and
   coarsely mashed
4 green chillies, finely chopped
50g/2oz fresh coriander (cilantro)
   leaves, finely chopped
7.5ml/1½ tsp ground cumin
5ml/1 tsp amchur (dry
   mango powder)
salt, to taste
vegetable oil, for shallow-frying

1 Make the spicy chickpeas. Heat the oil in a heavy pan and fry the coriander, cumin, turmeric, salt, sugar and flour paste, stirring frequently, until the oil has separated and the water evaporated.

2 Add the chickpeas to the spicy paste, then stir in the chillies, ginger, fresh coriander and tomatoes. Mix well and simmer for 5 minutes. Transfer to a serving dish and keep warm while you prepare the potato cakes.

3 To make the potato cakes, mix the mashed potato in a large bowl with the green chillies, coriander, ground cumin and amchur. Season with salt to taste. Mix well until all the ingredients are thoroughly combined.

4 Using your hands, shape the potato mixture into little cakes. Heat the oil in a shallow frying pan or griddle and fry the cakes on both sides until golden brown. Transfer to a serving dish and serve with the spicy chickpeas.

Rice Tortitas Energy 185kcal/776kJ; Protein 6.8g; Carbohydrate 17.6g, of which sugars 1.2g; Fat 10.4g, of which saturates 2.1g; Cholesterol 143mg; Calcium 56mg; Fibre 1.3g; Sodium 63mg.
Spicy Chickpeas Energy 163kcal/684kJ; Protein 5.2g; Carbohydrate 17.3g, of which sugars 1.6g; Fat 8.8g, of which saturates 1.1g; Cholesterol 0mg; Calcium 68mg; Fibre 3g; Sodium 96mg.

Potato Cakes with Black Pudding and Apple

This dish makes a deliciously rustic treat. The combination of crisp potato cake, tasty black pudding topped with apples and mushrooms is a real winner. Serve as an appetizer or as a light lunch.

Serves 4
4 large potatoes, peeled
45ml/3 tbsp olive oil

8 slices of black pudding
   (blood sausage)
115g/4oz cultivated mushrooms,
   such as oyster or shiitake
2 eating apples, peeled, cored and
   cut into wedges
15ml/1 tbsp sherry vinegar or
   wine vinegar
15g/1oz/2 tbsp butter
salt and ground black pepper

1 Grate the potatoes, putting them into a bowl of water as you grate them, drain and squeeze out the excess moisture.

2 Heat 30ml/2 tbsp olive oil in a large non-stick frying pan, add the grated potatoes and seasoning. Press the potatoes into the pan with your hands.

3 Cook the potatoes until golden brown on the underside, then turn over and cook the other side. When cooked, slide on to a warm plate.

4 Heat the remaining oil and fry the black pudding and mushrooms together for a few minutes. Remove from the pan and keep warm.

5 Add the apple wedges to the frying pan and gently cook until golden brown. Add the sherry or wine vinegar to the apples, and boil up the juices. Add the butter, stir with a wooden spatula until it has melted and season to taste with salt and ground black pepper.

6 Cut the potato cake into wedges and divide among four warmed plates. Arrange the black pudding and cooked mushrooms over the bed of potato cake, pour over the apples and the warm juices, and serve immediately.

Irish Potato Cakes

This is the traditional Irish method of making potato cakes on a griddle or heavy frying pan. Commercially made versions are available throughout Ireland as thin, pre-cooked potato cakes, which are fried for breakfast or occasionally, in the north of the country, for high tea. Griddle-cooked potato cakes were traditionally buttered and eaten hot topped with sugar, rather like pancakes.

Makes about 12
675g/1½lb potatoes, peeled
25g/1oz/2 tbsp unsalted
   (sweet) butter
about 175g/6oz/1½ cups plain
   (all-purpose) flour
salt

1 Boil the potatoes in a large pan until tender, then drain well and mash thoroughly. Salt the mash well, then mix in the butter and leave to cool a little.

2 Turn the mashed potatoes out on to a lightly floured work surface and knead in about one-third of their volume in flour, or as much as is needed to make a pliable dough. It will become easier to handle as the flour is incorporated, but try to avoid overworking it.

3 Roll out the dough to a thickness of about 1cm/½in and cut it into even triangles.

4 Heat a dry griddle pan or heavy frying pan over a low heat and cook the potato cakes for about 3 minutes on each side until browned. You will probably need to do this in batches; keep the cooked ones warm in a low oven. Serve hot with butter, or sugar, if you prefer.

> **Cook's Tip**
> *For authenticity look out for these Irish varieties of potato: Avalanche, a white-skinned early maincrop potato; Avondale, a beige-skinned maincrop; and Barna, an excellent red-skinned late maincrop.*

Black Pudding Energy 247kcal/1034kJ; Protein 4.2g; Carbohydrate 28.8g, of which sugars 5.4g; Fat 13.6g, of which saturates 4g; Cholesterol 13mg; Calcium 16mg; Fibre 2.4g; Sodium 132mg.
Irish Potato Cakes Energy 1276kcal/5392kJ; Protein 30.4g; Carbohydrate 249.1g, of which sugars 6.7g; Fat 24.1g, of which saturates 13.4g; Cholesterol 53mg; Calcium 282mg; Fibre 14g; Sodium 203mg.

Bacon and Potato Cakes

Golden and crisp, but soft when you bite into them, these potato cakes are wonderful for breakfast or supper, with or without anything else.

Serves 4

450g/1lb waxy potatoes, peeled
1 small onion, grated
4 slices streaky (fatty) bacon, finely chopped
30ml/2 tbsp self-raising (self-rising) flour
2 eggs, beaten
vegetable oil, for deep-frying
salt and ground black pepper
fresh parsley sprigs, to garnish

1 Coarsely grate the potatoes, rinse, drain and pat dry on kitchen paper, then mix with the onion, half the bacon, flour and eggs, and season with salt and black pepper.

2 Heat a 1cm/½in layer of oil in a frying pan until really hot, then add about 15ml/1 tbsp of the potato mixture and quickly spread the mixture out with the back of the spoon, taking care that it does not break up.

3 Add a few more spoonfuls of the mixture to the pan in the same way, leaving space between each one so they do not stick together, and fry them for 4–5 minutes until golden brown on the undersides.

4 Carefully turn the cakes over using a metal spatula and fry the other side until golden brown. Drain on kitchen paper, transfer to an ovenproof dish and keep warm in a low oven while frying the remainder.

5 Fry the remaining bacon pieces in the pan. Serve the cakes on individual plates and top with the fried bacon. Serve immediately, sprinkled with the parsley sprigs.

Variation
For a vegetarian alternative to this dish, omit the bacon and replace it with a seeded and chopped red (bell) pepper.

Gateshead Bacon and Potato Floddies

From Tyneside in northern England, floddies are traditionally cooked for breakfast in bacon fat, served with eggs and sausages. A kind of potato cake, floddies are said to have originated with canal workers, who cooked them over an open fire. They should be served crisp and golden brown, and are great as a snack or as part of a bigger breakfast feast.

Serves 4–6

250g/9oz potatoes, weighed after peeling
1 large onion
175g/6oz rindless streaky (fatty) bacon, finely chopped
50g/2oz/½ cup self-raising (self-rising) flour
2 eggs
oil, for frying
salt and ground black pepper

1 Grate the potatoes on to a clean dish towel, and then gather up the edges to make a pouch. Squeeze and twist the towel to remove the liquid.

2 Grate or finely chop the onion into a mixing bowl and add the grated potato, chopped bacon and flour. Season with salt and black pepper. Mix well with your hands until all the ingredients are thoroughly combined.

3 Beat the eggs in a separate bowl and stir them into the potato mixture. Heat some oil in a large frying pan.

4 Add generous tablespoonfuls of the potato mixture to the hot oil and flatten them slightly to make thin cakes. Cook over a medium heat for 3–4 minutes on each side until golden brown. Lift out, drain on kitchen paper and serve immediately.

Cook's Tips
• Push the floddies into oiled metal rings before frying if you wish, for a neat circular shape.
• Serve with grilled (broiled) sausages and fried eggs for a hearty and substantial breakfast treat.

Bacon and Potato Cakes Energy 363kcal/1512kJ; Protein 9.8g; Carbohydrate 25g, of which sugars 2.4g; Fat 25.6g, of which saturates 4.7g; Cholesterol 111mg; Calcium 53mg; Fibre 1.6g; Sodium 390mg.
Bacon Floddies Energy 214kcal/891kJ; Protein 8.8g; Carbohydrate 17.1g, of which sugars 3.5g; Fat 12.7g, of which saturates 3.4g; Cholesterol 82mg; Calcium 38mg; Fibre 1.4g; Sodium 397mg.

Curried Lamb and Potato Cakes

An unusual variation on burgers, these little lamb and potato triangles are easy and quick to make. They are really good served hot as part of a buffet, but they can also be eaten cold as a snack or taken on picnics.

Makes 12–15
450g/1lb new or small, firm potatoes
3 eggs
1 onion, grated
30ml/2 tbsp chopped fresh parsley
450g/1lb finely minced (ground) lean lamb
115g/4oz/2 cups fresh breadcrumbs
vegetable oil, for frying
salt and ground black pepper
sprigs of fresh mint, to garnish
pitta bread and herby green salad, to serve

1 Cook the potatoes in a large pan of boiling salted water for 20 minutes or until tender, then drain and leave to cool.

2 Beat the eggs in a large bowl. Add the onion, parsley and seasoning and beat together.

3 When the potatoes are cold, grate them coarsely and stir into the egg mixture, together with the minced lamb. Knead the mixture well for 3–4 minutes until all the ingredients are thoroughly blended.

4 Take a handful of the lamb mixture and roll it into a ball. Repeat this process until all the meat is used.

5 Roll the balls in the breadcrumbs and then mould them into fairly flat triangular shapes, about 13cm/5in long. Coat them in the breadcrumbs again.

6 Heat a 1cm/½in layer of oil in a frying pan over a medium heat. When the oil is hot, fry the potato cakes for 8–12 minutes until golden brown on both sides, turning occasionally. Drain on kitchen paper.

7 Serve immediately, garnished with mint and accompanied by pitta bread and salad.

Potato Blinis with Smoked Salmon

These crisp, light potato pancakes originated in Russia, where they are served with the finest caviar, but they are also good with salmon roe. They make great canapés to serve at a party.

Serves 6 as part of a buffet
1 potato, about 115g/4oz, boiled and mashed
15ml/1 tbsp easy-blend (rapid-rise) dried yeast
175g/6oz/1½ cups plain (all-purpose) flour
300ml/½ pint/1¼ cups lukewarm water
oil, for greasing
90ml/6 tbsp sour cream
6 slices smoked salmon
salt and ground black pepper
lemon slices, to garnish

1 Mix the mashed potato, yeast, flour, salt and pepper with the water to make a smooth dough. Cover with clear film (plastic wrap) and leave to rise in a warm place for 30 minutes or until doubled in bulk.

2 Heat a non-stick frying pan and add a little oil. Drop small spoonfuls of the blini dough on to the pan. Each blini should measure about 5cm/2in in diameter.

3 Cook the blinis for 2 minutes until lightly golden on the underside. Turn over using a metal spatula and cook the second side. Remove each batch as it cooks and keep them warm while you cook the remaining blinis.

4 To serve, top each blini with a little sour cream and a small folded slice of smoked salmon. Garnish with black pepper and a small slice of lemon.

> **Variation**
> For an alternative topping for the blinis, mix 200g/7oz/ scant 1 cup cream cheese with 15ml/1 tbsp chopped fresh parsley or dill. Spread over the blinis and top with the salmon. Add slivers of sweet pickled cherry chillies or a spoonful of salmon roe.

Lamb and Potato Cakes Energy 181kcal/760kJ; Protein 10.8g; Carbohydrate 13.9g, of which sugars 1.1g; Fat 9.6g, of which saturates 2.8g; Cholesterol 76mg; Calcium 31mg; Fibre 0.8g; Sodium 128mg.
Potato Blinis Energy 220kcal/930kJ; Protein 17.2g; Carbohydrate 26.3g, of which sugars 1.3g; Fat 5.9g, of which saturates 2.4g; Cholesterol 34mg; Calcium 66mg; Fibre 1.1g; Sodium 1024mg.

Smoked Salmon with Warm Potato Cakes

Although the ingredients are timeless, this combination makes an excellent modern dish, which is deservedly popular as a first course or as a substantial canapé to serve with drinks. It also makes a perfect brunch dish, served with lightly scrambled eggs and freshly squeezed orange juice. Choose wild fish if possible.

75g/3oz/²/₃ cup plain
  (all-purpose) flour
2 eggs, beaten
2 spring onions
  (scallions), chopped
a little freshly grated nutmeg
50g/2oz/¼ cup butter, melted
150ml/¼ pint/²/₃ cup sour cream
12 slices of smoked salmon
salt and ground black pepper
chopped fresh chives, to garnish

Serves 6
450g/1lb potatoes, cooked
  and mashed

1 Put the potatoes, flour, eggs and spring onions into a large bowl. Season with salt, black pepper and a little nutmeg, and add half the butter. Mix thoroughly and shape into 12 small potato cakes.

2 Heat the remaining butter in a non-stick frying pan and cook the potato cakes until browned on both sides.

3 To serve, mix the sour cream with some salt and pepper. Fold a piece of smoked salmon and place on top of each potato cake. Top the salmon with the cream and then the chives, and serve immediately.

Cook's Tip
If it is more convenient, you can make the potato cakes in advance and keep them overnight in the refrigerator. When required, warm them through in a hot oven 15 minutes before assembling and serving.

Herbed Plaice and Potato Croquettes

These tasty croquettes are made with a mixture of mashed potato and flaked fish. They are great as an appetizer and are very popular with children.

Serves 4–6
450g/1lb plaice fillets
300ml/½ pint/1¼ cups milk
450g/1lb cooked potatoes

1 fennel bulb, finely chopped
45ml/3 tbsp chopped
  fresh parsley
2 eggs
15g/½ oz/1 tbsp unsalted
  (sweet) butter
115g/4oz/2 cups white
  breadcrumbs
25g/1oz/2 tbsp sesame seeds
oil, for deep-frying
salt and ground black pepper

1 Gently poach the plaice fillets in the milk for approximately 15 minutes until the fish flakes. Drain and reserve the milk.

2 Peel the skin off the fish and remove any bones. In a food processor or blender, process the fish, potatoes, fennel, parsley, eggs and butter.

3 Add 30ml/2 tbsp of the reserved cooking milk and season with salt and ground black pepper. Mix well. Chill for 30 minutes, then shape into 20 croquettes with your hands.

4 Mix together the breadcrumbs and sesame seeds, then roll the croquettes in this mixture to form a good coating. Heat the oil in a large, heavy pan until it is hot enough to brown a cube of stale bread in 30 seconds.

5 Deep-fry the croquettes in batches for about 4 minutes until they are golden brown all over. Drain well on kitchen paper and serve the croquettes hot.

Cook's Tip
Serve these baby croquettes with a tartare sauce, if you like. Simply chop some capers and gherkins, and stir into home-made or good quality store-bought mayonnaise. Season to taste with salt and pepper.

Smoked Salmon Energy 326kcal/1365kJ; Protein 21.9g; Carbohydrate 22.9g, of which sugars 2.3g; Fat 17g, of which saturates 8.6g; Cholesterol 119mg; Calcium 70mg; Fibre 1.2g; Sodium 1315mg.
Croquettes Energy 397kcal/1673kJ; Protein 21.8g; Carbohydrate 45g, of which sugars 2.7g; Fat 15.8g, of which saturates 3.3g; Cholesterol 100mg; Calcium 138mg; Fibre 2.8g; Sodium 458mg.

Potato and Chive Pancakes with Pickled Herring and Onion Rings

Serve these moreish potato pancakes as an appetizer or as a light main course with salad.

Serves 6
275g/10oz potatoes, cooked and mashed
2 eggs, beaten
150ml/¼ pint/⅔ cup milk
40g/1½oz plain (all-purpose) flour
30ml/2 tbsp chopped fresh chives
vegetable oil or butter, for greasing
salt and ground black pepper

For the topping
2 small red or yellow onions, thinly sliced into rings
60ml/4 tbsp sour cream or crème fraîche
5ml/1 tsp wholegrain mustard
15ml/1 tbsp chopped fresh dill
6 pickled herring fillets

To garnish
fresh dill sprigs
fresh chives or chive flowers

1 Prepare the topping. Place the onions in a bowl and cover with boiling water. Set aside for 2–3 minutes, then drain and dry on kitchen paper. Mix the onions with the sour cream or crème fraîche, mustard and chopped dill. Season to taste. Cut the pickled herring fillets into 12–18 pieces. Set them aside.

2 Put the mashed potato in a bowl and beat in the eggs, milk and flour with a wooden spoon to make a batter. Season to taste with salt and pepper and whisk in the chopped chives.

3 Heat a frying pan over a medium heat and grease it with a little oil or butter. Spoon about 30ml/2 tbsp of batter into the pan to make a pancake, measuring about 7.5cm/3in across. Cook for 3–4 minutes, until the underside is set and brown.

4 Turn the pancake over and cook the other side for 3–4 minutes, until golden brown. Transfer to a plate and keep warm while you make the remaining pancakes.

5 Place two pancakes on each of six warmed plates and distribute the pickled herring fillets and onions equally among them. Garnish with dill sprigs, fresh chives and/or chive flowers. Season with black pepper and serve immediately.

Potato and Salt Cod Fritters

These bitesize fish and potato cakes, dipped into creamy aioli, are irresistible as an appetizer.

Serves 6
300ml/½ pint/1¼ cups milk
6 spring onions (scallions), finely chopped
450g/1lb salt cod, soaked for 24 hours in three changes of water
500g/1¼lb floury potatoes, cooked and mashed
30ml/2 tbsp extra virgin olive oil
30ml/2 tbsp chopped fresh parsley
juice of ½ lemon
2 eggs, beaten
plain (all-purpose) flour, for dusting
90g/3½oz/1¼ cups dried white breadcrumbs
olive oil, for shallow frying
lemon wedges and salad leaves, to serve
salt and ground black pepper

For the aioli
2 large garlic cloves, finely chopped
2 egg yolks
300ml/½ pint/1¼ cups olive oil
juice of ½ lemon, to taste

1 Simmer the milk in a pan with half the spring onions. Add the cod and poach gently for 10–15 minutes. Remove the cod and flake it with a fork into a bowl, discarding bones and skin.

2 Add 60ml/4 tbsp potato to the cod and mix well. Add the oil, then the remaining potato. Beat in the remaining spring onions and the parsley. Season with lemon juice and salt and pepper to taste. Beat one egg into the mixture, then chill until firm.

3 Shape the mixture into 12–18 balls, then flatten into small round cakes. Coat each one in flour, then dip in the remaining egg and coat with breadcrumbs. Chill until ready to fry.

4 Meanwhile, make the aioli. Pound the garlic with a little salt in a mortar and pestle. Whisk in the egg yolks. Beat in half the olive oil, a drop at a time. When the sauce is as thick as soft butter, beat in 5–10ml/1–2 tsp lemon juice. Continue adding oil until the aioli is thick. Season to taste.

5 Heat about 2cm/¾in oil in a large, heavy frying pan. Add the fritters and cook over a medium-hot heat for about 4 minutes on each side, until crisp and golden. Drain on kitchen paper, then serve with the aioli, lemon wedges and salad leaves.

Potato Pancakes Energy 164kcal/686kJ; Protein 5.8g; Carbohydrate 15.3g, of which sugars 3.1g; Fat 9.4g, of which saturates 2.5g; Cholesterol 75mg; Calcium 67mg; Fibre 0.8g; Sodium 78mg.
Salt Cod Fritters Energy 718kcal/2980kJ; Protein 21.1g; Carbohydrate 33.1g, of which sugars 1.9g; Fat 56.5g, of which saturates 8.3g; Cholesterol 165mg; Calcium 67mg; Fibre 1.6g; Sodium 196mg.

Salmon Fish Cakes

The secret of a good fish cake is to make it with freshly prepared fish and potatoes, home-made breadcrumbs and plenty of fresh herbs, such as dill and parsley or tarragon.

Serves 4
450g/1lb cooked salmon fillet
450g/1lb freshly cooked
 potatoes, mashed
25g/1oz/2 tbsp butter, melted or
 30ml/2 tbsp olive oil
10ml/2 tsp wholegrain mustard
15ml/1 tbsp each chopped fresh
 dill and chopped fresh parsley
 or tarragon
grated rind and juice of ½ lemon
15g/½oz/2 tbsp wholemeal
 (whole-wheat) flour
1 egg, lightly beaten
150g/5oz/2 cups dried
 breadcrumbs
60ml/4 tbsp sunflower oil
sea salt and ground black pepper
rocket (arugula) leaves and
 chives, to garnish
lemon wedges, to serve

1 Flake the cooked salmon, discarding any skin and bones. Put it in a bowl with the mashed potato, melted butter or oil and wholegrain mustard, and mix well.

2 Stir the herbs and the lemon rind and juice into the fish and potato mixture. Season to taste with plenty of sea salt and ground black pepper.

3 Divide the mixture into eight portions and shape each into a ball, then flatten into a thick disc. Dip the fish cakes first in flour, then in egg and finally in breadcrumbs, making sure that they are evenly coated with crumbs.

4 Heat the oil in a frying pan until it is very hot. Fry the fish cakes in batches until golden brown and crisp all over. As each batch is ready, drain on kitchen paper and keep hot. Garnish with rocket and chives and serve with lemon wedges.

Cook's Tip
Any fresh white or hot-smoked fish is suitable. Always buy organically farmed fish, or sustainably caught wild fish.

Haddock and Potato Fish Cakes

These tasty fish and potato cakes can be made slightly larger and served as substantial fish burgers, or made into smaller balls and served as tasty finger food at a party or buffet lunch.

Makes 20
450g/1lb skinned haddock,
 pollock or cod
2 medium potatoes, peeled
4 green chillies, finely chopped
5cm/2in piece fresh root ginger,
 finely crushed
a few fresh coriander (cilantro)
 and mint leaves, chopped
4 spring onions (scallions),
 finely chopped
2 eggs
breadcrumbs, for coating
vegetable oil, for shallow-frying
salt and ground black pepper
chilli sauce or sweet chutney,
 to serve

1 Place the fish in a lightly greased steamer and steam until cooked. The flesh should flake easily when tested with a fork or the tip of a knife. Remove from the heat but leave on the steaming tray to cool.

2 Meanwhile, cut the potatoes into chunks and cook in a pan with plenty of boiling water for 10–15 minutes until tender, then drain well and mash. Set aside.

3 When the fish is cool, flake it coarsely into a large bowl and add the potatoes, spices, coriander and mint, spring onions, seasonings and one of the eggs. Mix with a wooden spoon or your hands until the ingredients are thoroughly combined.

4 Shape into cakes. Beat the remaining egg and dip the cakes in it, then coat with the breadcrumbs. Heat the oil in a frying pan and cook the fish cakes until brown on all sides. Serve hot.

Cook's Tip
Any firm, white-fleshed fish can be used for making this dish. Haddock and pollock are cheaper than cod and they also tend to come from more sustainable stocks, making them the ideal choice for this recipe.

Fish Cakes Energy 586kcal/2453kJ; Protein 29.8g; Carbohydrate 49.9g, of which sugars 3.2g; Fat 31g, of which saturates 7.2g; Cholesterol 117mg; Calcium 79mg; Fibre 1.3g; Sodium 266mg.
Haddock Fish Cakes Energy 67kcal/284kJ; Protein 5.5g; Carbohydrate 6.9g, of which sugars 1.5g; Fat 2.2g, of which saturates 1.1g; Cholesterol 14mg; Calcium 30mg; Fibre 0.7g; Sodium 116mg.

Coquilles St Jacques

A classic French appetizer that calls for the best quality scallops and rich piped potato to ensure a wonderful result. You will need four scallop shells to serve these.

Serves 4
450g/1lb potatoes, chopped
50g/2oz/4 tbsp butter
4 large or 8 small scallops
120ml/4fl oz/½ cup fish stock

For the sauce
25g/1oz/2 tbsp butter
25g/1oz/¼ cup plain
    (all-purpose) flour
300ml/½ pint/1¼ cups milk
30ml/2 tbsp single (light) cream
115g/4oz/1 cup mature (sharp)
    Cheddar cheese, grated
salt and ground black pepper
dill sprigs, to garnish
grilled lemon wedges, to serve

1 Preheat oven to 200°C/400°F/Gas 6. Place the chopped potatoes in a large pan, cover with plenty of water and boil for about 10–15 minutes or until tender. Drain and mash well with the butter.

2 Spoon the mixture into a piping (pastry) bag fitted with a star nozzle. Pipe the potatoes around the outside of a cleaned scallop shell. Repeat the process, making four in total.

3 Simmer the scallops in a little fish stock for 3 minutes or until they are just firm. Drain well and slice the scallops finely. Set them aside.

4 To make the sauce, melt the butter in a small pan, add the flour and cook over a low heat for a couple of minutes, then gradually add the milk and cream, stirring constantly, and cook until thickened.

5 Stir in the cheese and cook until melted. Season to taste. Spoon a little sauce in the base of each shell. Divide the scallops between the shells and then pour the remaining sauce over the scallops.

6 Bake the scallops in the preheated oven for about 10 minutes, or until golden. Garnish with the dill sprigs. Serve with grilled lemon wedges.

Sweet Potato and Prawn Patties

You can make these delicious prawn and sweet potato patties any size: small for a snack or appetizer, or large for a main course; simply adjust the amount you spoon on to the spatula before frying. Traditionally, the patties are served with herb and lettuce leaves for wrapping and a sauce for dipping.

Serves 4
50g/2oz/½ cup plain
    (all-purpose) flour
50g/2oz/½ cup rice flour

scant 5ml/1 tsp baking powder
10ml/2 tsp sugar
2.5cm/1in fresh root ginger,
    peeled and grated
2 spring onions (scallions),
    finely sliced
175g/6oz small fresh prawns
    (shrimp), peeled and deveined
1 slim sweet potato, about
    225g/8oz, peeled and cut into
    fine matchsticks
vegetable oil, for deep-frying
salt and ground black pepper
chopped fresh coriander (cilantro),
    to garnish
nuoc cham or other dipping
    sauce, to serve

1 Sift the flours and baking powder into a bowl. Add the sugar and about 2.5ml/½ tsp each of salt and pepper. Gradually stir in 250ml/8fl oz/1 cup water, until thoroughly combined. Add the ginger and spring onions and leave to stand for 30 minutes.

2 Add the prepared prawns and sweet potato matchsticks to the batter and gently fold them in, making sure they are well coated. Heat enough vegetable oil for deep-frying in a wok or heavy pan.

3 Place a heaped tablespoon of the mixture on to a metal spatula and pat it down a little. Lower it into the oil, pushing it off the spatula so that it floats in the oil. Fry the patty for 2–3 minutes, turning it over so that it is evenly browned. Drain on kitchen paper. Continue with the rest of the batter, frying the patties in small batches.

4 Arrange the patties on a serving dish, or on lettuce leaves, garnish with coriander, and serve immediately with nuoc cham or another dipping sauce of your choice.

Coquilles St Jacques Energy 466kcal/1948kJ; Protein 24.2g; Carbohydrate 28.8g, of which sugars 5.7g; Fat 28.6g, of which saturates 18.3g; Cholesterol 103mg; Calcium 342mg; Fibre 1.3g; Sodium 496mg.
Sweet Potato Patties Energy 276kcal/1159kJ; Protein 11g; Carbohydrate 35g, of which sugars 6g; Fat 11g, of which saturates 1g; Cholesterol 85mg; Calcium 83mg; Fibre 81g; Sodium 0.2g.

Potato Salad with Capers and Black Olives

This dish from southern Italy is quick and easy to make. The combination of potatoes, olives, capers and anchovies is quite perfect.

Serves 4–6

900g/2lb large white potatoes
50ml/2fl oz/¼ cup white
   wine vinegar
75ml/5 tbsp olive oil

30ml/2 tbsp chopped flat
   leaf parsley
30ml/2 tbsp capers,
   finely chopped
50g/2oz/½ cup pitted black
   olives, chopped in half
3 garlic cloves, finely chopped
50g/2oz marinated
   anchovies (unsalted)
salt and ground black pepper

1 Boil the potatoes in their skins in a large pan of water for about 15–20 minutes or until they are just tender. Remove from the pan using a slotted spoon and place them in a separate bowl.

2 When the potatoes are cool enough to handle, carefully peel off the skins.

3 Cut the peeled potatoes into even chunks and place in a large, flat earthenware dish.

4 Mix together the white wine vinegar and olive oil, season to taste with salt and pepper and add the parsley, capers, olives and garlic. Toss carefully to combine and then pour over the potato chunks.

5 Lay the anchovies on top of the salad. Cover with a cloth and leave to settle for 30 minutes or so before serving to allow the flavours to permeate.

> **Variation**
> If you want to serve this dish to vegetarians, simply omit the anchovies; it tastes delicious even without them.

Tangy Potato Salad

If you like a good kick of mustard and the distinctive flavour of tarragon, you'll love the piquant dressing in this potato salad.

Serves 8

1.3kg/3lb small new or
   salad potatoes
30ml/2 tbsp white wine vinegar
15ml/1 tbsp Dijon mustard

45ml/3 tbsp vegetable or olive oil
75g/3oz/6 tbsp chopped
   red onion
120ml/4fl oz/½ cup mayonnaise
30ml/2 tbsp chopped fresh
   tarragon, or 7.5ml/1½ tsp
   dried tarragon
1 celery stick, thinly sliced
salt and ground black pepper
celery leaves and tarragon leaves,
   to garnish

1 Cook the potatoes in their skins in boiling salted water for about 10–15 minutes until tender. Drain well.

2 Mix together the vinegar and Dijon mustard, then slowly whisk in the oil.

3 When the potatoes are cool enough to handle, cut them into even slices and place them into a large bowl. Add the onion to the potatoes, then pour the dressing over them. Season with salt and pepper to taste, then toss gently to combine. Leave to stand for at least 30 minutes.

4 Mix together the mayonnaise and tarragon. Gently stir into the potatoes, together with the celery. Serve garnished with celery leaves and tarragon.

> **Cook's Tip**
> The delicious, distinctive tarragon flavour in this dish makes it the perfect partner to roast or grilled (broiled) chicken.

> **Variation**
> When available, use small red or even blue potatoes to give an interesting colour to the salad.

Olive Potato Salad Energy 282kcal/1174kJ; Protein 5g; Carbohydrate 24.4g, of which sugars 2.2g; Fat 18.9g, of which saturates 2.8g; Cholesterol 5mg; Calcium 54mg; Fibre 2g; Sodium 347mg.
Tangy Potato Salad Energy 283kcal/1182kJ; Protein 3.7g; Carbohydrate 32.4g, of which sugars 3.4g; Fat 16.2g, of which saturates 2.5g; Cholesterol 11mg; Calcium 18mg; Fibre 2.1g; Sodium 147mg.

Potato and Radish Salad

Crunchy radishes add a splash of peppery flavour and an appealing hint of colour to this subtle honey-scented salad. Unlike many potato salads, which are dressed in thick creamy sauces, this is quite light and cleanly flavoured with a truly tasty yet delicate dressing.

Serves 4–6
450g/1lb new or salad potatoes
45ml/3 tbsp olive oil
15ml/1 tbsp walnut or hazelnut oil (optional)
30ml/2 tbsp wine vinegar
10ml/2 tsp coarse-grain mustard
5ml/1 tsp honey
about 6–8 radishes, thinly sliced
30ml/2 tbsp chopped chives
salt and ground black pepper

1 Cook the potatoes in their skins in a large pan of boiling salted water for about 10–15 minutes until just tender. Drain well and leave to cool slightly. When cool enough to handle, cut the potatoes in half, but leave any small ones whole. Place in a large bowl and set aside.

2 To make the dressing, place the oils, vinegar, mustard and honey in a bowl and season to taste with salt and pepper. Whisk together until thoroughly combined.

3 Toss the dressing into the potatoes in the bowl while they are still cooling and leave to stand for 1–2 hours to allow the flavours to penetrate.

4 Finally, mix in the sliced radishes and chopped chives and chill in the refrigerator until ready to serve.

5 Just before serving, toss the salad mixture together again, as some of the dressing may have drained to the bottom, and adjust the seasoning.

> **Variation**
> Sliced celery stick, diced red onion and/or chopped walnuts would make good alternatives to the radishes if you are unable to obtain any.

Potato, Caraway Seed and Parsley Salad

This highly fragrant potato salad is enhanced with the distinctive flavours of garlic and caraway. Adding the garlic infused oil and the caraway seeds while the potatoes are still hot will help the potatoes to soak up the delicious flavours of the dressing.

Serves 4–6
675g/1½lb new potatoes, scrubbed
45ml/3 tbsp garlic-infused olive oil
15ml/1 tbsp caraway seeds, lightly crushed
45ml/3 tbsp chopped fresh parsley
salt and ground black pepper

1 Cook the potatoes in salted, boiling water for about 10 minutes, or until just tender. Drain thoroughly and transfer to a large bowl.

2 Add the garlic-infused oil, caraway seeds and some salt and ground black pepper to the hot potatoes, then mix until all of the ingredients are well combined. Set the bowl aside to allow the potatoes to cool a little.

3 When the potatoes are almost cold, stir in the chopped parsley and serve.

> **Cook's Tip**
> If the salad has stood for a while, give it a thorough mix before serving to ensure the dressing is evenly distributed. It will tend to settle to the bottom of the bowl over time.

> **Variation**
> This recipe is also delicious if made with the same quantity of sweet potatoes instead of new potatoes. Peel and roughly chop the sweet potatoes into chunks about the same size as new potatoes, then follow the recipe as before.

Potato and Radish Salad Energy 108kcal/451kJ; Protein 1.5g; Carbohydrate 13g, of which sugars 1.9g; Fat 5.9g, of which saturates 0.9g; Cholesterol 0mg; Calcium 8mg; Fibre 0.9g; Sodium 36mg.
Potato and Parsley Salad Energy 131kcal/549kJ; Protein 2.1g; Carbohydrate 18.3g, of which sugars 1.6g; Fat 5.9g, of which saturates 0.9g; Cholesterol 0mg; Calcium 22mg; Fibre 1.5g; Sodium 15mg.

Chef's Potato Salad

This delicious and flexible potato salad can be adapted to contain all of your favourite ingredients. It is also a good opportunity to use up any leftover vegetables and small pieces of cheese from the refrigerator. For these reasons, the quantities given are approximate.

Serves 6

450g/1lb cooked new potatoes, halved if large
2 carrots, grated coarsely
½ small fennel bulb or 2 sticks celery, sliced thinly
50g/2oz sliced button mushrooms
¼ cucumber, sliced or chopped
small green or red (bell) pepper, sliced
200g/7oz/1 cup cooked pulses, such as red kidney beans or green lentils
1 Little Gem (Bibb) or baby lettuce, or 1 head chicory (endive)
2–3 hard-boiled eggs, quartered and/or grated cheese, to serve
½ carton salad cress, chopped

For the dressing

60ml/4 tbsp mayonnaise
45ml/3 tbsp natural (plain) yogurt
30ml/2 tbsp milk
30ml/2 tbsp chopped fresh chives or spring onion (scallion) tops
salt and ground black pepper

1 Place all the vegetables and beans or lentils (except the lettuce or chicory) into a large mixing bowl.

2 Line a large serving platter or individual plates with the lettuce or chicory leaves – creating a nest for the other salad ingredients to sit in.

3 In a separate bowl, mix all the dressing ingredients together until well combined. Pour over the vegetables and beans or lentils in the mixing bowl.

4 Toss the salad thoroughly in the dressing, season well with salt and ground black pepper, then pile into the centre of the lettuce nest on the serving platter.

5 Top the salad with the hard-boiled egg quarters, cheese or both, and then sprinkle over the chopped cress. Serve the salad lightly chilled.

Watercress and Potato Salad

New potatoes are equally good hot or cold, and this colourful, nutritious salad is an ideal way of making the most of them. This recipe is for making in the microwave but it can easily be made on the stove by boiling the potatoes in a pan of water.

Serves 4

450g/1lb small new or salad potatoes, skin on
45ml/3 tbsp water
1 bunch watercress
200g/7oz/1½ cups cherry tomatoes, halved
30ml/2 tbsp pumpkin seeds
45ml/3 tbsp low-fat fromage frais or low-fat cream cheese
15ml/1 tbsp cider vinegar
5ml/1 tsp soft light brown sugar
salt and ground black pepper
pinch of paprika

1 Place the potatoes and water in a microwave-proof bowl. Cover and microwave on the high setting for 7–10 minutes, stirring halfway through cooking. Leave to stand, covered, for 3 minutes, then drain and leave to cool.

2 Put the potatoes in a large mixing bowl. Add the watercress, tomatoes and pumpkin seeds and mix together until the ingredients are well combined.

3 Place the fromage frais or cream cheese, vinegar, sugar, salt, pepper and paprika to taste in a screw-top jar and shake well to mix. Pour over the salad just before serving.

> **Variation**
> To make a spinach and potato salad, substitute about 225g/8oz fresh baby spinach leaves for the watercress.

> **Cook's Tip**
> If you are preparing this salad in advance, mix the dressing in the jar and set aside until needed. Shake the dressing again and toss it into the salad just before serving.

Chef's Salad Energy 229kcal/956kJ; Protein 9g; Carbohydrate 24.1g, of which sugars 7.1g; Fat 11.5g, of which saturates 2.2g; Cholesterol 103mg; Calcium 93mg; Fibre 5.2g; Sodium 240mg.
Watercress Salad Energy 152kcal/644kJ; Protein 6.1g; Carbohydrate 23.1g, of which sugars 5.2g; Fat 4.6g, of which saturates 0.7g; Cholesterol 0mg; Calcium 114mg; Fibre 2.8g; Sodium 45mg.

Russian Potato Salad

This potato salad became fashionable in the hotel dining rooms of the 1920s and 1930s. Originally it consisted of lightly cooked vegetables, eggs, shellfish and mayonnaise. Today we find it diced in plastic pots in supermarkets. This version recalls better days and plays on the theme of the Fabergé egg.

Serves 4
115g/4oz large button
  (white) mushrooms
350g/12oz cooked peeled
  prawns (shrimp)
120ml/4fl oz/½ cup mayonnaise
15ml/1 tbsp lemon juice
1 large gherkin, chopped, or
  30ml/2 tbsp capers
115g/4oz broad (fava)
  beans, shelled
115g/4oz small new potatoes,
  scrubbed or scraped
115g/4oz young carrots, trimmed
  and peeled
115g/4oz baby corn
115g/4oz baby turnips, trimmed
15ml/1 tbsp olive oil, preferably
  French or Italian
4 eggs, hard-boiled and shelled
25g/1oz canned anchovy fillets,
  cut into fine strips
salt and ground black pepper
paprika, to garnish

1 Slice the mushrooms, then cut into matchsticks. Mix with the prawns. Combine the mayonnaise and lemon juice and fold half into the mushrooms and prawns, add the gherkin or capers and season with salt and pepper.

2 Bring a large pan of salted water to the boil, add the broad beans and cook for 3 minutes. Drain and cool under cold running water, then pinch the beans between thumb and forefinger to release them from their tough skins.

3 Boil the potatoes in a pan of water for about 20 minutes, and the remaining vegetables for 6 minutes. Drain and cool under running water.

4 Moisten the vegetables with olive oil and divide between four shallow serving bowls. Spoon the dressed prawns into the centre of each serving and place a hard-boiled egg in the centre. Decorate the egg with strips of anchovy and sprinkle with paprika. Serve the remaining mayonnaise separately so diners can help themselves.

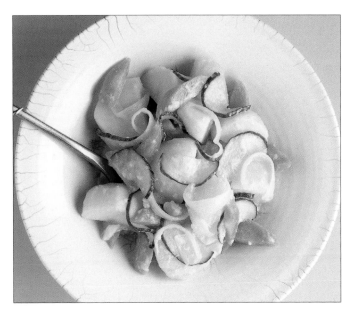

Japanese-style Potato Salad

In this Asian salad, the potatoes are stir-fried with carrots and onion, then cooked in stock before the egg is added.

Serves 4
4 medium potatoes
2 carrots
1 large mild onion
20ml/4 tsp oil
1 vegetable stock (bouillon) cube
20ml/4 tsp rice vinegar
10ml/2 tsp sugar
2.5ml/½ tsp salt, plus extra
  for the cucumber
2 eggs, beaten
½ cucumber

1 Cut the potatoes lengthways into four, then slice the pieces across into thick chunks. Soak the potatoes in cold water for 2 minutes and drain well.

2 Halve the carrots vertically, then slice them across into chunks. Cut the onion into thick wedges.

3 Heat the oil in a deep frying pan or pan. Stir-fry the potatoes, carrots and onion for 1 minute. Dissolve the vegetable stock cube in 200ml/7fl oz/scant 1 cup boiling water and pour it into the pan. Add the rice vinegar, sugar and salt. Cover and simmer for 5 minutes.

4 Uncover the pan and cook over a moderate heat until all the liquid has evaporated. Shake the pan gently occasionally to prevent the vegetables from sticking to the base of the pan as the liquid dries up.

5 Remove from the heat and allow to cool for 30 seconds, then add the beaten egg, stirring quickly until the egg sets. Transfer to a dish and leave to cool, then chill.

6 Meanwhile halve the cucumber vertically and cut it into thin slices. Place the cucumber in a colander or sieve (strainer) over a bowl. Sprinkle with a little salt and leave to stand for 10 minutes. Gently squeeze out the liquid from the cucumber.

7 Add the cucumber to the potato mixture and check the seasoning, adding more salt, if necessary. Serve chilled.

Russian Salad Energy 455kcal/1890kJ; Protein 28.1g; Carbohydrate 12.8g, of which sugars 5g; Fat 32.8g, of which saturates 5.7g; Cholesterol 387mg; Calcium 162mg; Fibre 4.3g; Sodium 963mg.
Japanese-style Salad Energy 206kcal/868kJ; Protein 6.3g; Carbohydrate 31.3g, of which sugars 8.5g; Fat 7.2g, of which saturates 1.4g; Cholesterol 95mg; Calcium 42mg; Fibre 2.8g; Sodium 62mg.

Baked Sweet Potato Salad

This sweet potato salad has a truly tropical taste and is ideal served with Asian or Caribbean dishes.

Serves 4–6
1kg/2¼lb sweet potatoes
1 red (bell) pepper, seeded and
  finely diced
3 celery sticks, finely diced
¼ red onion, finely chopped
1 fresh red chilli, finely chopped

salt and ground black pepper
coriander (cilantro) leaves,
  to garnish

For the dressing
45ml/3 tbsp chopped fresh
  coriander (cilantro)
juice of 1 lime
150ml/¼ pint/⅔ cup natural
  (plain) yogurt

1 Preheat the oven to 200°C/400°F/Gas 6. Wash the potatoes, and pierce them all over with a fork. Place in the oven and bake for about 40 minutes, or until tender.

2 Meanwhile, make the dressing. Whisk together the coriander, lime juice and yogurt in a small bowl and season to taste with salt and pepper. Chill in the refrigerator while you prepare the remaining salad ingredients.

3 In a large bowl, mix the diced red pepper, celery, chopped onion and chilli together.

4 Remove the potatoes from the oven. As soon as they are cool enough to handle, peel and cut them into cubes. Add them to the bowl. Drizzle the dressing over and toss carefully. Taste and adjust the seasoning, if necessary. Serve, garnished with coriander leaves.

Cook's Tip
It is generally thought that the seeds are the hottest part of a chilli. In fact, the seeds contain no capsaicin – the hot element in chillies – but it is intensely concentrated in the membrane surrounding them. Removing the seeds from the chilli usually removes this extra-hot flesh.

Spicy Potato Salad

This tasty potato salad is quick to prepare, and makes a satisfying accompaniment to plainly cooked meat or fish.

Serves 6
900g/2lb potatoes
2 red (bell) peppers, seeded
  and diced
1 shallot, finely chopped
2 or 3 spring onions (scallions),
  finely chopped
1 green chilli, seeded and
  finely chopped

2 celery sticks, finely chopped
1 garlic clove, crushed
10ml/2 tsp finely chopped
  fresh chives
10ml/2 tsp finely chopped
  fresh basil
15ml/1 tbsp finely chopped
  fresh parsley
15ml/1 tbsp single (light) cream
30ml/2 tbsp salad cream
15ml/1 tbsp mayonnaise
5ml/1 tsp prepared mild mustard
7.5ml/1½ tsp sugar
salt
chopped fresh chives, to garnish

1 Peel the potatoes. Boil in salted water for 10–12 minutes, until tender. Drain and cool, then cut into cubes and place in a large mixing bowl.

2 Add the chopped red peppers, shallot, spring onions, green chilli and celery to the potatoes, together with the crushed garlic and chopped herbs. Stir gently until the ingredients are thoroughly combined.

3 To make the dressing, blend the cream, salad cream, mayonnaise, mustard and sugar in a small bowl, stirring until the mixture is well combined.

4 Pour the dressing over the salad and toss gently to coat evenly. Serve garnished with the chopped chives.

Variation
If you prefer, leave out the salad cream and increase the amount of mayonnaise by 30ml/2 tbsp. To turn the salad into a light lunch dish, add some diced ham and a handful of cooked green beans that have been refreshed under cold running water.

Sweet Potato Salad Energy 176kcal/750kJ; Protein 4g; Carbohydrate 40.4g, of which sugars 14.1g; Fat 1g, of which saturates 0.3g; Cholesterol 0mg; Calcium 116mg; Fibre 5.2g; Sodium 103mg.
Spicy Potato Salad Energy 178kcal/749kJ; Protein 3.9g; Carbohydrate 31.4g, of which sugars 8.7g; Fat 4.9g, of which saturates 1g; Cholesterol 5mg; Calcium 48mg; Fibre 3.3g; Sodium 118mg.

Chicken and Potato Salmagundi

Salads, with the ingredients elaborately arranged, were fashionable in 16th-century England, containing chopped meat, anchovies, potatoes and eggs, garnished with onions, lemon juice, oil and other condiments. This variation of the dish is thought to come from Northumbria.

large sprig of thyme
10 black peppercorns
500g/1¼lb new or baby potatoes
225g/8oz carrots, cut into
    small sticks
225g/8oz sugar snap peas
4 eggs
½ cucumber, thinly sliced
8–12 cherry tomatoes
8–12 green olives stuffed
    with pimento

Serves 4–6

1 large chicken, weighing
    about 2kg/4½lb
1 onion
1 carrot
1 celery stick
2 bay leaves

For the dressing

75ml/5 tbsp olive oil
30ml/2 tbsp lemon juice
2.5ml/½ tsp sugar
1.5ml/¼ tsp ready-made English
    (hot) mustard
salt and ground black pepper

1 Put the chicken in a deep pan with the onion, carrot, celery, bay leaves, thyme and peppercorns. Add water to cover by at least 2.5cm/1in. Bring to the boil and simmer gently for 45 minutes or until the chicken is cooked, then leave to cool in the stock for several hours to keep it moist.

2 Whisk together the ingredients for the dressing. Set aside.

3 Using a separate pan for each, cook the potatoes, carrots and peas in lightly salted boiling water until just tender, drain and then rinse under cold water. Halve the potatoes. Hard-boil the eggs, cool, shell and cut into quarters.

4 Lift the chicken out of the stock, remove the meat and cut or tear into bitesize pieces.

5 Arrange the vegetables, chicken and eggs on a large platter, or in a large bowl, and add the tomatoes and olives. Just before serving, drizzle the salad dressing over the top.

Bacon and Potato Salad

Use either new or other waxy potatoes for this classic East European salad. They will hold their shape better than the floury variety when cooked.

10ml/2 tsp lemon juice
2 celery sticks, chopped
2 pickled sour cucumbers, diced
5ml/1 tsp Dusseldorf or
    German mustard
45ml/3 tbsp mayonnaise
30ml/2 tbsp chopped fresh chives
15ml/1 tbsp chopped fresh dill
salt and ground black pepper
chopped fresh chives and dill,
    to garnish
lettuce leaves, to serve

Serves 6

675g/1½lb potatoes, scrubbed
45ml/3 tbsp olive oil
4 smoked streaky (fatty) bacon
    rashers (strips), rinded
    and chopped

1 Cook the potatoes in a pan of boiling salted water for 15 minutes, until just tender. Drain, allow to cool for 5 minutes, then slice thickly and set aside in a bowl.

2 Meanwhile, heat 15ml/1 tbsp of the oil in a frying pan and fry the bacon for about 5 minutes, until crispy. Remove the bacon and set aside.

3 Stir the remaining oil and lemon juice into the pan, then pour over the sliced warm potatoes. Add the chopped celery, cucumber and half the crispy bacon and mix until all the ingredients are well combined. Leave to cool.

4 Blend the mustard in a small bowl with the mayonnaise, herbs and a little seasoning. Add to the potatoes and toss well to coat. Spoon the potatoes into a serving dish and sprinkle with the remaining bacon. Garnish with the fresh herbs and serve with lettuce leaves.

> **Cook's Tip**
> *German mustard is typically dark with a medium heat and a slightly sweet flavour; it is an ideal accompaniment for sausages, ham and bacon.*

Salmagundi Energy 397kcal/1664kJ; Protein 41.2g; Carbohydrate 24.9g, of which sugars 8.7g; Fat 15.5g, of which saturates 3g; Cholesterol 220mg; Calcium 63mg; Fibre 4.6g; Sodium 155mg.
Bacon and Potato Salad Energy 206kcal/863kJ; Protein 2.8g; Carbohydrate 24.3g, of which sugars 2.1g; Fat 11.5g, of which saturates 1.7g; Cholesterol 0mg; Calcium 22mg; Fibre 1.8g; Sodium 19mg.

Warm Potato Salad with Bacon and Shallot Dressing

This warm potato salad with bacon makes a fine accompaniment for grilled sausages or delicious smoked mackerel. Vinegar, mustard and finely chopped herbs make a punchy dressing.

Serves 6
900g/2lb small new or
    salad potatoes
90ml/6 tbsp olive oil
200g/7oz dry-cure streaky (fatty)
    bacon, smoked or unsmoked,
    cut into strips

3 shallots, chopped
1 small garlic clove,
    finely chopped
30ml/2 tbsp white wine vinegar
30ml/2 tbsp dry white vermouth
    or white wine
5ml/1 tsp French mustard
45–60ml/3–4 tbsp chopped fresh
    herbs, such as chervil, parsley
    and tarragon
15ml/1 tbsp chopped fresh chives
salt and ground black pepper
whole chives, to garnish

1 Cook the potatoes in boiling, salted water for between 15–20 minutes until tender. Drain, leave to cool a little, then peel. Slice the potatoes directly into a bowl and add 45ml/3 tbsp of the olive oil. Season with ground black pepper to taste. Stir the potatoes to coat, then set aside.

2 Heat a further 30ml/2 tbsp of the olive oil in a heavy frying pan. Fry the bacon until crisp and lightly browned, then add the shallots and cook, stirring constantly, for 2–3 minutes. Add the garlic and cook for a further 1 minute. Scrape the contents of the pan over the potatoes and stir to mix.

3 Return the pan to the heat. Add the vinegar and vermouth or wine and reduce a little, then stir in the mustard. Immediately pour this mixture over the potatoes. Add most of the mixed herbs and stir to mix.

4 Spoon the salad into a large serving bowl or individual bowls. Drizzle the remaining oil over the top and sprinkle with the remaining herbs and the chives. Garnish with whole chives, then serve immediately.

Sweet Potato, Egg, Pork and Beetroot Salad

This dish is a delicious way to use up any leftover roast pork. The flavour of the sweet potato balances well with the bitterness of the salad leaves.

Serve 4
900g/2lb sweet potatoes
4 chicory (Belgian endive) heads
5 hard-boiled eggs, shelled

450g/1lb pickled young
    beetroot (beets)
175g/6oz cold roast pork
salt

For the dressing
75ml/5 tbsp groundnut (peanut)
    or sunflower oil
30ml/2 tbsp white wine vinegar
10ml/2 tsp Dijon mustard
5ml/1 tsp fennel seeds, crushed

1 Peel the sweet potatoes and dice into equal pieces. Add the diced sweet potatoes to a pan of boiling salted water. Bring back to the boil, then simmer for 10–15 minutes, or until the potatoes are soft. Drain and allow to cool.

2 To make the dressing, combine the groundnut or sunflower oil, vinegar, mustard and fennel seeds in a screw-top jar and shake vigorously to mix.

3 Separate the chicory leaves and arrange them around the edge of four individual plates.

4 Pour two-thirds of the dressing over the sweet potatoes, then stir to coat well. Spoon on top of the chicory leaves.

5 Slice the eggs and beetroot, and arrange in a circle on top of the sweet potato. Slice the pork, then cut into 4cm/1½in strips and moisten with the rest of the dressing. Pile the pork into the centre of each salad. Season with salt and serve.

> **Cook's Tip**
> To crush the fennel seeds, grind using a mortar and pestle. If you don't have these, use two dessertspoons instead.

Bacon Potato Salad Energy 318kcal/1319kJ; Protein 12.4g; Carbohydrate 10.9g, of which sugars 2.2g; Fat 25.4g, of which saturates 4g; Cholesterol 198mg; Calcium 106mg; Fibre 2.3g; Sodium 268mg.
Sweet Potato Salad Energy 507kcal/2132kJ; Protein 21.9g; Carbohydrate 56.7g, of which sugars 20.9g; Fat 23.3g, of which saturates 4.4g; Cholesterol 265mg; Calcium 119mg; Fibre 7.7g; Sodium 283mg.

Frankfurter and Potato Salad with Mustard Dressing

This is a last-minute potato salad that is ideal for serving as a midweek meal.

Serves 4

675g/1½lb small new potatoes, scrubbed or scraped
2 eggs
350g/12oz frankfurters
1 round (butterhead) or frisée lettuce

225g/8oz young spinach leaves, stems removed
salt and ground black pepper

For the dressing

45ml/3 tbsp safflower oil
30ml/2 tbsp olive oil
15ml/1 tbsp white wine vinegar
10ml/2 tsp mustard
5ml/1 tsp caraway seeds, crushed

1 Bring the potatoes to the boil in salted water and simmer for about 15 minutes, or until just tender. Drain, cover and keep warm. Hard-boil the eggs for 12 minutes. Refresh in cold water, shell and cut into quarters.

2 Score the frankfurter skins corkscrew fashion with a small knife, then cover with boiling water and simmer for about 5 minutes to heat through. Drain well, cover and keep warm.

3 To make the dressing, place all the ingredients in a screw-top jar and shake vigorously to combine.

4 Moisten the salad leaves with half the dressing and divide between four large serving plates. Moisten the warm potatoes and frankfurters with the remainder of the dressing and scatter over the salad.

5 Finish the salad with sections of hard-boiled egg, season with salt and black pepper and serve warm.

> **Cook's Tip**
> *This salad has a German slant to it and calls for a sweet-and-sour German-style mustard. American mustard is similar.*

Warm Salad of Bayonne Ham and New Potatoes

With a lightly spiced nutty dressing, this warm potato salad is as delicious as it is fashionable, and it will make an excellent choice for informal entertaining.

Serves 4

225g/8oz new potatoes, halved if large
50g/2oz green beans
115g/4oz young spinach leaves

2 spring onions (scallions), sliced
4 eggs, hard-boiled and quartered
50g/2oz Bayonne ham, cut into strips
juice of ½ lemon
salt and ground black pepper

For the dressing

60ml/4 tbsp olive oil
5ml/1 tsp ground turmeric
5ml/1 tsp ground cumin
50g/2oz/⅓ cup shelled hazelnuts

1 Cook the potatoes in boiling salted water for 10–15 minutes, or until tender, then drain well.

2 Cook the green beans in boiling water for 2 minutes or until just tender, then drain.

3 Toss the potatoes and beans with the spinach and spring onions in a bowl.

4 Arrange the hard-boiled egg quarters on the salad and sprinkle the strips of ham over the top. Sprinkle with the lemon juice and season with plenty of salt and pepper.

5 To make the dressing, heat all the ingredients in a large frying pan and continue to cook, stirring frequently, until the nuts have just turned golden. Pour the hot, nutty dressing over the salad. Serve immediately.

> **Variation**
> *Replace the potatoes with a 400g/14oz can mixed beans and pulses. Drain and rinse the beans and pulses, then drain again. Toss lightly with the green beans and spring onions.*

Frankfurter Salad Energy 561kcal/2336kJ; Protein 20.5g; Carbohydrate 31g, of which sugars 5.9g; Fat 40.4g, of which saturates 11g; Cholesterol 162mg; Calcium 160mg; Fibre 3.9g; Sodium 1014mg.
Bayonne Ham and Potatoes Energy 323kcal/1341kJ; Protein 12.4g; Carbohydrate 10.9g, of which sugars 2.2g; Fat 25.8g, of which saturates 4.2g; Cholesterol 199mg; Calcium 105mg; Fibre 2.3g; Sodium 270mg.

Bacon and New Potato Salad

A rich mustard sauce gives the new potatoes added flavour and colour.

Serves 4–6

5 eggs
30–45ml/2–3 tbsp Dijon mustard
200g/7oz mayonnaise
3 celery sticks, finely chopped
115g/4oz bacon lardons
900g/2lb small new potatoes
30ml/2 tbsp chopped fresh flat leaf parsley
salt and ground black pepper

1 Place the eggs carefully into a pan of water and bring to the boil. Simmer for 5–8 minutes, drain and plunge the eggs straight into a bowl containing cold water.

2 Peel the eggs and mash three in a large bowl with a fork. Stir in the mustard, mayonnaise and celery. Season with salt and pepper. Thin down the dressing with a little water, if you wish.

3 Fry the bacon pieces in a dry frying pan until crisp and golden brown. Toss half of the bacon into the mayonnaise dressing. Reserve the remainder.

4 Cook the potatoes in boiling water for 20 minutes until tender. Drain and leave to cool.

5 Toss the cooled potatoes into the mayonnaise dressing and spoon on to a serving platter. Slice the remaining eggs and sprinkle over the salad with the reserved bacon pieces. Scatter the chopped parsley over the top and serve immediately.

Cook's Tip
Use firm salad potatoes, cut into even pieces, or use whole baby new potatoes. Cook with mint sprigs for extra flavour.

Variation
Experiment with flavour and texture by replacing the bacon with cooked peeled prawns (shrimp).

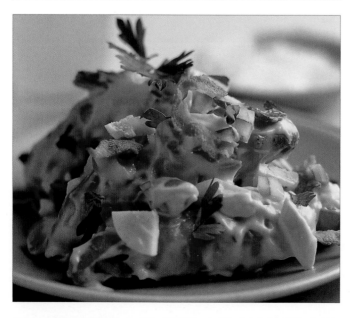

Potato Salad with Garlic Sausage

In this delicious and hearty salad, the potatoes are moistened with a little white wine before adding the vinaigrette. Great served as part of a cold spread.

Serves 4

450g/1lb small waxy potatoes
30–45ml/2–3 tbsp dry white wine
2 shallots, finely chopped
15ml/1 tbsp chopped fresh parsley
15ml/1 tbsp chopped fresh tarragon
175g/6oz cooked garlic sausage
fresh flat leaf parsley sprig, to garnish

For the vinaigrette
10ml/2 tsp Dijon mustard
15ml/1 tbsp tarragon vinegar or white wine vinegar
75ml/5 tbsp extra virgin olive oil
salt and ground black pepper

1 Scrub the potatoes. Boil in salted water for 10–15 minutes, until tender. Drain and refresh under cold running water.

2 Peel the potatoes if you like, or leave in their skins, and cut into 5mm/¼in slices. Sprinkle with the wine and shallots.

3 To make the vinaigrette, mix the mustard and vinegar in a small bowl, then whisk in the oil, 15ml/1 tbsp at a time. Season with salt and pepper and pour over the potatoes.

4 Add the chopped parsley and tarragon to the potatoes and toss until well mixed.

5 Slice the garlic sausage thinly and toss with the potatoes to combine. Season the salad with salt and pepper to taste.

6 Serve at room temperature, garnished with a sprig of parsley.

Variation
The potatoes are also delicious served on their own, simply dressed with vinaigrette, and perhaps accompanied by marinated herrings.

Bacon and Potato Salad Energy 446kcal/1854kJ; Protein 11.7g; Carbohydrate 25.3g, of which sugars 2.9g; Fat 33.9g, of which saturates 6.5g; Cholesterol 194mg; Calcium 46mg; Fibre 1.7g; Sodium 677mg.
Potato with Garlic Sausage Energy 315kcal/1313kJ; Protein 8.3g; Carbohydrate 22.3g, of which sugars 3.1g; Fat 21.6g, of which saturates 4.4g; Cholesterol 50mg; Calcium 45mg; Fibre 2.3g; Sodium 372mg.

Fresh Tuna Salade Niçoise

Fresh tuna transforms this famous salad from the south of France into something really special.

Serves 4
4 tuna steaks, about
  150g/5oz each
30ml/2 tbsp olive oil
225g/8oz fine green beans
1 small cos or romaine lettuce or
  2 Little Gem (Bibb) lettuces
4 new potatoes, boiled
4 ripe tomatoes or
  12 cherry tomatoes

2 red (bell) peppers, seeded and
  cut into thin strips
4 hard-boiled eggs, sliced
8 drained anchovy fillets in oil,
  halved lengthwise
16 large black olives
salt and ground black pepper
12 fresh basil leaves,
  to garnish

For the dressing
15ml/1 tbsp red
  wine vinegar
90ml/6 tbsp olive oil
1 fat garlic clove, crushed

1 Brush the tuna on both sides with a little olive oil and season with salt and pepper. Heat a ridged griddle or the grill (broiler) until very hot, then grill (broil) the tuna steaks for 1–2 minutes on each side; they should still be pink and juicy in the middle. Set aside.

2 Cook the beans in a pan of lightly salted boiling water for 4–5 minutes or until just tender. Drain, refresh under cold water and drain again.

3 Separate the lettuce leaves and arrange them on four individual serving plates. Slice the potatoes and tomatoes, if large (leave cherry tomatoes whole) and divide them among the plates. Arrange the fine green beans and red pepper strips on top of them.

4 Shell the eggs and cut into thick slices. Place two slices on each plate with an anchovy fillet draped over. Scatter four olives on to each plate.

5 To make the dressing, whisk together the vinegar, olive oil and garlic and season to taste. Drizzle over the salads. Arrange the tuna steaks on top, scatter over the basil and serve.

Hake and Potato Salad

Hake is excellent served cold, and is delicious with potatoes in a piquant dressing.

Serves 4
450g/1lb hake fillets
150ml/¼ pint/⅔ cup fish stock
1 onion, thinly sliced
1 bay leaf
450g/1lb cooked baby potatoes
1 red (bell) pepper, seeded
  and diced
115g/4oz/1 cup petits pois (baby
  peas), cooked
2 spring onions (scallions), sliced
½ cucumber, unpeeled and diced

4 large red lettuce leaves
salt and ground black pepper

For the dressing
150ml/¼ pint/⅔ cup Greek
  (US strained plain) yogurt
30ml/2 tbsp olive oil
juice of ½ lemon
15–30ml/1–2 tbsp capers

For the garnish
2 hard-boiled eggs,
  finely chopped
15ml/1 tbsp finely chopped fresh
  flat leaf parsley
15ml/1 tbsp finely chopped chives

1 Put the hake in a shallow pan with the fish stock, onion slices and bay leaf. Bring to the boil over a medium heat. Lower the heat and poach the fish gently for about 10 minutes, until it flakes easily when tested with the tip of a sharp knife. Leave it to cool, then remove and discard the skin and any remaining bones, and separate the flesh into large flakes.

2 Halve the potatoes, unless they are tiny, and place in a large bowl with the diced red pepper, petits pois, sliced spring onions and diced cucumber. Stir in the flaked hake and season to taste with salt and pepper.

3 Stir all the dressing ingredients together in a mixing bowl. Season with salt and pepper and toss gently into the salad. Place a lettuce leaf on each plate and spoon the salad over it. Mix the hard-boiled eggs with the parsley and chives. Sprinkle the mixture over each salad.

> **Variation**
> *This is equally good made with halibut, monkfish or cod.*

Salade Niçoise Energy 542kcal/2260kJ; Protein 46.8g; Carbohydrate 14.3g, of which sugars 9.8g; Fat 33.7g, of which saturates 6.5g; Cholesterol 236mg; Calcium 132mg; Fibre 4.4g; Sodium 671mg.
Hake Salad Energy 373kcal/1561kJ; Protein 31.2g; Carbohydrate 29.1g, of which sugaars 8.8g; fat 15.8g, of which saturates 4.2g; Cholesterol 121mg; Calcium 129mg; Fibre 4.3g; Sodium 192mg.

Spiced Trout and Potato Salad

In this make-ahead salad, the trout is marinated in a mixture of coriander, ginger and chilli and served with cold baby roast potatoes.

Serves 4
2.5cm/1in piece fresh root
  ginger, peeled and finely
  grated (shredded)
1 garlic clove, crushed
5ml/1 tsp hot chilli powder
15ml/1 tbsp coriander seeds,
  lightly crushed
grated rind and juice of 2 lemons
60ml/4 tbsp olive oil
450g/1lb trout fillet, skinned
900g/2lb new potatoes
5–10ml/1–2 tsp sea salt
ground black pepper
15ml/1 tbsp whole or chopped
  fresh chives, to garnish

1 Mix the ginger, garlic, chilli powder, coriander seeds and lemon rind in a bowl. Whisk in the lemon juice with 15ml/ 1 tbsp of the olive oil to make a marinade.

2 Place the trout in a shallow, non-metallic dish and cover with the marinade. Turn the fish to make sure they are well coated, cover with clear film (plastic wrap) and chill.

3 Preheat the oven to 200°C/400°F/Gas 6. Place the potatoes in a roasting pan, toss them in 30ml/2 tbsp olive oil and season with salt and ground black pepper. Roast in the oven for about 45 minutes or until golden brown and tender. Remove from the oven and leave to cool for at least 2 hours.

4 Reduce the oven to 190°C/375°F/Gas 5. Remove the trout from the marinade and place in a roasting pan. Bake for 20 minutes until cooked. Remove from the oven and leave to cool.

5 Cut the potatoes into chunks, flake the trout into bitesize pieces and toss them together in a serving dish with the remaining olive oil. Sprinkle with the chives and serve.

Cook's Tip
Look for firm pieces of fresh root ginger, with smooth skin. If it is really fresh, it will keep for up to 2 weeks in a cool place.

Genoese Squid and Potato Salad

This Italian-style salad is good for summer days, when green beans and new potatoes are at their best.

Serves 4–6
450g/1lb prepared squid,
  cut into rings
4 garlic cloves, roughly chopped
300ml/½ pint/1¼ cups Italian
  red wine
450g/1lb Charlotte or new
  potatoes, scrubbed
225g/8oz green beans, trimmed
  and cut into short lengths
2–3 sun-dried tomatoes in oil,
  drained and thinly
  sliced lengthwise
60ml/4 tbsp extra virgin
  olive oil
15ml/1 tbsp red wine vinegar
salt and ground black pepper

1 Preheat the oven to 180°C/350°F/Gas 4. Put the squid rings in an earthenware dish with half the garlic, the wine and pepper to taste. Cover and cook for 45 minutes, or until the squid is tender.

2 Meanwhile, put the potatoes in a pan, cover with cold water and add a good pinch of salt. Bring to the boil, cover and simmer for about 15 minutes, until tender. Using a slotted spoon, lift out the potatoes and set aside. Add the beans to the boiling water and cook for 3 minutes. Drain.

3 When the potatoes are cool enough to handle, slice them thickly on the diagonal and place them in a bowl with the warm beans and sun-dried tomatoes. Whisk the oil, vinegar and the remaining garlic in a bowl and add salt and pepper to taste. Pour over the potato mixture.

4 Drain the squid and discard the liquid. Add the squid to the potato mixture and mix very gently until all the ingredients are well combined. Arrange on individual plates and season liberally with pepper before serving.

Cook's Tip
The French potato called Charlotte is perfect for this salad because it retains its shape when boiled.

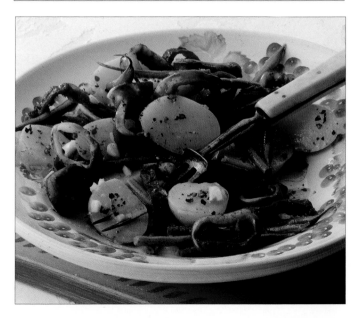

Spiced Trout Salad Energy 365kcal/1535kJ; Protein 26g; Carbohydrate 37.1g, of which sugars 2.9g; Fat 13.5g, of which saturates 1.5g; Cholesterol 0mg; Calcium 28mg; Fibre 2.3g; Sodium 580mg.
Genoese Squid Salad Energy 239kcal/999kJ; Protein 13.6g; Carbohydrate 14.3g, of which sugars 1.9g; Fat 10.9g, of which saturates 1.7g; Cholesterol 169mg; Calcium 31mg; Fibre 1.6g; Sodium 94mg

Lobster and Potato Salad

When you're in a decadent mood, this salad of potatoes and lobster will satisfy your every whim.

Serves 4

1 medium lobster, cooked
675g/1½lb new potatoes, scrubbed
½ frisée lettuce
175g/6oz lamb's lettuce (corn salad) leaves
60ml/4 tbsp extra virgin olive oil
200g/7oz can young artichokes in brine, quartered
4 oranges, peeled and divided into segments
2 ripe tomatoes, peeled, seeded and diced
1 small bunch fresh tarragon, chervil or flat leaf parsley
salt

For the dressing

30ml/2 tbsp frozen concentrated orange juice, thawed
75g/3oz/6 tbsp unsalted butter, diced
salt and cayenne pepper

1 Twist off the legs and claws of the lobster, and separate the tail from the body. Break the claws with a hammer and remove the meat. Cut the tail piece open from the underside, slice the meat and set aside.

2 Bring the scrubbed new potatoes to the boil in salted water and simmer for about 15 minutes, until just tender. Drain, cover and keep warm.

3 To make the dressing, measure the orange juice into a heatproof bowl and set it over a pan containing 2.5cm/1in simmering water. Heat the juice for 1 minute, turn off the heat, then whisk in the butter a little at a time until the dressing reaches a coating consistency.

4 Season to taste with salt and a pinch of cayenne pepper, cover and keep warm.

5 Dress the salad leaves with olive oil, then divide between four large serving plates. Moisten the potatoes, artichokes and orange segments with olive oil and distribute among the leaves. Lay the sliced lobster over the salad, spoon on the warm dressing, add the diced tomato and decorate with the fresh herbs. Serve at room temperature.

Potato, Mussel and Watercress Salad

The creamy, well-flavoured dressing enhances all the ingredients in this tasty potato salad.

Serves 4

675g/1½lb salad potatoes
1kg/2¼lb mussels, scrubbed and beards removed
200ml/7fl oz/scant 1 cup dry white wine
15g/½oz fresh flat leaf parsley, chopped
1 bunch of watercress or rocket (arugula)
salt and ground black pepper
chopped fresh chives or spring onion (scallion) tops, to garnish

For the dressing

105ml/7 tbsp olive oil
15–30ml/1–2 tbsp white wine vinegar
5ml/1 tsp strong Dijon mustard
1 large shallot, finely chopped
15ml/1 tbsp chopped fresh chives
45ml/3 tbsp double (heavy) cream
pinch of caster (superfine) sugar (optional)

1 Boil the potatoes in salted water for 15–20 minutes, or until tender. Drain, cool, then peel. Slice the potatoes into a bowl and toss with 30ml/2 tbsp of the oil for the dressing.

2 Discard any open mussels. Bring the white wine to the boil in a large, heavy pan. Add the mussels, cover and boil vigorously, shaking the pan occasionally, for 3–4 minutes, until the mussels have opened. Discard any that do not open. Drain and shell the mussels, reserving the cooking liquid.

3 Boil the reserved mussel cooking liquid until reduced to about 45ml/3 tbsp. Pour through a fine sieve (strainer) over the potatoes and toss to mix.

4 To make the dressing, whisk together the remaining oil with 15ml/1 tbsp of the vinegar, the mustard, shallot and chives. Add the cream and whisk again to form a thick dressing. Adjust the seasoning, adding more vinegar and/or a pinch of sugar to taste.

5 Toss the mussels with the potatoes, then gently mix in the dressing and chopped parsley. Arrange the watercress or rocket on a serving platter and top with the salad. Serve sprinkled with extra chives or a little spring onion.

Lobster Salad Energy 662kcal/2775kJ; Protein 51.5g; Carbohydrate 47.7g, of which sugars 22.7g; Fat 30.7g, of which saturates 12g; Cholesterol 260mg; Calcium 325mg; Fibre 6.9g; Sodium 900mg.
Potato and Mussel Salad Energy 459kcal/1918kJ; Protein 17.2g; Carbohydrate 29.2g, of which sugars 3.8g; Fat 27.7g, of which saturates 7g; Cholesterol 45mg; Calcium 222mg; Fibre 2.5g; Sodium 231mg.

Classic Fish Pie

Originally a fish pie was based on the 'catch of the day'. Now we can choose either the fish we like best, or the variety that offers best value for money.

Serves 4
butter, for greasing
450g/1lb mixed fish, such as
    cod or salmon fillets and
    peeled prawns (shrimp)

finely grated rind of 1 lemon
450g/1lb floury potatoes
25g/1oz/2 tbsp butter
salt and ground black pepper
1 egg, beaten

For the sauce
15g/½oz/1 tbsp butter
15ml/1 tbsp plain
    (all-purpose) flour
150ml/¼ pint/⅔ cup milk
45ml/3 tbsp chopped fresh parsley

1 Preheat the oven to 220°C/425°F/Gas 7. Grease an ovenproof dish and set aside. Cut the fish into bitesize pieces. Season the fish, sprinkle over the lemon rind and place in the base of the prepared dish. Set aside while you make the topping.

2 Cook the potatoes in a pan of boiling salted water for about 10–15 minutes until tender.

3 Meanwhile, make the sauce. Melt the butter in a pan, add the flour and cook, stirring, for a few minutes. Remove from the heat and gradually whisk in the milk. Return to the heat and bring to the boil, then reduce the heat to a simmer, whisking constantly, until the sauce has thickened and achieved a smooth consistency. Add the parsley and season to taste. Pour over the fish mixture.

4 Drain the potatoes well and then mash with the butter. Pipe or spoon the potatoes on top of the fish mixture. Brush the beaten egg over the potatoes. Bake for 45 minutes until the top is golden brown. Serve hot.

Cook's Tip
If using frozen fish defrost it thoroughly first, as lots of water from the fish will ruin your pie.

Fish Pie with Saffron Mash

This is the ultimate fish pie. Breaking through the golden potato crust reveals prawns and chunks of cod swathed in a creamy parsley sauce.

Serves 6
750ml/1¼ pints/3 cups milk
1 onion, chopped
1 bay leaf
2–3 peppercorns
450g/1lb each of fresh cod fillet
    and smoked haddock fillet

350g/12oz cooked tiger prawns
    (jumbo shrimp), shelled, with tails
75g/3oz/6 tbsp butter
75g/3oz/¾ cup plain
    (all-purpose) flour
60ml/4 tbsp chopped fresh parsley
1.3kg/3lb floury potatoes, peeled
large pinch saffron threads, soaked
    in 45ml/3 tbsp hot water
75g/3oz/6 tbsp butter
250ml/8fl oz/1 cup milk
45ml/3 tbsp chopped fresh dill
salt and ground black pepper

1 Put the milk, onion, bay leaf and peppercorns into a pan. Bring to the boil, simmer for about 10 minutes, and set aside. Lay the cod and haddock fillets, skin side up, in a large pan. Strain over the milk, place over a gentle heat and simmer for 5–7 minutes until just opaque. Lift the fish out of the milk and transfer to a plate. Reserve the milk.

2 When the fish is cool enough to handle, pull off the skin and flake the flesh into large pieces, removing any bones as you go. Transfer to a large bowl and add the shelled prawns.

3 Melt the butter in a small pan. Stir in the flour and cook for a minute or so, then gradually stir in the flavoured milk from the pan until you achieve a smooth consistency. Whisk well and simmer gently for 15 minutes until thick and a little reduced, then taste and season with salt and pepper. Stir in the parsley. Pour the sauce over the fish. Carefully mix together, transfer the mixture to a pie dish and leave to cool.

4 Preheat the oven to 180°C/350°F/Gas 4. Boil the potatoes in salted water until tender, drain and mash until smooth. Using an electric whisk, beat in the saffron and its soaking water, then the butter, milk and dill to make light, fluffy mashed potato. When the fish mixture has cooled and set, pile the mash on top. Bake for 30–40 minutes, or until the potato is golden and crisp.

Classic Fish Pie Energy 301kcal/1262kJ; Protein 26.5g; Carbohydrate 24.1g, of which sugars 2.6g; Fat 11.6g, of which saturates 6.2g; Cholesterol 132mg; Calcium 76mg; Fibre 1.6g; Sodium 173mg.
Fish Pie with Saffron Energy 458kcal/1921kJ; Protein 29.4g; Carbohydrate 32.8g, of which sugars 5.8g; Fat 25g, of which saturates 3.7g; Cholesterol 74mg; Calcium 216mg; Fibre 1g; Sodium 867mg.

Creamy Fish and Mushroom Pie

Fish pie is a healthy dish for a hungry family. To eke out the fish, mushrooms and potatoes provide both flavour and nourishment.

Serves 4

225g/8oz assorted wild and
  cultivated mushrooms, such as
  oyster, button (white), chanterelle
  or field (porcini) mushrooms,
  trimmed and quartered
675g/1½lb cod or haddock fillet,
  skinned and diced
600ml/1 pint/2½ cups milk, boiling

For the topping

900g/2lb floury potatoes, quartered
25g/1oz/2 tbsp butter
150ml/¼ pint/⅔ cup milk
salt and ground black pepper
grated nutmeg

For the sauce

50g/2oz unsalted butter
1 medium onion, chopped
½ celery stick, chopped
50g/2oz/½ cup plain
  (all-purpose) flour
10ml/2 tsp lemon juice
45ml/3 tbsp chopped fresh parsley

1 Preheat the oven to 200°C/400°F/Gas 6. Butter an ovenproof dish, sprinkle the mushrooms over the base, add the fish and season with salt and pepper to taste. Pour on the boiling milk, cover the dish and bake in the oven for 20 minutes.

2 Using a slotted spoon, transfer the fish and mushrooms to a 1.5 litre/2½ pint/6¼ cup baking dish. Pour the poaching liquid into a jug (pitcher) and set aside.

3 Meanwhile, cook the potatoes in lightly salted boiling water for 20 minutes. Drain and mash with the butter and milk. Season well with salt, pepper and nutmeg.

4 To make the sauce, melt the butter in a pan, add the chopped onion and celery and fry until soft, but not coloured. Stir in the flour, then remove from the heat.

5 Gradually add the reserved liquid, stirring until absorbed. Return to the heat, stir and simmer to thicken. Add the lemon juice and parsley, season, then add to the baking dish.

6 Top with the mashed potato and return to the oven for 30–40 minutes until the topping is golden brown.

Fish Pie with Sweet Potato Topping

This unusual fish pie is crowned with a subtly sweet topping of mashed potato and sweet potato.

Serves 4

175g/6oz/ 1 cup basmati rice
  450ml/¾ pint/scant 2 cups
  well-flavoured stock
175g/6oz/1½ cups podded
  broad (fava) beans
675g/1½lb cod fillets, skinned
450ml/¾ pint/scant 2 cups milk

For the sauce

40g/1½oz/3 tbsp butter

30–45ml/2–3 tbsp plain
  (all-purpose) flour
15ml/1 tbsp chopped fresh parsley
salt and ground black pepper

For the topping

450g/1lb sweet potatoes, peeled
  and cut in large chunks
450g/1lb floury white potatoes,
  peeled and cut in large chunks
milk and butter, for mashing
10ml/2 tsp freshly chopped parsley
5ml/1 tsp freshly chopped dill
15ml/1 tbsp single (light)
  cream (optional)

1 Preheat the oven to 190°C/375°F/Gas 5. Put the rice in a pan with the stock. Bring to the boil, then cover and simmer for 10 minutes until tender. Cook the beans in lightly salted water until tender. Drain thoroughly. When cool, remove their skins.

2 For the topping, cook the sweet and white potatoes separately in boiling salted water until tender. Drain, then mash with milk and butter and spoon into separate bowls. Beat the parsley and dill into the sweet potatoes, with the cream, if using.

3 Place the fish in a pan and pour in milk to cover. Dot with 15g/½oz/1 tbsp of the butter and season. Simmer for 5 minutes until tender. Remove from the pan. Make up the cooking liquid to 450ml/¾ pint/scant 2 cups with the remaining milk.

4 Make a white sauce. Melt the butter in a pan, stir in the flour and cook for 1 minute. Gradually add the milk mixture, stirring, until a white sauce forms. Stir in the parsley, taste and season.

5 Spread the rice on the bottom of a gratin dish. Add the beans and fish and pour over the sauce. Top with the potatoes in a pattern. Dot with butter and bake for 15 minutes until browned.

Creamy Fish Pie Energy 574kcal/2414kJ; Protein 41.3g; Carbohydrate 59.6g, of which sugars 15.5g; Fat 20.8g, of which saturates 12.5g; Cholesterol 115mg; Calcium 308mg; Fibre 4.1g; Sodium 480mg.
Fish Pie with Sweet Potato Energy 604kcal/2545kJ; Protein 41.6g; Carbohydrate 88g, of which sugars 8.6g; Fat 10.7g, of which saturates 5.7g; Cholesterol 99mg; Calcium 94mg; Fibre 6.9g; Sodium 223mg.

Fish Stew and Herby Mash

Herby mashed potato is the perfect partner to this flavoursome stew. It is delicious with a mix of sea bream, turbot and tuna.

Serves 4
45ml/3 tbsp olive oil
1 onion, finely chopped
2 garlic cloves, crushed
30ml/2 tbsp tomato purée (paste)
3 plum tomatoes, seeded and chopped
15ml/1 tbsp vinegar
1 bay leaf
15ml/1 tbsp chopped fresh flat leaf parsley
600ml/1 pint/2½ cups good fish stock
675–900g/1½–2lb mixed fish fillets, cut into 10cm/4in cubes
675g/1½lb old potatoes, peeled and cut into chunks
30ml/2 tbsp sour cream
salt and ground black pepper
chopped fresh flat leaf parsley, bay leaves and grated lemon rind, to garnish

1 Heat the oil in a large pan, and cook the onion and garlic for 2–3 minutes or until just soft. Add the tomato purée, tomatoes, vinegar, bay leaf and parsley. Stir in the fish stock. Bring to the boil.

2 Add the fish to the pan. Bring back to the boil, then reduce the heat and cook for about 30 minutes, stirring occasionally.

3 Meanwhile, place the potatoes in a large pan of lightly salted water. Bring to the boil and cook for 20 minutes. Drain well. Return to the pan, add the sour cream and a little pepper. Mash well with a fork.

4 Season the fish to taste. Serve with the mashed potato on individual plates or in bowls. Garnish with the parsley and bay leaves, and sprinkle grated lemon rind over the mash.

Cook's Tip
To make fish stock, place all the bones, trimmings, head and any leftover fish pieces in a pan. Add 1–2 carrots, 1 onion, sprigs of fennel or dill, a few peppercorns and a dash of dry white wine. Cover with cold water, bring to the boil then simmer for 20 minutes. Pour through a fine sieve (strainer).

Fisherman's Potato Casserole

This delicious seafood casserole combines fish fillets with shellfish and new potatoes in a creamy sauce.

Serves 4
500g/1¼lb mixed fish fillets, such as haddock, bass, red mullet or salmon
500g/1¼lb mixed shellfish, such as squid strips, mussels, cockles and prawns (shrimp)
15ml/1 tbsp oil
25g/1oz/2 tbsp butter
1 medium onion, finely chopped
1 carrot, finely chopped
3 celery sticks, finely chopped
30ml/2 tbsp plain (all-purpose) flour
600ml/1 pint/2½ cups fish stock
300ml/½ pint/1¼ cups dry (hard) cider
350g/12oz small new potatoes, halved
150ml/¼ pint/⅔ cup double (heavy) cream
small handful of chopped mixed herbs, such as parsley, chives and dill
salt and ground black pepper

1 Wash the fish fillets and dry on kitchen paper. Remove the skin and any bones. Cut the fish into large, even chunks.

2 Shell the prawns if necessary. Scrub the mussels and cockles, discarding any with broken shells or that do not close when given a sharp tap. Pull off the black beards on the mussels.

3 Heat the oil and butter in a large pan, add the onion, carrot and celery and cook over a medium heat, stirring occasionally, until beginning to soften. Add the flour, and cook for 1 minute.

4 Remove the pan from the heat and gradually stir in the fish stock and cider. Return the pan to the heat and cook, stirring constantly, until the mixture comes to the boil and thickens.

5 Add the potatoes. Bring the sauce back to the boil, then cover and simmer gently for 10–15 minutes until the potatoes are nearly tender. Add all the fish and shellfish and stir in gently.

6 Stir in the cream. Bring back to a gentle simmer, then cover and cook gently for 5–10 minutes or until the fish is cooked through and all the shells have opened. Adjust the seasoning to taste and gently stir in the herbs. Serve immediately.

Fish Stew Energy 466kcal/1949kJ; Protein 35.3g; Carbohydrate 32.4g, of which sugars 7.1g; Fat 22.4g, of which saturates 9.3g; Cholesterol 111mg; Calcium 53mg; Fibre 2.9g; Sodium 219mg.
Casserole Energy 583kcal/2439kJ; Protein 49.3g; Carbohydrate 25.3g, of which sugars 6.1g; Fat 30.2g, of which saturates 16.5g; Cholesterol 354mg; Calcium 199mg; Fibre 2.5g; Sodium 404mg.

Salmon with Potatoes and Dill

Creamy potatoes and dill are the ideal partners for the salty salmon in this dish.

Serves 6–8
200g/7oz/2 cups sea salt
50g/2oz/¼ cup caster
   (superfine) sugar
1kg/2¼lb salmon, scaled, filleted
   and boned
1 litre/1¾ pints/4 cups water
675–900g/1½–2lb new potatoes

*For the béchamel and
dill sauce*
25g/1oz/2 tbsp butter
45ml/3 tbsp plain
   (all-purpose) flour
750ml/1¼ pints/3 cups milk
120ml/4fl oz/½ cup double
   (heavy) cream
a little freshly grated
   nutmeg (optional)
25g/1oz/¼ cup chopped fresh dill
salt and ground black pepper

1 Mix together 100g/4oz/1 cup of the salt and the sugar. Cover the salmon fillets all over with the mixture and place them in a plastic bag. Seal the bag and put the fish on a plate in the refrigerator overnight.

2 The next day, make a brine by mixing the remaining salt and the water in a bowl. Place the salmon in the brine and leave in the refrigerator for another night.

3 Remove the salmon from the brine and cut into 5mm/¼in slices. If large, cut the potatoes in half then cook in boiling water for about 20 minutes until tender.

4 Meanwhile, make the béchamel sauce. Melt the butter in a pan, add the flour and cook over a low heat for 1 minute, stirring constantly to make a roux. Remove from the heat and slowly add the milk, stirring constantly, to form a smooth sauce. Return to the heat and cook, stirring constantly, for between 2–3 minutes until the sauce has thickened and is just starting to boil. Stir in the double cream and the grated nutmeg, if you are using. Season with salt and pepper to taste and heat gently.

5 Drain the cooked potatoes and add to the sauce with the chopped dill. Serve the salted salmon with the potatoes in béchamel and dill sauce.

Smoked Salmon and Potato Pudding

This mouthwateringly rich winter warmer – a classic dish from Sweden – is an excellent way to use up any leftover smoked salmon or gravlax. This is a good alternative to fish pie, with similar ingredients, but prepared very differently, with the potatoes sliced and layered at the the base of the dish rather than as a mashed topping.

Serves 8
250g/9oz new potatoes
25g/1oz/2 tbsp butter
1 leek, sliced
200g/7oz gravlax, about 8 slices
a little chopped fresh dill
2 eggs
250ml/8fl oz/1 cup milk
30ml/2 tbsp double
   (heavy) cream
salt and ground black pepper

1 Cook the potatoes in boiling salted water for 15–20 minutes until tender. Drain and leave to cool.

2 Meanwhile, melt the butter in a pan. Add the sliced leek and cook gently for about 5–7 minutes, stirring occasionally, until softened but not browned.

3 Preheat the oven to 180°C/350°F/Gas 4. Thinly slice the cooled potatoes and place in a layer in the bottom of a terrine. Add one to three slices of gravlax and then add a layer of the cooked leeks. Repeat these layers, using all the ingredients, finishing with a neat layer of potatoes. Sprinkle over the chopped dill.

4 Beat the eggs in a jug (pitcher) or bowl. Add the milk and cream and beat together, then season with salt and pepper. Pour the egg mixture into the terrine. Bake in the oven for about 30 minutes until golden brown. Serve in slices.

> **Variation**
> *If you like, the terrine can be finished with a garnish of 25g/1oz melted butter to which 30ml/2 tbsp chopped fresh parsley has been added.*

Salmon Dill Energy 407kcal/1699kJ; Protein 26.4g; Carbohydrate 22.6g, of which sugars 5.9g; Fat 24g, of which saturates 9.7g; Cholesterol 85mg; Calcium 155mg; Fibre 1g; Sodium 118mg.
Salmon Pudding Energy 137kcal/573kJ; Protein 9.9g; Carbohydrate 7.2g, of which sugars 2.4g; Fat 7.8g, of which saturates 3.9g; Cholesterol 70mg; Calcium 59mg; Fibre 0.8g; Sodium 525mg.

Salmon Baked with Potatoes and Thyme

This is a very simple and absolutely delicious dish. Pepper-crusted salmon fillets are baked on a bed of potatoes and onions braised in thyme-flavoured vegetable or fish stock. It is ideal as a quick and easy midweek meal, or special enough for a dinner party.

Serves 4

675g/1½lb waxy potatoes, thinly sliced
1 onion, thinly sliced
10ml/2 tsp fresh thyme leaves
450ml/¾ pint/scant 2 cups vegetable or fish stock
40g/1½oz/3 tbsp butter, finely diced
4 salmon fillets, each about 150g/5oz, skinned
30ml/2 tbsp olive oil
15ml/1 tbsp black peppercorns, roughly crushed
salt and ground black pepper
fresh thyme, to garnish
mangetouts (snow peas) or sugar snap peas, to serve

1 Preheat the oven to 190°C/375°F/Gas 5. Layer the potato and onion slices in a shallow baking dish, such as a lasagne dish, seasoning each layer and sprinkling with thyme.

2 Pour the stock over the potato and onion slices to just cover. Scatter the surface liberally with cubes of butter, cover with foil and place in the oven.

3 Bake the potatoes and onions for about 40 minutes, then remove the foil and bake for a further 20 minutes, or until they are almost cooked.

4 Meanwhile, brush the salmon fillets with olive oil and coat with crushed black peppercorns, pressing them into the fish, if necessary, with the back of a spoon.

5 Place the salmon on top of the potatoes, cover with foil and bake for a further 15 minutes, or until the salmon is opaque, removing the foil for the last 5 minutes of cooking. Garnish the fish with the fresh thyme sprigs and serve with mangetouts or sugar snap peas.

Salmon and Potato Bake

Subtly flavoured with fresh dill and onion, this warming fish and potato bake from Finland uses graavilohi – salmon that has been pressed with salt, dill and brandy for 24 hours.

Serves 4

25g/1oz/2 tbsp unsalted (sweet) butter, softened
8 potatoes, thinly sliced
300g/11oz Pressed Salmon with Dill, sliced (see below)
1 onion, finely chopped
30ml/2 tbsp chopped fresh dill
3 eggs, beaten
400ml/14fl oz/1⅔ cups milk
5ml/1 tsp salt
2.5ml/½ tsp ground white pepper

For the pressed salmon with dill (graavilohi)

90ml/6 tbsp coarse sea salt
90ml/6 tbsp sugar
90ml/6 tbsp chopped fresh dill
30ml/2 tbsp brandy
5ml/1 tsp ground black pepper
1 small or ½ large fresh salmon, filleted

1 To make the pressed salmon with dill, put the salt, sugar, dill, brandy and pepper in a bowl and mix together. Rub the mixture over both sides of the salmon fillets. Place the flesh sides of the fillets together, so that the skin sides are on the outside, to form a whole fish and wrap in foil.

2 Place the wrapped fish in a deep dish or roasting pan and place a heavy weight or weights, such as cans, on the top. Put in the refrigerator and leave for 12 hours. Turn the fish over, replace the weights and leave for a further 12 hours. Scrape off the marinade and pat the fish dry with kitchen paper.

3 To prepare the salmon bake, preheat the oven to 200°C/400°F/Gas 6. Grease a deep, ovenproof dish with a little of the butter.

4 Arrange half the potato slices over the base of the dish, then add a layer of salmon and a layer of onion. Sprinkle over the dill and end with a layer of the remaining potato slices.

5 Mix the eggs, milk, salt and pepper together and pour over the dish. Dot the remaining butter on top. Bake in the oven for 1 hour, until the potatoes are tender. Serve immediately.

Salmon and Thyme Energy 517kcal/2160kJ; Protein 33.4g; Carbohydrate 28.4g, of which sugars 3.1g; Fat 30.8g, of which saturates 9g; Cholesterol 96mg; Calcium 47mg; Fibre 1.9g; Sodium 147mg.
Salmon Bake Energy 338kcal/1413kJ; Protein 24.3g; Carbohydrate 17.9g, of which sugars 10.2g; Fat 19.4g, of which saturates 7g; Cholesterol 199mg; Calcium 167mg; Fibre 0.7g; Sodium 665mg.

Salmon with Warm Potato Salad

The salmon's savoury taste shines through this dish, enriched by the wine and lemon juice flavours in the poaching liquid. This is perfect served, as here, with a warm potato salad.

Serves 6
3 bunches fresh dill
6 salmon steaks, each 2.5cm/1in thick (1.3kg/3lb total weight)
475ml/16fl oz/2 cups water
250ml/8fl oz/1 cup dry white wine
15ml/1 tbsp white vinegar or lemon juice
5ml/1 tsp salt
5 whole allspice berries
2 bay leaves
6 small dill sprigs, to garnish
6 lemon slices, to garnish

For the warm potato salad
1.2kg/2½lb potatoes, peeled
175g/6oz chopped onion
175ml/6fl oz/¾ cup water
45ml/3 tbsp cider vinegar
10ml/2 tsp caster (superfine) sugar
5ml/1 tsp mustard powder
salt and ground white pepper
25g/1oz/2 tbsp butter
45ml/3 tbsp chopped parsley

1 Place the dill sprigs in the bottom of a large, heavy pan and arrange the salmon on top. Combine the water with the wine, vinegar or lemon juice and salt and add the allspice berries and bay leaves. Pour over the salmon. Bring the liquid to a simmer, then lower the heat, cover and cook for around 10–15 minutes.

2 Boil the potatoes in lightly salted water for 20–25 minutes, until tender. To make the dressing, place the chopped onion in a pan with the water. Bring to the boil, and then simmer for 5 minutes, until the onion is transparent. Stir in the vinegar, sugar and mustard and season to taste, adding a little more water if necessary. Stir in the butter until melted and keep warm.

3 Drain the potatoes. While they are still warm, cut them into 1cm/½in slices and layer them in a large bowl. Pour over the dressing, add the parsley and mix to coat the potatoes evenly.

4 When the fish is opaque and flakes easily with a fork, skim off any scum and lift out the fish, drain and allow to cool slightly. Remove the skin from the salmon before placing on a serving platter or on individual plates. Garnish with dill sprigs and lemon slice twists, and serve with the warm potato salad.

Flaky Smoked Salmon with Warm New Potatoes

A type of smoked salmon that has remained true to itself down the ages while retaining its distinctive flavour is Salar, made on the island of South Uist in the Outer Hebrides of Scotland. It is a flaky smoked salmon and this is achieved by smoking the fish closer to the heat source. The result is a delicious, moist, full-flavoured smoked fish, perfect in this dish.

Serves 4
12 small new potatoes
4 x Salar flaky salmon steaks, about 75g/3oz each
mixed salad leaves
a little olive oil
a few fresh basil leaves, torn, to garnish

For the dressing
10ml/2 tsp balsamic vinegar
20ml/4 tsp virgin olive oil

1 Cook the potatoes until just done, about 15 minutes, then drain and leave to cool until you can handle them.

2 Meanwhile, for the dressing, mix the balsamic vinegar and olive oil together. Toss the mixed salad leaves in the dressing then divide between four individual serving plates.

3 Cut the potatoes in two and mix with a little olive oil. The warmth of the potatoes will create a great smell and bring out the flavour.

4 Arrange the potatoes over the salad leaves and place the smoked salmon on top. Garnish with a few torn fresh basil leaves and serve with crusty bread.

> **Cook's Tip**
> Choose small, tasty new potatoes, such as baby Maris Piper or King Edwards. Make sure that they are not overcooked as they need to retain some crispness.

Salmon with Salad Energy 578kcal/2420kJ; Protein 47.6g; Carbohydrate 36.3g, of which sugars 6g; Fat 27.9g, of which saturates 6.5g; Cholesterol 117mg; Calcium 67mg; Fibre 2.4g; Sodium 146mg.
Flaky Salmon Energy 651kcal/2,710kJ; Protein 35.8g; Carbohydrate 23.2g, of which sugars 3.3g; Fat 46.8g, of which saturates 23.2g; Cholesterol 159mg; Calcium 222mg; Fibre 2g; Sodium 359mg.

Smoked Salmon Quiche with Potato Pastry

The ingredients in this light quiche perfectly complement the melt-in-the-mouth pastry made with potatoes.

Serves 6

For the pastry
115g/4oz floury maincrop
    potatoes, diced
225g/8oz/2 cups plain
    (all-purpose) flour, sifted
115g/4oz/½ cup butter, diced
½ egg, beaten
10ml/2 tsp chilled water

For the filling
275g/10oz smoked salmon
6 eggs, beaten
150ml/¼ pint/⅔ cup full-cream
    (whole) milk
300ml/½ pint/1¼ cups double
    (heavy) cream
30–45ml/2–3 tbsp chopped
    fresh dill
30ml/2 tbsp capers, chopped
salt and ground black pepper
salad leaves and chopped fresh
    dill, to serve

1 Boil the potatoes in a pan of salted water for 15 minutes or until tender. Drain well and return to the pan. Mash the potatoes until smooth and set aside to cool completely.

2 Place the flour in a bowl and rub in the butter to form fine crumbs. Beat in the potatoes and egg. Bring the mixture together, adding chilled water if needed.

3 Roll the pastry out on a floured surface and use to line a deep 23cm/9in round, loose-based, fluted flan tin (pan). Chill for 1 hour.

4 Preheat the oven to 200°C/400°F/Gas 6. Place a baking sheet in the oven to preheat it. Chop the salmon into bitesize pieces and set aside.

5 For the filling, beat the eggs, milk and cream together, then stir in the dill and capers and season with pepper. Add in the salmon and stir to combine.

6 Prick the base of the pastry case (pie shell) well and pour the mixture into it. Bake on a baking sheet for 35–45 minutes until cooked through. Serve warm with salad leaves and dill.

Grilled Salmon and Spring Vegetable Salad

Spring is the time to enjoy sweet, young vegetables. To make the most of their fresh flavour, toss in a simple dressing and serve with a lightly grilled salmon topped with sorrel and quail's eggs.

Serves 4
350g/12oz small new potatoes,
    scrubbed or scraped
4 quail's eggs
115g/4oz young carrots
115g/4oz baby corn on the cob
115g/4oz sugar snap peas
115g/4oz fine green (French) beans
115g/4oz young
    courgettes (zucchini)
115g/4oz patty-pan
    squash (optional)
120ml/4fl oz/½ cup
    French dressing
4 salmon fillets, about
    150g/5oz each, skinned
115g/4oz sorrel, stems removed
salt and ground black pepper

1 Bring the potatoes to the boil in salted water and cook for about 15 minutes, until tender. Drain, cover and keep warm.

2 Cover the quail's eggs with boiling water and cook for 8 minutes. Refresh under cold running water, shell and cut in half.

3 Bring a pan of salted water to the boil, add the carrots, corn, sugar snap peas, beans, courgettes and squash, if using, and cook for 2–3 minutes. Drain well. Place the hot vegetables with the potatoes in a bowl, moisten with a little French dressing and allow to cool. Preheat the grill (broiler).

4 Brush the salmon fillets with some of the French dressing and grill (broil) for 6 minutes, turning once.

5 Place the sorrel in a stainless-steel or enamel pan with 30ml/2 tbsp French dressing. Cover and soften over a gentle heat for 2 minutes. Strain and cool to room temperature.

6 Divide the potatoes and vegetables among four large serving plates. Add a piece of salmon to each plate and top with a spoonful of sorrel and two pieces of quail's egg. Season with salt and pepper to taste before serving.

Salmon Quiche Energy 338kcal/1413kJ; Protein 24.3g; Carbohydrate 17.9g, of which sugars 10.2g; Fat 19.4g, of which saturates 7g; Cholesterol 199mg; Calcium 167mg; Fibre 0.7g; Sodium 665mg.
Grilled Salmon Salad Energy 545kcal/2264kJ; Protein 32.3g; Carbohydrate 20.1g, of which sugars 6.3g; Fat 31g, of which saturates 6g; Cholesterol 110mg; Calcium 131mg; Fibre 4.2g; Sodium 739mg.

Cod Ceviche with Red Onion, Avocado and Sweet Potato

Ceviche is a South American dish of fish marinated in citrus juice and onion, which has a similar effect to cooking, served here with sweet potato for a truly exotic meal.

Serves 6 as an appetizer or 4 as a main course
500–675g/1¼–1½lb cod fillets, skinned
1 red onion, thinly sliced
pinch of dried red chilli flakes
grated rind of 1 small lime and juice of 5 limes
450–500g/1–1¼lb sweet potatoes
75ml/5 tbsp mild olive oil
15–25ml/3–5 tsp rice vinegar
2.5–5ml/½–1 tsp caster (superfine) sugar
2.5ml/½ tsp ground toasted cumin seeds
½–1 fresh red or green chilli, seeded and finely chopped
1 large or 2 small avocados, peeled, stoned (pitted) and sliced
225g/8oz peeled cooked prawns (shrimp)
45ml/3 tbsp chopped fresh coriander (cilantro)
30ml/2 tbsp roasted peanuts, chopped
salt and ground black pepper

1 Cut the fish into strips or chunks. Sprinkle half the onion over the base of a glass dish and lay the fish on top. Sprinkle on the dried red chilli flakes and pour in the lime juice. Cover and chill for 2–3 hours, spooning the lime juice over the fish once or twice. Drain, and discard the onion.

2 Steam or boil the sweet potatoes for 20–25 minutes, or until just tender. Peel and slice, or cut into wedges.

3 Place the oil in a bowl and whisk in the rice vinegar and sugar to taste, then add the cumin, season, and whisk in the fresh chilli and grated lime rind.

4 In a glass bowl, mix together the fish, sweet potatoes, avocado, prawns and most of the coriander, and the dressing.

5 Toss in the remaining half of the red onion slices and then sprinkle with the remaining chopped coriander and the peanuts. Serve immediately.

Cod Fillet Baked with Sliced Potatoes

Cod fillet bakes perfectly, its mild flavour enhanced by the herbs and its juices giving flavour to the sliced potatoes underneath.

Serves 4
2 large potatoes, sliced
600ml/1 pint/2½ cups water or fish stock
900g/2lb cod fillet, skinned and cut into 4 pieces
1 small bunch dill
1 small leek, shredded
50g/2oz/¼ cup butter
olive oil, to drizzle
salt and ground black pepper

For the sauce
150ml/¼ pint/⅔ cup single (light) cream
shredded leek, to garnish
chopped dill, to garnish

1 Preheat the oven to 200°C/400°F/Gas 6. Cook the potatoes in the water or fish stock for 7–10 minutes or until tender. Drain and reserve the stock.

2 Season the cod pieces. Divide the potatoes into four portions. Arrange each one in an overlapping fan shape on a greased non-stick roasting pan.

3 Season the potatoes and cut some of the dill over each fan, reserving a little for the sauce. Sprinkle over the leeks, reserving some for the sauce, and add a knob of the butter.

4 Lay the fish over the potatoes. Sprinkle the remaining leeks and sliced potatoes on top of the fish and drizzle with the olive oil. Bake, uncovered, for 15–20 minutes.

5 Meanwhile, to make the sauce, rapidly boil the reserved stock in a pan for 10 minutes or until reduced by two-thirds. Stir in the cream and the remaining dill. Boil for 5 minutes to thicken slightly.

6 Remove the fish from the oven and garnish with the shredded leek and chopped dill. Place the individual portions on plates and serve with the sauce.

Ceviche Energy 309kcal/1292kJ; Protein 24.7g; Carbohydrate 17.9g, of which sugars 5.4g; Fat 15.8g, of which saturates 2.6g; Cholesterol 111mg; Calcium 78mg; Fibre 3.2g; Sodium 155mg.
Cod Fillet Energy 428kcal/1788kJ; Protein 44.7g; Carbohydrate 19.1g, of which sugars 4g; Fat 19.5g, of which saturates 11.6g; Cholesterol 153mg; Calcium 74mg; Fibre 2.1g; Sodium 259mg.

Cod with Chilli and Potato

White-fleshed fish, such as cod and haddock, and potatoes, are the perfect foil for the flavours of robust spices, as is the case with the chilli and mustard seeds in this delicious dish.

Serves 4
30ml/2 tbsp olive oil
5ml/1 tsp mustard seeds
1 large potato, cubed
2 slices of Serrano ham, shredded
1 onion, thinly sliced
2 garlic cloves, thinly sliced
1 red chilli, seeded and sliced
115g/4oz skinless, boneless cod, cubed
120ml/4fl oz/½ cup vegetable stock
50g/2oz/½ cup grated tasty cheese, such as Manchego or Cheddar
salt and ground black pepper

1 Heat the oil in a heavy frying pan. Add the mustard seeds. Cook for 1–2 minutes, until the seeds begin to pop and splutter, then add the potato, ham and onion.

2 Cook the mixture, stirring regularly, for about 10–15 minutes, until the cubes of potato are brown and almost tender.

3 Add the garlic and chilli to the pan and cook for a further 2 minutes, stirring frequently.

4 Stir the cod cubes into the pan and cook for 2–3 minutes, until the fish turns white, then add the stock and plenty of salt and ground black pepper. Cover the pan and cook for a further 5 minutes, until the fish is just cooked and the potatoes are tender. The fish should be opaque and flake easily when tested with a knife.

5 Transfer the fish and potato mixture to a flameproof baking dish. Sprinkle over the grated cheese and place under a hot grill (broiler) for about 2–3 minutes, until the cheese is golden.

> **Cook's Tip**
> *If you prefer a crisp topping, replace half the cheese with wholemeal (whole-wheat) breadcrumbs.*

Sweet Potato Cod Rolls

The flavour of the sweet potatoes is offset perfectly by the tartness of the lemon butter sauce served over these fish rolls.

Serves 4
2 large sweet potatoes
450g/1lb cod fillet
300ml/½ pint/1¼ cups milk
300ml/½ pint/1¼ cups water
30ml/2 tbsp chopped parsley
rind and juice of 1 lemon
2 eggs, beaten

For the coating
175g/6oz/3 cups fresh white breadcrumbs
5ml/1 tsp Thai 7-spice seasoning
vegetable oil, for frying

For the sauce
50g/2oz/¼ cup butter
150ml/¼ pint/⅔ cup single (light) cream
15ml/1 tbsp chopped fresh dill
lemon zest, to serve

1 Scrub the sweet potatoes and cook them in their skins in lightly salted boiling water for 45 minutes or until very tender. Drain and cool. When cool, peel the skins and mash the flesh.

2 Place the cod in a frying pan and pour over the milk and water. Cover and poach for 10 minutes or until the fish starts to flake.

3 Drain and discard the milk, and then remove the skin and the bones from the fish. Flake the fish into the potatoes in a large bowl, stir in the parsley, the rind and juice of half of the lemon and one egg. Chill for 30 minutes.

4 Divide and shape the mixture into eight sausages. Dip each in the remaining egg. Mix the breadcrumbs with the seasoning. Roll the dipped fish rolls in the breadcrumbs.

5 Heat the oil and shallow-fry in batches for 7 minutes, until evenly browned. Remove and drain on kitchen paper. Keep hot.

6 To make the sauce, melt the butter in a small pan and add the remaining lemon juice and rind. Cook for a few seconds.

7 Remove from the heat and add the cream and chopped dill. Whisk to prevent the sauce curdling and serve with the fish rolls.

Sweet Potato Rolls Energy 613kcal/2568kJ; Protein 29.7g; Carbohydrate 56.1g, of which sugars 7.7g; Fat 31.5g, of which saturates 12.9g; Cholesterol 146mg; Calcium 133mg; Fibre 3.4g; Sodium 544mg.
Cod with Chilli Energy 178kcal/744kJ; Protein 11.8g; Carbohydrate 9.4g, of which sugars 1.6g; Fat 10.4g, of which saturates 3.7g; Cholesterol 33mg; Calcium 103mg; Fibre 0.7g; Sodium 264mg.

Indian Cod and Potato Stew

A spicy fish stew made with potatoes, peppers and traditional Indian spices.

Serves 4
30ml/2 tbsp oil
5ml/1 tsp cumin seeds
1 onion, chopped
1 red (bell) pepper, thinly sliced
1 garlic clove, crushed
2 red chillies, finely chopped
2 bay leaves

2.5ml/½ tsp salt
5ml/1 tsp ground cumin
5ml/1 tsp ground coriander
5ml/1 tsp chilli powder
400g/14oz can
    chopped tomatoes
2 large potatoes, cut into
    2.5cm/1in chunks
300ml/½ pint/1¼ cups
    fish stock
4 cod fillets
chapatis, to serve

1 Heat the oil in a large, deep-sided frying pan and fry the cumin seeds for about 2 minutes until they begin to splutter. Add the onion, pepper, garlic, chillies and bay leaves and fry for 5–7 minutes until the onions have browned.

2 Add the salt, ground cumin, ground coriander and chilli powder and cook for 3–4 minutes. Stir in the tomatoes, potatoes and fish stock. Bring to the boil and simmer for a further 10 minutes.

3 Add the fish, then cover and simmer for 10 minutes, or until the fish is tender. Serve with chapatis.

Variations
• In place of chapatis, serve this fish curry with pilau or plain rice with a few chopped herbs added.
• If you prefer another fish, try haddock or another firm fish such as monkfish or hake.
• For a change, use 450ml/¾ pint/scant 2 cups coconut milk in place of the chopped tomatoes.
• To vary the flavours, replace the red chillies with green chillies. Deseed and finely chop them.
• Add another vegetable or replace the potatoes with two bulbs of fennel, sliced.

Classic Cod and Chips

Quintessentially English, this is fish and chips as it should be cooked, with tender flakes of fish in a crisp batter, and home-made chips.

Serves 4
450g/1lb potatoes
groundnut (peanut) oil, for
    deep-frying

4 x 175g/6oz cod fillets, skinned
    and any tiny bones removed

For the batter
75g/3oz/⅔ cup plain
    (all-purpose) flour
1 egg yolk
10ml/2 tsp oil
175ml/6fl oz/¾ cup water
salt

1 To make the chips (French fries), cut the potatoes into slices about 5mm/¼in thick. Then cut the slices into 5mm/¼in fingers or chips. Rinse the slices thoroughly, drain well and then dry in a clean dish towel.

2 Heat the oil in a deep fat fryer to 180°C/350°F. Add the chips in the basket to the fryer and cook for 3 minutes. Lift out and shake off excess fat.

3 To make the batter, sift the flour into a bowl. Add a pinch of salt. Make a well in the middle of the flour and add the egg yolk, oil and a little of the water. Mix the yolk with the liquid, then add the remaining water and incorporate the surrounding flour to make a smooth batter. Cover and set aside.

4 Reheat the oil in the fryer and cook the chips again for about 5 minutes, until they are golden and crisp. Drain on kitchen paper and season with salt. Keep hot in a low oven.

5 Dip the pieces of fish fillet into the batter and turn them to make sure they are evenly coated. Allow any excess batter to drip off before carefully lowering the fish into the hot oil.

6 Cook the fish for 5 minutes, turning once, if necessary, so that the batter browns evenly all over. The batter should be crisp and golden. Remove with a slotted spoon and drain well on kitchen paper. Serve immediately, with lemon wedges and the chips.

Indian Stew Energy 332kcal/1396kJ; Protein 36.9g; Carbohydrate 27.6g, of which sugars 7.9g; Fat 9.2g, of which saturates 1.3g; Cholesterol 81mg; Calcium 59mg; Fibre 2.9g; Sodium 132mg.
Cod and Chips Energy 645kcal/2700kJ; Protein 32.6g; Carbohydrate 54.3g, of which sugars 0.7g; Fat 34.5g, of which saturates 4.2g; Cholesterol 0mg; Calcium 130mg; Fibre 3.4g; Sodium 294mg.

Cod, Basil, Tomato and Potato Pie

Natural and smoked fish make a great combination and are served here with potatoes and a subtle hint of tasty tomato and basil. Served with a green salad, this makes an ideal dish for lunch or a family supper.

Serves 8
1kg/2¼lb smoked cod
1kg/2¼lb white cod
900ml/1½ pints/3¾ cups milk
1.2litres/2 pints/5 cups water
2 basil sprigs
1 lemon thyme sprig
150g/5oz/10 tbsp butter
1 onion, chopped
75g/3oz/⅔ cup plain
   (all-purpose) flour
30ml/2 tbsp chopped fresh basil
4 firm plum tomatoes, peeled
   and chopped
12 medium floury potatoes
salt and ground black pepper
crushed black peppercorns,
   to garnish
lettuce leaves, to serve

1 Place both kinds of fish in a roasting pan with 600ml/1 pint/ 2½ cups of the milk, the water and the herb sprigs. Bring to a simmer and cook gently for about 3–4 minutes. Leave the fish to cool in the liquid for about 20 minutes. Drain the fish, reserving the cooking liquid for use in the sauce. Flake the fish, removing any skin and bone.

2 Melt 75g/3oz/6 tbsp of the butter in a large pan, add the onion and cook for about 5 minutes until softened and tender but not browned. Sprinkle over the flour and half the chopped basil. Gradually add the reserved fish cooking liquid, adding a little more milk if necessary to make a fairly thin sauce, stirring constantly to make a smooth consistency. Bring to the boil, season with salt and pepper, and add the remaining basil.

3 Remove the pan from the heat, then add the fish and tomatoes and stir gently to combine. Pour into an ovenproof dish. Preheat the oven to 180°C/350°F/Gas 4.

4 Cook the potatoes in boiling water until tender. Drain, then add the remaining butter and milk, and mash. Season to taste and spoon over the fish mixture, using a fork to create a pattern. Bake for 30 minutes until the top is golden. Sprinkle with the crushed peppercorns and serve hot with lettuce.

Cod, Tomato and Potato Bake

The wonderful sun-drenched flavours of the Mediterranean are brought together in this appetizing, potato-topped bake. Lightly cooked courgettes make a tasty accompaniment to this dish.

Serves 4
450g/1lb potatoes, cut into
   thin slices
30ml/2 tbsp olive oil
1 red onion, chopped
1 garlic clove, crushed
1 red (bell) pepper, seeded
   and diced
1 yellow (bell) pepper, seeded
   and diced
225g/8oz mushrooms, sliced
400g/14oz and 225g/8oz cans
   chopped tomatoes
150ml/¼ pint/⅔ cup dry
   white wine
450g/1lb skinless, boneless cod
   fillet, cut into 2cm/¾in cubes
50g/2oz/½ cup pitted black
   olives, chopped
15ml/1 tbsp chopped fresh basil
15ml/1 tbsp chopped
   fresh oregano
salt and ground black pepper
fresh oregano sprigs, to garnish
cooked courgettes (zucchini),
   to serve

1 Preheat the oven to 200°C/400°F/ Gas 6. Par-boil the potatoes in a pan of lightly salted, boiling water for 4 minutes. Drain thoroughly, then add 15ml/1 tbsp of the oil and toss together to mix. Set aside.

2 Heat the remaining oil in a heavy pan, add the onion, garlic and red and yellow peppers and cook for about 5 minutes, stirring occasionally.

3 Stir in the mushrooms, tomatoes and wine, bring to the boil and boil for a few minutes until the sauce has reduced slightly. Add the fish, olives, herbs and seasoning to the tomato mixture.

4 Spoon the mixture into a lightly greased casserole and arrange the potato slices over the top, covering the fish mixture completely.

5 Bake, uncovered, for about 45 minutes until the fish is cooked and tender and the potato topping is browned. Garnish with fresh oregano sprigs and serve with courgettes.

Cod and Pepper Bake Energy 318kcal/1334kJ; Protein 25.8g; Carbohydrate 28.8g, of which sugars 11.4g; Fat 9.1g, of which saturates 1.5g; Cholesterol 52mg; Calcium 74mg; Fibre 5.4g; Sodium 383mg.
Cod and Potato Pie Energy 474kcal/1989kJ; Protein 49.6g; Carbohydrate 30.7g, of which sugars 4.6g; Fat 17.8g, of which saturates 10.2g; Cholesterol 155mg; Calcium 62mg; Fibre 2.5g; Sodium 1672mg.

Salt Cod with Potato Mash Gratin

This recipe is reminiscent of the well-known French salt cod purée, brandade. Many similar dishes are produced around the Mediterranean, using salt or dried cod, which is also known as stockfish. Served with potatoes, garlic and cream, this traditional ingredient is transformed into a sophisticated main course or, in smaller portions, an elegant appetizer.

Serves 8
1kg/2¼lb potatoes, unpeeled
800g/1¾lb salt cod, soaked
105ml/7 tbsp olive oil
200ml/7fl oz/scant 1 cup single
    (light) cream
2 garlic cloves, chopped
1 small bunch of parsley, chopped
pinch of freshly grated nutmeg
salt

1 Cook the potatoes in a large pan of lightly salted boiling water for 20–30 minutes, until tender.

2 Drain the potatoes thoroughly, then peel and mash with a fork. Meanwhile, preheat the oven to 200°C/400°F/Gas 6.

3 Bring another large pan of water to the boil. Add the fish and bring the water back to the boil, then immediately remove the pan from the heat. Leave to stand for 5 minutes.

4 Remove the fish from the pan with a slotted spoon and leave to cool slightly. When cool enough to handle, remove and discard the skin and bones from the fish.

5 Mix the fish with the potatoes, then blend in the olive oil, cream and garlic. Stir in the parsley and nutmeg and season with salt, if necessary. Spoon the mixture into an ovenproof dish and bake for about 20 minutes. Serve hot.

Variation
This dish could also be made with sweet potatoes, if you like. Simply replace the white potatoes with the same quantity of sweet potatoes and prepare in the same way.

Salt Cod and Potato Casserole

Nowadays there is no longer any need to salt cod to preserve it, but the distinctive flavour of salted cod means that it is still an essential ingredient in many traditional recipes. This succulent Norwegian casserole recipe is made with salt cod layered with potatoes and onions in a delicate tomato and chilli sauce.

Serves 4
1kg/2¼lb salt cod
about 500g/1¼lb potatoes, sliced
1 onion, sliced
100ml/3½fl oz/scant ½ cup
    water
100ml/3½fl oz/scant ½ cup
    olive oil
75ml/2½fl oz/⅓ cup
    strained tomatoes
a little chopped red chilli

1 Soak the salt cod in cold water for two days, changing the water at least three times a day.

2 Drain the cod thoroughly and remove the skin and bones, then cut the fish into pieces, each measuring approximately 5cm/2in square.

3 Layer the fish, potatoes and finally the onion in a lightly oiled flameproof casserole.

4 Put the water, oil, strained tomatoes and the chilli in a separate pan and bring the mixture to the boil. Pour into the casserole, over the fish, potatoes and onions.

5 Return the liquid to the boil, reduce the heat, cover and simmer for about 1½–2 hours, until the potatoes are tender. Serve immediately.

Cook's Tip
It helps to have two sharp knives for preparing the salt cod; a small one to cut away the flesh from the bones, and a larger, flexible-bladed one to slide, in a sawing motion, between the flesh and the skin. A little salt on the fingers will help to get a firm grip on the skin.

Salt Cod Gratin Energy 366kcal/1535kJ; Protein 35.9g; Carbohydrate 21.4g, of which sugars 2.4g; Fat 15.8g, of which saturates 4.7g; Cholesterol 73mg; Calcium 65mg; Fibre 1.7g; Sodium 423mg.
Cod Casserole Energy 55kcal/231kJ; Protein 7.8g; Carbohydrate 2g, of which sugars 0.3g; Fat 1.8g, of which saturates 0.3g; Cholesterol 14mg; Calcium 6mg; Fibre 0.2g; Sodium 95mg.

Salt Cod with Scrambled Eggs, Onion and Potatoes

Salt cod is a traditional ingredient in Mediterranean and north European countries. This succulent salt cod recipe is a classic Portuguese dish: thin strips of cod are combined with onions, alongside a mixture of thin strips of potatoes and scrambled eggs.

Serves 4

400g/14oz salt cod, soaked
50ml/2fl oz/¼ cup olive oil
3 onions, thinly sliced
500g/1¼lb potatoes, cut into
    thin matchsticks (julienne)
    and deep-fried
8 eggs, lightly beaten
1 small bunch of parsley, chopped
12 black olives

1 Bring a pan of water to the boil. Add the fish and bring back to the boil, then immediately remove the pan from the heat. Leave to stand for 5 minutes.

2 Remove the fish from the pan with a slotted spatula and leave to cool slightly. When cool enough to handle, remove and discard the skin and bones.

3 Heat the olive oil in a large pan. Add the onions and cook over a low heat, stirring occasionally, for 5 minutes, until softened but not browned.

4 Add the fish, then the potatoes and, finally, the beaten eggs to the pan. Stir gently until all the ingredients are thoroughly combined but the eggs are still soft. Serve the dish straight away, sprinkled with the chopped parsley and black olives.

> **Variation**
> Another recipe called Bacalhau à Gomes de Sá originates in Porto (Oporto), and has the same ingredients but a different preparation technique. In this dish, the onions are cooked in olive oil, and mixed with cooked potatoes and salt cod marinated in milk. The dish is then served with parsley, cooked eggs and black olives.

Baked Salt Cod with Potatoes and Olives

This quintessentially Greek recipe, with its delicious mingling of salt cod, potatoes, tomatoes and olives, is resonant of afternoons spent languishing in the warm sun and the cool sea breeze. A true taste of the Mediterranean.

Serves 4

675g/1½lb salt cod
800g/1¾lb potatoes, cut
    into wedges
1 large onion, finely chopped
2 or 3 garlic cloves, chopped
leaves from 1 fresh
    rosemary sprig
30ml/2 tbsp chopped
    fresh parsley
120ml/4fl oz/½ cup olive oil
400g/14oz can
    chopped tomatoes
15ml/1 tbsp tomato purée (paste)
300ml/½ pint/1¼ cups hot water
5ml/1 tsp dried oregano
12 black olives
ground black pepper

1 Soak the cod in cold water overnight, changing the water as often as possible during the evening and morning. The cod does not have to be skinned for this dish, but you may prefer to remove the skin, especially if there is a lot of it on the fish. You should also remove any obvious fins or bones. After soaking, drain the cod and cut it into 7.5cm/3in squares.

2 Preheat the oven to 180°C/350°F/Gas 4. Mix the potatoes, onion, garlic, rosemary and parsley in a large roasting pan with plenty of black pepper. Add the olive oil and toss until coated.

3 Arrange the pieces of salt cod between the oil coated vegetables and spread the tomatoes evenly over the surface. Stir the tomato purée into the hot water until dissolved, then pour the mixture over the contents of the pan. Sprinkle the oregano on top. Bake for 1 hour, basting the fish and potatoes occasionally with the pan juices.

4 Remove the roasting pan from the oven, sprinkle the olives on top, and then cook for 30 minutes more, adding a little more hot water if the mixture seems to be drying out. Garnish with fresh parsley. Serve hot or cold.

Salt Cod with Eggs Energy 484kcal/2032kJ; Protein 49.1g; Carbohydrate 30.4g, of which sugars 8.9g; Fat 19.7g, of which saturates 4.4g; Cholesterol 440mg; Calcium 151mg; Fibre 4g; Sodium 843mg.
Baked Salt Cod Energy 624kcal/2,624kJ; Protein 61g; Carbohydrate 45.6g, of which sugars 12.9g; Fat 23.3g, of which saturates 3.5g; Cholesterol 100mg; Calcium 98mg; Fibre 4.8g; Sodium 918mg.

Hake with Turnip Tops and Sautéed Potatoes

Hake is highly prized in many regions of Europe and is served in numerous different ways. Here, sautéed potatoes and leafy turnip tops are paired with this delicate fish for a truly stunning result. Serve with spinach or broccoli for an elegant supper.

Serves 4

105ml/7 tbsp olive oil
2 small onions, chopped
2 garlic cloves, chopped
5ml/1 tsp sweet paprika
1 bay leaf
15ml/1 tbsp white wine vinegar
150ml/¼ pint/⅔ cup fish stock
  or water
4 hake steaks, about
  225g/8oz each
200g/7oz turnip tops (the green
  part of the turnip)
8 potatoes, boiled without peeling
4 hard-boiled eggs, halved

1 Preheat the oven to 180°C/350°F/Gas 4. Heat 30ml/2 tbsp of the olive oil in a flameproof casserole. Add the onions, garlic, paprika and bay leaf and cook over a low heat, stirring occasionally, for 5 minutes, until the onions have softened.

2 Add the vinegar and the stock or water, then place the hake in the casserole and season with salt. Cover and cook in the oven for 15 minutes.

3 Meanwhile, steam the turnip tops or cook in a little boiling water for 3–5 minutes, then drain if necessary. Press them through a sieve (strainer) into a bowl, mix with 15ml/1 tbsp of the remaining olive oil and keep warm.

4 Peel the potatoes and cut into quarters. Heat the remaining olive oil in a sauté pan or frying pan, add the potatoes and cook, turning occasionally, over a medium-low heat for around 7–8 minutes until light golden brown.

5 Using a slotted spatula, transfer the fish to a large serving plate. Add the potatoes, turnip tops and eggs and spoon over the onion sauce. Serve immediately.

Baked Monkfish with Potatoes and Garlic

Firm-fleshed monkfish and crispy, golden potatoes are the perfect canvas for the complex flavours in this dish.

Serves 4

1kg/2¼lb potatoes, cut into chunks
50g/2oz/¼ cup butter
2 onions, thickly sliced
4 garlic cloves
few fresh thyme sprigs
2–3 fresh bay leaves
450ml/¾ pint/scant 2 cups
  fish stock, plus 45ml/3 tbsp
900g/2lb monkfish tail, skin and
  membrane removed
30–45ml/2–3 tbsp white wine
50g/2oz/1 cup fresh
  white breadcrumbs
15g/½oz fresh parsley, chopped
15ml/1 tbsp olive oil
salt and ground black pepper

1 Preheat the oven to 190°C/375°F/Gas 5. Put the chunks of potato in an ovenproof dish. Melt half the butter in a large frying pan and cook the onions gently for 5–6 minutes. Add the onions to the potatoes and mix.

2 Slice 2–3 of the garlic cloves and add to the potatoes with the thyme and bay leaves, and season with salt and pepper.

3 Pour in the main batch of stock over the potatoes and bake, stirring once or twice, for 50–60 minutes, until the potatoes are just tender.

4 Push the monkfish into the potatoes and season. Bake for 10–15 minutes. Mix the 45ml/3 tbsp stock with the wine and use to baste the monkfish a couple of times during cooking.

5 Finely chop the remaining garlic. Melt the remaining butter and toss it with the breadcrumbs, chopped garlic, most of the chopped parsley and seasoning. Spoon over the monkfish, pressing it down gently with the back of a spoon.

6 Drizzle the olive oil over the fish, return the dish to the oven and bake for a final 10–15 minutes, until the breadcrumbs are crisp and golden and the liquid has been absorbed. Sprinkle the remaining parsley on to the potatoes and serve immediately.

Hake with Potatoes Energy 614kcal/2571kJ; Protein 51g; Carbohydrate 36.2g, of which sugars 5.7g; Fat 30.7g, of which saturates 5.2g; Cholesterol 242mg; Calcium 102mg; Fibre 3.4g; Sodium 326mg.
Baked Monkfish Energy 529kcal/2230kJ; Protein 45.8g; Carbohydrate 54g, of which sugars 6.5g; Fat 15g, of which saturates 7.4g; Cholesterol 63mg; Calcium 67mg; Fibre 3.5g; Sodium 245mg.

Sea Bream and Potato Parcels

Each of these little fish and potato parcels is a meal in itself and can be prepared several hours in advance, which makes the recipe ideal for entertaining. Serve the parcels with a mixed leaf salad.

Serves 4
8 small waxy salad potatoes, preferably red-skinned
200g/7oz sorrel, stalks removed
30ml/2 tbsp extra virgin olive oil
16 filo pastry sheets, thawed if frozen
4 sea bream fillets, about 175g/6oz each, scaled but not skinned
50g/2oz/¼ cup butter, melted
120ml/4fl oz/½ cup fish stock
250ml/8fl oz/1 cup whipping cream
salt and ground black pepper
finely diced red (bell) pepper, to garnish

1 Preheat the oven to 200°C/400°F/Gas 6. Cook the potatoes in a pan of lightly salted boiling water for about 15–20 minutes, or until just tender. Drain and leave to cool. Set about half the sorrel leaves aside. Shred the remaining leaves by piling up six or eight at a time, rolling them up like a fat cigar and slicing them with a sharp knife. Thinly slice the potatoes lengthways.

2 Brush a baking sheet with a little of the oil. Lay a sheet of filo pastry on the sheet, brush it with oil, then lay a second sheet crossways over the first. Repeat with two more sheets. Arrange a quarter of the sliced potatoes in the centre, season and add a quarter of the shredded sorrel. Lay a bream fillet on top, skin side up. Season with salt and ground black pepper.

3 Loosely fold the filo pastry up and over to make a neat parcel, then repeat to make three more. Place the parcels on the baking sheet and brush with half the butter. Bake for about 20 minutes, or until the filo is puffed up and golden brown.

4 Meanwhile, make the sorrel sauce. Heat the remaining butter in a pan, add the reserved sorrel and cook gently for 3 minutes, stirring, until it wilts. Stir in the stock and cream. Heat almost to boiling point, stirring continuously so that the sorrel breaks down. Season to taste and keep hot until the fish parcels are ready. Serve garnished with red pepper. Pass round the sauce separately.

Smoked Haddock and Potato Flan

The classic combination of potatoes and smoked fish is here reworked in pastry for this delicious flan.

Serves 4
For the pastry
225g/8oz/2 cups plain (all-purpose) flour
pinch of salt
115g/4oz/1½ cup cold butter, cut into chunks
cold water, to mix

For the filling
2 undyed smoked haddock fillets, approximately 200g/7oz
600ml/1 pint/2½ cups full-fat (whole) milk
3–4 black peppercorns
sprig of fresh thyme
150ml/¼ pint/⅔ cup double (heavy) cream
2 eggs
200g/7oz potatoes, peeled and diced
ground black pepper

1 Preheat the oven to 200°C/400°F/Gas 6. Use a food processor to make the pastry. Put the flour, salt and butter into the food processor bowl and process until the mixture resembles fine breadcrumbs. Pour in a little cold water (you will need about 40ml/8 tsp) and continue to process until the mixture forms a ball. If this takes longer than 30 seconds, add a dash or two more water. Take the pastry ball out of the food processor, wrap in clear film (plastic wrap) and leave to rest in a cool place for about 30 minutes.

2 Roll out the dough and use to line a 20cm/8in flan tin (pan). Prick the base of the pastry all over with a fork, then bake blind in the preheated oven for 20 minutes.

3 Put the haddock in a pan with the milk, peppercorns and thyme. Poach for 10 minutes. Remove the fish from the pan and flake into small chunks. Allow the poaching liquor to cool.

4 Whisk the cream and eggs together thoroughly, then whisk in the cooled poaching liquid.

5 Layer the pastry case (pie shell) with the flaked fish and diced potato, seasoning with black pepper. Pour the cream mixture over the top. Put the flan in the oven and bake for 40 minutes, until lightly browned on top and set. Serve hot.

Sea Bream Energy 651kcal/2,710kJ; Protein 35.8g; Carbohydrate 23.2g, of which sugars 3.3g; Fat 46.8g, of which saturates 23.2g; Cholesterol 159mg; Calcium 222mg; Fibre 2g; Sodium 359mg.
Haddock Flan Energy 734kcal/3064kJ; Protein 23.8g; Carbohydrate 58.4g, of which sugars 8.2g; Fat 46.8g, of which saturates 27.9g; Cholesterol 225mg; Calcium 280mg; Fibre 2.3g; Sodium 636mg.

Smoked Haddock and Potato Pie

Smoked haddock has a salty flavour and can be bought either dyed or undyed. The dyed fish has a strong yellow colour while the undyed is almost creamy in colour.

Serves 4

450g/1lb smoked haddock fillet
475ml/16fl oz/2 cups
  semi-skimmed (low-fat) milk
2 bay leaves
1 onion, quartered
4 cloves
450g/1lb new potatoes
butter, for greasing
30ml/2 tbsp cornflour (cornstarch)
60ml/4 tbsp double (heavy) cream
30ml/2 tbsp chopped fresh chervil
salt and ground black pepper
mixed vegetables, to serve

1 Preheat the oven to 200°C/400°F/Gas 6. Place the haddock in a deep-sided frying pan. Pour the milk over and add the bay leaves. Stud the onion with the cloves and place it in the pan with the fish and milk. Cover the top and leave to simmer for about 10 minutes or until the fish starts to flake.

2 Remove the fish with a slotted spoon and set aside to cool. Strain the liquid from the pan into a separate pan and set aside.

3 Cut the potatoes into fine even slices, leaving the skins on. Blanch in a pan of lightly salted water for 5 minutes, then drain.

4 Grease the base and sides of a 1.2 litre/2 pint/5 cup ovenproof dish. Then, using a knife and fork, flake the fish.

5 Reheat the milk in the pan. Mix the cornflour with a little water to form a paste and stir in the cream and the chervil. Add to the milk in the pan and cook until thickened.

6 Arrange one-third of the potatoes over the base of the dish and season with pepper. Lay half of the fish over. Repeat the layering, finishing with a layer of potatoes on top.

7 Pour the sauce over the top, making sure that it sinks down through the mixture. Cover with foil and cook for 30 minutes. Remove the foil and cook for a further 10 minutes to brown the surface. Serve with a selection of mixed vegetables.

Trout with Fennel and Potatoes

Cooking trout, fennel and potatoes together in one pan makes for an easy supper. Add your favourite steamed green vegetables to complete the meal.

Serves 2

1 small fennel bulb, about
  175g/6oz, with fronds
25g/1oz/2 tbsp butter, plus extra
  for greasing
350g/12oz potatoes, peeled and
  thinly sliced
1 bay leaf
60ml/4 tbsp dry vermouth
60ml/4 tbsp water
2 trout, about 225g/8oz
  each, cleaned
lemon and lime slices, to garnish
steamed green vegetables,
  to serve

1 Preheat the oven to 180°C/350°F/Gas 4. Cut the feathery green fronds from the fennel, chop very finely and set aside. Slice the fennel bulb thinly. Grease a shallow baking dish with butter and spread out the fennel bulb slices to cover the base of the dish.

2 Spread out the potato slices on top of the fennel and top with the bay leaf. Pour the vermouth and water over the vegetables. Season to taste. Cover the dish tightly with foil and bake in the oven for 35–40 minutes.

3 Remove the dish from the oven and lift off the foil. Place the trout on top of the vegetables and dot generously with butter. Replace the foil and bake for 20–25 minutes more, until the trout are cooked and the vegetables are tender.

4 Remove the foil and sprinkle the remaining chopped fennel over the fish. Garnish with the lemon and lime slices. Serve immediately, with the steamed green vegetables.

Cook's Tip
Dry vermouth has a concentrated flavour that works well in this recipe, and the herbs that are an intrinsic part of it are more than a match for the robust flavour of the fennel.

Smoked Haddock Pie Energy 300kcal/1266kJ; Protein 23.9g; Carbohydrate 32.4g, of which sugars 1.9g; Fat 9.3g, of which saturates 5.3g; Cholesterol 61mg; Calcium 56mg; Fibre 1.5g; Sodium 881mg.
Trout with Fennel Energy 461kcal/1937kJ; Protein 38.8g; Carbohydrate 31.4g, of which sugars 5.4g; Fat 17.7g, of which saturates 8.5g; Cholesterol 173mg; Calcium 90mg; Fibre 3.9g; Sodium 259mg.

Burbot and Potato Chowder

Burbot is a large freshwater fish with soft, well-flavoured flesh. This fish and potato chowder can be served on its own as a tasty appetizer or with fresh crusty bread for a sustaining main meal.

Serves 4

1kg/2¼lb burbot or monkfish, with their bones, if filleted
20g/¾oz/1½ tbsp unsalted butter
1 onion, chopped
1 small celery stick, chopped
1 small leek, chopped
1 bay leaf
10 whole allspice
5 white peppercorns
1.5 litres/2½ pints/6¼ cups water
1 carrot, finely diced
500g/1¼lb potatoes, cubed
5ml/1 tsp plain white (all-purpose) flour
200ml/7fl oz/scant 1 cup double (heavy) cream
salt and ground white pepper
dill sprigs, to garnish

1 Fillet the fish or, if the fishmonger fillets it for you, ask him to reserve the bones and head. Cut the fish into large chunks.

2 Heat the butter in a pan, add the onion, celery, leek, fish bones, fish head and any fish trimmings. Fry for 5 minutes until the vegetables soften. Add the bay leaf, allspice, peppercorns, 15ml/1 tbsp salt and 1 litre/1¾ pints/4 cups of the water. Bring to the boil, then simmer very gently for 30 minutes.

3 Strain the stock through a sieve (strainer) into a clean pan. (There should still be about 1 litre/1¾ pints/4 cups of liquid. Add extra water, if necessary, to make up the correct amount.)

4 Add the carrot and potato to the stock and bring to the boil. Lower the heat and simmer until the potato is nearly cooked. The timing will depend on the size of the potato cubes.

5 Add the fish to the pan and return to simmering point, then sprinkle over the flour and continue to simmer for a further 5 minutes, or until the fish is just cooked.

6 Stir in the cream, then taste and add salt and pepper according to taste. Pour into individual serving dishes and serve hot, garnished with a sprig of dill.

Mediterranean Fish and Potato Bake

This fish and potato bake uses the delicious combination of potatoes, wine, garlic, tomatoes and fresh fish to produce a fragrant and elegant main course dish, perfect for alfresco dining on long summer evenings.

Serves 4

3 potatoes
2 onions, halved and sliced
30ml/2 tbsp olive oil, plus extra for greasing and drizzling
2 garlic cloves, very finely chopped
675g/1½ lb thick skinless fish fillets, such as turbot or sea bass
1 bay leaf
1 thyme sprig
3 tomatoes, peeled and thinly sliced
30ml/2 tbsp orange juice
60ml/4 tbsp dry white wine
2.5ml/½ tsp saffron strands, steeped in 60ml/4 tbsp boiling water
salt and ground black pepper

1 Cook the potatoes in boiling salted water for 15 minutes, then drain. When the potatoes are cool enough to handle, peel off the skins and slice the potatoes thinly.

2 Meanwhile, in a heavy frying pan, fry the onions in the oil over a medium-low heat for about 10 minutes, stirring frequently. Add the garlic and continue cooking for a few minutes until the onions are soft and golden.

3 Preheat the oven to 190°C/375°F/Gas 5. Oil a 2 litre/3½ pint/ 8 cup baking dish and cover the base with a layer of half of the cooked potato slices. Cover with half the onions and season well with salt and black pepper.

4 Place the fish fillets on top of the vegetables and tuck the herbs in between them. Top with the tomato slices and then the remaining onions. Finish with a second layer of potatoes, arranging them neatly.

5 Pour over the orange juice, white wine and saffron liquid, season with salt and black pepper and drizzle a little extra olive oil on top. Bake the fish uncovered for about 30 minutes, until the potatoes are tender and the fish is cooked. Serve hot.

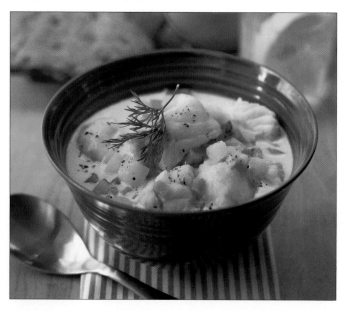

Burbot Chowder Energy 582kcal/2431kJ; Protein 47.6g; Carbohydrate 25.8g, of which sugars 6.4g; Fat 32.6g, of which saturates 19.7g; Cholesterol 119mg; Calcium 77mg; Fibre 2.8g; Sodium 117mg.
Fish Bake Energy 342kcal/1440kJ; Protein 35.1g; Carbohydrate 33.1g, of which sugars 11.7g; Fat 7.5g, of which saturates 1.2g; Cholesterol 78mg; Calcium 61mg; Fibre 3.8g; Sodium 127mg.

Potato and Mackerel Pilaki

Pilaki are popular dishes from Turkey, where the most common dishes are made with firm-fleshed fish. The classic one is made with bonito, but mackerel and sea bass are equally good. Potatoes are always used.

Serves 4–6

2 good-sized fresh mackerel, gutted and rinsed
120ml/4fl oz/½ cup good quality olive oil
2 onions, chopped
3–4 garlic cloves, chopped
1 mild fresh green chilli, seeded and chopped
2–3 carrots, diced
2–3 potatoes, diced
1 medium celeriac, weighing about 450g/1lb, peeled, trimmed and diced
2 large tomatoes, skinned and chopped, or 400g/14oz can chopped tomatoes, drained
5ml/1 tsp sugar
2–3 bay leaves
juice of 2 lemons
1 small bunch of fresh flat leaf parsley
salt and ground black pepper

1 Preheat the oven to 160°C/325°F/Gas 3. Cut the fish crossways into 2cm/¾in slices, keeping it intact at the backbone.

2 Heat the oil in a heavy pan. Stir in the onions, garlic and chilli and cook until soft. Add the carrots, potatoes and celeriac and cook for 2 minutes, then add the tomatoes, sugar and bay leaves.

3 Pour in 600ml/1 pint/2½ cups water and bring to the boil. Cover the pan, then simmer for 5–10 minutes, until the vegetables are just tender. Season with salt and pepper.

4 Spoon half the vegetables over the bottom of an ovenproof dish, place the fish on top and spoon the remaining vegetables over them. Sprinkle with the lemon juice and lay a few sprigs of parsley on top.

5 Cover with baking parchment that has been soaked in water and squeezed out. Bake for 20 minutes until the fish is cooked.

6 Remove the paper and parsley sprigs and serve hot, garnished with a little chopped parsley. Alternatively, leave the pilaki to cool in the dish and serve at room temperature.

Halibut and Sweet Potato Curry

Although the rice is simply boiled, it is an integral part of this dish and takes on the delicious and complex flavours of the fragrant sweet potato sauce with which it is served.

Serves 4

2 halibut steaks, total weight about 500–675g/1¼–1½lb
30ml/2 tbsp groundnut (peanut) oil
2 cardamom pods
1 cinnamon stick
6 allspice berries
4 cloves
1 large onion, chopped
3 garlic cloves, crushed
10–15ml/2–3 tsp grated fresh root ginger
10ml/2 tsp ground cumin
5ml/1 tsp ground coriander
2.5ml/½ tsp cayenne pepper or to taste
4 tomatoes, peeled, seeded and chopped
1 sweet potato, about 225g/8oz, cut into 2cm/¾in cubes
475ml/16fl oz/2 cups fish stock
115g/4oz piece of creamed coconut or 120ml/4 fl oz/½ cup coconut cream
1 bay leaf
225g/8oz/generous 1 cup white long grain rice
salt

1 Rub the halibut steaks well with salt and set aside. Heat the oil in a flameproof casserole and stir-fry the cardamom pods, cinnamon stick, allspice berries and cloves for 3 minutes.

2 Add the onion, garlic and ginger. Continue cooking for 4–5 minutes over a gentle heat, until the onion is fairly soft, stirring frequently, then add the cumin, coriander and cayenne pepper and cook briefly, stirring constantly.

3 Stir in the tomatoes, sweet potato, stock or water, coconut and bay leaf. Season with salt. Bring to the boil, then cover and simmer for 15–18 minutes, until the sweet potato is tender.

4 Cook the rice according to your preferred method. Meanwhile, add the fish steaks to the pan of sauce and spoon the sauce over them. Cover the pan with a lid and simmer for about 10 minutes, until the fish is just tender and flakes easily.

5 Spoon the rice into a warmed serving dish, spoon over the sauce and arrange the steaks on top. Serve immediately.

Mackerel Pilaki Energy 270kcal/1127kJ; Protein 17.3g; Carbohydrate 22.9g, of which sugars 11.2g; Fat 12.7g, of which saturates 2.7g; Cholesterol 40mg; Calcium 76mg; Fibre 4.1g; Sodium 115mg.
Halibut Curry Energy 639kcal/2669kJ; Protein 34.1g; Carbohydrate 62g, of which sugars 8.3g; Fat 28.4g, of which saturates 18.7g; Cholesterol 44mg; Calcium 74mg; Fibre 2.4g; Sodium 115mg.

Basque-style Tuna and Potatoes

This traditional Spanish stew is made in a slow cooker and is packed with robust, fiery flavours which are soaked up by tasty chunks of potato and meaty tuna.

Serves 4
30ml/2 tbsp olive oil
1 onion, finely chopped
1 garlic clove, finely chopped
75ml/2½ fl oz/⅓ cup white wine, preferably Spanish
200g/7oz can chopped tomatoes
150ml/¼ pint/⅔ cup boiling fish or vegetable stock
5ml/1 tsp paprika
2.5ml/½ tsp dried crushed chillies
450g/1lb waxy new potatoes, cut into 1cm/½ in chunks
1 red and 1 yellow (bell) pepper, seeded and chopped
1 small sprig of fresh rosemary
1 bay leaf
450g/1lb fresh tuna, cut into 2.5cm/1in chunks
salt and ground black pepper
crusty bread, to serve

1 Heat the oil in a large frying pan, add the onion and fry gently for 10 minutes until soft and translucent. Stir in the garlic, followed by the wine, stock, tomatoes, paprika and chillies. Bring to just below boiling point, then carefully pour the mixture into the ceramic cooking pot of a slow cooker.

2 Add the chunks of potato, red and yellow pepper, rosemary and bay leaf to the pot and stir to combine. Cover the slow cooker with the lid and cook on high for 2–2½ hours, or until the potatoes are just tender, then season the sauce to taste with salt and a little ground black pepper.

3 Stir the chunks of tuna into the sauce. Cover and cook for 15–20 minutes until the fish is firm and opaque.

4 Remove the rosemary and bay leaf, then ladle the stew into warmed dishes, grind over a little more black pepper and serve with crusty bread.

> **Cook's Tip**
> For a more economical store cupboard dish, use a drained 200g/7oz can of tuna in place of the fresh fish.

Tuna and Potato Marmitako

This traditional Spanish fisherman's stew, of tuna and potatoes, is wonderfully balanced by the flavours of sweet peppers and cider. It takes its name from the French cooking pot known as a 'marmite'.

Serves 4
60ml/4 tbsp olive oil
1 onion, chopped
2 garlic cloves, finely chopped
3 green (bell) peppers, seeded and chopped
½ dried hot chilli, seeded and chopped
4 light tuna or bonito steaks about 150g/5oz each
400g/14oz can tomatoes with juice
10ml/2 tsp paprika
3 potatoes, diced
350ml/12 fl oz/1½ cups dry (hard) cider
salt and ground black pepper
30ml/2 tbsp chopped fresh parsley, to garnish

1 Heat half the oil in a shallow flameproof casserole big enough to take the fish. Fry the onion gently until softened, then add the garlic. Add the peppers and chilli and stir-fry gently.

2 Season the fish steaks. Heat the remaining oil in a frying pan and fry the fish steaks for 2 minutes on each side over a high heat.

3 Add the tomatoes to the casserole and stir briefly. Add the paprika, then season with salt and pepper to taste.

4 Slip the fish steaks into the sauce, moving the peppers into the spaces between them. Cover with the potatoes, pushing them as flat as possible. Add the cider and bring to a simmer. Cover and cook very gently for about 45 minutes, or until the potatoes are done.

5 Check the seasoning, sprinkle with the chopped parley and serve immediately, straight from the casserole.

> **Variation**
> Veal chops can be used in the same way. Fry for 5 minutes on each side in step 2, then continue as with the fish.

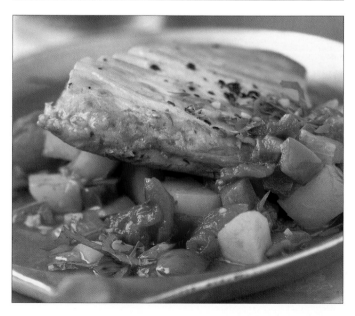

Basque Tuna Energy 862kcal/3634kJ; Protein 55.2g; Carbohydrate 95.5g, of which sugars 0.6g; Fat 31.6g, of which saturates 12.3g; Cholesterol 209mg; Calcium 126mg; Fibre 13.6g; Sodium 1711mg.
Tuna Marmitako Energy 393kcal/1648kJ; Protein 42.8g; Carbohydrate 13.8g, of which sugars 12.4g; Fat 16.8g, of which saturates 3.4g; Cholesterol 47mg; Calcium 64mg; Fibre 3.4g; Sodium 121mg.

Baked Tuna with Golden Potatoes

This delicious dish makes the most of tender, succulent tuna. Crisp, golden potatoes, which are baked alongside the fish, are the perfect accompaniment.

Serves 4

105ml/7 tbsp extra virgin olive oil
juice of 1 large lemon
3 garlic cloves, crushed
4 medium-thick tuna steaks, total weight about 800g/1¾lb
45ml/3 tbsp chopped fresh parsley
15ml/1 tbsp fresh oregano
500g/1¼lb potatoes, peeled and cut into small cubes
450g/1lb ripe tomatoes, peeled and chopped
150ml/¼ pint/⅔ cup hot water
salt and ground black pepper
fresh green salad tossed in olive oil, to serve

1 Mix the oil with the lemon juice and garlic, in a shallow dish that will hold all the tuna steaks snugly in a single layer. Stir in salt and pepper, then add the tuna steaks. Sprinkle over the herbs and turn the steaks to thoroughly coat in the marinade. Leave to marinate for 1–2 hours. Lift the steaks out and lay them in a roasting pan.

2 Preheat the oven to 180°C/350°F/Gas 4. Drop the cubes of potato into the marinating dish and turn to coat them thoroughly in the oil and lemon mixture.

3 Arrange the coated potatoes around the tuna steaks, drizzle over any remaining marinade and sprinkle the peeled and chopped tomatoes over the top. Pour the hot water into the roasting pan.

4 Bake the tuna for 40 minutes, turning it over halfway through and stirring the potatoes and other ingredients.

5 Lift the tuna out of the pan. Place on a warmed plate and cover with foil to keep warm. Increase the oven to 200°C/400°F/Gas 6 and add a little more hot water to the pan.

6 Cook the potatoes for about 15 minutes more to brown them and make them crisp. Serve the tuna and potato mixture with a green salad.

Tuna, Mascarpone and Potato Bake

This substantial one-dish meal, ideal for informal midweek entertaining, embraces the smoky flavour of seared tuna. The sweet and herby Italian sauce, a combination of mascarpone, tomatoes, basil and garlic, is a wonderful foil for the deliciously robust chunks of meaty fish and grated potato.

Serves 4

4 x 175g/6oz tuna steaks
400g/14oz can chopped tomatoes, drained
2 garlic cloves, crushed
30ml/2 tbsp chopped fresh basil
250g/9oz/generous 1 cup mascarpone cheese
3 large potatoes
25g/1oz/2 tbsp butter, diced
salt and ground black pepper

1 Preheat the oven to 200°C/400°F/Gas 6. Heat a griddle pan on the hob and sear the fish steaks for 2 minutes on each side, seasoning with a little black pepper. Set aside while you prepare the sauce.

2 Mix the chopped tomatoes, garlic, basil and cheese together in a bowl and season to taste with salt and plenty of ground black pepper.

3 Peel the potatoes, then grate half of them and dice the other half. Blanch them in separate pans of lightly salted water for about 3 minutes. Drain thoroughly and set aside to cool slightly. When the grated potato is cool enough to handle, squeeze out any excess moisture.

4 Lightly grease a 1.75 litre/3 pint/7½ cup ovenproof dish. Spoon over a little of the sauce and some of the grated potato. Lay the tuna over with more sauce and the remaining grated potato. Sprinkle the diced butter and the diced potatoes over the top. Bake for 30 minutes until cooked through and brown on top.

> **Variation**
> This dish can easily be made into a side dish, simply leave out the tuna and prepare the other ingredients as above.

Baked Tuna Energy 556kcal/2330kJ; Protein 50.7g; Carbohydrate 24g, of which sugars 5.4g; Fat 29.3g, of which saturates 5.4g; Cholesterol 56mg; Calcium 73mg; Fibre 3g; Sodium 122mg.
Tuna Bake Energy 520kcal/2185kJ; Protein 51g; Carbohydrate 29.3g, of which sugars 6.9g; Fat 22.9g, of which saturates 11.2g; Cholesterol 89mg; Calcium 65mg; Fibre 2.6g; Sodium 178mg.

Jansson's Temptation

Named after a well-known Swedish opera singer who liked to serve it to his guests after a performance, this warming baked dish of grated potatoes, cream and canned anchovies is the perfect antidote to the mid-winter blues.

Serves 6
6 large potatoes
1 Spanish (Bermuda) onion, thinly sliced
120ml/4fl oz/½ cup milk
250ml/8fl oz/1 cup double (heavy) cream
100g/3½oz can Swedish anchovies
salt and ground black pepper

1 Preheat the oven to 180°C/350°F/Gas 4. Peel and grate the potatoes. Put in a sieve (strainer) and wash under cold running water to remove any excess starch. Drain well and put in a bowl.

2 Add a sliced onion to the potatoes and mix together, then put in a greased, shallow, ovenproof dish.

3 Mix together the milk and cream. Put both the liquid and the fish from the can of anchovies into the milk mixture and stir together.

4 Pour the mixture over the potatoes and season with salt and pepper. Bake in the oven for 50 minutes until golden brown and bubbling.

Cook's Tips
• Swedish anchovies can be found at well-stocked delicatessens. If they are not readily available you can use ordinary salted anchovies and soak them in milk for a couple of hours to remove the saltiness.
• To make this recipe in individual portions, divide the ingredients on to large squares of buttered foil. Gather up the foil around the ingredients and bring the edges together. Bake for 40 minutes.
• This dish is delicious served on its own or with a salad and is also perfect when eaten with cold sliced ham.

Creamy Anchovy and Potato Bake

This tasty dish of potatoes, onions and anchovies cooked with cream makes a hearty winter lunch or simple supper, served with a refreshing salad. It could also be served as a hot appetizer.

Serves 4
1kg/2¼lb maincrop potatoes
2 onions
25g/1oz/2 tbsp butter
2 x 50g/2oz cans anchovy fillets
150ml/¼ pint/⅔ cup single (light) cream
150ml/¼ pint/⅔ cup double (heavy) cream
15ml/1 tbsp chopped fresh parsley
freshly ground black pepper
fresh crusty bread, to serve

1 Peel the potatoes and cut into slices slightly thicker than 1cm/½in. Cut the slices into strips slightly more than 1cm/½in wide. Peel the onions and cut into very thin rings.

2 Use half of the butter to grease the base and sides of the ceramic cooking pot, and layer half the potatoes and onions in the base of the dish.

3 Drain the anchovies, reserving 15ml/1 tbsp of the oil. Cut the anchovies into thin strips and lay these over the potatoes and onions, then layer the remaining potatoes and onions on the top.

4 Combine the single cream and anchovy oil in a small jug (pitcher) and season with a little ground black pepper. Pour the mixture over the potatoes and dot the surface with butter.

5 Cover and cook on high for 3½ hours, or until the potatoes and onions are tender. Brown under a hot grill (broiler), if you like, then drizzle over the double cream and sprinkle with parsley and pepper. Serve with fresh crusty bread.

Cook's Tip
This recipe can also be served as an appetizer for six, or as a side dish to accompany a main meal.

Jansson's Temptation Energy 400kcal/1669kJ; Protein 9.4g; Carbohydrate 36.5g, of which sugars 6.1g; Fat 25.1g, of which saturates 14.6g; Cholesterol 69mg; Calcium 115mg; Fibre 2.5g; Sodium 696mg.
Creamy Bake Energy 378kcal/1580kJ; Protein 11.3g; Carbohydrate 37.9g, of which sugars 6.4g; Fat 21.2g, of which saturates 11.4g; Cholesterol 54mg; Calcium 1460mg; Fibre 11.5g; Sodium 133mg.

Pilchard and Leek Potato Cakes

This is a simple supper using a selection of basic store-cupboard ingredients, which makes it ideal for a quick and easy midweek meal. Using canned pilchards that come in tomato sauce gives a greater depth of flavour to the finished dish.

Serves 6
225g/8oz potatoes, diced
425g/15oz can pilchards
   in tomato sauce, boned
   and flaked
1 small leek, very finely chopped
5ml/1 tsp lemon juice
salt and ground black pepper

For the coating
1 egg, beaten
75g/3oz/1½ cups fresh
   white breadcrumbs
vegetable oil for frying
salad leaves, cucumber ribbons
   and lemon wedges, to garnish
mayonnaise, to serve

1 Cook the potatoes in a pan of lightly salted boiling water for about 10–15 minutes or until tender. Drain thoroughly, then mash, and set aside to cool.

2 Add the pilchards and their tomato sauce, the leek and lemon juice to the cooled mashed potato. Season with salt and ground black pepper and then beat well with a wooden spoon until you have formed a smooth paste. Chill in the refrigerator for 30 minutes.

3 Divide the mixture into six pieces and shape into cakes. Dip each cake in the egg and then the breadcrumbs.

4 Heat the oil and shallow fry the fish cakes on each side for 5 minutes until golden brown. Drain on kitchen paper and garnish with salad leaves, cucumber ribbons and lemon wedges. Serve with mayonnaise.

Cook's Tip
Chilling the mixture in the refrigerator before shaping makes it easier to form into cakes prior to coating and frying.

Potatoes with Leeks and Herring

Potatoes and bread may seem like an unlikely combination, but this delicious open sandwich from Denmark proves that the two can be paired with triumphant results. Potatoes are an essential and valued part of the traditional Danish diet, and almost no meal is served without them.

Makes 4
40g/1½ oz/3 tbsp salted
   butter, softened
90g/3½oz leek, sliced
2 slices rye bread
2 round (butterhead)
   lettuce leaves
4–5 small new potatoes, peeled,
   boiled and thinly sliced
12–16 pieces pickled herring,
   about 2.5cm/1in square
10ml/2 tsp chopped chives

1 Melt 15g/½ oz/1 tbsp of the butter in a heavy frying pan. Stir in the leeks and cook over a medium heat, stirring constantly, for about 5 minutes, until wilted and softened slightly. Remove the pan from the heat and leave aside to cool.

2 Spread the slices of rye bread with the remaining butter, making sure to cover one side of each slice right up to the edge. Top the buttered rye bread with the lettuce leaves and cut each slice evenly in half.

3 Transfer each half slice of bread to a serving plate and layer between four to six slices of potato over the lettuce on each sandwich, making sure to cover the bread evenly.

4 Arrange three or four herring pieces down the centre of the potatoes and spoon 30ml/2 tbsp of the cooled fried leeks over the herring on each sandwich.

5 Generously sprinkle over the chopped chives and serve the sandwiches immediately.

Cook's Tip
After the bread has been sliced, move the slices to a serving plate or individual plates before arranging the toppings and garnish.

Pilchard Cakes Energy 294kcal/1229kJ; Protein 16.9g; Carbohydrate 17.1g, of which sugars 1.9g; Fat 18.1g, of which saturates 2.4g; Cholesterol 71mg; Calcium 243mg; Fibre 1.3g; Sodium 374mg.
Herring and Leeks Energy 196kcal/819kJ; Protein 6.6g; Carbohydrate 17.2g, of which sugars 4.2g; Fat 11.5g, of which saturates 5.3g; Cholesterol 32mg; Calcium 27mg; Fibre 1.7g; Sodium 347mg.

Eel with Potatoes in Cream Sauce

This dish is a great way to enjoy fried eel. Served with these delicious potatoes and accompanied by a cold beer, this seasonal dish is a summer speciality.

Serves 4
1kg/2¼lb eel, skinned and cleaned
1 egg
5ml/1 tsp water
25g/1oz/½ cup fine
   breadcrumbs, toasted
10ml/2 tsp salt
2.5ml/½ tsp white pepper

40g/1½oz/3 tbsp butter
2 lemons, sliced into wedges,
   to garnish

For the potatoes
800g/1¾lb potatoes, peeled
5ml/1 tsp salt
40g/1½oz/3 tbsp butter
20g/¾oz/4 tbsp plain
   (all-purpose) flour
475ml/16fl oz/2 cups single
   (light) cream
salt and white pepper, to taste
45ml/3 tbsp chopped fresh
   parsley, to garnish

1 Using a sharp knife, cut the skinned eel into 10cm/4in lengths. Whisk together the egg and water in a shallow dish. Place the breadcrumbs in a second shallow dish. Dip the eel first into the egg mixture, then into the breadcrumbs to coat both sides evenly. Sprinkle with salt and pepper. Leave the fish aside to rest for at least 10 minutes.

2 Melt the butter in a large pan over a medium-high heat. Add the eel pieces and cook, turning once, for around 10 minutes on each side, depending on thickness, until the coating is golden brown and the eel is tender. Remove from the pan and drain on kitchen paper. Keep warm.

3 Meanwhile, boil the potatoes in salted water for about 20 minutes. Drain, slice and keep warm. Melt the butter in a pan and stir in the flour. Cook, stirring, for 5 minutes until the roux is pale beige. Slowly stir in the cream and cook for about 5 minutes, stirring constantly, until the sauce has thickened. Season to taste.

4 Stir the potato slices into the cream sauce. Serve with the fried eel on warmed plates, sprinkled with parsley and garnished with lemon wedges.

Eel and Potato Stew

This hearty eel and potato stew is both filling and full of flavour. The firm-fleshed eel and slices of potato soak up all the delicious flavours of the fragrant broth. This can also be made with a variety of other fish. One delicious variation is to combine several types of fish, such as sardines, skate or conger eel.

Serves 4
1kg/2½lb eel fillets, cut into
   4cm/1½in slices

500g/1¼lb potatoes, cut into
   5mm/¼in slices
2 onions, very thinly sliced
2 bay leaves, torn into pieces
2 garlic cloves, chopped
50ml/2fl oz/¼ cup white wine
105ml/7 tbsp olive oil
1 bunch of parsley, chopped
5–7.5ml/1–1½ tsp ground ginger
salt
bread, to serve

1 If you haven't asked your fishmonger to prepare the eels, prepare them yourself by cutting off the heads and sprinkling the skin with salt so you can pull it off. Then rinse them well in cold running water.

2 Make a layer of potatoes in a large pan, then make a layer of onions, followed by a layer of fish. Season with pieces of bay leaf, some garlic, a little wine and olive oil and a sprinkling of parsley, ginger and salt. Continue making layers in this way until all the ingredients have been used up.

3 Sprinkle in 100ml/3½fl oz/scant ½ cup water, cover and cook on a low heat for about 30 minutes, until the fish is cooked through and the vegetables are tender. Serve with fresh bread.

Variations
• You can add some green and red (bell) pepper between the layers, if you like.
• The eels can also be cooked in 4cm/1½in boned pieces, in which case make the potato slices thicker as the eel will take longer to cook.

Fried Eel Energy 978kcal/4074kJ; Protein 50.2g; Carbohydrate 43.7g, of which sugars 5.6g; Fat 68.2g, of which saturates 32.3g; Cholesterol 483mg; Calcium 184mg; Fibre 2.3g; Sodium 448mg.
Eel Stew Energy 738kcal/3074kJ; Protein 45.5g; Carbohydrate 30.4g, of which sugars 9g; Fat 48.3g, of which saturates 10.1g; Cholesterol 375mg; Calcium 113mg; Fibre 3.6g; Sodium 245mg.

Cuttlefish with Potatoes

Sautéed cuttlefish is sweeter and more tender than squid, provided you buy small or medium specimens. If the only ones available are very large, cook them for a little longer than stated in the recipe below. Serve as a sumptuous main course or a tasty meze dish.

Serves 4 as a main course; 6 as a first course

1kg/2¼lb fresh
    cuttlefish, cleaned
150ml/¼ pint/⅔ cup extra virgin
    olive oil
1 large onion, about
    225g/8oz, chopped
175ml/6fl oz/¾ cup white wine
300ml/½ pint/1¼ cups
    hot water
500g/1¼lb potatoes, peeled
    and cubed
4–5 spring onions
    (scallions), chopped
juice of 1 lemon
60ml/4 tbsp chopped fresh dill
salt and ground black pepper

1 Rinse and drain the cleaned cuttlefish well, then slice them into 2cm/¾in wide ribbons.

2 Heat the oil in a heavy pan, add the onion and cook for about 5 minutes until light golden.

3 Add the cuttlefish to the onions and cook, stirring occasionally, until all the water they exude has evaporated and the flesh starts to change colour. This will take approximately 10–15 minutes.

4 Pour the white wine into the pan and allow to simmer briskly. When it has evaporated, add the water. Cover the pan and simmer gently for 10 minutes.

5 Add the potatoes, spring onions and lemon juice to the pan. Season with salt and ground black pepper. There should be enough water in the pan almost to cover the ingredients; top up if necessary.

6 Cover and cook gently for 40 minutes, or until the cuttlefish is tender. Add the dill and cook for 5 minutes. Serve the cuttlefish immediately on oven warmed plates.

Squid and Potato Casserole

This hearty stew is ideal on a cold evening. The potatoes disintegrate to thicken and enrich the sauce, making a warming, comforting main course packed with taste.

Serves 6

800g/1¾lb squid
45ml/3 tbsp olive oil
5 garlic cloves, crushed
4 fresh jalapeño chillies, seeded
    and finely chopped
2 celery sticks, diced
500g/1¼lb small new potatoes
    or baby salad potatoes,
    scrubbed, scraped or peeled
    and quartered
400ml/14fl oz/1⅔ cups dry
    white wine
400ml/14fl oz/1⅔ cups fish stock
4 tomatoes, diced
30ml/2 tbsp chopped fresh flat
    leaf parsley
salt
white rice or corn bread,
    to serve

1 Clean the squid under cold water. Pull the tentacles away from the body. The squid's entrails should come out easily. Remove the cartilage from inside the body cavity and discard it. Wash the body thoroughly.

2 Pull away the membrane that covers the body. Cut between the tentacles and head, discarding both the head and entrails. Leave the tentacles whole but discard the hard beak in the middle. Cut the body into thin rounds.

3 Heat the oil, add the garlic, chillies and celery and cook for 5 minutes. Stir in the potatoes, then add the wine and stock. Bring to the boil, then simmer, covered, for 25 minutes.

4 Remove from the heat and stir in the squid, tomatoes and parsley. Cover the pan and leave to stand until the squid is cooked. Serve immediately with boiled white rice or cornbread.

Cook's Tip
Adding the tomatoes and parsley at the end of cooking gives a real freshness to the sauce. If you want an even heartier dish, add these ingredients to the pan with the potatoes.

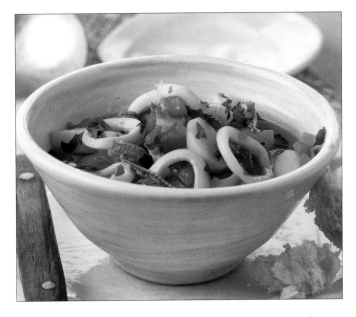

Cuttlefish Energy 540kcal/2254kJ; Protein 43.3g; Carbohydrate 24.7g, of which sugars 5.1g; Fat 27.3g, of which saturates 4.2g; Cholesterol 275mg; Calcium 176mg; Fibre 2.2g; Sodium 943mg.
Squid Casserole Energy 273kcal/1150kJ; Protein 22.7g; Carbohydrate 17.5g, of which sugars 3.6g; Fat 8.3g, of which saturates 1.5g; Cholesterol 300mg; Calcium 53mg; Fibre 2g; Sodium 173mg.

Indonesian Prawns with Sliced Potatoes

With a fresh-tasting combination of prawns and potatoes, cooked Indonesian style with satay sauce, this dish makes a deliciously rich and filling main course.

Serves 4

2 large waxy potatoes, peeled and cut in half
120ml/4fl oz/½ cup vegetable oil
1 bunch spring onions (scallions), finely sliced
2 red chillies, seeded and diced
450g/1lb peeled cooked prawns (shrimp)
45ml/3 tbsp crunchy peanut butter
200ml/7fl oz/scant 1 cup coconut cream
15ml/1 tbsp dark soy sauce
1 bunch chopped fresh coriander (cilantro)
salt

1 Boil the potatoes in lightly salted water for 15 minutes until tender. Drain, and when cool enough to handle, cut into 3mm/⅛in slices. Heat the oil in a frying pan and fry the potatoes for 10 minutes, turning occasionally until browned. Drain on kitchen paper and keep hot.

2 Drain off almost all of the oil from the pan and fry the spring onions and half the chillies in the pan for 1 minute. Add the peeled prawns and toss for a few seconds.

3 Beat together the peanut butter, coconut cream, soy sauce and remaining chilli. Add this sauce to the prawns and cook for a further minute or two until heated through.

4 Lightly grease a large serving platter and arrange the potatoes evenly around the base. Spoon the prawn mixture over until the potatoes are mostly covered. Top with the coriander.

Cook's Tip
For a more luxurious version, replace the prawns (shrimp) with fresh raw, shelled king prawns (jumbo shrimp).

Prawn and New Potato Stew

New potatoes with plenty of flavour, such as Jersey Royals, Maris Piper or Nicola, are essential for this effortless stew. Use a good quality jar of tomato and chilli sauce; there are now plenty available in the supermarkets. For a really easy supper dish, serve with warm, crusty bread to mop up the delicious sauce, and a mixed green salad.

Serves 4

675g/1½lb small new or salad potatoes, scrubbed
15g/½oz/½ cup fresh coriander (cilantro)
350g/12oz jar tomato and chilli sauce
300g/11oz cooked peeled prawns (shrimp), thawed and drained if frozen

1 Cook the potatoes in lightly salted, boiling water for 15 minutes, until tender. Drain and return to the pan.

2 Finely chop half the fresh coriander and add to the pan along with the tomato and chilli sauce and about 90ml/6 tbsp water. Bring the mixture to the boil, reduce the heat, cover and simmer gently for 5 minutes.

3 Stir the prawns into the potatoes and sauce and heat briefly until they are warmed through. Do not overheat the prawns or they will quickly shrivel, becoming tough and tasteless.

4 Spoon the stew into shallow bowls and serve sprinkled with the remaining coriander, torn into pieces.

Cook's Tip
If you prefer, you can make your own tomato and chilli sauce for this dish. Gently fry some finely chopped onion in a little oil for 10 minutes until soft. Add 2 red chillies, that have been seeded and finely chopped, to the pan and cook for a further 3–5 minutes. Pour in a 400g/14oz can of chopped tomatoes and season with salt and pepper. Simmer for 10–15 minutes then use as specified in the recipe above.

Indonesian Prawns Energy 577kcal/2396kJ; Protein 26.7g; Carbohydrate 20.5g, of which sugars 4.6g; Fat 43.4g, of which saturates 18.4g; Cholesterol 219mg; Calcium 119mg; Fibre 2g; Sodium 489mg.
Prawn Stew Energy 218kcal/924kJ; Protein 16.9g; Carbohydrate 30.4g, of which sugars 5.4g; Fat 4.1g, of which saturates 0.7g; Cholesterol 146mg; Calcium 84mg; Fibre 2.9g; Sodium 171mg.

Sweet Potato, Pumpkin and Prawn Cakes

This unusual Asian combination of sweet potato, pumpkin and prawn makes a delicious dish which needs only a salty fish or soy sauce to dip into as an accompaniment. Serve with noodles or fried rice for a more substantial meal.

Serves 4

200g/7oz/1¾ cups strong white
    bread flour
2.5ml/½ tsp salt
2.5ml/½ tsp dried yeast
175ml/6fl oz/¾ cup warm water
1 egg, beaten
200g/7oz raw prawns (shrimp)
225g/8oz pumpkin, peeled,
    seeded and grated
150g/5oz sweet potato, grated
2 spring onions
    (scallions), chopped
50g/2oz water
    chestnuts, chopped
2.5ml/½ tsp chilli sauce
1 garlic clove, crushed
juice of ½ lime
vegetable oil, for deep-frying
lime wedges, to serve

1 Sift together the flour and salt into a large bowl and make a well in the centre. In a separate container, dissolve the yeast in the water until creamy, then pour into the centre of the flour and salt mixture. Pour in the egg and set aside for a few minutes until bubbles appear. Mix to form a smooth batter.

2 Peel the prawns, if necessary, then place in a pan with just enough boiling water to cover. Simmer for about 2 minutes or until the prawns have turned pink. Drain, rinse in cold water and drain again well. Coarsely chop the prawns, then place in a bowl with the pumpkin and sweet potato.

3 Add the spring onions, water chestnuts, chilli sauce, garlic and lime juice and mix well. Fold into the batter mixture carefully until evenly mixed.

4 Heat a 1cm/½ in layer of oil in a large frying pan until really hot. Spoon in the batter in heaps, leaving space between each one, and cook until golden brown on both sides. Drain well on kitchen paper and keep warm as you cook the rest. Serve hot with the lime wedges.

Prawn and Potato Omelette

Similar to a Spanish tortilla, this potato dish makes a delicious and filling lunch when served with a fresh leafy green salad. The sweet prawns are cooked gently inside the omelette, staying tender and succulent.

Serves 6

200g/7oz potatoes, peeled
    and diced
30ml/2 tbsp olive oil
1 onion, finely sliced
2.5ml/½ tsp paprika
2 large tomatoes, peeled, seeded
    and chopped
200g/7oz peeled raw
    prawns (shrimp)
6 eggs
2.5ml/½ tsp baking powder
salt

1 Cook the potatoes in a pan of salted boiling water for about 10 minutes or until tender.

2 Meanwhile, pour the oil into a 23cm/9in frying pan which can safely be used under the grill (broiler). Place the pan over a medium heat.

3 Add the onion slices and stir well to coat evenly in the oil. Cook for 5 minutes until the onions begin to soften but not turn brown. Sprinkle over the paprika and cook for a further 1 minute, stirring constantly.

4 Stir in the tomatoes. Drain the cooked potatoes thoroughly, then add them to the pan. Stir gently to mix. Increase the heat and cook for 10 minutes, or until the mixture has thickened and the potatoes have absorbed the flavour of the tomatoes.

5 Remove the pan from the heat. Add the prawns and stir gently to combine with the other ingredients.

6 Preheat the grill. Beat the eggs in a separate bowl, stir in the baking powder and salt. Pour the egg mixture into the pan and mix thoroughly.

7 Cover the pan and cook for 8–10 minutes until the omelette has almost set, then finish under the grill. Serve hot in wedges.

Prawn Cakes Energy 317kcal/1346kJ; Protein 18.2g; Carbohydrate 57.6g, of which sugars 9.1g; Fat 3.2g, of which saturates 0.9g; Cholesterol 145mg; Calcium 216mg; Fibre 6g; Sodium 383mg.
Prawn Omelette Energy 247kcal/1031kJ; Protein 19.6g; Carbohydrate 10.8g, of which sugars 3g; Fat 14.5g, of which saturates 3.3g; Cholesterol 383mg; Calcium 93mg; Fibre 1.2g; Sodium 211mg.

Chilli Crab and Potato Cakes

Crab meat makes wonderful fish and potato cakes, as shown by these gutsy morsels. Served with a rich tomato dip, they make great party food.

Makes about 15
225g/8oz white crab meat (fresh, frozen or canned)
115g/4oz cooked potatoes, mashed
30ml/2 tbsp fresh herb seasoning
2.5ml/½ tsp mild mustard
2.5ml/½ tsp ground black pepper
½ fresh hot chilli, finely chopped
5ml/1 tsp fresh oregano
1 egg, beaten
plain (all-purpose) flour, for dredging

vegetable oil, for frying
lime wedges and coriander (cilantro) sprigs, to garnish
fresh whole chilli peppers, to garnish

For the tomato dip
15g/½oz/1 tbsp butter or margarine
½ onion, finely chopped
2 canned plum tomatoes, chopped
1 garlic clove, crushed
150ml/¼ pint/⅔ cup water
5–10ml/1–2 tsp malt vinegar
15ml/1 tbsp chopped fresh coriander (cilantro)
½ hot fresh chilli, chopped

1 Mix together the crab meat, potatoes, herb seasoning, mustard, pepper, chilli, oregano and egg in a large bowl. Chill the mixture for at least 30 minutes.

2 Meanwhile, make the tomato dip. Melt the butter or margarine in a small pan over a medium heat. Add the onion, tomatoes and garlic and cook for about 5 minutes until the onion is tender. Add the water, vinegar, coriander and fresh chilli.

3 Bring to the boil, reduce the heat and simmer for about 10 minutes. Transfer the mixture to a food processor or blender and blend to a smooth purée.

4 Shape the chilled crab mixture into rounds and dredge with flour, shaking off the excess. Heat a little oil in a frying pan and fry, a few cakes at a time, for 2–3 minutes on each side. Drain on kitchen paper and keep warm in a low oven while cooking the remainder. Garnish with lime wedges, coriander sprigs and whole chillies and serve immediately with the tomato dip.

Baked Mussels and Potatoes

This imaginative shellfish and potato casserole uses some of the best Italian flavours – tomatoes, garlic, basil and, of course, plump, juicy mussels.

Serves 2–3
800g/1¾lb large mussels, in their shells

225g/8oz small firm potatoes
75ml/5 tbsp olive oil
2 garlic cloves, finely chopped
8 fresh basil leaves, torn into pieces
2 medium tomatoes, peeled and thinly sliced
45ml/3 tbsp breadcrumbs
ground black pepper
basil leaves, to garnish

1 Cut off the 'beards' from the mussels. Scrub and soak in several changes of cold water. Discard any with broken shells or ones that are open.

2 Place the mussels with a cupful of water in a large pan over a medium heat. As soon as the mussel shells open, lift them out of the water. Remove and discard the empty half shells, leaving the mussels in the other half. (Discard any mussels that do not open at this stage.) Strain any cooking liquid remaining in the pan through a layer of kitchen paper, and reserve to add at the final stage.

3 Cook the potatoes in a large pan of boiling water for about 10–12 minutes or until they are almost tender. Drain well and leave to cool. When they have cooled enough to handle, peel and slice them.

4 Preheat the oven to 180°C/350°F/Gas 4. Spread 30ml/2 tbsp of the olive oil in the bottom of a shallow ovenproof dish. Cover the base of the dish with the potato slices in one layer. Add the mussels in their half shells in a single layer on top of the potato slices. Sprinkle with the garlic and basil. Cover with a layer of sliced tomato.

5 Sprinkle with breadcrumbs and black pepper, the reserved mussel cooking liquid and the remaining olive oil. Bake for about 20 minutes until the tomatoes are soft and the breadcrumbs are golden brown. Serve hot directly from the baking dish, and garnish with basil.

Chilli Crab Cakes Energy 70kcal/290kJ; Protein 3.5g; Carbohydrate 2.9g, of which sugars 0.7g; Fat 5g, of which saturates 1.1g; Cholesterol 26mg; Calcium 24mg; Fibre 0.3g; Sodium 95mg.
Baked Mussels Energy 348kcal/1457kJ; Protein 16.7g; Carbohydrate 25.8g, of which sugars 3.4g; Fat 20.5g, of which saturates 3g; Cholesterol 30mg; Calcium 178mg; Fibre 1.7g; Sodium 288mg.

Potato and Smoked Mussel Bake

This recipe uses smoked mussels, which have a creamy texture and rich flavour, delicious with sour cream, chives and potatoes. You can easily substitute smoked oysters for the mussels.

Serves 4

2 large maincrop potatoes, cut in half

butter, for greasing
2 shallots, finely diced
2 x 85g/3¼oz cans smoked mussels
1 bunch chives, chopped
300ml/½ pint/1¼ cups sour cream
175g/6oz/1½ cups mature (sharp) Cheddar cheese, grated
salt and ground black pepper
mixed vegetables, to serve

1 Preheat the oven to 180°C/350°F/Gas 4. Cook the potatoes in a large pan of lightly salted boiling water for 15 minutes until they are just tender. Drain and leave to cool slightly. When cool enough to handle, cut the potatoes into even 3mm/⅛in slices.

2 Grease the base and sides of a 1.2 litre/2 pint/5 cup casserole dish. Lay a few potato slices over the base of the dish. Sprinkle a few shallots over and season well.

3 Drain the oil from the mussels into a bowl. Slice the mussels and add them again to the reserved oil. Stir in the chives and sour cream with half of the cheese. Spoon a little of the sauce over the layer of potatoes.

4 Continue to layer the sliced potatoes, shallots and the sauce. Finish with a layer of potatoes and sprinkle over the remainder of the grated cheese.

5 Bake in the oven for 30–45 minutes. Remove from the oven and serve while hot with a selection of mixed vegetables.

Cook's Tip
To serve this dish for a dinner party, rather than serve it in a large dish, once it has cooked, stamp out rounds using a 5cm/2in cutter and serve on a bed of salad leaves.

Clam and Potato Stovies

Clams are now harvested in the lochs of Scotland, especially in Loch Fyne where some of the best Scottish clams are grown on ropes. Here, they are layered with sliced potatoes and slow-cooked in a delicious and hearty baked dish.

Serves 4

2.5 litres/4 pints/10 cups clams
potatoes (see step 3)
oil, for greasing
chopped fresh flat leaf parsley, to garnish
50g/2oz/¼ cup butter
salt and ground black pepper

1 Wash the clams and soak them overnight in fresh cold water. This will clean them out and get rid of any grains of sand and other detritus.

2 Preheat the oven to 190°C/375°F/Gas 5. Put the clams into a large pan, cover with water and bring to the boil. Add a little salt, then simmer until the shells open. Reserve the cooking liquor. Shell the clams, reserving a few whole.

3 Weigh the shelled clams. You will need approximately three times the weight of the clams in unpeeled potatoes.

4 Peel and slice the potatoes thinly. Lightly oil the base and sides of a flameproof, ovenproof dish. Arrange a layer of sliced potatoes in the base of the dish, then add a layer of the clams and season with a little salt and ground black pepper. Repeat the layering process until the ingredients are all used, finishing with a layer of potatoes on top. Finally, season lightly with more salt and black pepper.

5 Pour in some of the reserved cooking liquor to come about halfway up the dish. Dot the top with the butter, then cover the dish tightly with foil. Bring to the boil on top of the stove over a medium-high heat, then transfer to the preheated oven and bake for about 2 hours until the potatoes are tender and the top is golden brown.

6 Serve the bake immediately, garnished with chopped fresh flat leaf parsley.

Mussel Bake Energy 454kcal/1890kJ; Protein 23.1g; Carbohydrate 20.7g, of which sugars 4.5g; Fat 30.6g, of which saturates 19.2g; Cholesterol 115mg; Calcium 424mg; Fibre 1.1g; Sodium 577mg.
Clam Stovies Energy 320kcal/1348kJ; Protein 17.3g; Carbohydrate 36.7g, of which sugars 3.3g; Fat 12.6g, of which saturates 7g; Cholesterol 57mg; Calcium 188mg; Fibre 2.9g; Sodium 262mg.

Smoked Venison with Garlic Potatoes

Smoked venison makes a delicious change from the more common meats. This warming dish makes an ideal supper or lunch, accompanied by creamy potatoes flavoured with plenty of garlic.

Serves 4
675g/1½lb peeled potatoes

175ml/6fl oz/¾ cup milk
1 garlic clove
10ml/2 tsp sea salt
olive oil, for greasing and
  to serve
75ml/2½fl oz/⅓ cup double
  (heavy) cream
115g/4oz sliced smoked venison
salad leaves, such as rocket
  (arugula) to garnish

1 Preheat the oven to 180°C/350°F/Gas 4. Thinly slice the potatoes and place in a pan. Pour in the milk. Using the side of a knife, crush the garlic with the sea salt. Stir the mixture into the potatoes. Bring to the boil over a gentle heat, stirring occasionally, until the milk begins to thicken.

2 Grease the inside of a large gratin dish with a little olive oil. Add the cream to the potatoes and, stirring gently so the potatoes don't break up, combine well. Allow to just come to the boil again, then pour the mixture carefully into the ovenproof gratin dish.

3 Place the dish in the preheated oven for about 1 hour or until the potatoes are lightly browned and tender. To serve, place a scoop of the potato on to a warmed plate and put a pile of smoked venison on top, adding a splash of olive oil over each serving. Garnish with salad leaves.

Cook's Tips
• Use good tasty potatoes, such as King Edward or Maris Piper, for this dish.
• If you cannot find smoked venison in your local supermarket or delicatessen, many smokehouses have websites that offer a mail order delivery service.
• If you are feeling generous, you could use more smoked venison.

Rack of Lamb with Vegetables

Gathering with family members and sharing a feast featuring a magnificent rack of lamb, is one of the real pleasures in life. The red potatoes make an exciting change from the usual white variety.

Serves 8–10
1.8–2kg/4–4½lb rack of lamb,
  fat trimmed from bones

900g/2lb red potatoes, peeled
  and halved
3 medium onions, quartered
900g/2lb carrots, halved
  lengthways
40g/1½oz/⅓ cup plain
  (all-purpose) flour
250ml/8fl oz/1 cup good
  lamb stock
salt and ground black pepper
chopped parsley, to garnish

1 Preheat the oven to 220°C/425°F/Gas 7. To prepare the meat, make a slit in the membrane on each rib and arrange the racks in a circle with the bone ends curving outward.

2 Tie the ribs with fine string to secure them in the crown position. (You can ask your butcher to prepare the crown roast for you.) Wrap the bone ends with foil to prevent them from burning. Rub the meat with salt and pepper, and place the crown on a rack in a roasting pan.

3 Place the lamb in the preheated oven and immediately lower the temperature to 180°C/350°F/Gas 4. Roast for 1½ hours. Do not cover or baste while cooking.

4 Remove the pan from the oven and arrange the potatoes, onions and carrots around the base of the crown. Cook for about 30 minutes more, or until the meat is done to your liking and the vegetables are tender.

5 Transfer the lamb and vegetables to a serving dish and keep warm. Skim the fat from the pan juices. To make the gravy, pour 45ml/3 tbsp pan juices into a pan over a medium heat. Whisk the flour into the pan juices and cook for 3–4 minutes until all of the flour is absorbed. Slowly stir in the remaining pan juices and the stock; cook until thickened. Season to taste with salt and ground black pepper. Serve alongside the lamb and vegetables.

Roast Lamb with Potatoes

This simple roast with potatoes owes its wonderful flavour to the addition of fresh rosemary and garlic. Serve with one or two lightly cooked fresh vegetables, such as broccoli, spinach or carrots.

Serves 4

½ leg of lamb, about 1.3kg/3lb
2 garlic cloves, cut lengthways into thin slivers
105ml/7 tbsp olive oil
leaves from 4 sprigs of fresh rosemary, finely chopped
about 250ml/8fl oz/1 cup lamb or vegetable stock
675g/1½ lb potatoes, cut into 2.5cm/1in cubes
a few fresh sage leaves, chopped
salt and ground black pepper

1 Preheat the oven to 230°C/450°F/Gas 8. Using the point of a sharp knife, make several deep incisions in the lamb, especially near the bone, and insert a sliver of garlic into each.

2 Place the lamb in a roasting pan and rub it all over with 45ml/3 tbsp of the oil. Sprinkle over about half of the chopped rosemary, patting it on firmly, and season with plenty of salt and pepper. Roast for 30 minutes, turning once.

3 Lower the temperature to 190°C/375°F/Gas 5. Turn the lamb over again. Pour in 125ml/4fl oz/½ cup of the stock.

4 Roast for a further 1¼–1½ hours until the lamb is tender, turning the joint two or three times more and adding the rest of the stock in two or three batches. Baste the lamb each time it is turned.

5 Meanwhile, put the potatoes in a separate roasting pan and toss with the remaining oil and rosemary and the sage. Roast the potatoes on the same shelf as the lamb, if possible, for 45 minutes, turning the potatoes several times until golden and tender.

6 Transfer the lamb to a carving board, cover with foil and leave for 10 minutes before carving. Serve with the roast potatoes and accompany with green vegetables, baby carrots or roasted Mediterranean vegetables.

Gigot Boulangère

A delicious pairing of lamb, garlic and potatoes, this is a trouble-free choice for Sunday lunch.

Serves 6

50g/2oz/¼ cup butter, plus extra for greasing
4–6 garlic cloves
2 yellow onions, thinly sliced
12–18 thyme or rosemary sprigs
2 fresh bay leaves
1.8kg/4lb red potatoes, thinly sliced
450ml/¾ pint/scant 2 cups hot lamb or vegetable stock
2kg/4½lb leg of lamb
30ml/2 tbsp olive oil
salt and ground black pepper

1 Preheat the oven to 190°C/375°F/Gas 5. Use a little butter to grease a large ovenproof dish, about 6cm/2½in deep. Finely chop half the garlic and sprinkle a little over the prepared dish.

2 Fry the onions in 25g/1oz/2 tbsp of the butter for 5–8 minutes, until softened. Roughly chop half the thyme or rosemary and crush the bay leaves.

3 Arrange a layer of potatoes in the dish, season and sprinkle with half the remaining garlic, rosemary or thyme, one bay leaf and the onions. Add the remaining potatoes, garlic and herbs.

4 Pour in the stock and add a little hot water to bring the liquid to just below the level of the potatoes. Dot with the remaining butter, cover with foil and cook in the oven for 40 minutes. Increase the temperature to 200°C/400°F/Gas 6.

5 Meanwhile, cut the rest of the garlic into slivers. Make slits all over the lamb with a narrow, sharp knife and insert slivers of garlic and sprigs of thyme or rosemary into the slits. Season the lamb well with salt and pepper.

6 Uncover the potatoes and sprinkle a few rosemary or thyme sprigs over them. Rest a roasting rack or ovenproof cooling rack over the dish and place the lamb on it. Rub the olive oil over the meat, then return the dish to the oven. Cook, turning the lamb once or twice, for 1½–1¾ hours, depending on how well done you prefer lamb. Leave the lamb to rest for 20 minutes in a warm place before carving.

Roast Lamb Energy 493kcal/2050kJ; Protein 25.6g; Carbohydrate 28.7g, of which sugars 10.7g; Fat 31.5g, of which saturates 15.1g; Cholesterol 97mg; Calcium 62mg; Fibre 3.9g; Sodium 113mg.
Gigot Boulangère Energy 980kcal/4114kJ; Protein 101.8g; Carbohydrate 52.3g, of which sugars 6.8g; Fat 41.9g, of which saturates 19.3g; Cholesterol 384mg; Calcium 82mg; Fibre 3.7g; Sodium 358mg.

Garlic-spiked Lamb with Potatoes

This is the Greek equivalent of the Sunday roast, but everything is cooked in a single dish so that all the flavours meld together. The fragrant lemon and garlic lamb is deliciously tender and the beautifully crisp potatoes, roasted in with the lamb, take on all the delicious flavours and aromas of the traditional Mediterranean ingredients.

Serves 6–8

1 leg of lamb, about 2kg/4¹/₂lb
3 garlic cloves, quartered
lengthways, plus 6–8 whole,
    unpeeled garlic cloves, or
    1–2 heads of garlic, halved
900g/2lb potatoes, peeled and
    quartered lengthways
juice of 1 lemon
45ml/3 tbsp extra virgin
    olive oil
450ml/³/₄ pint/scant 2 cups
    hot water
5ml/1 tsp dried
    Greek oregano
2.5ml/¹/₂ tsp dried Greek thyme
    or 5ml/1 tsp chopped
    fresh thyme
salt and ground black pepper

1 Preheat the oven to 220°C/425°F/Gas 7. Place the meat in a large roasting pan. Make several incisions in it and insert one or two quarters of garlic into each one.

2 Arrange the potatoes and whole garlic cloves or halved heads of garlic around the meat, pour the lemon juice and olive oil over, and add half the water to the dish. Sprinkle over half the herbs, and some seasoning.

3 Roast the lamb for 15 minutes, then reduce the oven temperature to 190°C/375°F/Gas 5. Roast for 1 hour.

4 Turn the meat over to brown the other side, sprinkle over the rest of the herbs and seasoning, and turn the potatoes over gently. Add the remaining hot water to the pan and cook for another 25–30 minutes, basting occasionally with the pan juices.

5 Cover the meat with a clean dish towel and let it rest for 10 minutes before serving. The cloves of garlic can be popped out of their skins and eaten with the meat; they will be deliciously creamy.

Middle Eastern Roast Lamb and Potatoes

When the aroma of garlic and saffron come wafting out of the oven, this deliciously garlicky lamb served with potatoes and onions won't last very long. It makes a welcome change from the traditional roast on a Sunday afternoon.

Serves 6–8

2.75kg/6lb leg of lamb
4 garlic cloves, halved
60ml/4 tbsp olive oil
juice of 1 lemon
2–3 saffron strands, soaked in
    15ml/1 tbsp boiling water
5ml/1 tsp mixed dried herbs
450g/1lb baking potatoes,
    thickly sliced
2 large onions, thickly sliced
salt and ground black pepper
fresh thyme, to garnish

1 Make eight incisions in the skin of the leg of lamb with a sharp knife, press the garlic cloves into the slits and place the lamb in a non-metallic dish.

2 In a bowl, mix together the olive oil, lemon juice, saffron mixture and dried herbs. Rub this mixture over the lamb and marinate for 2 hours. Turn the lamb in the marinade a couple of times, rubbing the marinade all over.

3 Preheat the oven to 180°C/350°F/Gas 4. Layer the potatoes and onions in a large roasting pan.

4 Lift the lamb out of the marinade and place the lamb on top of the potatoes and onions, fat side up, and season well with plenty of salt and ground black pepper.

5 Pour any remaining marinade over the lamb and roast in the preheated oven for about 2 hours. Baste the lamb with the juices that gather two or three times during the cooking process to keep the lamb moist.

6 Remove the pan from the oven, cover with foil and leave to rest for 10–15 minutes before carving. Garnish with fresh thyme and serve.

Garlic Lamb Energy 750kcal/3132kJ; Protein 73.4g; Carbohydrate 24.3g, of which sugars 2.1g; Fat 40.4g, of which saturates 17.3g; Cholesterol 273mg; Calcium 37mg; Fibre 1.8g; Sodium 175mg.
Roast Lamb Energy 270kcal/1124kJ; Protein 27.9g; Carbohydrate 4.9g, of which sugars 1.3g; Fat 15.4g, of which saturates 6.6g; Cholesterol 106mg; Calcium 12mg; Fibre 0.5g; Sodium 64mg.

Traditional Lancashire Lamb and Potato Hotpot

This famous lamb and potato hotpot was traditionally cooked in a farmhouse or communal bread oven, in time for supper at the end of the day. The ingredients would have been layered straight into the pot, but here the meat is first browned to add colour and flavour to the dish.

Serves 4

15–30ml/1–2 tbsp oil

8–12 lean best end of neck (cross rib) lamb chops
about 175g/6oz lamb's kidneys, skin and core removed and cut into pieces
2 medium onions, thinly sliced
few sprigs of fresh thyme or rosemary
900g/2lb potatoes, thinly sliced
600ml/1 pint/2½ cups lamb or vegetable stock
25g/1oz/2 tbsp butter, cubed
salt and ground black pepper

1 Preheat the oven to 180°C/350°F/Gas 4. Heat the oil in a large frying pan and brown the lamb chops quickly on all sides. Remove the meat from the pan and set aside.

2 Add the pieces of kidney to the hot pan and brown lightly over a high heat. Lift out.

3 In a casserole, layer the chops and kidneys with the onions, herbs and potatoes, seasoning each layer.

4 Finish off with a layer of potatoes. Pour over the stock, sprinkle with herbs and dot the top with butter. Cover, put into the preheated oven and cook for 2 hours. Remove the lid, increase the oven temperature to 220°C/425°F/Gas 7 and cook, uncovered, for a further 30 minutes until the potatoes on top are crisp.

> **Variation**
> Add sliced carrots or mushrooms to the layers of meat and potato. Replace 150ml/¼ pint/⅔ cup of the stock with dry (hard) cider or dry white wine.

Mutton and Potato Hotpot

Another traditional cottage favourite, this mutton and potato hotpot would have been a Sunday treat in days gone by. Mutton is hard to find today but it really is worth looking out for. Try your local farmers' market or ask your butcher if they could get it for you. It often has a far superior flavour to traditional lamb, although it does require much longer, slower cooking.

Serves 6

6 mutton chops
6 lamb's kidneys
1 large onion, sliced
450g/1lb potatoes, sliced
600ml/1 pint/2½ cups dark stock
salt and ground black pepper

1 Preheat the oven to 180°C/350°F/Gas 4. Trim the mutton chops, leaving a little fat but no bone. Slice the lamb's kidneys in two horizontally, and remove the fat and core with a pair of sharp scissors.

2 Place three of the chops in a deep casserole and season well with salt and ground black pepper.

3 Add a layer of half the kidneys, then half the onion and finally half the potatoes. Season lightly.

4 Repeat the process, seasoning as you go and making sure that you finish with an even layer of potatoes.

5 Heat the stock and pour it into the casserole, just about covering everything but leaving the potatoes just showing at the top. Cover and cook in the preheated oven for 1½ hours.

6 Remove the lid from the casserole and cook for 30 minutes more to allow the potatoes to brown. Serve immediately.

> **Variation**
> If you prefer, you can use lamb chops instead. Use two chops per person and reduce the cooking time by 30 minutes as lamb does not need 2 hours.

Hotpot Energy 810kcal/3400kJ; Protein 76.7g; Carbohydrate 43.7g, of which sugars 9.3g; Fat 37.8g, of which saturates 13.2g; Cholesterol 363mg; Calcium 140mg; Fibre 6.2g; Sodium 285mg.
Mutton Hotpot Energy 626kcal/2629kJ; Protein 76.9g; Carbohydrate 23.1g, of which sugars 5g; Fat 25.8g, of which saturates 11.6g; Cholesterol 374mg; Calcium 76mg; Fibre 2g; Sodium 269mg.

Lamb with Shallots and Potatoes

This lamb and potato casserole is finished with a topping of garlic, parsley and lemon rind.

Serves 6

1kg/2¼lb boneless shoulder
   of lamb, cut into 5cm/2in cubes
1 garlic clove, finely chopped
finely grated rind of ½ lemon and
   juice of 1 lemon
90ml/6 tbsp olive oil
45ml/3 tbsp plain (all-purpose)
   flour, seasoned
1 large onion, sliced
5 anchovy fillets in olive oil, drained
2.5ml/½ tsp caster (superfine) sugar

300ml/½ pint/1¼ cups white wine
475ml/16fl oz/2 cups lamb stock
   or half stock and half water
1 bouquet garni, made from
   1 fresh bay leaf, 1 fresh thyme
   sprig and 1 fresh parsley sprig
500g/1¼lb small new potatoes
250g/9oz shallots, peeled but whole
45ml/3 tbsp double (heavy)
   cream (optional)
salt and ground black pepper

For the topping
shredded rind of ½ lemon
45ml/3 tbsp chopped fresh flat
   leaf parsley
1 garlic clove, chopped

1 Mix the lamb, garlic, rind and half the lemon juice. Season, then add 15ml/1 tbsp olive oil and marinate for between 12–24 hours. When ready to cook, chop the topping ingredients together.

2 Drain the lamb, reserving the marinade. Preheat the oven to 180°C/350°F/Gas 4. Heat the oil in a frying pan, toss the lamb in the seasoned flour, then brown in the pan. Transfer to a flameproof casserole. Fry the onion for 10 minutes. Add the anchovies and sugar, mashing the fish well. Add the marinade, wine and stock. Bring to the boil, then simmer for 5 minutes. Pour over the lamb.

3 Add the bouquet garni to the casserole and season. Cover and cook in the oven for 1 hour. Add the potatoes, re-cover, and cook for 20 minutes. Brown the shallots in the frying pan and add to the casserole. Cover and cook for 30–40 minutes. Transfer the lamb and vegetables to a serving dish. Discard the herbs.

4 Boil the cooking juices on the stove to reduce them. Add the cream, if using, and heat through. Season and add lemon juice to taste. Pour over the lamb, sprinkle on the topping and serve.

Irish Lamb and Potato Stew

Simple yet delicious, this potato and lamb main course is quintessentially Irish. Traditionally mutton chops are used, but as they can be hard to find you can use lamb chops instead. The results will still be wonderful.

Serves 4

1.2kg/2½lb boneless lamb chops
15ml/1 tbsp vegetable oil

3 large onions, quartered
4 large carrots, thickly sliced
900ml/1½ pints/3¾ cups water
4 large firm potatoes, cut
   into chunks
1 large thyme sprig
15g/½oz/1 tbsp butter
15ml/1 tbsp chopped
   fresh parsley
salt and ground black pepper
Savoy cabbage, to serve
   (optional)

1 Trim any excess fat from the lamb chops. Heat the vegetable oil in a large flameproof casserole, add the lamb and brown on both sides. Remove from the pan.

2 Add the onions and carrots to the casserole and cook for 5 minutes until the onions are browned. Return the lamb to the pan with the water. Season with salt and pepper. Bring to a boil, then reduce the heat, cover and simmer for 1 hour.

3 Add the potatoes to the pan with the thyme, cover again, and simmer for a further hour.

4 Leave the stew to settle for a few minutes. Remove the fat from the liquid with a ladle, then pour off the liquid into a clean pan. Bring to a simmer and stir in the butter, then the parsley.

5 Season well with salt and pepper and pour back into the casserole. Serve with cabbage, boiled or steamed, if you like.

Cook's Tip
If you can't find boneless chops, use the same weight of middle neck (US shoulder or breast) of lamb. Ask the butcher to chop the meat into cutlets, which should then be trimmed of any excess fat before cooking.

Lamb with Shallots Energy 553kcal/2311kJ; Protein 37g; Carbohydrate 26.2g, of which sugars 5.3g; Fat 30.6g, of which saturates 10.4g; Cholesterol 128mg; Calcium 79mg; Fibre 2.7g; Sodium 261mg.
Irish Stew Energy 823kcal/3453kJ; Protein 80g; Carbohydrate 50.3g, of which sugars 10.4g; Fat 34.9g, of which saturates 14.8g; Cholesterol 266mg; Calcium 137mg; Fibre 4.4g; Sodium 540mg.

Minty Lamb, Leek and Potato Bake

This is especially good with new season's lamb and organically grown leeks, and the deliciously crisp potato crust hides a treasure trove of exciting flavours. If you have some home-made chicken stock it boosts the flavour tremendously; if not, use a good quality ready-made stock rather than a dried bouillon cube.

Serves 6

30ml/2 tbsp sunflower oil
2kg/4¹/₂lb fillet or boned leg of
    lamb, cubed
10 spring onions (scallions),
    thickly sliced
3 leeks, thickly sliced
15ml/1 tbsp flour
150ml/¹/₄ pint/²/₃ cup white wine
300ml/¹/₂ pint/1¹/₄ cups
    chicken stock
15ml/1 tbsp tomato purée (paste)
15ml/1 tbsp sugar
30ml/2 tbsp fresh mint leaves,
    finely chopped, plus a few more
    to garnish
115g/4oz/²/₃ cup dried
    pears, chopped
1kg/2¹/₄lb potatoes, peeled
    and sliced
25g/1oz/2 tbsp melted butter
salt and ground black pepper

1 Preheat the oven to 180°C/350°F/Gas 4. Heat the oil in a large heavy frying pan and cook the cubed lamb fillet or leg for a few minutes, turning occasionally, to seal it. Transfer to a large casserole dish.

2 Add the sliced onions and leeks and cook for 3–5 minutes. Stir in the flour and cook for another minute. Add the wine and stock and bring to the boil.

3 Add the tomato purée and sugar, and season with salt and ground pepper. Stir in the chopped mint leaves and pears and then pour into the casserole. Stir the mixture well to combine the ingredients. Arrange the sliced potatoes on top and brush with the melted butter.

4 Cover the casserole with a tight-fitting lid and bake in the preheated oven for 1¹/₂ hours. Then increase the oven temperature to 200°C/400°F/Gas 6, and cook for a further 30 minutes, uncovered, to brown the potatoes. Garnish with mint leaves and serve immediately.

Moussaka

This classic Greek dish with lamb, potatoes and aubergine (eggplant) is layered through with a rich, cheesy topping to make a substantial meal.

Serves 6

30ml/2 tbsp olive oil
30ml/2 tbsp chopped
    fresh oregano
1 large onion, finely chopped
675g/1¹/₂lb lamb, minced (ground)
1 large aubergine (eggplant), sliced
2 x 400g/14oz cans
    chopped tomatoes
45ml/3 tbsp tomato purée (paste)
1 lamb stock cube, crumbled
2 floury main crop
    potatoes, halved
115g/4oz/1 cup Cheddar
    cheese, grated
150 ml/¹/₂ pint/²/₃ cup single
    (light) cream
salt and ground black pepper
fresh bread, to serve

1 Preheat the oven to 180°C/350°F/Gas 4. Heat the olive oil in a large deep-sided frying pan. Fry the oregano and onions over a low heat, stirring frequently, for about 5 minutes or until the onions have softened.

2 Stir in the lamb and cook for 10 minutes until browned. Meanwhile, grill the aubergine slices for 5 minutes until browned, turning once.

3 Stir the tomatoes and purée into the mince mixture, and crumble the stock cube over it, stir well, season with salt and pepper and simmer uncovered for a further 15 minutes.

4 Meanwhile, cook the potatoes in lightly salted boiling water for 5–10 minutes until just tender. Drain, and when cool enough to handle, cut into thin slices.

5 Layer the aubergine, mince and potatoes in a 1.75 litre/3 pint/7¹/₂ cup oval ovenproof dish, finishing with a layer of potatoes.

6 Mix the cheese and cream together in a bowl and pour over the top of the other ingredients in the dish. Cook for around 45–50 minutes until the moussaka is bubbling and golden on the top. Serve straight from the dish, while hot, with plenty of fresh, crusty bread.

Minty Lamb Energy 846kcal/3542kJ; Protein 70.3g; Carbohydrate 37.3g, of which sugars 10.1g; Fat 45.5g, of which saturates 20.3g; Cholesterol 263mg; Calcium 75mg; Fibre 4.5g; Sodium 347mg.
Moussaka Energy 588Kcal/2444kJ; Protein 37.9g; Carbohydrate 14.8g, of which sugars 3.7g; Fat 40.9g, of which saturates 18.2g; Cholesterol 206mg; Calcium 379mg; Fibre 2.4g; Sodium 506mg.

Mutton and Potato Pies

These meat and potato pies make a nutritious portable meal and are ideal for family picnics.

Makes 6 small pies
450g/1lb boneless mutton or lamb
1 large onion, diced
2 carrots, diced
1 potato, diced
2 celery sticks, diced
1 egg, beaten
salt and ground black pepper

For the shortcrust pastry
500g/1¼lb/5 cups plain
  (all-purpose) flour
250g/9oz/generous 1 cup butter,
  or half butter and half white
  vegetable fat (shortening)
120ml/4fl oz/½ cup very
  cold water

1 To make the pastry, sift the flour into a large bowl and add the butter. Rub the butter into the flour with the fingertips or a pastry blender, lifting the mixture as much as possible to aerate. Add the chilled water. Mix with a knife or fork until the mixture clings together. Turn it on to a floured surface and knead lightly once or twice until smooth. Wrap in baking parchment or foil and leave in the refrigerator to relax for 20 minutes before using.

2 Trim any fat or gristle from the meat and cut it up into very small pieces. Place in a large bowl and add the diced onion, carrots, potato and celery. Mix well and season with salt and ground black pepper.

3 Preheat the oven to 180°C/350°F/Gas 4. Cut a third off the ball of pastry and reserve to make the lids of the pies. Roll out the rest and, using a small plate as a guide and re-rolling the pastry as necessary, cut out six circles. Divide the meat and vegetable mixture between the circles, piling it in the middle of each.

4 Roll out the remaining pastry and cut out six smaller circles, about 10cm/4in across. Lay these on top. Dampen the edges of the pastry bases, bring the pastry up around the meat, pleat it to fit the lid and pinch the edges together.

5 Make a small hole in the top of each pie to let out the steam. Brush with beaten egg and slide the pies on to baking sheets. Bake in the oven for an hour. Serve hot or cold.

Shepherd's Pie

This potato topped dish was developed during Victorian days as an economical way of making the most of leftover meat. By the 1930s it had become a regular part of the British eating pattern, and was made with meat from the Sunday roast and served to the family on Monday or Tuesday. When it is made with beef it is known as cottage pie.

Serves 4
1kg/2¼lb potatoes, peeled
60ml/4 tbsp milk
about 25g/1oz/2 tbsp butter
15ml/1 tbsp oil
1 large onion, finely chopped
1 medium carrot, finely chopped
450g/1lb cold cooked lamb,
  minced (ground)
150ml/¼ pint/⅔ cup lamb or
  beef stock
30ml/2 tbsp chopped parsley
salt and ground black pepper

1 Preheat the oven to 190°C/375°F/Gas 5. Boil the potatoes in salted water for about 20 minutes or until soft. Drain, and mash with the milk, adding butter, salt and ground black pepper to taste.

2 Heat the oil in a heavy frying pan and add the onion and carrot. Cook over medium heat for about 5–10 minutes, stirring occasionally, until softened. Stir in the minced meat, lamb or beef stock and parsley.

3 Spread the meat mixture in an ovenproof dish and spoon the mashed potato evenly over the top, creating an attractive pattern with a fork, if you like. Cook in the hot oven for about 30 minutes until the potatoes are crisped and browned.

> **Variations**
> • Add extra ingredients to the meat base, if you like, such as a clove or two of chopped garlic, a few wild mushrooms, a spoonful of tomato purée (paste) or ketchup, or a splash of Worcestershire sauce.
> • You could also mix the potatoes with other vegetables, such as mashed parsnip, squash or swede (rutabaga), and grate over a layer of mature cheddar before cooking.

Mutton Pies Energy 784kcal/3275kJ; Protein 25.1g; Carbohydrate 74.6g, of which sugars 5.2g; Fat 44.9g, of which saturates 26.1g; Cholesterol 178mg; Calcium 155mg; Fibre 4g; Sodium 345mg.
Shepherd's Pie Energy 487kcal/2045kJ; Protein 29.4g; Carbohydrate 50.1g, of which sugars 15.2g; Fat 20.2g, of which saturates 8.4g; Cholesterol 69mg; Calcium 54mg; Fibre 5.3g; Sodium 379mg.

Lamb Pie with Mustard Potatoes

Shepherd's pie with a twist, the mustard gives a real tang to the potato topping.

Serves 4

800g/1¾lb floury potatoes, diced
60ml/4 tbsp milk
15ml/1 tbsp wholegrain or
    French mustard
a little butter
450g/1lb lamb, minced (ground)

1 onion, chopped
2 celery sticks, thinly sliced
2 carrots, diced
30ml/2 tbsp cornflour (cornstarch)
    blended into 150ml/¼ pint/⅔
    cup lamb stock
15ml/1 tbsp Worcestershire sauce
30ml/2 tbsp chopped fresh
    rosemary, or 10ml/2 tsp dried
salt and ground black pepper
fresh vegetables, to serve

1 Cook the potatoes in a large pan of boiling, lightly salted water until tender. Drain well and mash until smooth, then stir in the milk, mustard, butter and seasoning to taste. Meanwhile, preheat the oven to 200°C/400°F/Gas 6.

2 Fry the lamb in a non-stick pan, breaking it up with a fork, until lightly browned all over. Add the onion, celery and carrots to the pan and cook for 2–3 minutes, stirring, to stop the mixture sticking to the base.

3 Stir in the stock and cornflour mixture. Bring to the boil, stirring all the while, then remove from the heat. Stir in the Worcestershire sauce and rosemary and season with salt and pepper to taste.

4 Turn the lamb mixture into a 1.75 litre/3 pint/7 cup ovenproof dish and spread over the potato topping evenly, swirling with the edge of a palette knife. Bake for 30–35 minutes until golden on the top. Serve hot with a selection of fresh vegetables.

Variations
• This recipe can be adapted to make a cottage pie, simply follow the method above substituting lamb with minced (ground) beef.
• To vary the potato topping slightly, try adding horseradish – either creamed or for an even stronger flavour, freshly grated.

Lamb Pie with a Potato Crust

This tasty pie, topped with mashed potato, is cooked entirely in the microwave, making a quick and easy meal to prepare for all the family.

Serves 4

675g/1½lb potatoes, diced
45ml/3 tbsp water
30ml/2 tbsp skimmed milk
15ml/1 tbsp wholegrain or
    French mustard

1 onion, chopped
2 celery sticks, sliced
2 carrots, diced
450g/1lb lean minced
    (ground) lamb
150ml/¼ pint/⅔ cup beef stock
60ml/4 tbsp rolled oats
15ml/1 tbsp Worcestershire sauce
30ml/2 tbsp chopped
    fresh rosemary
salt and ground black pepper

1 Place the potatoes in a microwave-proof bowl with the water. Cover and microwave on HIGH for 8–10 minutes, until tender, stirring once. Drain and mash until smooth, then stir in the milk and mustard.

2 Place the onion, celery and carrots in a large microwave-proof bowl. Cover and microwave on HIGH for 5 minutes, stirring once. Add the minced lamb, mixing well. Microwave on HIGH for 2 minutes, stirring once.

3 Stir in the stock, oats, Worcestershire sauce and rosemary, and season to taste. Cover loosely and microwave on HIGH for 20–25 minutes, until cooked, stirring twice.

4 Turn the meat mixture into a 1.75 litre/3 pint/7½ cup microwave-proof dish that is suitable for grilling (broiling). Swirl the potato evenly over the top. Microwave, uncovered, on HIGH for 4–5 minutes until hot. Brown under a grill (broiler), if liked. Serve with freshly cooked vegetables.

Cook's Tip
This recipe is suitable for cooking in a combination microwave. Follow the oven manufacturer's timing guide for good results.

Lamb and Mustard Pie Energy 371kcal/1561kJ; Protein 26.5g; Carbohydrate 37.9g, of which sugars 7.7g; Fat 13.7g, of which saturates 6.2g; Cholesterol 86mg; Calcium 68mg; Fibre 3.3g; Sodium 194mg.
Lamb Pie Energy 408kcal/1716kJ; Protein 27.6g; Carbohydrate 44.1g, of which sugars 7.7g; Fat 14.7g, of which saturates 6.1g; Cholesterol 86mg; Calcium 65mg; Fibre 4.3g; Sodium 191mg.

Lamb, New Potato and Chilli Curry

This dish makes the most of an economical cut of meat by cooking it slowly until the meat is falling from the bone. Chillies, potatoes and coconut cream give it lots of flavour.

Serves 4

25g/1oz/2 tbsp butter

4 garlic cloves, crushed

2 onions, sliced into rings

2.5ml/½ tsp each ground cumin, ground coriander, turmeric and cayenne pepper

2–3 red chillies, seeded and finely chopped

300ml/½ pint/1¼ cups hot chicken stock

200ml/7fl oz/scant 1 cup coconut cream

4 lamb shanks, all excess fat removed

450g/1lb new potatoes, chopped into halves

6 ripe tomatoes, quartered

salt and ground black pepper

coriander (cilantro) leaves, to garnish

spicy rice, to serve

1 Preheat the oven to 160°C/325°F/Gas 3. Melt the butter in a large flameproof casserole dish, add the garlic and onions and cook over a low heat for 15 minutes, until soft and golden. Stir in the ground spices and chopped chillies, then cook for a further 2 minutes.

2 Stir in the hot stock and coconut cream. Place the lamb shanks in the liquid and cover the casserole dish with foil. Cook in the hot oven for around 2 hours, turning the shanks twice, first after about an hour or so and again about half an hour later. The meat should be beautifully tender and falling off the bone.

3 Par-boil the potatoes for 10 minutes, drain and add to the casserole dish with the tomatoes, then cook uncovered in the oven for a further 35 minutes. Season to taste and garnish with coriander leaves. Serve with the spicy rice.

> **Cook's Tip**
> *Make this dish a day in advance if possible. Cool and chill overnight, then skim off the excess fat that has risen to the surface. Reheat thoroughly before you serve it.*

Spicy Lamb and Potato Stew

Indian spices transform this simple lamb and potato stew into a mouthwatering dish fit for princes. Serve with a spicy dhal and some naan bread.

Serves 6

675g/1½lb lean lamb fillet

15ml/1 tbsp oil

1 onion, finely chopped

2 bay leaves

1 fresh green chilli, seeded and finely chopped

2 garlic cloves, finely chopped

10ml/2 tsp ground coriander

5ml/1 tsp ground cumin

2.5ml/½ tsp ground turmeric

2.5ml/½ tsp chilli powder

2.5ml/½ tsp salt

2 tomatoes, peeled and chopped

600ml/1 pint/2½ cups chicken stock

2 large potatoes, cut into bitesize chunks

chopped fresh coriander (cilantro), to garnish

1 Remove any visible fat from the lamb and cut the meat into neat 2.5cm/1in cubes.

2 Heat the oil in a large, heavy pan and fry the onion, bay leaves, chilli and garlic for 5 minutes.

3 Add the cubed meat and cook for about 6–8 minutes until lightly browned all over.

4 Add the ground coriander, ground cumin, ground turmeric, chilli powder and salt and cook the spices for 3–4 minutes, stirring constantly to prevent them from sticking to the bottom of the pan.

5 Add the tomatoes and stock to the pan. Bring the mixture to the boil, then reduce the heat, cover the pan and simmer for about 1 hour.

6 Add the bitesize chunks of potato to the simmering mixture, stir in well, and simmer gently for a further 30–40 minutes, or until the meat is tender, the potatoes are cooked and most of the excess juices have been absorbed, leaving a thick but minimal sauce. Garnish with the chopped fresh coriander and serve piping hot.

Lamb and Potato Curry Energy 364kcal/1528kJ; Protein 23.5g; Carbohydrate 30.5g, of which sugars 12.1g; Fat 17.4g, of which saturates 8.8g; Cholesterol 89mg; Calcium 58mg; Fibre 3.5g; Sodium 205mg.
Spicy Lamb Stew Energy 284kcal/1192kJ; Protein 24g; Carbohydrate 14.1g, of which sugars 3.1g; Fat 15.1g, of which saturates 6.3g; Cholesterol 86mg; Calcium 23mg; Fibre 1.3g; Sodium 109mg.

Lamb and Potato Parsi

This highly fragrant, delicately spiced lamb and potato dish is sure to impress.

Serves 6
900g/2lb lamb fillet, cubed
60ml/4 tbsp ghee or butter
2 onions, sliced
450g/1lb floury potatoes,
  cut into chunks
chicken stock or water (see method)
450g/1lb/2⅓ cups basmati
  rice, soaked

pinch of saffron threads, dissolved
  in 30ml/2 tbsp warm milk
fresh coriander (cilantro) sprigs,
  to garnish

For the marinade
475ml/16fl oz/2 cups natural
  (plain) yogurt
3–4 garlic cloves, crushed
10ml/2 tsp cayenne pepper
20ml/4 tsp garam masala
10ml/2 tsp ground cumin
5ml/1 tsp ground coriander

1 Make the marinade by mixing all the ingredients in a large bowl. Add the meat, stir to coat, then cover and leave for 3–4 hours in a cool place or overnight in the refrigerator.

2 Melt 30ml/2 tbsp of the ghee or butter in a large pan and cook the onions for 6–8 minutes. Transfer to a plate.

3 Melt a further 25ml/1½ tbsp of the ghee or butter in the pan. Cook the lamb, in batches, until brown. When all the lamb is browned, return it to the pan and add the remaining marinade.

4 Stir in the potatoes and add three-quarters of the cooked onions. Pour in stock or water to cover. Bring to the boil, then cover and simmer gently for 40–50 minutes, until the potatoes are cooked. Preheat the oven to 160°C/325°F/Gas 3.

5 Drain the rice. Cook it in a pan of boiling stock or water for 5 minutes. Meanwhile, spoon the lamb mixture into a casserole. Drain the rice and mound it on top of the lamb, then make a hole down the centre. Top with the leftover onions, pour the saffron milk over and dot with the remaining ghee or butter.

6 Cover the pan with a double layer of foil and a lid. Cook in the oven for 30–35 minutes, or until the rice is completely tender. Garnish with fresh coriander sprigs and serve.

Lamb Stew with Chilli Sauce

The chillies in this Mexican stew add depth and richness to the sauce, while the potato slices ensure that it is substantial enough to serve on its own.

Serves 6
6 dried guajillo chillies, seeded
2 dried pasilla chillies, seeded
250ml/8fl oz/1 cup hot water
3 garlic cloves, peeled

5ml/1 tsp ground cinnamon
2.5ml/½ tsp ground cloves
2.5ml/½ tsp ground black pepper
15ml/1 tbsp vegetable oil
1kg/2¼lb lean boneless lamb
  shoulder, cut into
  2cm/¾in cubes
400g/14oz potatoes, scrubbed and
  cut into 1cm/½in thick slices
salt
strips of red pepper and fresh
  oregano, to garnish

1 Snap or tear the dried chillies into large pieces, put them in a bowl and pour over the hot water. Leave to soak for 30 minutes, then tip the contents of the bowl into a food processor or blender. Add the garlic and spices. Process until smooth.

2 Heat the oil in a large pan. Add the lamb cubes, in batches and stir-fry over a high heat until the cubes are evenly browned on all sides.

3 Return all the lamb cubes to the pan, spread them out, then cover them with a layer of potato slices. Add salt to taste. Put a lid on the pan and cook over a medium heat for 10 minutes.

4 Pour the chilli mixture over the lamb and mix thoroughly. Replace the lid and simmer over a low heat for about 1 hour or until both the meat and potato are tender. Serve with a rice dish, and garnish with strips of red pepper and fresh oregano.

> **Cook's Tips**
> • When frying the lamb do not be tempted to cook too many cubes at one time, as the meat will steam rather than fry.
> • Both guajillo and pasilla chillies are dried at the time of harvest and it is important to wash them before use. They are available to buy from well-stocked supermarkets or online.

Lamb Parsi Energy 764kcal/3193kJ; Protein 41g; Carbohydrate 81.9g, of which sugars 9.8g; Fat 30.6g, of which saturates 16.1g; Cholesterol 147mg; Calcium 196mg; Fibre 1.5g; Sodium 295mg.
Lamb with Chilli Sauce Energy 367kcal/1536kJ; Protein 34g; Carbohydrate 11.8g; of which sugars 1.9g; Fat 20.8g; of which saturates 9g; Cholesterol 127mg; Calcium 19mg; Fibre 0.9g; Sodium 151mg.

Steak with Stout and Potatoes

The Irish way to braise beef is in stout, of course, and topped with thickly sliced potatoes. Bake it in a moderate oven for long, slow tenderizing if you prefer.

Serves 4
675g/1½lb stewing beef
15ml/1 tbsp vegetable oil
25g/1oz/2 tbsp butter
225g/8oz tiny white onions
175ml/6fl oz/¾ cup stout or
   dark beer
300ml/½ pint/1¼ cups
   beef stock
bouquet garni
675g/1½lb firm, waxy potatoes,
   cut into thick slices
225g/8oz/3 cups large
   mushrooms, sliced
15ml/1 tbsp plain
   (all-purpose) flour
2.5ml/½ tsp mild mustard
salt and ground black pepper
chopped thyme sprigs, to garnish

1 Trim any excess fat from the steak and cut into four pieces. Season the meat all over. Heat the oil and 10g/¼oz/1½ tsp of the butter in a large heavy pan. Add the steak and brown on both sides, taking care not to burn the butter. Remove from the pan and set aside.

2 Add the onions to the pan and cook for 3–4 minutes until lightly browned. Return the steak to the pan with the onions. Pour on the stout or beer and stock and season to taste.

3 Next add the bouquet garni and top with the potato slices, distributing them evenly over the surface to cover the steak. Bring to a boil, then cover and simmer gently for 1 hour.

4 Add the sliced mushrooms over the potatoes. Cover again and simmer for a further 30 minutes or so. Remove the steak and vegetables with a slotted spoon and arrange on a platter.

5 Mix the remaining butter with the flour. Whisk a little at a time into the cooking liquid in the pan. Stir in the mustard. Cook over a medium heat for 3 minutes, stirring, until thickened.

6 Season the sauce and pour over the steak. Garnish with plenty of thyme sprigs and serve the dish immediately.

Pot-roasted Brisket with Vegetables

This pot-roasted beef and potato dish includes a large, sausage-shaped dumpling, which is added to the pot and cooked with the meat.

Serves 6–8
5 onions, sliced
3 bay leaves
1–1.6kg/2¼–3½lb beef brisket
1 garlic head, broken into cloves
4 carrots, thickly sliced
5–10ml/1–2 tsp paprika
500ml/17fl oz/generous 2 cups
   beef stock
3–4 potatoes, peeled and quartered
salt and ground black pepper

For the dumpling
about 90cm/36in sausage casing
250g/9oz/2¼ cups plain
   (all-purpose) flour
120ml/4fl oz/½ cup semolina
   or couscous
10–15ml/2–3 tsp paprika
1 carrot, grated and 2 carrots,
   diced (optional)
250ml/8fl oz/1 cup rendered
   chicken fat
30ml/2 tbsp crisp, fried onions
½ onion, grated and 3 onions,
   thinly sliced
3 garlic cloves,
   finely chopped
salt and ground black pepper

1 Preheat the oven to 180°C/350°F/Gas 4. Put one-third of the onions and a bay leaf in an ovenproof dish, then top with the beef. Sprinkle over the garlic, carrots and the remaining bay leaves. Add salt, pepper and paprika, then top with the remaining onions. Pour in enough stock to fill the dish to about 5–7.5cm/ 2–3in and cover with foil. Cook in the oven for 2 hours.

2 Meanwhile, make the dumpling. In a bowl, combine all the ingredients and stuff the mixture into the casing, leaving enough space for the mixture to expand. Tie into sausage-shaped lengths.

3 When the meat has cooked for about 2 hours, add the dumpling and potatoes to the pan, re-cover and cook for a further 1 hour, or until the meat and potatoes are tender.

4 Remove the foil from the dish and increase the oven temperature to 190–200°C/375–400°F/Gas 5–6. Move the onions away from the top of the meat to the side of the dish and return to the oven for a further 30 minutes, or until the meat, onions and potatoes are beginning to brown and become crisp. Serve hot or cold.

Steak with Stout Energy 538kcal/2253kJ; Protein 43.4g; Carbohydrate 35.5g, of which sugars 6.2g; Fat 24.5g, of which saturates 10.2g; Cholesterol 111mg; Calcium 44mg; Fibre 3.2g; Sodium 172mg.
Pot-roasted Brisket Energy 586kcal/2453kJ; Protein 33.2g; Carbohydrate 55.5g, of which sugars 9.6g; Fat 27.3g, of which saturates 10.8g; Cholesterol 85mg; Calcium 93mg; Fibre 3.8g; Sodium 93mg.

Beef and Root Vegetable Stew

This slow-cooker dish features beans, grains, meat and root vegetables. The tasty addition of whole boiled eggs is a classic feature.

Serves 4
250g/9oz/1⅓ cups dried haricot (navy) beans
30ml/2 tbsp olive oil
1 onion, chopped
4 garlic cloves, finely chopped
50g/2oz pearl barley
15ml/1 tbsp ground paprika
pinch of cayenne pepper

1 celery stick, chopped
400g/14oz can chopped tomatoes
3 carrots, sliced
1 small turnip, diced
2 baking potatoes, peeled and cut into chunks
675g/1½lb mixture of beef brisket, stewing beef and smoked beef, cut into cubes
1 litre/1¾ pints/4 cups boiling beef stock
30ml/2 tbsp easy-cook (converted) white rice
4 eggs, at room temperature
salt and ground black pepper

1 Place the beans in a large bowl. Pour over cold water to cover and leave to soak for 8 hours, or overnight, if you like.

2 Drain the beans and place in a large pan, cover with fresh cold water and bring to the boil. Boil for 10 minutes, skimming off any froth from the surface, then drain well and set aside.

3 Meanwhile, heat the oil in a pan, add the onion and cook gently for about 10 minutes, or until soft. Transfer the onions to the ceramic cooking pot.

4 Add the garlic, beans, barley, paprika, cayenne pepper, celery, tomatoes, carrots, turnip, potatoes, beef and stock to the onions and stir to combine.

5 Cover the pot with the lid and cook on low for 5–6 hours, or until the meat and vegetables are tender. Add the rice, stir, and season with salt and pepper.

6 Rinse the eggs in tepid water, then lower them, one at a time, into the hot stock. Cover and cook for a further 45 minutes, or until the rice is cooked. Serve hot, making sure each portion contains a whole egg.

All-in-the-pot Beef Stew

This one-pot recipe of beef, potatoes, carrots and celery harks back to the idea of cooking everything in one pot over a fire in the hearth, the traditional way of preparing food in days gone by. It makes a superb alternative to a Sunday roast and is more forgiving as the beef, being boiled, can sit and wait while you have that extra glass of wine before lunch.

Serves 8
25g/1oz/2 tbsp butter, softened
25g/1oz/¼ cup plain (all-purpose) flour
1.6kg/3½lb silverside (pot roast), boned and rolled
450g/1lb small whole onions, peeled
450g/1lb small carrots, peeled and cut in two
8 celery sticks, peeled and cut into four pieces
12 small potatoes
30ml/2 tbsp chopped fresh parsley

1 Make a beurre manié by combining the butter and flour thoroughly. This will be used to thicken the sauce.

2 Put the beef in a large pan, pour in cold water to cover and put on the lid. Bring to the boil and simmer for 2 hours, topping up with boiling water.

3 After about 2 hours add the prepared vegetables to the pan and simmer for a further 30 minutes, until the vegetables are just cooked.

4 Remove the cooked beef and vegetables from the pan, arrange on a serving dish and keep warm. Ladle about 350ml/12fl oz/1½ cups of the cooking liquor into a clean pan and bring to the boil.

5 When the cooking liquor has come to the boil, whisk in the prepared beurre manié to thicken it and add the chopped fresh parsley.

6 When ready to eat, pour the sauce over the beef and vegetables, retaining some to pass round at the table. Serve the meat in thick slices, accompanied by a healthy serving of the cooked vegetables.

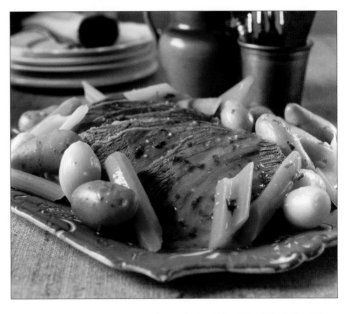

Root Veg Stew Energy 860kcal/3607kJ; Protein 58.9g; Carbohydrate 74.2g, of which sugars 13.7g; Fat 38.8g, of which saturates 12.7g; Cholesterol 341mg; Calcium 164mg; Fibre 10.9g; Sodium 639mg.
Beef Stew Energy 875kcal/3656kJ; Protein 89.8g; Carbohydrate 38.5g, of which sugars 16.7g; Fat 41.1g, of which saturates 17.7g; Cholesterol 231mg; Calcium 121mg; Fibre 6.3g; Sodium 358mg.

Traditional Beef Stew

A traditional casserole of beef cooked with potatoes and root vegetables makes this a complete meal in a pot. Cooking the vegetables separately from the meat for part of the time is an interesting technique, which allows them to keep more of their own flavour than would be possible if added to the meat at the beginning of the cooking.

Serves 4–6

1.2kg/2½lb stewing beef, cut into large cubes
1.2 litres/2 pints/5 cups beef stock
450g/1lb carrots, cut into bitesize pieces
1 small swede (rutabaga) or turnip
675g/1½lb potatoes, cut into bitesize pieces
1 onion, finely chopped
salt and ground black pepper

1 Put the beef in a large pan, add enough water to cover, season with salt and pepper and bring slowly to the boil. Lower the heat, cover and simmer for 1 hour.

2 When the beef has been cooking for 30 minutes, bring the stock to the boil in a flameproof casserole. Add the carrots and swede or turnip and simmer for 15 minutes. Add the potatoes and simmer for a further 15 minutes.

3 When the beef has been cooking for about 1 hour, strain the cubes, reserving the stock for a soup or another dish at a later date. Add the beef to the vegetables with the onion. Check the seasoning, adding salt and ground black pepper only if necessary.

4 Gently simmer the casserole for a further 15–30 minutes, depending on the quality of the meat, until the meat and vegetables are tender. Serve hot.

> **Cook's Tip**
> *Try to select beef with a good marbling of fat running through it as this will give a moister, more tender result than a very lean cut of meat.*

Braised Beef with Vegetables

Traditional stews like this were once the mainstay of many kitchens, when everything was left to cook gently all day in one large pot on the range or (in earlier times) the edge of the fire. Gentle simmering in a modern oven produces an equally delicious dish.

Serves 4–6

1kg/2¼lb lean stewing steak, cut into 5cm/2in cubes
45ml/3 tbsp plain (all-purpose) flour
45ml/3 tbsp oil
1 large onion, thinly sliced
1 large carrot, thickly sliced
2 celery sticks, finely chopped
300ml/½ pint/¼ cup beef stock
30ml/2 tbsp tomato purée (paste)
5ml/1 tsp dried mixed herbs
15ml/1 tbsp dark muscovado (molasses) sugar
225g/8oz baby potatoes, halved
2 leeks, thinly sliced
salt and ground black pepper

1 Preheat the oven to 150°C/300°F/Gas 2. Season the flour and use to coat the beef cubes.

2 Heat the oil in a large, flameproof casserole. Add a small batch of the cubed beef, cook quickly until browned on all sides and, with a slotted spoon, lift out. Repeat with the remaining beef, making sure not to cook too many cubes at once as the meat will steam rather than fry.

3 Add the onion, carrot and celery to the casserole. Cook over a medium heat for about 10 minutes, stirring frequently, until they begin to soften and brown slightly on the edges.

4 Return the meat to the casserole and add the stock, tomato purée, herbs and sugar, at the same time scraping up any sediment that has stuck to the casserole. Heat until the liquid nearly comes to the boil.

5 Cover with a tight-fitting lid and put into the hot oven. Cook for 2–2½ hours, or until the beef is tender.

6 Gently stir in the potatoes and leeks, cover and continue cooking for a further 30 minutes or until the potatoes are tender. Check the seasoning and serve immediately.

Beef Stew Energy 475kcal/1987kJ; Protein 48.4g; Carbohydrate 28.2g, of which sugars 10.8g; Fat 19.4g, of which saturates 7.8g; Cholesterol 116mg; Calcium 73mg; Fibre 4.3g; Sodium 170mg.
Braised Beef Energy 450kcal/1880kJ; Protein 41.3g; Carbohydrate 23.6g, of which sugars 10.3g; Fat 21.7g, of which saturates 7.3g; Cholesterol 97mg; Calcium 63mg; Fibre 3.5g; Sodium 137mg.

Sailor's Steak with Potato and Onion

Also known as seaman's beef, this dish used to be linked with sailors because it requires very few kitchen utensils and just one pot to make it. Cooking the meat, onion and potatoes together gives the dish a delicious stew-like combination of textures and flavours.

Serves 8

8 thin slices entrecôte (sirloin) steak, about 600g/1lb 6oz

8 medium potatoes
15g/½oz/1 tbsp butter
4 onions, chopped
1 sprig fresh thyme
2 bay leaves
500ml/17fl oz/generous 2 cups dark ale
salt and ground black pepper
15ml/1 tbsp chopped fresh parsley, to garnish
pickled beetroot (beet) or pickled gherkins, to serve

1 Preheat the oven to 180°C/350°F/Gas 4. Using a rolling pin or heavy wooden mallet, beat the steaks until flattened.

2 Peel the potatoes, cut them in half and then into slices about 1cm/½in thick.

3 Melt the butter in a large flameproof casserole. Add the onions and fry for about 10 minutes, stirring frequently, until golden brown.

4 Push the onions to one side of the dish, add the steaks and fry until sealed on both sides.

5 Add the sliced potatoes to the pan, followed by the thyme and bay leaves. Stir the ingredients until well combined. Season with salt and pepper.

6 Pour the ale over the ingredients in the casserole, cover with a tight-fitting lid and bake in the preheated oven for about 1 hour or until the potatoes are tender.

7 Ladle on to individual plates and sprinkle the chopped parsley over the top to garnish. Serve accompanied by pickled beetroot or pickled gherkins.

Smoked Beef with Potato Pancakes

This tasty and unusual recipe features potato pancakes and fine smoked meats.

Serves 4
500g/1¼lb trimmed beef fillet
oil, for chargrilling
salt and ground black pepper
herb sprigs, to garnish
broccoli florets, white turnip and courgettes (zucchini), to serve

For the potato pancakes
250g/9oz potatoes, cooked
50g/2oz/½ cup plain (all-purpose) flour

1 egg
freshly grated nutmeg
oil, for frying

For the sauce
4 shallots, finely diced
200ml/7fl oz/scant 1 cup chicken stock
120ml/4fl oz/½ cup dry white wine
200ml/7fl oz/scant 1 cup double (heavy) cream
15ml/1 tbsp chopped fresh herbs, such as flat leaf parsley, tarragon, chervil and basil
lemon juice, to taste

1 To make the potato pancakes, blend the potatoes with the flour and egg to make a thick paste. Add nutmeg and seasoning to taste. Lightly oil and heat a heavy pan, then use the potato mixture to make eight small pancakes, cooking them on both sides until golden brown. Keep warm.

2 To make the sauce, put the shallots, stock, wine and half the cream into a pan and cook over a medium heat until reduced by two-thirds. Purée the mixture and strain it, then mix in enough of the herbs to turn the sauce green.

3 Season the beef with salt and pepper. In a heavy, preheated pan, seal the meat on all sides over medium heat. Place the meat in a smoker for about 10 minutes until medium-rare. Or, to chargrill the meat, preheat a dry cast-iron ridged pan until very hot. Brush the meat with oil and cook for 3–5 minutes.

4 To serve, whip the remaining cream and fold it into the sauce. Adjust the seasoning and add lemon juice if required. Divide the sauce between four warm plates. Cut the beef into eight slices and place two on each plate. Add the pancakes and garnish with herbs. Serve with the broccoli, turnip and courgettes.

Sailor's Steak Energy 279kcal/1170kJ; Protein 19.4g; Carbohydrate 29.9g, of which sugars 9.7g; Fat 6.6g, of which saturates 3.2g; Cholesterol 50mg; Calcium 38mg; Fibre 2.3g; Sodium 70mg.
Smoked Beef Energy 683kcal/2834kJ; Protein 32.9g; Carbohydrate 23g, of which sugars 3g; Fat 49.5g, of which saturates 27.5g; Cholesterol 219mg; Calcium 82mg; Fibre 1.9g; Sodium 166mg.

Marinated Beef and Potato Salad

The beef steak needs to marinate overnight, but once that is done this dish is quick to assemble. The salad with potato balls makes an interesting side dish.

Serves 6
900g/2lb sirloin steak
3 large white potatoes
$1/2$ red (bell) pepper, seeded and diced
$1/2$ green (bell) pepper, seeded and diced
I small red onion, finely chopped
2 garlic cloves, crushed
4 spring onions (scallions), diagonally sliced
I small cos or romaine lettuce, leaves torn
salt and ground black pepper
olive oil, to serve
Parmesan cheese shavings, to serve

For the marinade
120ml/4fl oz/$1/2$ cup olive oil
120ml/4fl oz/$1/2$ cup red wine vinegar
90ml/6 tbsp soy sauce

I Place the beef in a large, non-metallic container. Mix together the ingredients for the marinade. Season with pepper and pour over the meat.

2 Cover the meat and leave to marinate for several hours, or preferably overnight.

3 Drain the marinade from the meat and pat the joint dry. Preheat a frying pan, cut the steak carefully into thin slices and fry for a few minutes until just cooked on each side, but still slightly pink. Set aside to cool.

4 Peel the potatoes. Using a melon baller, carefully scoop out rounds from each potato. Boil in lightly salted water for about 5 minutes or until just tender.

5 Drain the potatoes and transfer to a bowl. Add the peppers, onion, garlic, spring onions and lettuce leaves. Season with salt and pepper and toss together.

6 Transfer the potato and pepper mixture to a plate with the beef. Drizzle with a little extra olive oil and serve topped with Parmesan shavings.

Beef and Grilled Sweet Potatoes

This salad is absolutely delicious with a simple potato salad and some peppery leaves, such as watercress, mizuna or rocket.

Serves 6–8
800g/1$3/4$lb fillet of beef
5ml/I tsp black peppercorns, crushed
10ml/2 tsp chopped fresh thyme
60ml/4 tbsp olive oil
450g/Ilb orange-fleshed sweet potato, peeled
salt and ground black pepper

For the dressing
I garlic clove, chopped
15g/$1/2$oz flat leaf parsley
30ml/2 tbsp chopped fresh coriander (cilantro)
15ml/I tbsp small salted capers, rinsed
$1/2$–I fresh green chilli, seeded and chopped
10ml/2 tsp Dijon mustard
10–15ml/2–3 tsp white wine vinegar
75ml/5 tbsp extra virgin olive oil
2 shallots, finely chopped

I Roll the beef fillet in the crushed peppercorns and thyme, then set aside to marinate for a few hours. Preheat the oven to 200°C/400°F/Gas 6.

2 Heat half the oil in a frying pan. Add the beef and brown it all over, turning frequently, to seal it. Place on a baking tray and cook in the oven for 10–15 minutes. Remove the beef from the oven and cover with foil, then leave for 10–15 minutes.

3 Meanwhile, preheat the grill (broiler). Cut the sweet potatoes into 1cm/$1/2$in slices. Brush with the remaining oil, season to taste, and grill (broil) for 5–6 minutes on each side, until browned. Cut the slices into strips and place in a bowl. Cut the beef into slices or strips and toss with the sweet potato, then set the bowl aside.

4 For the dressing, process the garlic, parsley, coriander, capers, chilli, mustard and 10ml/2 tsp of the vinegar in a food processor or blender. With the motor still running, pour in the oil to make a smooth dressing. Season to taste. Stir in the shallots.

5 Toss the dressing into the sweet potatoes and beef and leave to stand for up to 2 hours before serving.

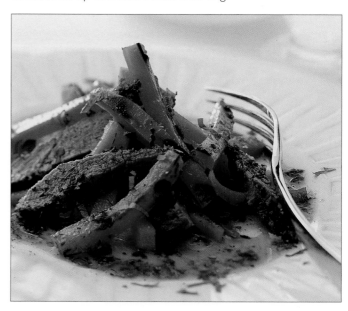

Marinated Beef Energy 296kcal/1247kJ; Protein 38g; Carbohydrate 20.1g, of which sugars 5g; Fat 7.6g, of which saturates 3.2g; Cholesterol 77mg; Calcium 40mg; Fibre 2.3g; Sodium 120mg.
Beef and Sweet Potatoes Energy 300kcal/1253kJ; Protein 21.9g; Carbohydrate 12g, of which sugars 3.2g; Fat 18.6g, of which saturates 4.6g; Cholesterol 61mg; Calcium 18mg; Fibre 1.4g; Sodium 67mg.

Spicy Corned Beef and Potato Hash

This is real nursery, or comfort, food at its best. Whether you remember Gran's version, or prefer this American-style potato hash, it turns corned beef into a supper fit for any guest.

Serves 4

30ml/2 tbsp vegetable oil
25g/1oz/2 tbsp butter
1 onion, finely chopped
1 green (bell) pepper, diced
2 large firm boiled potatoes, cut into small chunks
350g/12oz can corned beef, cut into small cubes
1.5ml/¼ tsp grated nutmeg
1.5ml/¼ tsp paprika
4 eggs
salt and ground black pepper
deep-fried parsley, to garnish
sweet chilli sauce or tomato sauce, to serve

1 Heat the oil and butter together in a large frying pan. Add the onion and fry for 5–6 minutes until softened.

2 In a bowl, mix together the green pepper, potatoes, corned beef, nutmeg and paprika and season well. Add to the pan and toss gently to distribute the cooked onion. Press down lightly and fry without stirring on a medium heat for about 3–4 minutes until a golden brown crust has formed on the underside.

3 Stir the mixture through to distribute the crust, then repeat the frying twice, until the mixture is well browned.

4 Make four wells in the hash and carefully crack an egg into each. Cover and cook gently for about 4–5 minutes until the egg whites are set.

5 Sprinkle generously with deep-fried parsley and cut into quarters. Serve hot with sweet chilli sauce or tomato sauce.

Cook's Tips
• Chill the can of corned beef for about half an hour before use – it will be easier to cut it into cubes.
• Smoked paprika makes an interesting alternative to the regular variety, offering a mellow smoky flavour.

Beef and Potato Rydberg

The Hotel Rydberg, which overlooked the Royal Palace in Stockholm, Sweden, closed in 1914 but is still remembered for this recipe that was popularly served there at the turn of the century. Using fillet steak (instead of the original kidneys) and potatoes, it is a luxury version of the classic Swedish beef hash.

Serves 6

8 large potatoes
600g/1lb 6oz fillet steak (beef tenderloin)
2 onions
50g/2oz/¼ cup butter
15ml/1 tbsp vegetable oil
salt and ground black pepper
6 very fresh eggs, to serve
Brown sauce, Worcestershire sauce, mustard and tomato ketchup, to serve

1 Peel and cut the potatoes into small cubes measuring about 3mm/⅛in. Cut the steak and onions into cubes the same size as the potatoes.

2 Heat the butter and oil in a frying pan, add the onions and fry for 8–10 minutes until golden brown. Using a slotted spoon, remove from the pan. Add the potatoes, adding more butter if necessary, and fry for about 20 minutes until golden brown. Remove from the pan.

3 Just before serving, so that the steak is not overcooked, add the steak cubes to the pan and fry for less than a minute, until sealed but still rare.

4 Arrange small piles of the fried steak cubes, the fried potatoes and the fried onions on individual serving plates. Break the eggs, one at a time, separating the yolks from the whites, and putting the egg yolks in half the broken shell in the middle of the plates.

5 Serve immediately, accompanied by the brown sauce, Worcestershire sauce, mustard and tomato ketchup so that each person can season the dish at the table according to their own taste. Diners should then mix all the ingredients together themselves and combine them with the raw egg yolk from the shell on their plate.

Beef Hash Energy 421kcal/1758kJ; Protein 30.8g; Carbohydrate 16.9g, of which sugars 5.4g; Fat 26.15g, of which saturates 10.6g; Cholesterol 277mg; Calcium 65mg; Fibre 1.7g; Sodium 870.8mg.
Beef Rydberg Energy 407kcal/1711kJ; Protein 26.4g; Carbohydrate 46.9g, of which sugars 6.3g; Fat 13.9g, of which saturates 7.4g; Cholesterol 79mg; Calcium 34mg; Fibre 3.4g; Sodium 125mg.

Cornish Beef and Potato Pasties

The original portable lunch, pasties made a satisfying midday meal for intrepid Cornish tin miners, who could use the crimped pastry join across the top as a handle when their hands were filthy. These contain the traditional filling of chopped steak, potatoes and other root vegetables.

Makes 6

500–675g/1¼–1½lb
    shortcrust pastry
450g/1lb chuck steak, cubed
1 potato, about 175g/6oz, cubed
175g/6oz swede
    (rutabaga), cubed
1 onion, finely chopped
2.5ml/½ tsp dried mixed herbs
beaten egg, to glaze
salt and ground black pepper

1 Preheat the oven to 220°C/425°F/Gas 7. Divide the pastry into six equal pieces, then roll out each piece to form a rough circle, measuring about 20cm/8in.

2 Mix together the steak, vegetables and herbs. Season with salt and black pepper. Spoon an equal amount of the mixture on to one half of each pastry circle.

3 Brush the edges of the pastry with a little water, then fold the pastry over the filling. Crimp the edges firmly together on the top.

4 Use a metal spatula to transfer the pasties to a non-stick baking sheet, then brush the top of each one with a little beaten egg.

5 Put into the hot oven and cook for 15 minutes, then reduce the oven temperature to 160°C/325°F/Gas 3 and cook for a further 1 hour.

Variation
Swede (rutabaga) is the traditional vegetable in Cornish pasties, along with potatoes, but other vegetables could be used in its place, if you prefer. Turnip, carrot or celery will all be suitable additions to the pasties.

Cottage Pie

This classic dish features minced beef mixed with onion and carrot and then topped with a crispy, golden layer of mashed potato.

Serves 4

50g/2oz/¼ cup butter
1 large onion, finely chopped
1 celery stalk, finely diced
1 large carrot, finely diced
450g/1lb lean minced
    (ground) beef
15ml/1 tbsp plain (all-purpose) flour
250ml/8fl oz/1 cup hot
    beef stock
30ml/2 tbsp chopped fresh parsley
15ml/1 tbsp tomato purée (paste)
900g/2lb floury potatoes, peeled
30–45ml/2–3 tbsp milk
10ml/2 tsp Dijon mustard
salt and ground black pepper

1 Melt ½oz (15g) of the butter in a frying pan over moderate heat. Add the chopped onion, celery and carrot and cook until the onion is soft, stirring occasionally. Add the beef and fry, stirring, until it is brown and crumbly.

2 Sprinkle the flour evenly over the surface, stir it into the meat and vegetables and cook for a minute or two. Gradually add the stock, stirring well. Stir in the parsley and tomato purée. Season with salt and ground black pepper.

3 Bring the mixture to a simmer, then cover with a tight-fitting lid and cook over very low heat, stirring occasionally, for about 45 minutes.

4 Meanwhile, cook the potatoes in boiling salted water for about 10–15 minutes or until they are tender. Drain well.

5 While the potatoes are still warm, place them in a bowl and mash them thoroughly. Add the remaining butter and just enough milk to make a soft fluffy texture. Season to taste with plenty of salt and ground black pepper. Preheat the oven to 200°C/400°F/Gas 6.

6 Stir the mustard into the beef mixture, then turn it into a baking dish. Cover with a neat layer of potatoes and seal to the sides of the dish. Mark a pattern with a fork, if you like. Bake in the oven for 20–25 minutes. Serve hot.

Cornish Pasties Energy 414kcal/1731kJ; Protein 10.4g; Carbohydrate 38.8g, of which sugars 1.4g; Fat 25.3g, of which saturates 9.2g; Cholesterol 51mg; Calcium 93mg; Fibre 1.4g; Sodium 620mg.
Cottage Pie Energy 281kcal/1179kJ; Protein 7.2g; Carbohydrate 34.6g, of which sugars 6.2g; Fat 13.7g, of which saturates 5.1g; Cholesterol 22mg; Calcium 50mg; Fibre 2.9g; Sodium 132mg.

Beef, Lentil and Potato Pie

This microwave dish features lentils and minced meat with a potato and parsnip mash topping.

Serves 4

175g/6oz/1 cup green lentils
1 onion, chopped
2 celery sticks, chopped
1 large carrot, chopped
1 garlic clove, crushed
225g/8oz lean minced (ground) beef
400g/14oz can chopped tomatoes
10ml/2 tsp yeast extract
1 bay leaf

For the topping

450g/1lb potatoes, peeled and cut into large chunks
450g/1lb parsnips, peeled and cut into large chunks
60ml/4 tbsp low-fat natural (plain) yogurt
45ml/3 tbsp chopped chives
20ml/4 tsp freshly grated Parmesan cheese
2 tomatoes, sliced
25g/1oz/1/4 cup pine nuts (optional)

1 Place the lentils in a microwave-proof bowl and pour in boiling water to cover. Cover and microwave on HIGH for 6 minutes and set aside. Place the onion, celery, carrot and garlic in a large microwave-proof bowl. Cover, microwave on HIGH for 4 minutes and stir once. Add the mince, stir and microwave on HIGH for 2 minutes. Mix in the tomatoes.

2 Drain the lentils, reserving 250ml/8fl oz/1 cup of the cooking water in a measuring jug (cup). Add the lentils to the meat mixture, then dissolve the yeast extract in the cooking water and stir it in with the bay leaf. Cover loosely, then microwave on HIGH for 12–15 minutes, stirring twice.

3 Make the topping: place the potatoes and parsnips in a microwave-proof bowl with 75ml/5 tbsp water. Cover and microwave on HIGH for 11–13 minutes, stirring once, until tender. Mash together and stir in the yogurt and chives.

4 Remove the bay leaf and place the mixture in a large heatproof dish. Spoon over the potato mixture, sprinkle with Parmesan and garnish with tomato slices. Sprinkle with pine nuts, if using, and grill (broil) until the topping is crisp and golden.

Baked Beef with a Potato Crust

This recipe makes the best of braising beef by marinating it in red wine and topping it with a cheesy grated potato crust that bakes to a golden, crunchy consistency.

Serves 4

675g/1½lb stewing beef, diced
300ml/½ pint/1¼ cups red wine
3 juniper berries, crushed
slice of orange peel
30ml/2 tbsp olive oil
2 onions, cut into chunks
2 carrots, cut into chunks

1 garlic clove, crushed
225g/8oz/3 cups button (white) mushrooms
150ml/¼ pint/2/3 cup beef stock
30ml/2 tbsp cornflour (cornstarch)
salt and ground black pepper

For the crust

450g/1lb potatoes, grated
15ml/1 tbsp olive oil
30ml/2 tbsp creamed horseradish
50g/2oz/½ cup mature (sharp) Cheddar cheese, grated
salt and ground black pepper

1 Place the diced beef in a large, non-metallic bowl. Add the red wine, juniper berries, and orange peel and season with black pepper. Mix the ingredients together until thoroughly combined and then cover and leave to marinate for at least 4 hours or overnight, if possible.

2 Preheat the oven to 160°C/325°F/Gas 3. Drain the beef, making sure to reserve the marinade. Heat the oil in a large flameproof casserole dish and fry the meat in small batches for around 5 minutes until sealed on all sides.

3 Add the onions, carrots and garlic and cook for 5 minutes. Stir in the mushrooms, red wine marinade and beef stock. Simmer. Mix the cornflour with water to make a smooth paste. Stir into the pan. Season, cover and cook for 1½ hours.

4 Make the crust 30 minutes before the end of the cooking time for the beef. Start by blanching the potatoes in boiling water for 5 minutes. Drain and then squeeze out the extra liquid.

5 Stir in the remaining ingredients and then sprinkle over the beef. Increase the oven to 200°C/400°F/Gas 6 and bake for a further 30 minutes so that the top is crisp and browned.

Beef and Lentil Pie Energy 455kcal/1926kJ; Protein 31.7g; Carbohydrate 64g, of which sugars 15.7g; Fat 9.9g, of which saturates 4g; Cholesterol 37mg; Calcium 192mg; Fibre 10.3g; Sodium 293mg.
Baked Beef Energy 641kcal/2678kJ; Protein 45.9g; Carbohydrate 36.6g, of which sugars 10.8g; Fat 29.6g, of which saturates 10.6g; Cholesterol 111mg; Calcium 152mg; Fibre 4.2g; Sodium 306mg.

Potato, Beef and Mushroom Gratin

This medley of potatoes, beef and mushrooms offers an appealing mix of flavours and produces a hearty and rewarding main meal.

Serves 4

30ml/2 tbsp vegetable oil
I small onion, chopped
15ml/I tbsp plain
　(all-purpose) flour
150ml/¼ pint/⅔ cup
　vegetable stock
225g/8oz cooked beetroot (beets),
　drained well and chopped
15ml/I tbsp creamed horseradish

15ml/I tbsp caraway seeds
3 shallots, or I onion, chopped
450g/Ilb frying steak, cut into
　thin strips
225g/8oz assorted wild or
　cultivated mushrooms, sliced
10–15ml/2–3 tsp hot mustard
60ml/4 tbsp sour cream
45ml/3 tbsp chopped fresh parsley

For the potato border

900g/2lb floury potatoes, cooked
150ml/¼ pint/⅔ cup milk
25g/Ioz/2 tbsp butter
15ml/I tbsp chopped fresh dill
salt and ground black pepper

I Preheat the oven to 190°C/375°F/Gas 5. Lightly oil a gratin dish. Heat 15ml/I tbsp of the oil in a large pan, add the onion and fry until softened. Stir in the flour and gradually add the stock, stirring until blended and thickened. Add the beetroot (reserving a little for the topping), horseradish and caraway seeds. Mix gently, then set aside.

2 Mash the cooked potatoes with the milk and butter. Add the chopped dill, if using, and season to taste. Spoon the potatoes into the prepared dish and push well up the sides, making a large hollow in the middle. Spoon the beetroot mixture into the well, evening it out with the back of a spoon, and set aside.

3 Heat the remaining oil in a frying pan, add the shallots or onion and fry until softened. Add the steak and stir-fry quickly until browned. Add the mushrooms and fry quickly for about 2–3 minutes. Gently stir in the mustard, sour cream, seasoning to taste and half the parsley until well blended.

4 Spoon the steak mixture over the beetroot mixture in the dish, sprinkling the reserved beetroot on top, then cover and bake for 30 minutes. Sprinkle with the remaining parsley and serve.

Meatball and Potato Pie

The breadcrumb and potato crust of this pie hides a delicious and surprising filling of beef and pork meatballs in a Madeira wine gravy.

Serves 4

250g/9oz minced (ground) beef
250g/9oz minced (ground) pork
I large egg, lightly beaten
25g/Ioz/½ cup crushed rusks or
　dry breadcrumbs
2.5ml/½ tsp freshly ground nutmeg
30ml/2 tbsp mild paprika
40g/I½oz/3 tbsp butter

I onion, chopped
150g/5oz mushrooms
40g/I½oz/⅓ cup plain
　(all-purpose) flour
50ml/2fl oz/¼ cup Madeira
480g/I7oz can browned beans,
　drained and rinsed
30 ml/2 tbsp finely chopped
　fresh parsley
800g/I¾lb waxy potatoes

For the topping

25g/Ioz/2 tbsp butter, melted
30ml/2 tbsp crushed rusks or
　breadcrumbs

I Put the meat in a bowl with the egg, rusks, nutmeg, ½ tsp black pepper and salt. Knead until combined. Form the mixture into about 30 small balls then roll the meatballs in the paprika.

2 Melt the butter in a large frying pan, add the meatballs and cook over a high heat, turning frequently, for about 8 minutes, until evenly browned. Add the onion and mushrooms and cook, stirring frequently, for 2–3 minutes. Sprinkle in the flour and cook, stirring constantly, for 2 minutes, until it is lightly coloured.

3 Gradually stir in 400ml/14fl oz/1⅔ cups water, then stir in the Madeira. Lower the heat, cover and simmer for 10 minutes. Add the beans and transfer the mixture to an ovenproof dish. Sprinkle with parsley. Preheat the oven to 200°C/400°F/Gas 6.

4 Par-boil the potatoes in salted boiling water for 5–7 minutes, then drain. Evenly slice the potatoes and arrange the slices, overlapping slightly, on top of the pie. Drizzle with the melted butter and sprinkle with the rusks or breadcrumbs.

5 Bake for around 40–45 minutes until golden brown on top. Serve immediately with brussel sprouts sprinkled with toasted almonds and apple sauce.

Potato Gratin Energy 560kcal/2346kJ; Protein 34.1g; Carbohydrate 49.5g, of which sugars 12g; Fat 26.4g, of which saturates 10.8g; Cholesterol 91mg; Calcium 111mg; Fibre 4.6g; Sodium 354mg.
Meatball Pie Energy 774kcal/3247kJ; Protein 42.4g; Carbohydrate 77g, of which sugars 9.4g; Fat 33.9g, of which saturates 16g; Cholesterol 161mg; Calcium 185mg; Fibre 11.1g; Sodium 813mg.

Beef and Sweet Potato Stew

The tender beef cooked in red wine balances the sweetness of the peaches, pumpkin and sweet potatoes.

Serves 8
1 large pumpkin, about 5kg/11lb
60ml/4 tbsp olive oil
1kg/2¼lb braising steak, cut into 2.5cm/1in cubes
1 large onion, finely chopped
3 fresh red chillies, chopped
2 garlic cloves, crushed
1 large tomato, roughly chopped
2 fresh bay leaves
600ml/1 pint/2½ cups beef stock
350ml/12fl oz/1½ cups red wine
500g/1¼lb potatoes, peeled and cut into 2cm/¾in cubes
500g/1¼lb sweet potatoes, peeled and cut into 2cm/¾in cubes
1 corn cob, cut widthways into 6 slices
3 peaches, peeled, stoned (pitted) and cut into thick wedges
salt and ground black pepper

1 Cut a slice off the top of the pumpkin, 6cm/2½in from the stem, to make a lid. Scoop out the seeds and stringy fibres and discard. Scoop out some of the flesh, leaving a shell about 2cm/¾in thick. Dice the removed flesh into 1cm/½in pieces. Brush the inside and the flesh of the lid with oil and season. Place pumpkin and lid on a baking sheet, flesh side up. Set aside.

2 Preheat the oven to 200°C/400°F/Gas 6. Heat half the remaining oil in a pan over a high heat. Add the beef, season and cook until browned. Set aside. Lower the heat and add the remaining oil to the pan. Stir in the onion and chillies, and cook for 5 minutes. Add the garlic and tomato for 2 minutes.

3 Return the meat to the pan and add the bay leaves, stock and red wine. Bring to the boil, then lower the heat to a gentle simmer. Cook for 1 hour or until the meat is tender.

4 Bake the pumpkin and lid in the oven for 30 minutes. Add the potatoes, sweet potatoes, pumpkin pieces and corn to the stew. Bring to the boil, then simmer, covered, for 15 minutes.

5 Finally add the peach wedges and season to taste. Spoon the stew into the partially cooked pumpkin, cover with the lid and bake for 15 minutes or until tender. To serve, ladle the stew on to plates, then cut the empty pumpkin into eight wedges.

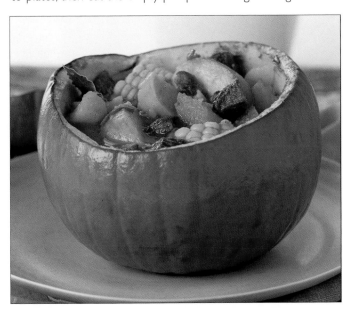

Mussaman Beef and Potato Curry

This delicious meat and potato curry is traditionally based on beef, but chicken, lamb or tofu can be used instead, if you prefer.

Serves 4–6
675g/1½lb stewing steak
600ml/1 pint/2½ cups coconut milk
250ml/8fl oz/1 cup coconut cream
45ml/3 tbsp Mussaman curry paste
30ml/2 tbsp Thai fish sauce
15ml/1 tbsp palm sugar (jaggery) or light muscovado (brown) sugar
60ml/4 tbsp tamarind juice, made by soaking tamarind paste in warm water
6 green cardamom pods
1 cinnamon stick
1 large potato, about 225g/8oz, cut into even chunks
1 onion, cut into wedges
50g/2oz/½ cup roasted peanuts

1 Trim off any excess fat from the stewing steak, then, using a sharp knife, cut it into 2.5cm/1in chunks.

2 Pour the coconut milk into a large, heavy pan and bring to the boil over a medium heat. Add the chunks of beef, reduce the heat to low, partially cover the pan and simmer gently for about 40 minutes, or until tender.

3 Pour the coconut cream into a separate pan. Cook over a medium heat, stirring constantly, for about 5 minutes, or until it separates. Stir in the Mussaman curry paste and cook rapidly for 2–3 minutes, until fragrant and thoroughly blended.

4 Add the coconut cream and curry paste mixture to the pan with the beef and stir until thoroughly blended. Simmer for a further 4–5 minutes, stirring occasionally.

5 Stir the fish sauce, sugar, tamarind juice, cardamom pods, cinnamon stick, potato chunks and onion wedges into the beef curry. Continue to simmer for a further 15–20 minutes, or until the potato is cooked and tender.

6 Add the roasted peanuts to the pan and mix well to combine. Cook for about 5 minutes more, then transfer to warmed individual serving bowls and serve immediately.

Beef Stew Energy 380kcal/1600kJ; Protein 31.4g; Carbohydrate 28.9g, of which sugars 14.9g; Fat 13.1g, of which saturates 3.8g; Cholesterol 0mg; Calcium 133mg; Fibre 6.2g; Sodium 65mg.
Mussaman Curry Energy 626kcal/2610kJ; Protein 44.6g; Carbohydrate 24.8g, of which sugars 15.4g; Fat 39.3g, of which saturates 22.7g; Cholesterol 98mg; Calcium 74mg; Fibre 1.6g; Sodium 288mg.

Beef and Potatoes in Peanut Sauce

This slow-cooked stew has a uniquely Asian flavour. Potatoes, rice and peanuts are used to thicken the juices, yielding a rich and glossy sauce.

Serves 4–6
900g/2lb braising steak
30ml/2 tbsp vegetable oil
15ml/1 tbsp annatto seeds
2 medium onions, chopped
275g/10oz celeriac,
   roughly chopped
2 garlic cloves, crushed
475ml/16fl oz/2 cups
   beef stock
375g/12oz new potatoes, peeled
   and cut into large dice
15ml/1 tbsp fish sauce
30ml/2 tbsp tamarind sauce
10ml/2 tsp sugar
1 bay leaf
1 fresh thyme sprig
45ml/3 tbsp long grain rice
30ml/2 tbsp peanut butter
15ml/1 tbsp white wine vinegar
salt and ground black pepper

1 Cut the beef into 2.5cm/1in cubes and set aside. Heat the oil in a flameproof casserole, add the annatto seeds and stir until the oil is dark red in colour. Remove the seeds with a slotted spoon and discard.

2 Add the onions, celeriac and garlic to the casserole and fry for 3–5 minutes, until softened but not coloured. Add the beef and fry until lightly and evenly browned.

3 Add the stock, potatoes, fish sauce, tamarind sauce, sugar, bay leaf and thyme to the stew. Bring to a simmer, cover with a tight-fitting lid and cook for 2 hours.

4 Meanwhile, soak the rice in cold water for 30 minutes. Drain the rice and grind with the peanut butter in a mortar with a pestle or in a food processor.

5 When the beef is tender, add 60ml/4 tbsp of the cooking liquid to the rice and nut mixture. Blend until smooth, then stir into the casserole.

6 Simmer gently, uncovered, for about 15–20 minutes, until thickened. Stir in the wine vinegar, and spoon into warmed bowls. Serve immediately.

Tex-Mex Baked Potatoes with Chilli

Classic chilli beef tops crisp, floury-centred baked potatoes. Easy to prepare and great for a simple yet substantial family supper.

Serves 4
2 large baking potatoes
15ml/1 tbsp vegetable oil, plus
   more for brushing
1 garlic clove, crushed
1 small onion, chopped
½ red (bell) pepper, chopped
225g/8oz lean minced
   (ground) beef
½ small fresh red chilli, seeded
   and chopped
5ml/1 tsp ground cumin
pinch of cayenne pepper
200g/7oz can chopped tomatoes
30ml/2 tbsp tomato
   purée (paste)
2.5ml/½ tsp fresh oregano
2.5ml/½ tsp fresh marjoram
200g/7oz can red kidney
   beans, drained
15ml/1 tbsp chopped fresh
   coriander (cilantro)
salt and ground black pepper
chopped fresh marjoram,
   to garnish
lettuce leaves, to serve
60ml/4 tbsp sour cream,
   to serve

1 Preheat the oven to 220°C/425°F/Gas 7. Brush or rub the potatoes with a little of the oil and then pierce them with skewers. Place the potatoes on the top shelf of the oven and bake them for 30 minutes before beginning to cook the chilli.

2 Heat the oil in a large heavy pan and add the garlic, onion and pepper. Fry gently for 4–5 minutes until softened.

3 Add the beef and fry until browned, then stir in the chilli, cumin, cayenne pepper, tomatoes, tomato purée, 60ml/4 tbsp water and the herbs. Bring to a boil, then reduce the heat, cover and simmer for about 25 minutes, stirring occasionally.

4 Stir in the kidney beans and cook, uncovered, for 5 minutes. Remove from the heat and stir in the chopped coriander. Season well and set aside.

5 Cut the baked potatoes in half and place them in serving bowls. Top with the chilli mixture and a dollop of sour cream. Garnish with chopped fresh marjoram and serve hot accompanied by a few lettuce leaves.

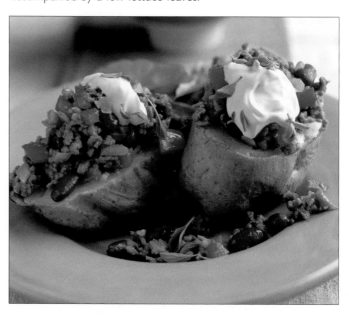

Beef in Peanut Sauce Energy 365kcal/1529kJ; Protein 30.8g; Carbohydrate 17.5g, of which sugars 16.4g; Fat 19.6g, of which saturates 6.2g; Cholesterol 65mg; Calcium 64mg; Fibre 1.2g; Sodium 238mg.
Tex-mex Potatoes Energy 327kcal/1369kJ; Protein 17.7g; Carbohydrate 30.6g, of which sugars 8.2g; Fat 15.7g, of which saturates 6.4g; Cholesterol 43mg; Calcium 71mg; Fibre 5.2g; Sodium 277mg.

Spicy Meat and Potato Fritters

These tasty meat and
potato balls are spiced
with coriander and cumin
seeds and then lightly fried.
Serve simply with a dipping
sauce or chutney as a snack
or with rice and salad for a
more substantial meal.

Makes 30

450g/1lb floury potatoes, such as
   Maris Piper or King Edward
450g/1lb lean minced
   (ground) beef
1 onion, quartered
1 bunch spring onions
   (scallions), chopped
3 garlic cloves, crushed
5ml/1 tsp ground nutmeg
15ml/1 tbsp coriander seeds,
   dry-fried and ground
10ml/2 tsp cumin seeds,
   dry-fried and ground
4 eggs, beaten
oil for shallow-frying
salt and ground black pepper

1 Cook the potatoes in a large pan of boiling salted water for
15–20 minutes, or until tender, then drain well and leave to one
side to cool slightly.

2 While the potatoes are still warm, mash them in the pan
until they are well broken up. Add to the minced beef and mix
well together.

3 Finely chop the onion, spring onions and garlic. Add to the
meat and potato mixture with the ground nutmeg, coriander
and cumin. Stir in enough of the beaten egg to give a soft
consistency that can be formed into fritters. Season to taste
with salt and ground black pepper.

4 Heat enough oil in a large frying pan for shallow-frying.
Using a dessertspoon, scoop out 6–8 oval-shaped fritters and
drop them into the hot oil. Leave to cook without turning so
that they keep their shape (this will take about 3–5 minutes)
and then turn over and cook for a further minute until they
are evenly browned all over.

5 Drain the fritters well on kitchen paper and keep warm
while cooking the remaining fritters. When the mixture is used
up, transfer the fritters to a large platter and serve hot.

Beef Tagine with Sweet Potatoes

This warming dish of tender
beef and succulent sweet
potatoes is eaten during the
winter in Morocco, where it
can get surprisingly cold.

Serves 4

675–900g/1½–2lb braising or
   stewing beef
30ml/2 tbsp sunflower oil
a good pinch of ground turmeric
1 large onion, chopped
1 red or green chilli, seeded
   and chopped
7.5ml/1½ tsp paprika
a good pinch of cayenne pepper
2.5ml/½ tsp ground cumin
450g/1lb sweet potatoes
15ml/1 tbsp chopped
   fresh parsley
15ml/1 tbsp chopped fresh
   coriander (cilantro)
15g/½ oz/1 tbsp butter
salt and ground black pepper

1 Cube the beef. Heat the oil in a flameproof casserole and fry
the meat, with the turmeric and seasoning, for 3–4 minutes
until evenly brown, stirring frequently.

2 Cover the pan with a tight-fitting lid and cook for 15 minutes
over a fairly gentle heat, without lifting the lid. Preheat the oven
to 180°C/350°F/Gas 4.

3 Add the onion, chilli, paprika, cayenne pepper and cumin
to the casserole, with just enough water to cover the meat.
Cover tightly and cook in the oven for 1–1½ hours until the
meat is very tender, checking occasionally and adding a little
extra water to keep the stew moist.

4 Meanwhile, peel the sweet potatoes and slice them straight
into a bowl of salted water. Transfer to a pan, bring to the boil
and simmer for 3 minutes until just tender. Drain.

5 Stir the herbs into the meat. Arrange the potato slices over
the top of the meat and dot with the butter. Cover and bake
for 10 minutes more.

6 Increase the oven temperature to 200°C/400°F/Gas 6 or
heat the grill (broiler). Remove the lid of the casserole and
cook in the oven or under the grill for a further 5–10 minutes
until the potatoes are golden.

Spicy Meat Fritters Energy 83kcal/346kJ; Protein 4.1g; Carbohydrate 2.9g, of which sugars 0.4g; Fat 6.3g, of which saturates 1.6g; Cholesterol 35mg; Calcium 10mg; Fibre 0.2g; Sodium 24mg.
Beef Tagine Energy 301kcal/1254kJ; Protein 21.9g; Carbohydrate 12g, of which sugars 3.2g; Fat 18.7g, of which saturates 4.6g; Cholesterol 61mg; Calcium 18mg; Fibre 1.4g; Sodium 67mg.

Roast Pork and Glazed Potatoes

For this pork and potato recipe, select a bone-in pork loin with the skin left on for the crackling.

Serves 8–10

2.25kg/5lb bone-in pork loin,
10ml/2 tsp mustard powder
15 whole cloves
2 bay leaves
900ml/1½ pints/3¾ cups water
175ml/6fl oz/¾ cup single (light)
   cream (optional)
salt and white pepper
braised red cabbage, to serve

For the glazed potatoes

900g/2lb small potatoes
50g/2oz/¼ cup caster
   (superfine) sugar
65g/2½ oz/5 tbsp butter

For the apples with redcurrant jelly

750ml/1¼ pints/3 cups water
115g/4oz/generous ½ cup soft
   light brown sugar
5ml/1 tsp lemon juice
4–5 tart apples, peeled, cored
   and halved
60–75ml/4–5 tbsp redcurrant jelly

1 Preheat the oven to 200°C/400°F/Gas 6. Score the pork skin and rub with the salt, pepper and mustard powder. Push the cloves and bay leaves into the skin. Place the pork, skin side up, on a rack in a roasting pan and cook for 1 hour, until the skin is crisp. Pour the water into the pan and cook for 30 minutes.

2 Boil the potatoes in salted water for 15–20 minutes, or until soft. Drain, peel and keep warm. Melt the sugar in a frying pan over a low heat until it turns light brown. Add the potatoes and butter and cook for 6–8 minutes. Keep warm.

3 Bring the water for the apples to the boil in a pan and stir in sugar, lemon juice and apple halves. Lower the heat and simmer until the apples are just tender. Remove the apples and spoon 7.5ml/1½ tsp jelly into the hollow of each half. Keep warm.

4 Transfer the pork to a serving dish and rest in a warm place for 15 minutes before carving. Meanwhile, make the gravy: pour the roasting pan juices into a pan and reduce over a medium heat. Whisk in a little cream if you wish, and season to taste.

5 Remove the crackling from the pork. Serve the pork with the gravy, potatoes, poached apple halves and crackling.

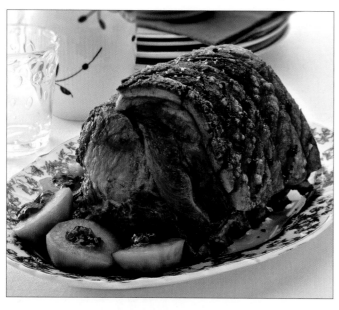

Pork and Potato Hotpot

Making this dish in the slow cooker makes the pork chops meltingly tender and allows the potato slices to soak up all the delicious juices from the meat.

Serves 4

25g/1oz/2 tbsp butter
15ml/1 tbsp oil

1 large onion, very thinly sliced
1 garlic clove, crushed
225g/8oz/generous 3 cups button
   (white) mushrooms, sliced
1.5ml/¼ tsp dried mixed herbs
900g/2lb potatoes, thinly sliced
4 thick pork chops
750ml/1¼ pints/3 cups vegetable
   or chicken stock
salt and ground black pepper

1 Use 15g/½oz/1 tbsp of the butter to grease the base and halfway up the sides of the ceramic cooking pot.

2 Heat the oil in a frying pan, add the sliced onion and cook gently for about 5 minutes, until softened and translucent. Add the garlic and mushrooms to the pan and cook for a further 5 minutes until softened. Remove the pan from the heat and stir in the mixed herbs.

3 Spoon half the mushroom mixture into the base of the ceramic cooking pot, then arrange half the potato slices on top and season with salt and ground black pepper.

4 Using a sharp knife, trim as much fat as possible from the pork chops, then place them on top of the potatoes in a single layer. Pour about half the stock over the top to cover the potatoes and prevent them discolouring.

5 Continue to layer the mushroom mixture and the sliced potatoes, finishing with a layer of neatly overlapping potatoes. Pour over the remaining stock; it should just cover the top layer of potatoes, so use a little more or less if necessary. Dot the remaining butter on top of the potatoes and cover with the lid.

6 Cook the stew on high for 4–5 hours, or until the potatoes and meat are tender when pierced with a thin skewer. If you like, place the hotpot under a medium grill (broiler) for 5–10 minutes to brown before serving.

Roast Pork Energy 654kcal/2735kJ; Protein 36.9g; Carbohydrate 39.5g, of which sugars 26.2g; Fat 39.9g, of which saturates 16.1g; Cholesterol 124mg; Calcium 36mg; Fibre 1.5g; Sodium 152mg.
Pork Hotpot Energy 511kcal/2132kJ; Protein 17.9g; Carbohydrate 41.5g, of which sugars 6.5g; Fat 31.5g, of which saturates 12.1g; Cholesterol 67mg; Calcium 40mg; Fibre 3.7g; Sodium 529mg.

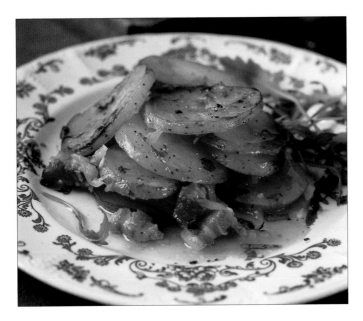

Oven-cooked Potatoes with Bacon

This traditional Welsh potato dish is often called Miser's Feast, referring to the fact that it could have been cooked over a log fire and eaten over several days. This is delicious served with a crisp salad or stir-fried vegetables, or as an ideal accompaniment to grilled sausages.

Serves 4
15ml/1 tbsp oil
25g/1oz/2 tbsp butter
8 thick rindless bacon rashers
  (strips), chopped
2 onions, thinly sliced
1kg/2¼lb potatoes, thinly sliced
600ml/1 pint/2½ cups chicken or
  vegetable stock
ground black pepper
chopped fresh parsley, to garnish

1 Preheat the oven to 190°C/375°F/Gas 5. Heat the oil and butter in a wide flameproof casserole, add the bacon rashers and cook over a medium heat, stirring occasionally, until the bacon is just beginning to brown at the edges.

2 Add the thinly sliced onions and the cooked bacon to the casserole. Cook for between 5–10 minutes, making sure to stir occasionally, until the onions have slightly softened and turned a rich golden brown.

3 Add the potatoes and stir well. Pour in the stock and level the surface, pushing the potatoes and onions into the liquid. Season with black pepper.

4 Bring to the boil, cover and put into the hot oven. Cook for 30–40 minutes or until the vegetables are soft.

5 Remove the cover. Raise the oven temperature to 220°C/425°F/Gas 7 and cook for a further 15–20 minutes, until the top is crisp and golden brown. Garnish with some chopped parsley.

> **Variation**
> *Try adding a little chopped fresh sage, shredded wild garlic or leeks, or some grated mature cheese in step four.*

Prosciutto with Potato Rémoulade

Rémoulade is a classic piquant dressing based on mayonnaise. The traditional French version is flavoured with mustard, gherkins, capers and herbs, but simpler variations are seasoned only with mustard. This recipe pairs this tasty cream-enriched dressing with matchstick potatoes and delicate prosciutto for a light and elegant main course.

150ml/¼ pint/⅔ cup mayonnaise
150ml/¼ pint/⅔ cup double
  (heavy) cream
5–10ml/1–2 tsp Dijon mustard
juice of ½ lime
30ml/2 tbsp olive oil
12 prosciutto slices
450g/1lb asparagus
  spears, halved
salt and ground black pepper
25g/1oz wild rocket (arugula),
  to garnish
extra virgin olive oil, to serve

Serves 4
2 potatoes, each weighing about
  175g/6oz, quartered lengthways

1 Put the potatoes in a large pan. Add water to cover and bring to the boil. Add salt, then simmer for about 15 minutes, or until the potatoes are tender, but do not let them get too soft. Drain thoroughly and leave to cool and then cut into long, thin strips.

2 Beat together the mayonnaise, cream, mustard, lime juice and seasoning in a large bowl. Add the potatoes and stir carefully to coat them with the dressing.

3 Heat the oil in a griddle or frying pan and cook the prosciutto in batches until crisp and golden. Use a slotted spoon to remove the ham, draining each piece well.

4 Add the asparagus to the pan and cook in the fat remaining in the pan for about 3 minutes, or until just tender and golden.

5 Put a generous spoonful of potato rémoulade on each plate and top with several slices of prosciutto. Add the asparagus and garnish with rocket. Serve immediately, offering olive oil to drizzle over.

Potatoes with Bacon Energy 396kcal/1659kJ; Protein 42.7g; Carbohydrate 19.2g, of which sugars 4.4g; Fat 16.9g, of which saturates 6.7g; Cholesterol 177mg; Calcium 29mg; Fibre 1.5g; Sodium 310mg.
Rémoulade Energy 612kcal/2530kJ; Protein 13.1g; Carbohydrate 18.6g, of which sugars 5.4g; Fat 56.5g, of which saturates 16.8g; Cholesterol 99mg; Calcium 74mg; Fibre 3.1g; Sodium 693mg.

Potato, Pancetta and Parmesan Galette

This richly flavoured, potato-topped 'pie' is a perfect winter warmer. A mandolin will make quick work of the potatoes, slicing them thinly, but be careful of your fingers because the blade is sharp.

Serves 4

30ml/2 tbsp garlic-infused olive oil
450g/1lb waxy potatoes, peeled and very thinly sliced
6 pancetta slices
50g/2oz/²⁄₃ cup freshly grated Parmesan cheese
salt and ground black pepper

1 Preheat the oven to 180°C/350°F/Gas 4. Brush a 20cm/8in ovenproof dish with some of the oil.

2 Arrange one-third of the sliced potatoes in the bottom of the ovenproof dish, season with salt and pepper and lay three slices of pancetta over the top. Sprinkle over a little cheese and arrange another layer of potatoes on the top.

3 Lay the remaining pancetta on top of the potatoes, sprinkle with a little more of the Parmesan and season with more salt and pepper.

4 Top with the remaining potatoes, season with salt and pepper and drizzle over the remaining olive oil. Press the potatoes down firmly and cover the tin with foil.

5 Bake for 30–35 minutes, then uncover and sprinkle with the remaining Parmesan. Bake for a further 15–20 minutes, or until golden brown on top.

6 Leave to rest for about 10–15 minutes, then cut into wedges and serve immediately.

Cook's Tip
Flavouring olive oil with garlic is very simple, it is ready to use in 2 weeks and it can be stored in a cool, dry place for 3–6 months.

Shropshire Bacon and Potato Pie

This classic combination of potatoes, onions, apples and bacon is packed inside a pastry crust and would have been typical of the thrifty and filling food that was fed to farm workers at the end of a long hard day in the fields.

Serves 4–5

75g/3oz plain (all-purpose) flour
75g/3oz plain wholemeal (whole-wheat) flour
pinch of salt
40g/1½oz/3 tbsp lard, diced
40g/1½oz/3 tbsp butter, diced
15ml/1 tbsp oil
225g/8oz lean bacon or gammon (smoked or cured ham), cut into small strips
2 medium onions, thinly sliced
450g/1lb potatoes, thinly sliced
10ml/2 tsp sugar
2 medium cooking apples, peeled cored and sliced
4 fresh sage leaves, finely chopped
salt and ground black pepper
300ml/½ pint/1¼ cups vegetable stock or medium dry (hard) cider
beaten egg or milk, to glaze

1 Sift the two flours and salt into a bowl and rub in the fats until the mixture resembles fine crumbs. Mix in enough cold water to bind the mixture, gathering it into a ball of dough. Chill for 30 minutes.

2 Preheat the oven to 180°C/350°F/Gas 4. Heat the oil in a pan and cook the bacon until crisp. Transfer to a mixing bowl.

3 Add the onions, potatoes and sugar to the hot pan and brown until beginning to soften. Add to the bowl.

4 Add the apple slices to the bowl. Stir in the sage, season with salt and pepper and mix well. Transfer the mixture into a 1.5 litre/2½ pint/6¼ cup pie dish, level the surface and pour the stock or cider over.

5 Roll out the pastry on a lightly floured surface to a shape large enough to cover the dish. Brush the edges of the dish with milk or beaten egg. Lay the pastry lid over the top, trim the edges and make a slit in the centre. Brush with beaten egg or milk.

6 Put into the hot oven and cook for about 1 hour, until the crust is golden brown and the filling is cooked through.

Potato Galette Energy 286kcal/1191kJ; Protein 9.8g; Carbohydrate 18.1g, of which sugars 1.5g; Fat 19.9g, of which saturates 5.8g; Cholesterol 25mg; Calcium 158mg; Fibre 1.1g; Sodium 385mg.
Shropshire Pie Energy 436kcal/1824kJ; Protein 12.7g; Carbohydrate 42.7g, of which sugars 8.2g; Fat 25g, of which saturates 10.7g; Cholesterol 48mg; Calcium 43mg; Fibre 4g; Sodium 754mg.

Pork Escalopes with Potato Rösti

The juices from the pork cook into the apples and potatoes, giving them a wonderful flavour as well as making a delicious sauce.

Serves 4
2 large potatoes, finely grated
1 medium Bramley apple, grated
2 garlic cloves, crushed
1 egg, beaten
butter, for greasing

15ml/1 tbsp olive oil
4 large slices prosciutto
4 pork escalopes, about
    175g/6oz each
4 sage leaves
1 medium Bramley apple,
    cut into thin wedges
25g/1oz/2 tbsp unsalted
    butter, diced
salt and ground black pepper
caramelized apple wedges,
    to serve

1 Preheat the oven to 200°C/400°F/Gas 6. Squeeze out all the excess liquid from the grated potatoes and apple. Mix the grated ingredients together with the garlic, egg and seasoning.

2 Divide the potatoes into four portions and spoon each quarter on to a baking sheet that has been lined with foil and greased. Form a circle with the potatoes and flatten out slightly with the back of a spoon. Drizzle with a little olive oil. Bake for 10 minutes.

3 Meanwhile, lay the prosciutto on a clean surface and place a pork escalope on top. Lay a sage leaf and a quarter of the apple wedges over each escalope and top each piece with the butter. Wrap the prosciutto around each piece of meat, making sure it is covered completely.

4 Remove the potatoes from the oven, place each pork parcel on top and return to the oven for 20 minutes. Carefully lift the pork and potatoes off the foil and serve with caramelized wedges of apple and any cooking juices on the side.

Cook's Tips
• *Be careful not to overcook the pork as it will start to dry out.*
• *Do not grate the potato until just before it is needed: if left for a prolonged period it will take on an unappetizing grey hue.*

Bacon and Herb Potato Rösti

This version of the traditional potato dish from Switzerland is enhanced by the addition of bacon and plenty of fresh herbs.

Serves 4
450g/1lb potatoes, left whole
    and unpeeled

30ml/2 tbsp olive oil
1 red onion, finely chopped
4 lean back bacon rashers
    (strips), rinded and diced
15ml/1 tbsp potato flour
30ml/2 tbsp chopped fresh
    mixed herbs
salt and ground black pepper
fresh parsley sprigs, to garnish

1 Lightly grease a baking sheet. Par-boil the potatoes in a pan of lightly salted, boiling water for about 6 minutes. Drain the potatoes and set aside to cool slightly.

2 Once cool enough to handle, peel the potatoes and coarsely grate them into a bowl. Set aside.

3 Heat 15ml/1 tbsp of the oil in a frying pan, add the onion and bacon and cook gently for 5 minutes, stirring occasionally. Preheat the oven to 220°C/425°F/Gas 7.

4 Remove the pan from the heat. Stir the onion mixture, remaining oil, potato flour, herbs and seasoning into the grated potatoes and mix well.

5 Divide the mixture into eight small piles and spoon them on to the prepared baking sheet, leaving a little space between each pile of the mixture.

6 Bake in the oven for about 20–25 minutes until the rösti are crisp and golden brown. Serve immediately, garnished with sprigs of fresh parsley.

Variation
This dish is also delicious when made with either chopped streaky (fatty) bacon or cooked ham in place of the lean back bacon, if you prefer.

Pork Escalopes Energy 396kcal/1659kJ; Protein 42.7g; Carbohydrate 19.2g, of which sugars 4.4g; Fat 16.9g, of which saturates 6.7g; Cholesterol 177mg; Calcium 29mg; Fibre 1.5g; Sodium 310mg.
Bacon Rösti Energy 245kcal/1025kJ; Protein 10.7g; Carbohydrate 23.6.g, of which sugars 1.8g; Fat 12.6g, of which saturates 2.9g; Cholesterol 146mg; Calcium 32mg; Fibre 2.6g; Sodium 572mg.

Chorizo Sausage, Potato and Spring Onion Hash

This moreishly spicy dish is really easy to make and is a great way to use up any leftover boiled potatoes, if you have them. The potatoes will absorb some of the delicious spicy flavours of the chorizo.

Serves 4
450g/1lb fresh chorizo sausages
15ml/1 tbsp olive oil
450g/1lb cooked potatoes, cut into small chunks
1 bunch of spring onions (scallions), sliced
salt and ground black pepper

1 Heat a large frying pan over a medium heat and add the chorizo sausages. Cook for around 8–10 minutes, turning occasionally, until cooked through. Remove the sausages from the pan and set aside.

2 Add the olive oil to the sausage fat in the pan and when hot add the chunks of potato. Cook them over a low heat for between 5–8 minutes, turning occasionally until golden brown and coated in the chorizo juices.

3 Meanwhile, cut the chorizo sausages into bitesize chunks and add to the pan with the potatoes.

4 Add the spring onions to the pan and cook for a couple more minutes, until they are piping hot. Season with salt and pepper, and serve immediately.

> **Cook's Tips**
> • Fresh chorizo sausages are available from good butchers or from Spanish delicatessens and larger supermarkets. They often come in different varieties, with some being hotter and spicier than others – choose those that match your taste.
> • If you don't have any leftover cooked potatoes then simply boil some from scratch in plenty of salted water until tender. Leave them aside to cool completely before cutting into small chunks and adding them to the frying pan, as specified above.

Mushroom, Bacon and Potato Rösti

Dried ceps or porcini mushrooms have a wonderful woody, earthy aroma and taste. With salty bacon lardons, they turn potato rösti into a memorable supper.

Serves 4
675g/1½lb floury potatoes
10g/¼oz dried ceps or porcini mushrooms
225g/8oz very thick smoked bacon, cut into lardons or thin strips
2 fresh thyme sprigs, chopped
30ml/2 tbsp chopped fresh parsley
30ml/2 tbsp vegetable oil
4 large eggs, to serve
1 bunch watercress, to garnish
crushed black peppercorns, to garnish

1 Cook the potatoes in a pan of boiling salted water for 5 minutes and no longer, as they need to remain firm enough to grate at the next stage.

2 Meanwhile, cover the mushrooms with boiling water and leave to soften for 5–10 minutes. Drain and chop.

3 Fry the bacon gently in a non-stick pan until all the fat has run out. Remove the bacon using a slotted spoon and reserve the fat for later.

4 Drain the potatoes and leave to cool. When they are cool enough to handle, grate them coarsely, then pat dry thoroughly on kitchen paper to remove all moisture. Place them in a large bowl and add the mushrooms, thyme, parsley and bacon. Mix together well.

5 Heat the bacon fat with a little of the oil in the frying pan until it is really hot. Spoon in the rösti mixture in heaps and flatten out. Fry in small batches for about 6 minutes until crisp and golden on both sides, turning once. Drain off excess oil on kitchen paper and keep warm in a low oven.

6 Heat the remaining oil in the hot pan and fry the eggs as you like them. Serve the rösti immediately with the eggs, watercress and crushed peppercorns.

Wild Mushroom Rösti Energy 387kcal/1616kJ; Protein 18.5g; Carbohydrate 27.2g, of which sugars 2.2g; Fat 23.6g, of which saturates 6.4g; Cholesterol 220mg; Calcium 42mg; Fibre 1.7g; Sodium 955mg.
Chorizo Hash Energy 522kcal/2172kJ; Protein 14.4g; Carbohydrate 29.6g, of which sugars 3.8g; Fat 39.3g, of which saturates 14.3g; Cholesterol 53mg; Calcium 63mg; Fibre 2.1g; Sodium 869mg.

Eggs Baked in Ham and Potato Hash

This dish is based on the traditional hash, but with ham replacing the more common corned beef. It is a great way to use up any leftover meat or potatoes.

Serves 6
50g/2oz/2 tbsp butter
1 large onion, chopped
350g/12oz cooked ham, diced
450g/1lb cooked potatoes, diced
115g/4oz mature (sharp) Cheddar
    cheese, grated
30ml/2 tbsp tomato ketchup
15–30ml/1–2 tbsp
    Worcestershire sauce
6 eggs
few drops of Tabasco sauce
salt and ground black pepper
15ml/1 tbsp chopped fresh
    parsley, to garnish

1 Preheat the oven to 325°F/170°C/Gas 3. Melt half of the butter in a frying pan. Cook the onion until soft, stirring occasionally.

2 Place the onion in a mixing bowl. Add the ham, potatoes, cheese, ketchup and Worcestershire sauce. Season with salt and pepper. Stir the mixture to combine.

3 Spread the hash in a lightly greased baking dish in a layer about 2.5cm/1in deep. Bake for 10 minutes.

4 Make six hollows in the hash. Break an egg into each hollow.

5 Melt the remaining butter in a small pan. Season with a few drops of Tabasco sauce to taste. Drizzle the seasoned butter over the eggs and hash.

6 Bake for 15–20 minutes or until the eggs are set and cooked to your taste. Serve immediately, in the dish, garnished with the chopped parsley.

Cook's Tip
If you prefer your food a little spicier then simply add a little more of the Tabasco sauce into the butter.

Swedish Pork and Potato Hash

This Swedish potato hash was originally introduced as an economy dish made with leftovers. Its popularity has meant that it is invariably now made using only fresh ingredients.

Serves 3–4
4 large potatoes
about 25g/1oz/2 tbsp butter
15ml/1 tbsp vegetable oil
1 large onion, finely chopped
150g/5oz gammon (smoked
    or cured ham) or bacon,
    finely chopped
100g/4oz smoked frankfurters,
    finely chopped
500g/1¼lb cold cooked lamb or
    beef, cubed
salt and ground black pepper
3–4 very fresh eggs, to serve
Worcestershire sauce, to serve
chopped fresh parsley, to garnish

1 Peel and cut the potatoes into small cubes measuring about 3mm/⅛in. Heat the butter and oil in a large frying pan, add the potato cubes and fry for about 20 minutes, stirring frequently, until golden brown. Remove from the pan with a slotted spoon, put in a bowl and keep warm.

2 Put the onion in the pan, adding more butter if necessary, and fry until golden brown. Remove from the pan and add to the potatoes. Add the gammon or bacon and the frankfurter sausages, fry until cooked and put them in the bowl.

3 Fry the beef or lamb until heated through and add to the other fried ingredients. Season the mixture with salt and pepper to taste and mix together.

4 Serve the mixture on warmed, individual plates. Break the eggs, one at a time, separating the yolks from the whites, and putting an egg yolk in half its shell in the centre of each plate. Garnish with parsley and serve with Worcestershire sauce.

Cook's Tip
Make sure that the eggs are fresh and, because the recipe contains raw egg yolks, do not serve the dish to infants, the elderly, pregnant women, and convalescents.

Egg Hash Energy 305kcal/1275kJ; Protein 19.7g; Carbohydrate 18.2g, of which sugars 5.9g; Fat 17.2g, of which saturates 9.9g; Cholesterol 135mg; Calcium 180mg; Fibre 1.5g; Sodium 1020mg.
Swedish Hash Energy 930kcal/3866kJ; Protein 55.9g; Carbohydrate 18.7g, of which sugars 3.6g; Fat 70.9g, of which saturates 28.8g; Cholesterol 427mg; Calcium 68mg; Fibre 1.3g; Sodium 1992mg.

Pork and Leek Sausages with Mustard Mashed Potato and Gravy

Tangy mustard, mashed potato and rich onion gravy are the perfect partners to delicious grilled sausages.

Serves 4

12 pork and leek sausages
salt and ground black pepper

For the onion gravy
30ml/2 tbsp olive oil
25g/1oz/2 tbsp butter
8 onions, sliced
5ml/1 tsp caster (superfine) sugar
15ml/1 tbsp plain
  (all-purpose) flour
300ml/½ pint/1¼ cups beef stock

For the mash
1.5kg/3¼lb potatoes
50g/2oz/¼ cup butter
150ml/¼ pint/⅔ cup double
  (heavy) cream
15ml/1 tbsp wholegrain mustard

1 Heat the oil and butter in a large pan until foaming. Add the onions and mix well to coat them in the fat. Cover and cook gently for about 30 minutes, stirring frequently. Add the sugar and cook for a further 5 minutes, or until the onions are softened, reduced and caramelized.

2 Remove the pan from the heat and stir in the flour, then gradually stir in the stock. Return the pan to the heat. Bring to the boil, stirring, then simmer for 3 minutes, or until thickened. Season.

3 Meanwhile, cook the potatoes in a pan of boiling salted water for 20 minutes, or until tender.

4 While the potatoes are cooking, preheat the grill (broiler) to medium. Arrange the sausages in a single layer in the grill pan and cook, turning occasionally, for around 15–20 minutes, or until cooked and evenly brown.

5 Drain the potatoes well and mash them with the butter, double cream and wholegrain mustard. Season with salt and pepper to taste.

6 Serve the sausages with the creamy mustard mash and plenty of onion gravy.

Potato and Sausage Casserole

You will find numerous variations of this delicious supper dish throughout Britain, but the basic ingredients are the same wherever you go – potatoes, sausages and bacon. It is a great dish to feed the family.

Serves 4

15ml/1 tbsp vegetable oil
4 bacon rashers (strips), cut into
  2.5cm/1in pieces
2 large onions, chopped
2 garlic cloves, crushed
8 large pork sausages
4 large baking potatoes,
  thinly sliced
1.5ml/¼ tsp fresh sage
300ml/½ pint/1¼ cups
  vegetable stock
salt and ground black pepper
soda bread, to serve

1 Preheat the oven to 180°C/350°F/Gas 4. Grease a large ovenproof dish and set aside.

2 Heat the oil in a frying pan. Add the bacon and fry for 2 minutes. Add the onions and fry for 5–6 minutes until golden. Add the garlic and fry for 1 minute, making sure that it doesn't burn, then remove the mixture from the pan and set aside.

3 Add the sausages to the empty pan and fry for 5–6 minutes until golden brown.

4 Arrange the potatoes in the base of the prepared dish. Spoon the bacon and onion mixture on top. Season with the salt and pepper and sprinkle with the fresh sage.

5 Pour on the stock and top with the sausages. Cover and bake for 1 hour. Serve hot with fresh soda bread.

Cook's Tip
The success of this dish will depend on the quality of the sausages you use. Try to use the best you can find – a local butcher will usually make their own, which will often be of better quality than those from a supermarket.

Pork Sausages Energy 939kcal/3913kJ; Protein 19.9g; Carbohydrate 85g, of which sugars 16.7g; Fat 60g, of which saturates 28.6g; Cholesterol 133mg; Calcium 179mg; Fibre 6.6g; Sodium 942mg.
Sausage Casserole Energy 553kcal/2305kJ; Protein 17.4g; Carbohydrate 48.7g, of which sugars 10g; Fat 33.4g, of which saturates 11.8g; Cholesterol 51mg; Calcium 74mg; Fibre 4g; Sodium 1019mg.

Pork and Garlic Sausage Casserole with Potatoes and Apple

This hearty and filling slow-cooked casserole contains a variety of pork cuts along with flavoursome onion, sauerkraut and potatoes. The light ale helps to tenderize the meat, and adds a robust flavour to the sauce.

Serves 6

45ml/3 tbsp sunflower oil
225g/8oz lean, smoked bacon, rinded and diced
450g/1lb lean shoulder of pork, trimmed and cut into 2.5cm/1in cubes
1 large onion, sliced
900g/2lb potatoes, thickly sliced
250ml/8fl oz/1 cup light ale
225g/8oz/2 cups German garlic sausage, skinned and sliced
500g/1¼lb/2¼ cups sauerkraut, drained
2 red eating apples, cored and sliced
5ml/1 tsp caraway seeds
salt and ground black pepper

1 Preheat the oven to 180°C/350°F/Gas 4. Heat 30ml/2 tbsp of the sunflower oil in a flameproof casserole. Fry the bacon for 2–3 minutes, stirring frequently, until beginning to colour.

2 Add the cubes of pork and cook for 4–5 minutes until lightly browned on all sides. Remove the bacon and pork cubes from the pan and set aside.

3 Add the remaining oil to the pan and gently cook the onion for 6–8 minutes, until soft. Return the meat to the pan and add the sliced potatoes, stirring to mix.

4 Pour the ale into the pan and stir gently to mix. Bring the mixture to the boil, then reduce the heat. Cover the pan with a tight-fitting lid and cook in the preheated oven for 45 minutes.

5 Stir the garlic sausage, drained sauerkraut, sliced apple and caraway seeds into the pan. Season with salt and ground black pepper to taste.

6 Return the casserole to the oven and cook for a further 30 minutes, or until the meat is tender. Serve immediately.

Dublin Potato and Sausage Coddle

This truly Irish dish combines bacon and sausages, two foods known since the earliest Irish literature, and is said to have been the favourite meal of Jonathan Swift, the 18th-century Irish author of *Gulliver's Travels*. Leeks and oatmeal were originally used but potatoes and onion are popular nowadays. As with very simple dishes, the success of coddle lies in the superiority of the ingredients selected.

Makes 4 large or 8 small portions

8 x 8mm/⅓in thick ham or dry-cured bacon slices
8 best-quality lean pork sausages
4 large onions, thinly sliced
900g/2lb potatoes, peeled and sliced
90ml/6 tbsp chopped fresh parsley
salt and ground black pepper

1 Cut the ham or bacon into large chunks and cook with the sausages in 1.2 litres/2 pints/5 cups boiling water for about 5 minutes. Drain, but reserve the cooking liquor.

2 Put the meat and sausages into a pan or ovenproof dish with the sliced onions, potatoes and the chopped parsley. Season with salt and ground black pepper, and add just enough of the reserved cooking liquor to cover. Cover with a tight-fitting lid; lay a piece of buttered foil or baking parchment on top before putting on the lid.

3 Simmer gently over a low heat for about 1 hour, or until the liquid is reduced by half and all the ingredients are cooked but not too mushy. Serve immediately with the vegetables on top, with the traditional accompaniments of fresh soda bread and a glass of stout, if you like.

Cook's Tip
The traditional accompaniments to this dish are fresh soda bread and glasses of stout, but a crisp green vegetable, such as lightly cooked Brussels sprouts or purple sprouting broccoli, makes a nice contrast.

Garlic Sausage Energy 472kcal/1976kJ; Protein 32g; Carbohydrate 37.7g, of which sugars 11.7g; Fat 21.6g, of which saturates 6.2g; Cholesterol 110mg; Calcium 91mg; Fibre 5.3g; Sodium 1449mg.
Dublin Coddle Energy 432kcal/1809kJ; Protein 20.6g; Carbohydrate 52g, of which sugars 10.2g; Fat 17.2g, of which saturates 6.1g; Cholesterol 45mg; Calcium 83mg; Fibre 5.7g; Sodium 1.27g.

Chorizo with Garlic Potatoes

A classic tapas recipe, this simple dish can be served in small quantities as a snack or, as here, in slightly larger proportions for a lunch. The bitesized chunks of potato are the perfect foil to the spicy chorizo and soak up all the delicious smoky flavours of the sausage.

Serves 4

450g/1lb potatoes
3 eggs, hard-boiled and
*   quartered*
175g/6oz chorizo sausage, sliced
150ml/¼ pint/⅔ cup mayonnaise
150ml/¼ pint/⅔ cup sour cream
2 garlic cloves, crushed
salt and ground black pepper
30ml/2 tbsp chopped fresh
*   coriander (cilantro), to garnish*

1 Cook the potatoes in a pan of boiling salted water for about 15–20 minutes, or until tender. Drain them well and set aside to cool slightly.

2 Cut the potatoes into bitesize pieces. Place them in a large serving dish with the eggs and chorizo sausage, and season to taste with salt and pepper.

3 In a small bowl, mix together the mayonnaise, sour cream and garlic until well combined. Season to taste with salt and ground black pepper.

4 Spoon the sour cream and mayonnaise mixture over the potato and chorizo mixture in the serving dish.

5 Toss the salad gently to thoroughly coat all the ingredients with the sour cream and mayonnaise dressing, then sprinkle over some chopped coriander to garnish. Divide between four plates and serve immediately.

Variation
To give this dish a more piquant flavour, add about 15ml/ 1 tbsp finely chopped cornichons and 4 finely chopped anchovy fillets. If coriander isn't available, then use 15ml/1 tbsp fresh marjoram instead.

Spicy Spanish Potato, Chorizo and Cheese Tortilla

The classic Spanish tortilla contains only onions and potatoes, gently stewed in olive oil then stirred into eggs to make a thick cake-like omelette fried in a pan, then baked in the oven. Here, the combination of sliced potatoes with chilli and chorizo makes a potato cake with a real kick to it.

Serves 4

15ml/1 tbsp vegetable oil
½ onion, sliced
1 small green (bell) pepper,
*   cut into rings*
1 garlic clove, finely chopped
1 tomato, chopped
6 pitted black olives, chopped
275g/10oz cooked firm, waxy
*   potatoes, sliced*
225g/8oz sliced chorizo,
*   in strips*
1 fresh green chilli, chopped
50g/2oz/½ cup Cheddar
*   cheese, grated*
6 eggs
45ml/3 tbsp milk
1.5ml/¼ tsp ground cumin
1.5ml/¼ tsp dried oregano
1.5ml/¼ tsp paprika
salt and ground black pepper
rocket (arugula) leaves, to garnish

1 Preheat the oven to 190°C/375°F/Gas 5. Line the base of a 23cm/9in round cake tin (pan) with baking parchment.

2 Heat the oil in a large non-stick frying pan. Add the onion, green pepper and garlic and cook over a medium heat for 5–8 minutes until softened.

3 Spoon the onion mixture into the prepared tin with the tomato, olives, potatoes, chorizo and chilli. Mix the ingredients together until well combined and sprinkle the grated cheese over the top.

4 In a small bowl, whisk together the eggs and milk until frothy. Add the cumin, oregano, paprika and salt and pepper to taste. Pour the mixture on to the vegetables, tilting the tin so that the egg mixture spreads evenly.

5 Bake for 30 minutes until set and lightly golden. Serve in wedges, hot or cold, with rocket leaves.

Chorizo with Potatoes Energy 631kcal/2613kJ; Protein 12.7g; Carbohydrate 24.3g, of which sugars 4g; Fat 54.4g, of which saturates 15.5g; Cholesterol 214mg; Calcium 84mg; Fibre 1.4g; Sodium 582mg.
Spanish Tortilla Energy 439kcal/1824kJ; Protein 23.6g; Carbohydrate 13.1g, of which sugars 1.8g; Fat 32.4g, of which saturates 9.5g; Cholesterol 328mg; Calcium 285mg; Fibre 2.4g; Sodium 669mg.

Spring Onion, Potato and Pepperoni Tortilla

Cooked potatoes are delicious with spicy pepperoni in this thick Spanish-style omelette. Salad and crusty bread are excellent accompaniments.

Serves 4
30ml/2 tbsp olive oil
75g/3oz pepperoni, sliced

225g/8oz potatoes, cooked and
  cut into cubes
3 spring onions (scallions), sliced
115g/4oz Fontina cheese, cut
  into cubes
115g/4oz/1 cup frozen
  peas, thawed
6 eggs
30ml/2 tbsp chopped parsley
salt and ground black pepper

1 Heat the oil in a non-stick frying pan and add the potatoes, pepperoni and spring onions. Cook over a high heat for about 5 minutes, stirring occasionally, until the pepperoni releases some of its fat and the onions have softened. Add the cheese and peas, and stir to combine.

2 In a medium bowl, beat the eggs with the parsley and seasoning, then pour the mixture over the ingredients in the frying pan. Stir well to evenly distribute the egg mixture around the ingredients. Cook gently, without stirring, for about 10 minutes, or until the egg mixture is golden underneath.

3 When the mixture has almost set, cover the pan with a large plate and carefully invert the pan and its cover to turn out the tortilla. Slide the tortilla back into the pan and continue cooking for a further 10 minutes, or until browned underneath.

4 Carefully turn out the tortilla on to a large, flat serving platter and serve hot or warm, cut into slices.

> **Cook's Tip**
> If you do not have the confidence to invert the tortilla and replace it in the pan, simply finish cooking it under a preheated grill (broiler) for 5–8 minutes, or until just set.

Heaven and Earth Potatoes

This dish from Germany, whose name translates as 'heaven and earth', combines apples 'from heaven' and potatoes 'from the earth', and is served with slices of black pudding and crisp onion rings.

Serves 4
450g/1lb floury potatoes, peeled
  and quartered

350g/12oz cooking apples, cored,
  peeled and chopped
50g/2oz/¼ cup butter
2 cloves
pinch of nutmeg
30ml/2 tbsp sunflower oil
350g/12oz blutwurst or black
  pudding (blood sausage), cut
  into 1cm/½in slices
1 onion, sliced into rings
salt and ground black pepper

1 Put the potatoes in a large pan. Add water to cover and bring to the boil. Add salt, then simmer for about 15 minutes, or until the potatoes are tender, but do not let them get too soft. Drain thoroughly and leave to cool.

2 Meanwhile, put the chopped apples and 15g/½oz/1 tbsp of the butter in a small pan along with the cloves. Heat gently and simmer for about 10 minutes, until they are just soft but do not let them get too mushy. Leave to cool slightly.

3 Discard the cloves, then add the cooked apple to the pan with the cooked potato. Add the remaining butter, nutmeg and a little salt and ground black pepper.

4 Mash the mixture until smooth and creamy with a potato masher or pass it all through a food mill. Pile on to a serving plate and keep warm.

5 Meanwhile, heat the oil in a heavy frying pan and cook the slices of blutwurst or black pudding for 5 minutes, or until crisp. Remove from the pan with a slotted spoon and arrange to one side of the purée.

6 Add the onion rings to the pan and fry for 12–15 minutes, until lightly browned and crispy. Pile on top of the purée and serve immediately.

Potato Tortilla Energy 443kcal/1848kJ; Protein 16g; Carbohydrate 32.4g, of which sugars 3.6g; Fat 28.1g, of which saturates 12.3g; Cholesterol 49mg; Calcium 226mg; Fibre 1.9g; Sodium 728mg.
Heaven and Earth Energy 281kcal/1180kJ; Protein 15.6g; Carbohydrate 29.5g, of which sugars 4.5g; Fat 12g, of which saturates 6.1g; Cholesterol 25mg; Calcium 80mg; Fibre 1.7g; Sodium 1050mg.

Chicken with Summer Vegetables and Tarragon

This is an all-in-the-pot dish, with the chicken cooking liquid providing the stock for the potatoes and other vegetables as well as the sauce.

Serves 4
1.8kg/4lb boiling fowl
  (stewing chicken)
1 onion, peeled, studded with
  6 cloves
1 bay leaf

a sprig each of thyme and parsley
10 black peppercorns
12 small potatoes, washed
8 small shallots, peeled
vegetables of your choice, such as
  carrots, courgettes (zucchini),
  broad (fava) beans and peas,
  mangetouts (snowpeas)
25g/1oz/2 tbsp butter
30ml/2 tbsp plain
  (all-purpose) flour
60ml/4 tbsp chopped
  fresh tarragon

1 Wash the chicken and dry with kitchen paper. Place in a large pan with the onion, bay leaf, thyme, parsley and peppercorns, with water to cover. Bring to the boil, then reduce the heat and simmer gently for 1½ hours.

2 Remove the chicken from the pan and keep warm. Remove all the seasonings, either with a slotted spoon or by straining the mixture, then bring the cooking liquid back to the boil, skimming off any fat that may have appeared on the top.

3 Cook the vegetables in the liquid, putting the potatoes in first for a few minutes, then adding the shallots and carrots, if using, and finally any green vegetables that take no time at all. When the vegetables are cooked, place the chicken on a serving dish and surround with all the vegetables.

4 In a small pan, melt the butter, add the flour and stir to create a roux. Slowly add some liquor from the large pan until a sauce is created – about 600ml/1 pint/2½ cups – and allow to simmer for a few minutes to reduce down and strengthen the flavour. At the last moment stir in the chopped fresh tarragon, then ladle the sauce over the chicken and vegetables. Serve immediately.

Roast Chicken with Potatoes and Lemon

This is a lovely, easy dish for a family meal. As with other roasts, everything is baked together so that the potatoes absorb all the different flavours, especially that of the lemon.

Serves 4
1.6kg/3½lb chicken
2 garlic cloves, peeled,
  but left whole

15ml/1 tbsp chopped fresh thyme
  or oregano, or 5ml/1 tsp dried,
  plus 2–3 fresh sprigs of thyme
  or oregano
800g/1¾lb potatoes
juice of 1 lemon
60ml/4 tbsp extra virgin
  olive oil
300ml/½ pint/1¼ cups
  hot water
salt and ground black pepper

1 Preheat the oven to 200°C/400°F/Gas 6. Place the chicken, breast side down, in a large roasting pan, then tuck the garlic cloves and the thyme or oregano sprigs inside the bird.

2 Peel the potatoes and quarter them lengthways. If they are very large, slice them lengthways into thinner pieces. Arrange the potatoes around the chicken, then pour the lemon juice over the chicken and potatoes. Season with salt and pepper, drizzle the olive oil over the top and add about three-quarters of the chopped fresh or dried thyme or oregano. Pour the hot water into the roasting pan.

3 Roast the chicken and potatoes for 30 minutes, then remove the roasting pan from the oven and turn the chicken over.

4 Season the bird with a little more salt and pepper, sprinkle over the remaining fresh or dried herbs, and add a little more hot water, if needed. Reduce the oven temperature to 190°C/375°F/Gas 5.

5 Return the chicken and potatoes to the oven and roast them for another hour, or slightly longer, by which time both the chicken and the potatoes will be a golden colour. Serve with a crisp leafy salad.

Chicken and Tarragon Energy 713kcal/2973kJ; Protein 51.2g; Carbohydrate 39.3g, of which sugars 13g; Fat 40g, of which saturates 12.9g; Cholesterol 261mg; Calcium 103mg; Fibre 5.4g; Sodium 251mg.
Roast Chicken Energy 767kcal/3,195kJ; Protein 53.3g; Carbohydrate 32.5g, of which sugars 2.9g; Fat 47.7g, of which saturates 11.8g; Cholesterol 264mg; Calcium 51mg; Fibre 2.6g; Sodium 206mg.

Roast Lime Chicken with Sweet Potatoes

This chicken, delicately flavoured with garlic, turmeric and coriander, would traditionally be spit-roasted. However, it works very well as a conventional roast, and, cooked this way, it can be accompanied by the succulent addition of sweet potatoes flavoured with the delicious juices from the chicken.

Serves 4

4 garlic cloves, 2 finely chopped
  and 2 bruised but left whole
small bunch coriander (cilantro),
  with roots, coarsely chopped
10ml/2 tsp salt
5ml/1 tsp ground turmeric
5cm/2in piece fresh turmeric
1 roasting chicken, about
  1.5kg/3¼lb
1 lime, cut in half
4 medium/large sweet potatoes,
  peeled and cut into
  thick wedges
300ml/½ pint/1¼ cups chicken
  or vegetable stock
30ml/2 tbsp soy sauce
salt and ground black pepper

1 Preheat the oven to 190°C/375°F/Gas 5. Calculate the cooking time for the chicken, allowing 20 minutes per 500g/1¼lb, plus 20 minutes. Using a mortar and pestle or food processor, grind the chopped garlic, coriander, salt and turmeric to a paste.

2 Place the chicken in a roasting pan and smear it with the herb and spice paste. Squeeze the lime juice over and place the lime halves and garlic cloves in the cavity. Cover with foil and roast in the oven.

3 Meanwhile, bring a pan of water to the boil and par-boil the sweet potatoes for 10–15 minutes, until just tender. Drain well and place them around the chicken in the roasting pan. Baste with the cooking juices and sprinkle with salt and pepper. Replace the foil and return the chicken to the oven.

4 About 20 minutes before the end of the cooking time, remove the foil and baste the chicken with the juices. Turn the sweet potatoes over.

5 At the end of the calculated roasting time, check that the chicken is cooked. Lift it out of the roasting pan, tip it so that all the juices collected in the cavity drain into the pan, then place the bird on a carving board. Cover it with tented foil and leave it to rest before carving. Transfer the sweet potatoes to a serving dish and keep them hot in the oven while you make the gravy.

6 Pour away the oil from the roasting pan but retain the meat juices. Place the roasting pan on top of the stove and heat it until the juices are bubbling. Pour in the stock. Bring the mixture to the boil, stirring constantly with a wooden spoon and scraping the base of the pan to incorporate the residue.

7 Stir in the soy sauce and check the seasoning before straining the gravy into a jug (pitcher). Serve it with the carved chicken and the sweet potatoes.

Escalopes of Chicken with Baby Vegetables

This is a quick and light dish – ideal for summer, when it is too hot to slave over the stove for hours or to eat heavy meals. Flattening the chicken breast fillets thins and tenderizes the meat and also speeds up the cooking process. The fresh tomato mayonnaise brings out the sweet flavour of the potatoes.

Serves 4

4 skinless chicken breast fillets,
  each weighing 175g/6oz
juice of 1 lime
120ml/4fl oz/½ cup olive oil
675g/1½lb mixed baby potatoes,
  carrots, fennel (sliced if large),
  asparagus and peas
sea salt and ground black pepper
fresh flat leaf parsley sprigs,
  to garnish

For the tomato mayonnaise
150ml/¼ pint/⅔ cup mayonnaise
15ml/1 tbsp sun-dried
  tomato paste

1 Lay the chicken portions between two sheets of clear film (plastic wrap) or baking parchment and beat them flat with a rolling pin. Season the chicken with salt and pepper and sprinkle with the lime juice.

2 Heat 45ml/3 tbsp of the oil in a frying pan or griddle pan and fry the chicken for 10 minutes on each side, or until cooked.

3 Meanwhile, put the potatoes and carrots in a pan with the remaining oil and season with sea salt. Cover and cook over a medium heat for 10–15 minutes, stirring frequently. Add the fennel and cook for a further 5 minutes, stirring frequently. Finally, add the asparagus and peas and cook for 5 minutes more, or until all the vegetables are tender.

4 To make the sauce, mix together the mayonnaise and sun-dried tomato paste in a small bowl. Spoon the vegetables on to a warmed large serving platter or individual plates and arrange the chicken on top. Serve the tomato mayonnaise with the chicken and vegetables. Garnish with sprigs of flat leaf parsley.

Roast Lime Chicken Energy 620kcal/2581kJ; Protein 47g; Carbohydrate 21.3g, of which sugars 5.7g; Fat 38.9g, of which saturates 11.4g; Cholesterol 240mg; Calcium 43mg; Fibre 2.4g; Sodium 228mg.
Escalopes of Chicken Energy 513kcal/2143kJ; Protein 44g; Carbohydrate 18.9g, of which sugars 9g; Fat 29.6g, of which saturates 4.7g; Cholesterol 141mg; Calcium 41mg; Fibre 3.2g; Sodium 251mg.

Chicken and Vegetable Pot Au Feu

A lovely wine and herb-scented stock contains tender morsels of chicken and baby vegetables in this light and aromatic seasonal version of the French casserole.

Serves 4
1 chicken, about 2.25kg/5lb
1 parsley sprig
15ml/1 tbsp black peppercorns
1 bay leaf
300g/11oz baby carrots, washed and left whole
175g/6oz baby leeks, washed and left whole
25g/1oz/2 tbsp butter
15ml/1 tbsp olive oil
300g/11oz large shallots, halved
200ml/7fl oz/scant 1 cup dry white wine
800g/1¾lb baby new potatoes, scrubbed
120ml/4fl oz/½ cup double (heavy) cream
salt and ground black pepper
small bunch parsley or tarragon, chopped, to garnish

1 Joint the chicken into eight pieces and place the carcass in a large stockpot. Add the parsley sprig, peppercorns, bay leaf and the carrot and leek trimmings. Cover with cold water and bring to the boil. Simmer for about 45 minutes, then strain, reserving the stock for later.

2 Meanwhile, melt the butter with the olive oil in a frying pan, then add the chicken pieces. Add seasoning, and brown the chicken all over.

3 Transfer the chicken pieces to a plate and add the shallots to the pan. Cook over a low heat for 20 minutes, stirring occasionally, until softened, but not browned.

4 Return the chicken pieces to the pan and pour over the white wine. Scoop up any juices from the base of the pan with a wooden spoon.

5 Add the carrots, leeks and potatoes to the pan. Pour in enough stock to just cover the ingredients. Bring the mixture to the boil, then cover the pan and simmer for 20 minutes.

6 Stir the cream into the casserole. Transfer to a serving dish and garnish with the herbs. Serve immediately.

Chicken and Mushroom Potato Bake

This rich, creamy dish is simple to make in the slow cooker and is a hearty supper on a cold winter's day. The sauce combines with juices from the mushrooms and chicken during cooking to make a well-flavoured gravy that is soaked up by the potatoes.

Serves 4
4 large skinless chicken breast fillets, cut into chunks
15ml/1 tbsp olive oil
40g/1½oz/3 tbsp butter
1 leek, finely sliced into rings
25g/1oz/¼ cup plain (all-purpose) flour
550ml/18fl oz/2½ cups milk
5ml/1 tsp Worcestershire sauce (optional)
5ml/1 tsp wholegrain mustard
1 carrot, finely diced
225g/8oz/3 cups button (white) mushrooms, thinly sliced
900g/2lb potatoes, thinly sliced
salt and ground black pepper

1 Heat the olive oil in a large pan. Add the chicken and fry gently until beginning to brown. Remove the chicken from the pan using a slotted spoon, leaving any juices behind. Set aside.

2 Add 25g/1oz/2 tbsp of the butter to the pan and heat gently until melted. Stir in the leeks and fry gently for about 5 minutes. Sprinkle the flour over the leeks, then turn off the heat and gradually blend in the milk until smooth. Slowly bring the mixture to the boil, stirring all the time, until thickened.

3 Remove the pan from the heat and stir in the Worcestershire sauce, if using, mustard, diced carrot, mushrooms and chicken. Season generously.

4 Arrange enough potato slices to cover the base of the ceramic cooking pot. Spoon one-third of the chicken mixture over the top, then cover with another layer of potatoes. Repeat layering, finishing with a layer of potatoes. Dot the remaining butter on top.

5 Cover and cook on high for 4 hours, or until the potatoes are cooked and tender when pierced with a skewer. If you like, place the dish under a moderate grill (broiler) for 5 minutes to brown, then serve immediately.

Chicken Pot Au Feu Energy 613kcal/2563kJ; Protein 53.1g; Carbohydrate 36.4g, of which sugars 17.9g; Fat 25g, of which saturates 11.1g; Cholesterol 196mg; Calcium 128mg; Fibre 5.3g; Sodium 396mg.
Chicken and Potato Bake Energy 359kcal/1511kJ; Protein 31g; Carbohydrate 33.6g, of which sugars 7.8g; Fat 12.1g, of which saturates 6g; Cholesterol 92mg; Calcium 130mg; Fibre 3.1g; Sodium 193mg.

Stoved Chicken and Potatoes

'Stovies' were originally potatoes slowly cooked on the stove, with onions and dripping or butter, until falling to pieces. This version includes a delicious layer of bacon and chicken hidden in the middle of the vegetables.

Serves 4

butter, for greasing
1kg/2¼lb baking potatoes, cut
   into 5mm/¼in slices
2 large onions, thinly sliced
15ml/1 tbsp chopped fresh thyme
25g/1oz/2 tbsp butter
15ml/1 tbsp vegetable oil
2 large bacon slices, chopped
4 large chicken joints, halved
600ml/1 pint/2½ cups
   chicken stock
1 bay leaf
salt and ground black pepper

1 Preheat the oven to 150°C/300°F/Gas 2. Arrange a thick layer of half the potato slices in the bottom of a large, lightly greased heavy casserole, then cover with half the onions. Sprinkle with half of the thyme, and season with salt and pepper to taste.

2 Heat the butter and oil in a large heavy frying pan, add the bacon and chicken, stirring frequently, and brown on all sides. Using a slotted spoon, transfer the chicken and bacon to the casserole. Reserve the fat in the pan.

3 Sprinkle the remaining thyme over the chicken, season with salt and pepper, then cover with the remaining onion slices, followed by a neat layer of overlapping potato slices. Season the dish well with salt and pepper.

4 Pour the stock into the casserole, add the bay leaf and brush the potatoes with the reserved fat. Cover the pan with a tight-fitting lid and bake in the oven for about 2 hours until the chicken is very tender.

5 Preheat the grill (broiler). Take the cover off the casserole and place it under the grill until the slices of potato are beginning to turn golden brown and crisp. Remove the bay leaf and serve hot.

Spinach and Potato Stuffed Chicken

This dish consists of large chicken breasts, filled with a herby spinach and potato mixture, then topped with butter and baked until mouth-wateringly tender.

Serves 6

115g/4oz floury potatoes, diced
115g/4oz spinach leaves,
   finely chopped
1 egg, beaten
30ml/2 tbsp chopped fresh
   coriander (cilantro)
4 large skinless chicken
   breast fillets
50g/2oz/¼ cup butter

For the sauce
400g/14oz can
   chopped tomatoes
1 garlic clove, crushed
150ml/¼ pint/⅔ cup hot
   chicken stock
30ml/2 tbsp chopped
   fresh coriander (cilantro)
salt and ground black pepper
fried mushrooms, to serve

1 Preheat the oven to 180°C/350°F/Gas 4. Boil the potatoes in a large pan of boiling water for 15 minutes or until tender. Drain the potatoes, place them in a large bowl and roughly mash with a fork. Stir the spinach into the potato with the egg and coriander. Season with salt and pepper to taste.

2 Cut almost all the way through the chicken breast fillets and open out to form a pocket in each. Spoon the filling into the centre and fold the chicken back over again. Secure with cocktail sticks (toothpicks) and place in a roasting pan.

3 Dot with butter and cover with foil. Bake for 25 minutes. Remove the foil and cook for a further 10 minutes until the chicken is golden.

4 Meanwhile, to make the sauce, heat the tomatoes, garlic and stock in a pan and cook for 10 minutes. Season and stir in the coriander. Serve the chicken with the sauce and fried mushrooms.

> **Cook's Tip**
> Young spinach leaves have a sweeter flavour and are ideal for using in this dish.

Stoved Chicken Energy 630kcal/2653kJ; Protein 69.2g; Carbohydrate 48.2g, of which sugars 8.9g; Fat 19.2g, of which saturates 7.2g; Cholesterol 195mg; Calcium 56mg; Fibre 3.9g; Sodium 574mg.
Spinach and Potato Energy 212kcal/888kJ; Protein 26.6g; Carbohydrate 5.7g, of which sugars 2.8g; Fat 9.4g, of which saturates 5g; Cholesterol 119mg; Calcium 60mg; Fibre 1.5g; Sodium 159mg.

Chicken with Potato Dumplings

Slowly poaching chicken pieces in a creamy sauce topped with light herb and potato dumplings makes a delicate yet hearty and warming meal.

Serves 6
1 onion, chopped
300ml/½ pint/1¼ cups
   vegetable stock
120ml/4fl oz/½ cup white wine
4 large chicken breast fillets
300ml/½ pint/1¼ cups single
   (light) cream

15ml/1 tbsp chopped
   fresh tarragon
salt and ground black pepper

For the dumplings
225g/8oz maincrop potatoes,
   boiled and mashed
175g/6oz/1¼ cups suet
115g/4oz/1 cup self-raising
   (self-rising) flour
50ml/2fl oz/¼ cup water
30ml/2 tbsp chopped mixed
   fresh herbs
salt and ground black pepper

1 Place the onion, stock and wine in a deep-sided frying pan. Add the chicken and simmer, covered, for 20 minutes.

2 Remove the chicken from the stock, cut it into chunks and set aside. Strain the stock and discard the onion. Return the stock to the pan and boil until reduced by one-third. Stir in the single cream and tarragon, and simmer until just thickened. Stir in the chicken and season with salt and ground black pepper.

3 Spoon the mixture into a 900ml/1½ pint/3¾ cup ovenproof dish. Preheat the oven to 190°C/375°F/Gas 5.

4 Mix together the dumpling ingredients to make a soft dough. Divide into six and shape into balls with floured hands.

5 Place the dumplings on top of the chicken mixture and bake uncovered for 30 minutes until cooked. Serve immediately.

Cook's Tip
Make sure that you do not reduce the sauce too much before cooking in the oven as the dumplings absorb quite a lot of liquid.

Chicken and Pesto Jacket Potatoes

Although it is usually served with pasta, pesto also gives a wonderful lift to rice, bread and potato dishes – all good starchy carbohydrates. Here, it is combined with chicken and yogurt to make a tasty topping for jacket potatoes.

Serves 4
4 baking potatoes
2 chicken breast fillets, skin on
15ml/1 tbsp pesto sauce
250ml/8fl oz/1 cup plain
   (natural) yogurt
fresh basil sprigs, to garnish

1 Preheat the oven to 200°C/400°F/Gas 6. Prick the potatoes all over with a fork and bake in the oven for about 1¼ hours until soft.

2 About 20 minutes before the end of the cooking time for the potatoes, place the chicken fillets in an ovenproof dish and bake in the oven until cooked through.

3 Meanwhile, place the pesto sauce into a bowl. Add the natural yogurt and stir well until the ingredients are thoroughly combined.

4 Skin and slice the chicken fillets. Cut the potatoes open and fill with the chicken slices. Top with the pesto-flavoured yogurt and garnish with basil sprigs.

Cook's Tips
• The chicken fillets and potatoes can be cooked in the microwave, if you like. Microwave the chicken fillets on HIGH for 3–4 minutes, turning over halfway through cooking. Microwave the potatoes on HIGH for 12–15 minutes, turning over once halfway during cooking. Leave to stand for 3–4 minutes.
• A good technique for ensuring that the insides of the jacket potatoes are particularly fluffy is to place a dish towel over them and break them open by stamping them with the palm of the hand. This opens them up quicker than cutting with a knife, which means the air escapes faster, resulting in beautifully light and airy potato inside.

Chicken with Dumplings Energy 552kcal/2300kJ; Protein 28.2g; Carbohydrate 26.5g, of which sugars 2.6g; Fat 37.4g, of which saturates 21g; Cholesterol 121mg; Calcium 83mg; Fibre 1.3g; Sodium 80mg.
Chicken and Pesto Energy 272kcal/1151kJ; Protein 26.1g; Carbohydrate 36.9g, of which sugars 7.3g; Fat 3.3g, of which saturates 1.5g; Cholesterol 57mg; Calcium 180mg; Fibre 2g; Sodium 160mg.

Rice with Chilli Chicken and Potatoes

This Indian dish is so tasty that it is generally reserved for special occasions.

Serves 4 to 6

1.3kg/3lb skinless chicken breast
   fillet, cut into large pieces
60ml/4 tbsp biryani masala paste
2 green chillies, chopped
15ml/1 tbsp crushed fresh
   root ginger
15ml/1 tbsp crushed garlic
50g/2oz coriander (cilantro)
   leaves, chopped
6–8 mint leaves, chopped
150ml/¼ pint/⅔ cup natural
   (plain) yogurt, beaten
30ml/2 tbsp tomato purée (paste)
4 onions, finely sliced, deep-fried
   and crushed
salt, to taste
450g/1lb basmati rice, washed

5ml/1 tsp black cumin seeds
5cm/2in cinnamon stick
4 green cardamoms
2 black cardamoms
vegetable oil, for shallow-frying
4 large potatoes, peeled
   and quartered
175ml/6fl oz/¾ cup milk,
   mixed with 75ml/2½fl oz/
   ⅓ cup water
1 sachet saffron powder, mixed
   with 90ml/6 tbsp milk
30ml/2 tbsp ghee or unsalted
   (sweet) butter

For the garnish

ghee or unsalted (sweet) butter,
   for shallow-frying
50g/2oz cashew nuts
50g/2oz sultanas (golden raisins)
2 hard-boiled eggs, quartered
deep-fried onion slices

1 Mix the chicken with the next 10 ingredients and marinate for 2 hours. Place in a pan and cook for 10 minutes. Set aside. Boil a pan of water and soak the rice with the cumin seeds, cinnamon stick and cardamoms for 5 minutes. Drain well. Heat the oil for frying. Cook the potatoes until browned. Set aside.

2 Place half the rice on top of the chicken, then an even layer of potatoes. Add the remaining rice on the potatoes. Sprinkle the milky water all over the rice. Make a few holes through the rice and pour in a little saffron milk. Dot the surface with ghee or butter, cover and cook over a low heat for 35–45 minutes.

3 Make the garnish. Heat the ghee or butter and fry the nuts and sultanas until they swell. Set aside. When the rice is ready, gently toss the layers together. Garnish with the nut mixture, eggs and onion slices and serve immediately.

Devil's Chicken and Potato Curry

Every Eurasian household in Malaysia has its own version of this devilishly hot chicken and potato curry. Served as a meal on its own with bread to mop up the sauce, it is often eaten at family celebration meals.

Serves 6

4–6 skinless chicken breast fillets,
   cut into chunks
60ml/4 tbsp vegetable oil
1 onion, halved and sliced
25g/1oz fresh root ginger, peeled
   and cut into julienne strips
4 garlic cloves, cut into strips
30–45ml/2–3 tbsp vinegar
10ml/2 tsp sugar
3 medium potatoes, cut into
   bitesize pieces
2 courgettes (zucchini), halved
   lengthways, seeded and sliced
8 Chinese leaves (Chinese
   cabbage), cut into squares

10ml/2 tsp brown mustard seeds,
   ground and mixed to a paste
   with a little water
salt
fresh crusty bread, to serve

For the spice paste

10 dried chillies, soaked in warm
   water, seeded and patted dry
6 fresh red chillies, seeded
   and chopped
8 shallots, chopped
6 garlic cloves, chopped
25g/1oz fresh root ginger, peeled
   and chopped
6 candlenuts or macadamia nuts
10ml/2 tsp ground turmeric

For the marinade

15ml/1 tbsp light soy sauce
15ml/1 tbsp dark soy sauce
10ml/2 tsp rice or white
   wine vinegar
10ml/2 tsp caster
   (superfine) sugar

1 Mix together the ingredients for the marinade and rub it into the chicken pieces. Leave to marinate for 30 minutes. Using a mortar and pestle or food processor, grind the chillies, shallots, garlic, ginger and nuts to a paste. Stir in the turmeric.

2 Heat the oil in a wok or heavy pan. Stir in the onion, ginger and garlic and fry until golden. Add the spice paste, stir, toss in the chicken and stir until it browns. Pour in water to cover.

3 Bring up to the boil, then add the vinegar, sugar and potatoes. Reduce to a simmer and cook until the potatoes are just tender. Add the sliced courgettes and cabbage and cook for 2 minutes. Stir in the mustard paste, season with salt and serve immediately.

Chicken and Rice Energy 940kcal/3944kJ; Protein 66g; Carbohydrate 107.1g, of which sugars 15.5g; Fat 28.4g, of which saturates 5.9g; Cholesterol 153mg; Calcium 166mg; Fibre 4.9g; Sodium 195mg.
Devil's Curry Energy 270kcal/1136kJ; Protein 32.5g; Carbohydrate 15.4g, of which sugars 4.6g; Fat 9.1g, of which saturates 1.3g; Cholesterol 88mg; Calcium 36mg; Fibre 1.8g; Sodium 441mg.

Japanese Chicken and Vegetables

As well as potatoes, this authentic Japanese dish features konnyaku, a black or white yam cake that is available from good Japanese supermarkets.

Serves 4

2 chicken thighs, about 200g/7oz, boned, with skin remaining
1 large carrot, trimmed
1 konnyaku

300g/11oz new potatoes
500g/1¼lb canned bamboo shoots, drained
30ml/2 tbsp vegetable oil
300ml/½ pint/1¼ cups dashi stock
salt

For the seasonings

75ml/5 tbsp shoyu
30ml/2 tbsp sake
30ml/2 tbsp caster (superfine) sugar
30ml/2 tbsp mirin

1 Cut the chicken into bitesize pieces. Chop the carrot into 2cm/¾in triangles. To do this, cut the carrot slightly diagonally and turn it 90 degrees each time you cut.

2 Boil the konnyaku in boiling water for 1 minute and drain under cold running water. Cool and slice it crossways into 5mm/¼in thick rectangular strips. Cut a 4cm/1½in slit down the centre of a strip without cutting the ends. Push the top of the strip through the slit to make a decorative tie. Repeat with all the konnyaku strips.

3 Peel and halve the new potatoes. Halve the canned bamboo shoots, then cut into the same shape as the carrot.

4 In a medium pan, heat the oil and stir-fry the chicken until the meat turns white. Add the carrot, konnyaku ties, potatoes and bamboo shoots. Stir well each time you add a new ingredient.

5 Add the dashi stock and bring to the boil. Cook on a high heat for 3 minutes, then reduce to medium-low. Add the shoyu, sake, caster sugar and mirin, cover the pan, then simmer for 15 minutes.

6 When the potatoes are soft, transfer the cooked chicken and vegetables to a large serving bowl. Serve immediately.

Chicken and Sweet Potato Curry with Coconut and Caramel Sauce

This typical South-east Asian chicken and sweet potato curry is simple to make and delicious to eat. Serve this curry with crusty baguettes for mopping up the sauce, or steamed fragrant rice or noodles.

Serves 4

45ml/3 tbsp Indian curry powder or garam masala
15ml/1 tbsp ground turmeric
500g/1¼lb skinless chicken thighs or chicken breast portions
25ml/1½ tbsp raw cane sugar

30ml/2 tbsp sesame oil
2 shallots, chopped
2 garlic cloves, chopped
4cm/1½in galangal, peeled and chopped
2 lemon grass stalks, chopped
10ml/2 tsp chilli paste or dried chilli flakes
1–2 medium sweet potatoes, peeled and cubed
45ml/3 tbsp Thai fish sauce
600ml/1 pint can coconut milk
1 small bunch each of fresh basil and coriander (cilantro), stalks removed
salt and ground black pepper

1 In a small bowl, mix together the curry powder or garam masala and the turmeric. Put the chicken thighs in a bowl and coat with half of the spice. Set aside.

2 To make the caramel sauce, heat the sugar in a small pan with 7.5ml/1½ tsp water, until the sugar dissolves and the syrup turns golden. Remove from the heat and set aside.

3 Heat a wok or wide heavy pan and add the oil. Stir-fry the shallots, garlic, galangal and lemon grass until they begin to smell fragrant. Stir in the rest of the turmeric and curry powder with the chilli paste or chilli flakes, followed by the chicken, moving it around the wok for 2–3 minutes.

4 Add the sweet potatoes, then the fish sauce, caramel sauce, coconut milk and 150ml/¼ pint/⅔ cup water, stirring well to combine the flavours. Bring the liquid to the boil, reduce the heat and cook for about 15 minutes or until the chicken is tender. Season with salt and pepper and stir half the basil and coriander through the curry. Garnish with the remaining herbs.

Japanese Chicken Energy 168kcal/705kJ; Protein 12.7g; Carbohydrate 15.8g, of which sugars 4.4g; Fat 6.4g, of which saturates 0.9g; Cholesterol 31mg; Calcium 46mg; Fibre 2.2g; Sodium 976mg.
Chicken and Coconut Curry Energy 387kcal/1632kJ; Protein 31g; Carbohydrate 38g, of which sugars 19g; Fat 14g, of which saturates 3g; Cholesterol 131mg; Calcium 1.8mg; Fibre 1g; Sodium 1g.

Chicken and Sweet Potato Curry with Rice Vermicelli

Lemon grass, garlic and sweet potatoes give this South-east Asian curry a wonderful aromatic flavour.

Serves 4
1 chicken, about 1.3–1.6kg/3–3¹/₂lb
225g/8oz sweet potatoes
60ml/4 tbsp vegetable oil
1 onion, finely sliced
3 garlic cloves, crushed
30–45ml/2–3 tbsp Thai
   curry powder
5ml/1 tsp sugar
10ml/2 tsp Thai fish sauce

600ml/1 pint/2¹/₂ cups
   coconut milk
1 lemon grass stalk, cut in half
350g/12oz rice vermicelli, soaked
   in hot water until soft
1 lemon, cut into wedges,
   to serve

For the garnish
115g/4oz beansprouts
2 spring onions (scallions), finely
   sliced diagonally
2 red chillies, seeded and
   finely sliced
8–10 mint leaves

1 Skin the chicken. Cut the flesh into small pieces and set aside. Peel the sweet potatoes and cut them into large chunks, about the same size as the chicken pieces.

2 Heat half the oil in a large heavy pan. Add the onion and garlic and fry until the onion softens.

3 Add the chicken pieces and stir-fry until they change colour. Stir in the curry powder. Season with salt and sugar and mix thoroughly, then stir in the fish sauce. Pour in the coconut milk and add the lemon grass. Cook over a low heat for 15 minutes.

4 Meanwhile, heat the remaining oil in a large frying pan. Fry the sweet potatoes until lightly golden. Using a slotted spoon, add them to the chicken. Cook for 10–15 minutes more, or until both the chicken and sweet potatoes are tender.

5 Drain the rice vermicelli and cook it in a pan of boiling water for 3–5 minutes. Drain well. Place in shallow bowls, with the chicken curry. Garnish with beansprouts, spring onions, chillies and mint leaves and serve with lemon wedges.

Chicken and Potato Ghiveci

This superb dish, with its colourful medley of sweet and crunchy vegetables, is one of the best potted chicken soups around. The secret of its success is when to add the vegetables so that they are cooked to perfection. For the best results, it is important to use fresh herbs rather than dried, although a mixture of fresh and dried herbs would not compromise the flavour too much.

Serves 6
60ml/4 tbsp vegetable oil, melted
   lard or white cooking fat
1 mild onion, thinly sliced
2 garlic cloves, crushed

2 red (bell) peppers, seeded
   and sliced
about 1.6kg/3¹/₂lb chicken, jointed
   into six pieces
90ml/6 tbsp tomato
   purée (paste)
3 potatoes, diced
5ml/1 tsp chopped
   fresh rosemary
5ml/1 tsp chopped
   fresh marjoram
5ml/1 tsp chopped fresh thyme
3 carrots, cut into chunks
¹/₂ small celeriac, cut
   into chunks
120ml/4fl oz/¹/₂ cup dry
   white wine
2 courgettes (zucchini), sliced
salt and ground black pepper
chopped fresh rosemary and
   marjoram, to garnish

1 Heat the oil in a large flameproof casserole. Add the onion and garlic and cook for 1–2 minutes until softened.

2 Add the peppers to the casserole and cook, stirring occasionally, for a further 2 minutes.

3 Place the chicken in the casserole and brown over the hob for about 15 minutes.

4 Add the tomato purée, potatoes, herbs, carrots, celeriac and white wine to the casserole, and season to taste with salt and pepper. Cook over a gentle heat, covered, for a further 40–50 minutes.

5 At 5 minutes before the end of cooking, add the courgettes. Adjust the seasoning to taste. Garnish with the herbs and serve with rye bread, if you like, or with herb bread or crusty rolls.

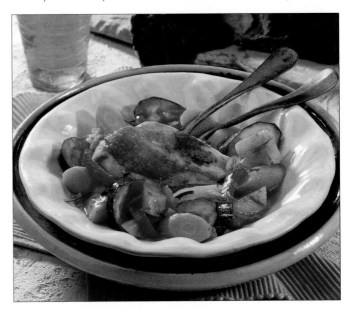

Chicken Vermicelli Curry Energy 763kcal/3199kJ; Protein 51.6g; Carbohydrate 92g, of which sugars 11.6g; Fat 21.3g, of which saturates 4.1g; Cholesterol 109mg; Calcium 170mg; Fibre 4g; Sodium 545mg.
Chicken Ghiveci Energy 430kcal/1807kJ; Protein 49.6g; Carbohydrate 28.5g, of which sugars 12.9g; Fat 12.3g, of which saturates 2.3g; Cholesterol 175mg; Calcium 61mg; Fibre 4.4g; Sodium 202mg.

Chicken, Pork and Potatoes in Peanut Sauce

This traditional Peruvian dish is made with dried potatoes, which break up when cooked to thicken the sauce. The same effect is achieved here by using floury potatoes.

Serves 6
75g/3oz/¾ cup unsalted peanuts
60ml/4 tbsp olive oil
3 chicken breast portions, halved
500g/1¼lb boneless pork loin, cut into 2cm/¾in pieces
1 large onion, chopped
30–45ml/2–3 tbsp water
3 garlic cloves, crushed
5ml/1 tsp paprika
5ml/1 tsp ground cumin
500g/1¼lb floury potatoes, peeled and thickly sliced
550ml/18fl oz/scant 2½ cups vegetable stock
salt and ground black pepper
cooked rice, to serve

For the garnish
2 hard-boiled eggs, sliced
50g/2oz/½ cup pitted black olives
chopped fresh flat leaf parsley

1 Place the peanuts in a large dry frying pan over a low heat. Toast for 2–3 minutes, until golden. Leave to cool, then process in a food processor until finely ground.

2 Heat half the oil in a heavy pan. Add the chicken pieces, season and cook for 10 minutes, until golden brown all over. Transfer the pieces of chicken to a plate, using a slotted spoon. Heat the remaining oil and cook the pork for 3–4 minutes, until brown. Transfer to the plate with the chicken pieces.

3 Lower the heat, add the onion and fry for 5 minutes. Add the garlic, paprika and cumin and fry for 1 minute. Stir in the sliced potatoes, cover the pan and cook for a further 3 minutes. Mix in the peanuts and stock. Simmer for 30 minutes.

4 Return the meat to the pan and bring to the boil. Lower the heat, replace the lid and simmer for 6–8 minutes.

5 Garnish the stew with the egg slices, black olives and chopped parsley. Serve with the rice.

Turkey Croquette Potatoes

These deliciously crisp patties of smoked turkey mixed with mashed potato and spring onions will be a firm family favourite.

Serves 4
450g/1lb potatoes, diced
3 eggs
30ml/2 tbsp milk
175g/6oz smoked turkey rashers (strips), finely chopped
2 spring onions (scallions), sliced
115g/4oz/2 cups fresh white breadcrumbs
vegetable oil, for deep fat frying

For the sauce
15ml/1 tbsp olive oil
1 onion, finely chopped
400g/14oz can tomatoes, drained
30ml/2 tbsp tomato purée (paste)
15ml/1 tbsp chopped fresh parsley
salt and ground black pepper

1 Boil the potatoes for 20 minutes or until tender. Drain and then return the pan to a low heat to evaporate the excess water.

2 Mash the potatoes with two eggs and the milk. Season well with salt and pepper. Stir in the turkey and spring onions. Chill for 1 hour.

3 Meanwhile, to make the sauce, heat the oil in a frying pan and fry the onion for 5 minutes until softened. Add the tomatoes and purée, stir and simmer for 10 minutes. Stir in the parsley, season to taste and keep the sauce warm until needed.

4 Remove the potato mixture from the refrigerator and divide into eight pieces. Shape each piece into a sausage shape and dip in the remaining beaten egg and then the breadcrumbs.

5 Heat the vegetable oil in a deep-fat fryer to 175°C/330°F and deep fry the croquettes for 5 minutes, or until golden and crisp. Serve immediately, accompanied with the sauce.

Cook's Tip
Test the oil temperature by dropping a cube of bread into it. If it sinks, rises and sizzles in 10 seconds, the oil is ready to use.

Chicken in Peanut Sauce Energy 394kcal/1651kJ; Protein 39.3g; Carbohydrate 16.7g, of which sugars 2.4g; Fat 19.4g, of which saturates 4.1g; Cholesterol 85mg; Calcium 33mg; Fibre 1.8g; Sodium 123mg.
Turkey Croquettes Energy 404kcal/1698kJ; Protein 19.4g; Carbohydrate 47g, of which sugars 7.7g; Fat 16.7g, of which saturates 2.4g; Cholesterol 73mg; Calcium 93mg; Fibre 3.3g; Sodium 315mg.

Roasted Duckling on a Bed of Honeyed Potatoes

The rich flavour of duck combined with these sweetened potatoes glazed with honey makes an excellent treat for a dinner party or special occasion.

Serves 4

1 duckling, giblets removed
60ml/4 tbsp light soy sauce
150ml/¼ pint/⅔ cup fresh
　orange juice
3 large floury potatoes, cut
　into chunks
30ml/2 tbsp clear honey
15ml/1 tbsp sesame seeds
salt and ground black pepper

1 Preheat the oven to 200°C/400°F/Gas 6. Place the duckling in a roasting pan. Prick the skin well.

2 Mix the soy sauce and orange juice together and pour over the duck. Cook in the oven for 20 minutes.

3 Place the potato chunks in a bowl and stir in the honey, toss to mix well. Remove the duckling from the oven and spoon the potatoes all around and under the duckling.

4 Roast for 35 minutes and remove from the oven. Toss the potatoes in the duck's juices so that they cook evenly, and turn the duckling over. Return the roasting pan to the oven and cook for a further 30 minutes.

5 Remove the duckling from the oven and carefully scoop off the excess fat, leaving the juices behind.

6 Sprinkle the sesame seeds over the potatoes, season and turn the duckling back over, breast side up, and cook for a further 10 minutes. Remove the duckling and potatoes from the oven and keep warm, allowing the duckling to stand for a few minutes.

7 Pour off the excess fat and simmer the juices on the hob for a few minutes. Serve the juices with the carved duckling and the potatoes.

Poussins and New Potato Pot roast

Pot roasts are traditionally associated with the colder months, but this delicious version is a simple summer dish that makes the most of new season potatoes.

Serves 4

2 poussins, about
　500g/1¼lb each
25g/1oz/2 tbsp butter
15ml/1 tbsp clear honey
500g/1¼lb small
　new potatoes
1 red onion, halved lengthwise
　and cut into thin wedges
4–5 small rosemary sprigs
2 bay leaves
1 lemon, cut into wedges
450ml/¾ pint/scant 2 cups hot
　chicken stock
salt and ground black pepper

1 Soak a clay chicken brick in cold water for 20 minutes, then drain. Cut the poussins in half, along the breast bone.

2 Melt the butter, mix it together with the honey and brush over the poussins. Season with salt and pepper.

3 Place the small new potatoes and onion wedges in the base of the chicken brick. Tuck the rosemary sprigs, bay leaves and lemon wedges in among the vegetables. Pour over the hot chicken stock (see Cook's Tip).

4 Place the halved poussins on top of the vegetables. Cover the chicken brick and place it in an unheated oven. Set the oven to 200°C/400°F/Gas 6 and cook for 55–60 minutes, or until the poussin juices run clear and the vegetables are tender. Uncover the chicken brick for the last 10 minutes of cooking to add more colour to the poussins, if necessary. Serve hot.

Cook's Tips
• Make sure the stock is hot, but not boiling, when it is added to the chicken brick, otherwise the chicken brick may crack.
• A poussin is a baby chicken – usually around 4–6 weeks old. Poussins can be cooked by grilling (broiling), roasting or pot-roasting, but are especially tender and moist cooked in a chicken brick.

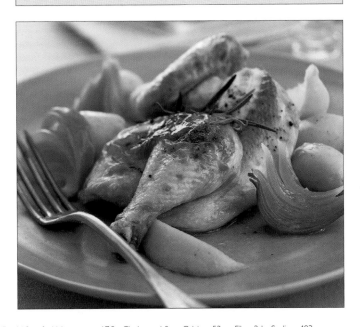

Roasted Duckling Energy 806kcal/3341kJ; Protein 20.8g; Carbohydrate 32.3g, of which sugars 6.4g; Fat 66.8g, of which saturates 17.9g; Cholesterol 0mg; Calcium 53mg; Fibre 2.1g; Sodium 403mg.
Poussins Energy 443kcal/1852kJ; Protein 30.1g; Carbohydrate 24.2g, of which sugars 5.4g; Fat 25.8g, of which saturates 8.9g; Cholesterol 158mg; Calcium 23mg; Fibre 1.5g; Sodium 153mg.

Potato, Leek and Tomato Bake

This simple potato dish is delicious for lunch or supper – a real winner with all the family. It is made in the microwave to make it even more convenient. Select the best tomatoes you can for a deliciously sweet flavour; if this means using small fruit, then add one or two extra.

Serves 4
675g/1½lb potatoes
2 leeks, trimmed and sliced
3 large tomatoes, sliced
a few fresh rosemary
    sprigs, crushed
1 garlic clove, crushed
300ml/½ pint/1¼ cups hot
    vegetable stock
15ml/1 tbsp olive oil
salt and ground black pepper

1 Scrub and thinly slice the potatoes. Layer them with the sliced leeks and tomatoes in a 1.2 litre/2 pint/5 cup microwave-proof dish that is also suitable for grilling (broiling). Sprinkle some of the crushed rosemary sprigs in between each layer and finish with a final layer of sliced potatoes on the top.

2 Add the crushed garlic to the vegetable stock, stir in the salt and ground black pepper to taste and pour over the dish of layered vegetables, ensuring that the mixture seeps down between every layer. Brush the top layer of sliced potatoes with the olive oil.

3 Cover and microwave on HIGH for 15–18 minutes or until the potatoes are tender.

4 Leave the dish to stand for around 5 minutes, then remove the cover. Cook under a preheated hot grill (broiler), if you like, until the top is crisp and brown all over. Serve immediately, straight from the dish at the table.

> **Cook's Tip**
> *This recipe is also suitable for cooking in a combination microwave. Follow the oven manufacturer's timing guide for the best results.*

Greek Tomato and Potato Bake

This is an adaptation of a classic Greek potato dish, which is usually cooked on the hob. This recipe has a richer flavour because it is stove-cooked first and then baked in the oven.

Serves 4
120ml/4fl oz/½ cup olive oil
1 large onion, finely chopped

3 garlic cloves, crushed
4 large ripe tomatoes, peeled,
    deseeded and chopped
1kg/2¼lb waxy new or
    salad potatoes
salt and ground black pepper
15ml/1 tbsp chopped fresh flat
    leaf parsley, to garnish

1 Preheat the oven to 180°C/350°F/Gas 4. Heat the oil in a flameproof casserole. Fry the onion and garlic for 5 minutes until softened and just starting to brown.

2 Add the tomatoes to the pan, season with salt and ground black pepper and cook for 1 minute.

3 Cut the potatoes into even wedges. Add to the pan and cook for about 10 minutes. Season again and cover the pan with a tight-fitting lid.

4 Place the covered casserole on the middle shelf of the preheated oven and cook for 45–60 minutes until the potatoes are tender. Garnish with flat leaf parsley and serve.

> **Variation**
> *To add to the Greek theme of this dish you could add a handful of pitted and chopped black olives. Look out for the superior kalamata olives in delicatessens and supermarkets.*

> **Cook's Tip**
> *Make sure that the potatoes are completely coated in the oil so that they cook evenly.*

Greek Bake Energy 399kcal/1670kJ; Protein 5.9g; Carbohydrate 49.3g, of which sugars 10.6g; Fat 21.2g, of which saturates 3.2g; Cholesterol 0mg; Calcium 41mg; Fibre 4.6g; Sodium 39mg.
Potato, Leek and Tomato Bake Energy 178kcal/752kJ; Protein 5g; Carbohydrate 32.4g, of which sugars 6.7g; Fat 4g, of which saturates 0.6g; Cholesterol 0mg; Calcium 39mg; Fibre 4.6g; Sodium 27mg.

Potato and Parsnip Dauphinois

Layers of potatoes and parsnips are baked slowly in creamy milk with a melted cheese topping. This is an ideal special side dish or light supper dish.

Serves 4–6

1kg/2lb potatoes, thinly sliced
1 onion, thinly sliced
450g/1lb parsnips, thinly sliced
2 garlic cloves, crushed
50g/2oz/4 tbsp butter
125g/4oz Gruyère or Cheddar
    cheese, grated
fresh nutmeg, grated
salt and ground black pepper
300ml/½ pint/1¼ cups single
    (light) cream
300ml/½ pint/1¼ cups milk

1 Lightly grease a large shallow ovenproof dish. Preheat the oven to 180°C/350°F/Gas 4.

2 Layer the potatoes in the dish with the onion and parsnips. In between each layer, dot the vegetables with pieces of garlic and butter.

3 Finish with a layer of potatoes and sprinkle over most of the grated cheese. Sprinkle with the fresh nutmeg and season well with salt and ground black pepper.

4 Heat the cream and milk together in a small pan until the mixture is hot but not boiling. Slowly pour the creamy milk over the vegetables in the dish. Shake the pan a little to make sure the sauce seeps underneath the vegetable layers.

5 Sprinkle the remaining cheese over the top of the vegetables and grate a little more nutmeg on top. Bake for about an hour or so until the potatoes are tender and the cheese topping is bubbling and golden. Serve immediately.

> **Cook's Tip**
> *For this dish you can use either waxy new potatoes, which will hold their shape better after cooking, or the floury variety, which will disintegrate a little bit. Either variety will absorb the delicious creamy garlic flavours of this dish.*

Baked Leek, Potato and Brie Gratin

Potatoes baked in a creamy cheese sauce make the ultimate comfort dish, whether served as an accompaniment to pork or fish dishes or, as here, with plenty of leeks and melted cheese as a main course. When preparing leeks, separate the leaves and rinse them thoroughly under cold running water, as soil and grit often get caught between the layers.

Serves 4–6

900g/2lb medium potatoes,
    thinly sliced
2 large leeks, trimmed
200g/7oz ripe Brie or Camembert
    cheese, sliced
450ml/¾ pint/scant 2 cups single
    (light) cream
salt and ground black pepper

1 Preheat the oven to 180°C/350°F/Gas 4. Cook the potatoes in plenty of lightly salted, boiling water for 3 minutes, until slightly softened, then drain.

2 Cut the leeks into 1cm/½in slices and blanch them in a pan of boiling water for 1–2 minutes, until softened, then drain them thoroughly.

3 Place half the potatoes into a lightly greased, shallow, ovenproof dish and spread them out to the edge. Cover the potatoes with about two-thirds of the leeks, then add the remaining potatoes on top.

4 Tuck the cheese and the remaining leeks in among the potatoes. Season with salt and pepper and pour the cream over.

5 Bake for 1 hour, until tender and golden. Cover with foil if the top starts to overbrown before the potatoes are tender.

> **Variation**
> *This dish can be made with vegetable stock in place of the cream if you are concerned about calories.*

Potato Dauphinois Energy 438kcal/1833kJ; Protein 12.6g; Carbohydrate 41.6g, of which sugars 11.6g; Fat 25.4g, of which saturates 15.8g; Cholesterol 70mg; Calcium 304mg; Fibre 5.3g; Sodium 291mg.
Leek Gratin Energy 383kcal/1597kJ; Protein 13.1g; Carbohydrate 28.2g, of which sugars 5.4g; Fat 24.2g, of which saturates 15.4g; Cholesterol 72mg; Calcium 181mg; Fibre 3.3g; Sodium 225mg.

Root Vegetable Casserole with Courgette and Caraway Dumplings

Light courgette dumplings spiced with caraway complete this warming slow-cooker dish.

Serves 3
300ml/½ pint/1¼ cups dry (hard) cider
175ml/6fl oz/¾ cup boiling vegetable stock
2 leeks, cut into 2cm/¾in slices
2 carrots, cut into chunks
2 parsnips, cut into chunks
225g/8oz potatoes, cut into chunks
1 sweet potato, cut into chunks

1 bay leaf
7.5ml/1½ tsp cornflour (cornstarch)
115g/4oz full-fat soft cheese with garlic and herbs
salt and ground black pepper

For the dumplings
115g/4oz/1 cup self-raising (self-rising) flour
5ml/1 tsp caraway seeds
50g/2oz/½ cup shredded vegetable suet (chilled, grated shortening)
1 courgette (zucchini), grated
about 75ml/5 tbsp cold water

1 Reserve 15ml/1 tbsp of the cider and pour the rest into the ceramic cooking pot with the stock. Cover and switch to high. Add the vegetables to the ceramic cooking pot with the bay leaf. Cover with the lid and cook for 3 hours.

2 In a small bowl, blend the cornflour with the reserved cider. Add the cheese and mix together until combined, then gradually blend in a few spoonfuls of the cooking liquid. Pour over the vegetables and stir until thoroughly mixed. Season with salt and black pepper. Cover and cook for a further 1–2 hours, or until the vegetables are almost tender.

3 Towards the end of the cooking time, make the dumplings. Sift the flour into a bowl and stir in the caraway seeds, suet, courgettes, salt and black pepper. Stir in the water, adding a little more if necessary, to make a soft dough. With floured hands, shape the mixture into 12 dumplings, about the size of walnuts.

4 Carefully place the dumplings on top of the casserole, cover and cook for a further hour, or until the vegetables and dumplings are cooked. Serve in warmed deep soup plates.

Winter Vegetable Casserole with Herb Dumplings

When the cold weather sets in, make this warming potato casserole with some hearty old-fashioned dumplings.

Serves 6
2 potatoes
2 carrots
1 small fennel bulb
1 small swede (rutabaga)
2 leeks
2 courgettes (zucchini)
50g/2oz/½ cup butter or margarine
30ml/2 tbsp plain (all-purpose) flour
1 x 425g/15oz can butter (lima) beans, with liquid

600ml/1 pint/2½ cups stock
30ml/2 tbsp tomato purée (paste)
1 cinnamon stick
10ml/2 tsp ground coriander
2.5ml/½ tsp ground ginger
2 bay leaves
salt and ground black pepper

For the dumplings
200g/7oz/1¾ cups plain (all-purpose) flour
115g/4oz vegetable suet (US chilled, grated shortening), or chilled butter, grated
5ml/1 tsp dried thyme
5ml/1 tsp salt
120ml/4 fl oz/½ cup milk

1 Cut all the vegetables into even, bitesize chunks, then fry gently in the butter or margarine for about 10 minutes. Stir in the flour, then the liquor from the beans, the stock, tomato purée, spices, bay leaves and seasoning. Bring to the boil, stirring. Cover and simmer for 10 minutes, then add the beans and cook for a further 5 minutes.

2 Meanwhile, make the dumplings. Mix the flour, suet or butter, thyme and salt to a firm but moist dough with the milk and knead with your hands until it is smooth. Divide the dough into 12 pieces, rolling each one into a ball with your fingers. Uncover the simmering stew and then add the dumplings, allowing space between each one for expansion.

3 Replace the lid and cook on a gentle simmer for a further 15 minutes. Do not remove the lid or you will let out all the steam. Be careful not to cook dumplings too fast, or they will break up. Remove the cinnamon stick and bay leaves before you serve this dish, steaming hot.

Vegetable Casserole Energy 616kcal/2584kJ; Protein 11.9g; Carbohydrate 74.9g, of which sugars 17.1g; Fat 28.9g, of which saturates 15.9g; Cholesterol 35mg; Calcium 256mg; Fibre 9.5g; Sodium 369mg.
Winter Casserole Energy 510kcal/2132kJ; Protein 12.5g; Carbohydrate 59.7g, of which sugars 9.9g; Fat 26.2g, of which saturates 13.7g; Cholesterol 20mg; Calcium 160mg; Fibre 8.3g; Sodium 358mg.

Creamy Beetroot and Potato Gratin with Wild Mushrooms

This delicious dish of mashed potato with beetroot and wild mushrooms captures the true spirit of autumn.

Serves 4

30ml/2 tbsp vegetable oil
1 medium onion, chopped
45ml/3 tbsp plain
　(all-purpose) flour
300ml/½ pint/¼ cups
　vegetable broth
675g/1½lb cooked beetroot
　(beets), peeled and chopped
75ml/5 tbsp single (light) cream
30ml/2 tbsp horseradish sauce
5ml/1 tsp hot mustard
15ml/1 tbsp wine vinegar

5ml/1 tsp caraway seeds
30ml/2 tbsp unsalted butter
1 shallot, chopped
225g/8oz/3 cups assorted wild
　and cultivated mushrooms, such
　as ceps, chanterelles, oyster,
　shiitake and field (portabello)
　mushrooms, trimmed
　and sliced
45ml/3 tbsp chopped
　fresh parsley

For the potato border

900g/2lb floury potatoes, peeled
150ml/¼ pint/⅔ cup milk
15ml/1 tbsp chopped fresh
　dill (optional)
salt and ground black pepper

1 Preheat the oven to 190°C/375°F/Gas 5. Oil a 23cm/9in round baking dish. Heat the oil in a large pan, add the onion and sauté until soft. Stir in the flour, then remove from the heat and gradually stir in the broth. Return to the heat and add the beetroot, cream, horseradish, mustard, vinegar and caraway seeds.

2 Bring the potatoes to a boil in salted water and cook for 20 minutes. Drain well and mash with the milk. Add the dill, if using, and season to taste with salt and pepper. Spoon the potatoes into the prepared dish and make a well in the centre. Spoon the beetroot mixture into the well and set aside.

3 Melt the butter in a large frying pan and cook the shallot until soft, but not browned. Add the mushrooms and cook, stirring, until their juices run. Increase the heat and boil off the moisture. When dry, season and stir in the chopped parsley. Spread the mushrooms over the beetroot mixture, cover and bake for 30 minutes. Serve hot.

Tomato and Rich Mediterranean Vegetable Hotpot

Here's a one-dish meal that's suitable for feeding large numbers of people. It's lightly spiced and has plenty of garlic – who could refuse?

Serves 4

60ml/4 tbsp extra virgin olive oil
　or sunflower oil
1 large onion, chopped
2 small or medium aubergines
　(eggplants), cut into small cubes
4 courgettes (zucchini), cut into
　small chunks
2 red, yellow or green (bell)
　peppers, seeded and chopped
115g/4oz/1 cup fresh or
　frozen peas

115g/4oz green beans
200g/7oz can flageolet (small
　cannellini) beans, rinsed
　and drained
450g/1lb new or salad potatoes,
　peeled and cubed
2.5ml/½ tsp ground cinnamon
2.5ml/½ tsp ground cumin
5ml/1 tsp paprika
4–5 tomatoes, peeled
400g/14oz can chopped tomatoes
30ml/2 tbsp chopped fresh parsley
3–4 garlic cloves, crushed
350ml/12fl oz/1½ cups
　vegetable stock
salt and ground black pepper
black olives and fresh parsley,
　to garnish

1 Preheat the oven to 190°C/375°F/ Gas 5. Heat 45ml/ 3 tbsp of the oil in a heavy pan, and cook the onion until golden. Add the aubergines, sauté for 3 minutes, then add the courgettes, peppers, peas, beans and potatoes, and stir in the spices and seasoning. Cook for 3 minutes, stirring constantly.

2 Cut the peeled tomatoes in half and scoop out the seeds. Finely chop the tomatoes and place them in a bowl. Stir in the canned tomatoes with the chopped fresh parsley, crushed garlic and the remaining olive oil. Spoon the cooked vegetable mixture into a shallow ovenproof dish and level the surface.

3 Pour the stock over the aubergine mixture and then spoon over the prepared tomato mixture.

4 Cover the dish with foil and bake for 30–45 minutes, until the vegetables are tender. Serve hot, garnished with black olives and parsley.

Creamy Beetroot Energy 445kcal/1874kJ; Protein 11.1g; Carbohydrate 64.4g, of which sugars 20.5g; Fat 17.8g, of which saturates 7.6g; Cholesterol 31mg; Calcium 140mg; Fibre 7g; Sodium 295mg.
Vegetable Hotpot Energy 365kcal/1529kJ; Protein 14.3g; Carbohydrate 48.2g, of which sugars 20.1g; Fat 14.1g, of which saturates 2.3g; Cholesterol 0mg; Calcium 141mg; Fibre 12.8g; Sodium 224mg.

Spicy Potato Strudel

Wrap up a tasty mixture of vegetables in a spicy, creamy sauce with crisp filo pastry. Serve with a good selection of chutneys or a spicy yogurt sauce.

Serves 4

1 onion, chopped
2 carrots, coarsely grated
1 courgette (zucchini), chopped
350g/12oz firm potatoes, finely chopped
65g/2½ oz/5 tbsp butter
10ml/2 tsp mild curry paste
2.5ml/½ tsp dried thyme
150ml/¼ pint/⅔ cup water
1 egg, beaten
30ml/2 tbsp single (light) cream
50g/2oz/¼ cup Cheddar cheese, grated
8 sheets filo pastry, thawed if frozen
sesame seeds, for sprinkling
salt and ground black pepper

1 In a large frying pan, cook the onion, carrots, courgette and potatoes in about 25g/1oz/2 tbsp of the butter for 5 minutes, tossing frequently so they cook evenly. Add the curry paste and stir in. Continue to cook the vegetables for a further minute.

2 Add the thyme, water and seasoning. Gradually bring to the boil, then reduce the heat and simmer for about 10 minutes until tender, stirring occasionally.

3 Remove from the heat and leave to cool. Transfer the mixture into a large bowl and then mix in the egg, cream and cheese. Chill until ready to fill the filo pastry.

4 Melt the remaining butter and lay out four sheets of filo pastry, slightly overlapping them to form a fairly large rectangle. Brush with some melted butter and fit the other sheets on top. Brush again.

5 Preheat the oven to 190°C/375°F/Gas 5. Spoon the filling along one long side, then roll up the pastry. Form it into a circle and set on a baking sheet. Brush again with the last of the butter and sprinkle over the sesame seeds.

6 Bake the strudel in the oven for about 25 minutes until golden and crisp. Leave to stand for 5 minutes before cutting.

Baked Potatoes and Three Fillings

Potatoes baked in their skins make an excellent and nourishing meal on their own. For an even better treat, add one of these three delicious and easy toppings.

Serves 4

4 medium baking potatoes
olive oil
sea salt
filling of your choice (see below)

Stir-fry vegetables
45ml/3 tbsp groundnut or sunflower oil
2 leeks, thinly sliced
2 carrots, cut into sticks
1 courgette (zucchini), thinly sliced
115g/4oz baby corn, halved
115g/4oz/1½ cup button (white) mushrooms, sliced
45ml/3 tbsp soy sauce
30ml/2 tbsp dry sherry or vermouth
15ml/1 tbsp sesame oil
sesame seeds, to garnish

Red bean chilli sauce
425g/15oz can red kidney beans, drained
200g/7oz/scant 1 cup low-fat cottage or cream cheese
30ml/2 tbsp mild chilli sauce
5ml/1 tsp ground cumin

Cheese and creamy corn
425g/15oz can creamed corn
115g/4oz/1⅓ cups hard cheese, grated
5ml/1 tsp mixed dried herbs
fresh parsley sprigs, to garnish

1 Preheat the oven to 200°C/400°F/Gas 6. Score the potatoes with a cross and rub all over with the oil. Bake for 45 minutes to 1 hour until tender. Cut the potatoes open along the score lines and push up the flesh. Season and top with a filling.

2 For the vegetables, heat the oil in a wok or frying pan until bubbling. Add the leeks, carrots, courgette and baby corn and stir-fry for about 2 minutes, then add the mushrooms and stir-fry for 1 minute. Add the soy sauce, sherry or vermouth and sesame oil. Heat through until bubbling and sprinkle with sesame seeds.

3 For the red beans, heat the beans in a pan and stir in the cottage or cream cheese, chilli sauce and cumin.

4 For the creamy corn, heat the corn gently in a pan with the cheese and herbs. Garnish with the parsley sprigs.

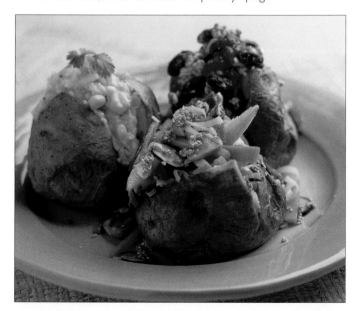

Spicy Strudel Energy 362kcal/1512kJ; Protein 9.8g; Carbohydrate 34.8g, of which sugars 6.5g; Fat 21.1g, of which saturates 12.7g; Cholesterol 98mg; Calcium 169mg; Fibre 3g; Sodium 227mg.
Baked Potatoes Energy 223kcal/941kJ; Protein 7.3g; Carbohydrate 38.6g, of which sugars 8.3g; Fat 4.5g, of which saturates 0.8g; Cholesterol 0mg; Calcium 55mg; Fibre 5.4g; Sodium 1150mg.

Peppers Filled with Vegetables

Nigella seeds have a mild, slightly nutty flavour and are best toasted for a few seconds in a dry frying pan before being used in a recipe. This helps to bring out their flavour.

Serves 6

6 large evenly shaped red or
   yellow (bell) peppers
500g/1¼lb waxy potatoes
1 small onion, chopped
4 or 5 garlic cloves, chopped
5cm/2in piece fresh root
   ginger, chopped
1 or 2 fresh green chillies,
   seeded and chopped
105ml/7 tbsp water
90–105ml/6–7 tbsp vegetable oil
1 aubergine (eggplant), diced
10ml/2 tsp cumin seeds
5ml/1 tsp nigella seeds
2.5ml/½ tsp ground turmeric
5ml/1 tsp ground coriander
5ml/1 tsp ground toasted
   cumin seeds
cayenne pepper
about 30ml/2 tbsp lemon juice
sea salt and ground black pepper
30ml/2 tbsp chopped fresh
   coriander (cilantro), to garnish

1 Cut the tops off the red or yellow peppers, then remove and discard the seeds. Cut a thin slice off the base of any wobbly peppers so that they stand upright. Bring a large pan of lightly salted water to the boil. Add the peppers to the water and cook for 5–6 minutes. Remove from the pan and leave them upside down in a colander to drain thoroughly.

2 Cook the potatoes in lightly salted, boiling water for 10–12 minutes until just tender. Drain, cool and peel, then cut into 1cm/½in dice.

3 Put the onion, garlic, ginger and green chillies in a food processor or blender with 60ml/4 tbsp of the water and process to a purée.

4 Heat 45ml/3 tbsp of the vegetable oil in a large, deep frying pan and cook the aubergine, stirring occasionally, until it is evenly browned. Remove the aubergine from the pan using a slotted spoon and set aside to cool. Add another 30ml/2 tbsp of the vegetable oil to the pan, then add the potatoes and cook until lightly browned. Remove the potatoes from the pan and set aside.

5 If necessary, add another 15ml/1 tbsp sunflower oil to the pan, then add the cumin and nigella seeds. Fry briefly until the seeds darken, then add the turmeric, coriander and ground cumin. Cook for 15 seconds. Stir in the onion and garlic purée and fry, scraping the pan with a spatula, until the onions begin to brown.

6 Return the potatoes and aubergine to the pan, season with salt, ground black pepper and one or two pinches of cayenne. Add the remaining water and 15ml/1 tbsp lemon juice and then cook, stirring, until the liquid evaporates. Preheat the oven to 190°C/375°F/Gas 5.

7 Fill the peppers with the spiced vegetable mixture and place on a lightly greased baking tray. Brush the peppers with a little oil and bake for 30–35 minutes until they are cooked. Leave to cool a little, then sprinkle with a little more lemon juice. Garnish with the coriander and serve.

Vegetables in Ashes with Salsa

Use a double layer of coals to start the barbecue so they will be deep enough to make a bed for the foil-wrapped vegetables.

Serves 4–6

2 small whole heads of garlic
2 butternut squash, halved
   lengthways and seeded
4–6 onions, with a cross cut in
   the top of each
4–6 baking potatoes
4–6 sweet potatoes
45ml/3 tbsp olive oil
fresh thyme, bay leaf and
   rosemary sprigs
salt and ground black pepper
2 handfuls of hickory wood chips
   soaked in cold water for at
   least 30 minutes

For the tomato salsa

500g/1¼lb tomatoes, quartered
   and seeded
2.5ml/½ tsp sugar
a pinch of chilli flakes
1.5ml/¼ tsp smoky
   chilli powder
30ml/2 tbsp tomato chutney

1 Prepare a barbecue with plenty of coals. Wrap the garlic, squash and onions separately in a double layer of foil, but do not seal. Wrap the potatoes in pairs, with one sweet and one ordinary potato. Drizzle olive oil over each packet, season and add a herb sprig. Spray with a little water and seal the parcels.

2 Once the flames have died down and the coals are hot, or with a light coating of ash, place the parcels on top of them. The garlic will take 20 minutes to cook, the squash 30 minutes, the onions 45 minutes and the potatoes 1 hour. As each vegetable cooks, remove the parcel and wrap in an extra layer of foil to keep warm. Set aside. Shortly before serving, loosen the tops of all the parcels, except the garlic, and put them all back on the coals so the vegetables dry out a little before serving.

3 Meanwhile, make the salsa. Heat an oiled grill rack. Sprinkle the tomatoes with sugar, chilli flakes and seasoning. Place them on the rack and cook, covered, for 5 minutes. Drain the hickory chips and place a handful on the coals, replace the cover and leave to smoke for 5 minutes. Add some more wood chips and grill for 10 minutes. Spoon the tomato flesh from the charred skins into a bowl, crush with a fork and mix in the other ingredients. Serve with the vegetables.

Filled Peppers Energy 222kcal/926kJ; Protein 3.6g; Carbohydrate 26.1g, of which sugars 13g; Fat 12.1g, of which saturates 2.5g; Cholesterol 0mg; Calcium 25mg; Fibre 4.4g; Sodium 17mg.
Vegetables in Ashes Energy 439kcal/1860kJ; Protein 9.5g; Carbohydrate 89.6g, of which sugars 21.5g; Fat 7.3g, of which saturates 1.3g; Cholesterol 0mg; Calcium 114mg; Fibre 9.6g; Sodium 118mg.

Potato and Onion Cakes with Beetroot Relish

These grated potato cakes are utterly irresistible. They are especially delicious with a sweet-sharp beetroot relish and sour cream.

Serves 4

500g/1 ¼lb potatoes (such as King Edward, Estima or Desirée)
1 small cooking apple, peeled, cored and coarsely grated
1 small onion, finely chopped
50g/2oz/½ cup plain (all-purpose) flour
2 large eggs, beaten
30ml/2 tbsp chopped chives
vegetable oil, for shallow frying
salt and ground black pepper

250ml/8fl oz/1 cup sour cream or crème fraîche
fresh dill sprigs and fresh chives or chive flowers, to garnish

For the beetroot relish
250g/9oz beetroot (beets), cooked, peeled and diced
1 large dessert apple, cored and finely diced
15ml/1 tbsp finely chopped red onion
15–30ml/1–2 tbsp tarragon vinegar
15ml/1 tbsp chopped fresh dill
15–30ml/1–2 tbsp light olive oil
pinch of caster (superfine) sugar (optional)

1 To make the relish, mix the beetroot with the apple and onion. Add 15ml/1 tbsp of the vinegar, the dill and 15ml/1 tbsp of oil. Season, adding more vinegar and oil if necessary, and a pinch of sugar to taste.

2 Coarsely grate the potatoes, then rinse, drain and dry them on a clean dish towel. Mix the potatoes, apple and onion in a bowl. Stir in the flour, eggs and chives. Season and mix again.

3 Heat about 5mm/¼in depth of oil in a frying pan and fry spoonfuls of the mixture. Flatten them to make pancakes 7.5–10cm/3–4in across and cook for 3–4 minutes on each side, until browned. Drain on kitchen paper and keep warm until the mixture is used up.

4 Serve a stack of cakes with spoonfuls of sour cream or crème fraîche, and relish. Garnish with dill sprigs and chives or chive flowers and season with black pepper just before serving.

Potato Cakes with Goat's Cheese

Goat's cheese makes a tangy, bubbling topping for these herby potato cakes. They are particularly delicious served with a flavoursome salad.

Serves 2–4

450g/1lb floury potatoes
10ml/2 tsp chopped fresh thyme
1 garlic clove, crushed
2 spring onions (scallions) (including the green parts), finely chopped

30ml/2 tbsp olive oil
50g/2oz/¼ cup unsalted butter
2 x 65g/2½oz firm goat's cheese
salt and ground black pepper
salad leaves, such as curly endive, radicchio and lamb's lettuce, tossed in walnut dressing, to serve
thyme sprigs, to garnish

1 Coarsely grate the potatoes. Using your hands, squeeze out as much of the thick starchy liquid as possible, then gently combine with the chopped thyme, garlic and spring onions. Season with salt and black pepper.

2 Heat half the oil and butter in a non-stick frying pan. Add two large spoonfuls of the potato mixture, spacing them well apart, and press firmly down with a spatula. Cook for 3–4 minutes on each side until golden.

3 Drain the potato cakes on kitchen paper and keep warm in a low oven. Heat the remaining oil and butter and fry two more potato cakes in the same way with the remaining mixture. Meanwhile preheat the grill (broiler).

4 Cut the cheese in half horizontally and place one half, cut side up, on each potato cake. Grill (broil) for 2–3 minutes until lightly golden. Serve on plates and arrange the salad leaves around them. Garnish with thyme sprigs.

> **Cook's Tip**
> These potato cakes make great party snacks. Make them half the size and serve warm on a large platter.

Beetroot Potato Cakes Energy 471kcal/1964kJ; Protein 10.3g; Carbohydrate 42.1g, of which sugars 13.4g; Fat 30.2g, of which saturates 10.6g; Cholesterol 152mg; Calcium 118mg; Fibre 3.7g; Sodium 125mg.
Goat's Cheese Cakes Energy 310kcal/1290kJ; Protein 7.9g; Carbohydrate 18.6g, of which sugars 2g; Fat 23.2g, of which saturates 12.6g; Cholesterol 54mg; Calcium 48mg; Fibre 1.3g; Sodium 272mg.

Raclette with New Potatoes

Traditional to both Switzerland and France, raclette melts to a velvety creaminess and warm golden colour and has a savoury taste with a hint of sweetness, perfect with delicate new potatoes.

Serves 4
For the pickle
2 red onions, sliced

5ml/1 tsp sugar
90ml/6 tbsp red wine vinegar
2.5ml/½ tsp salt
generous pinch of dried dill

For the potatoes
500g/1¼lb new or salad
   potatoes, halved if large
250g/9oz raclette cheese slices
salt and ground black pepper

1 To make the pickle, spread out the sliced onions in a glass dish, pour over enough boiling water to cover them, and set aside until cold.

2 Meanwhile, mix the sugar, red wine vinegar, salt and dill in a small pan. Heat gently, stirring, until the sugar has dissolved, then set aside to cool.

3 Drain the onions and return them to the dish, pour the vinegar mixture over, cover and leave for at least 1 hour, preferably overnight.

4 Cook the potatoes in their skins in boiling water until tender, then drain and place in a roasting tin (pan). Preheat the grill (broiler). Season the potatoes and arrange the raclette on top.

5 Place the pan under the grill until the cheese has melted. Serve hot. Drain the excess vinegar from the red onion pickle and serve the pickle with the potatoes.

Cook's Tip
To speed up the process, look for ready-sliced raclette for this dish. It is available from most large supermarkets and specialist cheese shops.

Potato, Smoked Mozzarella and Garlic Pizza

New potatoes, smoked mozzarella and garlic make this pizza unique.

Serves 2–3
350g/12oz small new or
   salad potatoes
45ml/3 tbsp olive oil
2 garlic cloves, crushed
1 pizza base, about 25–30cm/
   10–12in diameter

1 red onion, thinly sliced
150g/5oz/1¼ cups smoked
   mozzarella cheese, grated
10ml/2 tsp chopped fresh
   rosemary or sage
salt and ground black pepper
30ml/2 tbsp freshly grated
   Parmesan cheese, to garnish

1 Preheat the oven to 220°C/425°F/Gas 7. Put the potatoes in a large pan. Add water to cover and bring to the boil. Add salt, then simmer for about 5 minutes, or until the potatoes are just becoming tender. Drain thoroughly and leave to cool.

2 When the potatoes are cool enough to handle, peel and slice them thinly.

3 Heat 30ml/2 tbsp of the oil in a frying pan. Add the sliced potatoes and garlic and fry for 5–8 minutes, turning frequently until tender.

4 Brush the pizza base with the remaining oil. Sprinkle the onion over, then arrange the potatoes on top.

5 Sprinkle over the mozzarella and rosemary or sage and plenty of black pepper. Bake for 15–20 minutes until golden. Remove from the oven, sprinkle with Parmesan and more ground black pepper.

Variation
For non-vegetarians, you could add sliced smoked pork sausage or pastrami to the pizza to make it even more substantial.

Raclette Energy 327kcal/1366kJ; Protein 19.3g; Carbohydrate 27.1g, of which sugars 6.9g; Fat 15.9g, of which saturates 10.1g; Cholesterol 50mg; Calcium 508mg; Fibre 2.3g; Sodium 899mg.
Potato Pizza Energy 413kcal/1727kJ; Protein 14.1g; Carbohydrate 39.5g, of which sugars 3.7g; Fat 23.1g, of which saturates 8.5g; Cholesterol 29mg; Calcium 222mg; Fibre 2.1g; Sodium 302mg.

Pepper and Potato Tortilla

Tortilla is traditionally a Spanish egg and potato dish like a thick omelette, best eaten cold in chunky wedges. Use a hard Spanish cheese, like Mahón, or a goat's cheese, although sharp Cheddar makes a good substitute.

Serves 4
2 medium waxy potatoes

45ml/3 tbsp olive oil, plus more
  if necessary
1 large onion, thinly sliced
2 garlic cloves, crushed
2 (bell) peppers, one green
  and one red, seeded and
  thinly sliced
6 eggs, beaten
115g/4oz/1 cup mature (sharp)
  cheese, grated
salt and ground black pepper

1 Par-boil the potatoes in boiling water for about 10 minutes. Drain and leave to cool slightly. Slice them thickly. Preheat the grill (broiler).

2 In a large non-stick or well-seasoned frying pan, heat the oil over a medium heat. Add the onion, garlic and peppers and cook for 5 minutes until softened. Add the potatoes and cook, stirring occasionally, until the potatoes are tender.

3 Pour in half the beaten eggs, sprinkle half the cheese over this and then the remainder of the egg. Season with salt and pepper. Finish with a layer of cheese. Reduce the heat to low and continue to cook without stirring, half covering the pan with a lid to help set the eggs.

4 When the tortilla is firm, place the pan under the hot grill to seal the top just lightly. Leave the tortilla in the pan to cool. Serve at room temperature, cut into wedges.

> **Variation**
> *You can add any sliced and lightly cooked vegetable, such as mushrooms, courgette (zucchini) or broccoli, to this tortilla instead of the green and red (bell) peppers. Cooked pasta or brown rice are both excellent alternatives to the potatoes.*

Courgette and Potato Tortilla

Microwaves can be an incredibly convenient tool in the kitchen of a busy household. This delicious, chunky, omelette-style potato tortilla can be made in next to no time in the microwave. All it needs is a little browning under a hot grill at the end of cooking.

Serves 4
30ml/2 tbsp chopped
  fresh tarragon

4 eggs, beaten
30ml/2 tbsp olive oil
1 onion, finely chopped
450g/1lb potatoes, cut into
  small dice
1 garlic clove, crushed
2 courgettes (zucchini),
  thinly sliced
salt and ground black pepper
mixed leafy salad and crusty
  bread, to serve

1 Stir the tarragon into the eggs and season with salt and ground black pepper. Set aside.

2 Place the oil and onion in a large, shallow microwave-proof dish which is suitable for putting under the grill (broiler). Cover and microwave on HIGH for 3 minutes. Add the diced potatoes, garlic and sliced courgettes, cover again and microwave on HIGH for 10 minutes, stirring twice during the cooking process.

3 Pour the eggs over the vegetables, cover and microwave on HIGH for about 3–5 minutes, rotating the dish twice, until the eggs are beginning to set slightly. Meanwhile, preheat the grill.

4 Place the tortilla under the grill and cook for a few minutes until the top has set and is tinged golden. Cut into wedges and serve from the dish with a mixed salad and crusty bread.

> **Cook's Tip**
> *This recipe is also suitable for cooking in a combination microwave. Follow the oven manufacturer's timing guide for the best results.*

Pepper Tortilla Energy 321kcal/1333kJ; Protein 13.1g; Carbohydrate 19.6g, of which sugars 10.2g; Fat 21.1g, of which saturates 8.3g; Cholesterol 123mg; Calcium 256mg; Fibre 3g; Sodium 254mg.
Courgette Tortilla Energy 221kcal/923kJ; Protein 9.7g; Carbohydrate 20.7g, of which sugars 3.6g; Fat 11.7g, of which saturates 2.5g; Cholesterol 190mg; Calcium 58mg; Fibre 2g; Sodium 84mg.

Potato, Pepper and Mint Frittata

This fresh-tasting Italian version of the ever-popular omelette is filled with potatoes and plenty of fresh herbs. Try to use fresh mint in preference to the dried variety if you can find it. It is delicious served either hot or cold.

Serves 3–4

450g/1lb small new or
   salad potatoes
6 eggs
30ml/2 tbsp chopped fresh mint
30ml/2 tbsp olive oil
1 onion, chopped
2 garlic cloves, crushed
2 red (bell) peppers, seeded and
   roughly chopped
salt and ground black pepper
mint sprigs, to garnish

1 Cook the potatoes in their skins in boiling salted water until just tender. Drain and leave to cool slightly. When cool enough to handle, cut them into thick slices.

2 Whisk together the eggs and mint in a bowl. Season with salt and ground black pepper, then set aside. Heat the oil in a large frying pan.

3 Add the onion, garlic, peppers and potatoes to the pan and cook, stirring occasionally, for about 5–7 minutes, until the onion and peppers are soft but not browned.

4 Pour the beaten egg mixture over the vegetables in the frying pan and stir gently to distribute the egg evenly.

5 Push the mixture towards the centre of the pan as it cooks to allow any liquid egg to run on to the base and cook through. Meanwhile, preheat the grill (broiler).

6 When the frittata is lightly set on the bottom, place the pan under the hot grill for 2–3 minutes until the top is a light golden brown colour.

7 Serve hot or cold, cut into wedges piled high on a serving dish and garnished with sprigs of mint.

Spanish Potato Omelette

The traditional Spanish omelette consists simply of potatoes, onions and eggs. This one has other vegetables too, and makes a substantial vegetarian meal.

Serves 6

30ml/2 tbsp olive oil, plus extra
   for drizzling
1 Spanish onion, chopped
1 small red pepper, seeded
   and diced
2 celery sticks, chopped
225g/8oz potatoes, peeled, diced
   and cooked
400g/14oz can cannellini
   beans, drained
8 eggs
salt and ground black pepper

1 Heat the olive oil in a 30cm/12in frying pan or paella pan. Add the chopped onion, red pepper and celery, and cook over a medium heat for between 3–5 minutes until the vegetables are soft, but not coloured.

2 Add the potatoes and beans, and cook for several minutes to heat through.

3 In a small bowl, beat the eggs with a fork, then season well and pour over the ingredients in the pan.

4 Stir the egg mixture with a wooden spatula until it begins to thicken, then allow it to cook over a low heat for about 8 minutes. The omelette should be firm, but still slightly moist in the middle. Cool slightly, then very carefully invert on to a large serving plate.

5 Cut the omelette into thick wedges. Serve warm or cool with a green salad and olives and a little olive oil.

> **Cook's Tip**
> In Spain, this omelette is often served as a tapas dish or appetizer. It is delicious served cold, cut into bitesize pieces and accompanied with a chilli sauce or mayonnaise for dipping. Other sliced seasonal vegetables, baby artichoke hearts and chickpeas can also be used in this recipe.

Potato Frittata Energy 267kcal/1115kJ; Protein 12.2g; Carbohydrate 23.7g, of which sugars 6.8g; Fat 14.5g, of which saturates 3.3g; Cholesterol 285mg; Calcium 57mg; Fibre 2.5g; Sodium 121mg.
Spanish Omelette Energy 374kcal/1563kJ; Protein 16.7g; Carbohydrate 34.9g, of which sugars 11.3g; Fat 19.4g, of which saturates 4.5g; Cholesterol 381mg; Calcium 87mg; Fibre 3.9g; Sodium 162mg.

Sweet Potatoes with Gorgonzola

The contrast of colours in this dish looks stunning and the mixture of flavours tastes wonderful with the sharp, spicy tones of the cheese mingling deliciously with the sweet potato.

Serves 4

4 large sweet potatoes, scrubbed
30ml/2 tbsp olive oil
2 large leeks, washed and sliced
115g/4oz Gorgonzola cheese,
 thinly sliced
salt and ground black pepper

1 Preheat the oven to 190°C/375°F/Gas 5. Dry the sweet potatoes with kitchen paper and rub them all over with about 15ml/1 tbsp of the oil. Place them on a baking sheet and sprinkle with salt. Bake in the oven for about 45 minutes to 1 hour, or until tender.

2 Meanwhile, heat the remaining oil in a frying pan and add the sliced leeks. Cook for 3–4 minutes, or until softened and just beginning to turn golden.

3 Cut the potatoes in half lengthways and place them cut side up on the baking sheet. Top with the cooked leeks and season.

4 Lay the cheese slices on top and grill (broil) under a hot grill (broiler) for 2–3 minutes, until bubbling. Serve immediately.

Cook's Tip
Ensure that the potatoes are completely cooked by inserting a sharp knife or a metal skewer into the centre of the potato.

Variations
• *Use other cheeses if you like. Mature (sharp) Cheddar would work well, or go for another blue cheese, such as Stilton or Dolcelatte, if you prefer.*
• *The sweetness of the potato is key to the success of this recipe, but delicately flavoured chunks of sweet pumpkin or butternut squash would work just as well.*

Aubergine and Sweet Potato Stew

Inspired by Thai cooking, this aubergine and sweet potato stew cooked in a coconut sauce is scented with fragrant lemon grass, ginger and lots of garlic.

Serves 6

60ml/4 tbsp groundnut (peanut) oil
2 aubergines (eggplants), cut
 into chunks
225g/8oz Thai red shallots or
 other shallots
5ml/1 tsp fennel seeds,
 lightly crushed
4–5 garlic cloves, thinly sliced
25ml/1½ tbsp finely chopped
 fresh root ginger
475ml/16fl oz/2 cups vegetable
 stock
2 stems lemon grass, outer layers
 discarded, finely chopped
15g/½oz fresh coriander
 (cilantro), stalks and leaves
 chopped separately
3 kaffir lime leaves, lightly bruised
2–3 small red chillies
45–60ml/3–4 tbsp Thai green
 curry paste
675g/1½lb sweet potatoes, cut
 into thick chunks
400ml/14fl oz/1⅔ cups
 coconut milk
2.5–5ml/½–1 tsp light
 muscovado (brown) sugar
250g/9oz mushrooms, sliced
juice of 1 lime, to taste
salt and ground black pepper
18 fresh Thai basil leaves or
 ordinary basil, to garnish

1 Heat half the oil in a lidded frying pan. Add the aubergines and cook over a medium heat, stirring occasionally, until lightly browned on all sides. Remove from the pan and set aside.

2 Slice 4–5 of the shallots and set aside. Fry the remaining whole shallots in the pan, adding more oil if necessary, until browned. Set aside. Add the remaining oil to the pan and cook the sliced shallots, fennel, garlic and ginger until soft but not browned. Add the vegetable stock, lemon grass, coriander stalks, lime leaves and whole chillies. Cover and simmer for 5 minutes.

3 Stir in 30ml/2 tbsp of the curry paste and the sweet potatoes. Simmer for 10 minutes, return the aubergines and shallots to the pan and cook for a further 5 minutes. Stir in the coconut milk and sugar. Season to taste, then add the mushrooms and simmer for 5 minutes. Stir in more curry paste and lime juice to taste, followed by the chopped coriander leaves. Sprinkle with basil and serve.

Baked Sweet Potatoes Energy 338kcal/1425kJ; Protein 9.5g; Carbohydrate 44.8g, of which sugars 13.1g; Fat 14.8g, of which saturates 6.6g; Cholesterol 22mg; Calcium 206mg; Fibre 6.5g; Sodium 432mg.
Aubergine Stew Energy 234kcal/986kJ; Protein 3.5g; Carbohydrate 30.1g, of which sugars 12.3g; Fat 12.1g, of which saturates 2.3g; Cholesterol 0mg; Calcium 65mg; Fibre 5g; Sodium 126mg.

Sweet Potato and Pumpkin Curry

A hearty, soothing curry that is perfect for autumn or winter evenings. The cheerful colour of the sweet potato alone will brighten you up — and it tastes terrific.

Serves 4
30ml/2 tbsp vegetable oil
4 garlic cloves, crushed
4 shallots, finely chopped
30ml/2 tbsp yellow
   curry paste
600ml/1 pint/2½ cups
   vegetable stock
2 kaffir lime leaves, torn

15ml/1 tbsp chopped
   fresh galangal
450g/1lb pumpkin, peeled,
   seeded and diced
225g/8oz sweet potatoes, diced
90g/3½oz/scant 1 cup peanuts,
   roasted and chopped
300ml/½ pint/1¼ cups
   coconut milk
90g/3½oz/1½ cups chestnut
   mushrooms, sliced
15ml/1 tbsp soy sauce
30ml/2 tbsp mushroom ketchup
50g/2oz/⅓ cup pumpkin seeds,
   toasted, and fresh green chilli
   flowers, to garnish

1 Heat the oil in a large pan. Add the garlic and shallots and cook over a medium heat, stirring occasionally, for 10 minutes, until softened and golden. Do not let them burn.

2 Add the yellow curry paste and stir-fry over a medium heat for 30 seconds, until fragrant, then add the stock, lime leaves, galangal, pumpkin and sweet potatoes. Bring to the boil, stirring frequently, then reduce the heat to low and simmer gently for 15 minutes.

3 Add the peanuts, coconut milk and mushrooms to the pan. Stir in the soy sauce and mushroom ketchup and simmer for 5 minutes more. Spoon into warmed individual serving bowls, garnish with the pumpkin seeds and chillies and serve.

Cook's Tip
The well-drained vegetables from any of these curries would make a very tasty filling to be used in a pastry or pie. This may not be the most Eastern tradition, but it is a good example of modern fusion food.

Mixed Vegetables in Coconut Sauce

A vegetable dish is an essential part of an Indian meal, even for a simple occasion, where one or two vegetable dishes may be served with a lentil dhal, a raita, and bread or boiled rice. There are many ways to make a vegetable curry, but this recipe, in which the potatoes and other vegetables are simmered in coconut milk, is typical of South India.

Serves 4
225g/8oz potatoes, cut into
   5cm/2in cubes

115g/4oz green beans
150g/5oz carrots, scraped and
   cut into 5cm/2in cubes
500ml/17fl oz/2¼ cups
   hot water
1 small aubergine (eggplant),
   about 225g/8oz, quartered
   lengthways
75g/3oz coconut milk powder
5ml/1 tsp salt
30ml/2 tbsp vegetable oil
6–8 fresh or 8–10 curry leaves
1 or 2 dried red chillies,
   chopped into small pieces
5ml/1 tsp ground cumin
5ml/1 tsp ground coriander
2.5ml/½ tsp ground turmeric
rice, dhal or Indian bread, to serve

1 Put the cubed potatoes, green beans and carrots in a large pan, add 300ml/½ pint/1¼ cups of the hot water and bring to the boil. Reduce the heat a little, cover the pan and continue to cook for 5 minutes.

2 Cut the aubergine quarters into 5cm/2in pieces. Rinse and then add to the pan.

3 Blend the coconut milk powder with the remaining hot water and add to the vegetables, with the salt. Bring to a slow simmer, cover and cook for 6–7 minutes.

4 In a small pan, heat the oil over a medium heat and add the curry leaves and the dried red chillies. Immediately follow with the ground cumin, coriander and turmeric.

5 Stir-fry the spices together for 15–20 seconds and pour the entire contents of the pan over the vegetables. Stir to distribute the spices evenly and remove the pan from the heat. Serve the mixed vegetables with rice, dhal or any Indian bread.

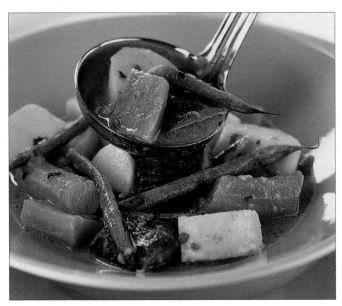

Pumpkin Curry Energy 337kcal/1404kJ; Protein 10.3g; Carbohydrate 21.7g, of which sugars 10.8g; Fat 23.8g, of which saturates 4g; Cholesterol 0mg; Calcium 168mg; Fibre 5.1g; Sodium 554mg.
Mixed Vegetables Energy 80kcal/335kJ; Protein 1.2g; Carbohydrate 5.6g, of which sugars 5.3g; Fat 6.1g, of which saturates 0.9g; Cholesterol 0mg; Calcium 29mg; Fibre 2.3g; Sodium 71mg.

Roast Potatoes

For crisp roasties with fluffy interiors, cook them in a single layer. Cooking potatoes in goose fat may seem decadent, but the results will be well worth the expense.

Serves 4
1.3kg/3lb floury potatoes
90ml/6 tbsp oil, lard, white cooking fat or goose fat
salt

1 Preheat the oven to 200°C/400°F/Gas 6. Peel the potatoes and cut into chunks. Boil in salted water for 5 minutes, drain, return to the pan, and shake them to roughen the surfaces.

2 Put the fat into a large roasting pan and put into the hot oven to heat the fat. Add the potatoes, coating them in the fat. Return to the oven and roast for 40–50 minutes, turning once or twice, until crisp, golden and cooked through.

Baked Jacket Potatoes

Once the potato, one of England's staple foods, is cooked in its skin in the oven it is transformed into the ultimate comfort food. The deliciously crispy skin masks a moreishly soft and fluffy interior. It can be served split and laced with butter or sour cream, or with a filling of grated cheese.

Serves 4
4 large floury potatoes of even size, such as King Edward or Maris Piper
a little oil
salt (optional)
butter or sour cream, to serve
chopped fresh parsley or chives, to serve

1 Preheat the oven to 200°C/400°F/Gas 6. Scrub and dry the potatoes, and prick the skins with a fork to prevent them bursting during cooking.

2 Rub the skins all over with a little oil and sprinkle with a little salt, if using.

3 Put the potatoes in the hot oven, either on a baking sheet or straight on to the oven shelf. Cook for about 1 hour or until soft throughout.

4 Leave the cooked potatoes to stand for 5 minutes before splitting them open. Be careful of the escaping steam.

5 Serve with a dollop of butter on top, or sour cream and a sprinkling of parsley or chives.

Chips

Chips, or French fries, are the ultimate potato classic. Fry these twice – once to cook them, and the second time to crisp them.

Serves 4
sunflower or vegetable oil, for deep frying
675g/1½lb potatoes
salt

1 Heat the oil to 150°C/300°F. Peel the potatoes and cut them into chips (French fries) about 1cm/½in thick. Rinse and dry.

2 Lower a batch of chips into the hot oil and cook for about 5 minutes or until tender but not browned. Lift out on to kitchen paper and leave to cool.

3 Just before serving, increase the temperature of the oil to 190°C/375°F. Add the par-cooked chips, in batches. Cook until crisp and golden.

4 Lift out of the fryer and drain on kitchen paper. Sprinkle the cooked chips with salt and serve immediately.

Cook's Tips
• *Cooking potatoes in the microwave is quicker and easier, but the results will be nowhere near as good. If you have the time to prepare baked potatoes as laid out above it is well worth the effort.*
• *Ensure that the potatoes are completely cooked by inserting a sharp knife or a metal skewer into the centre of the potato. You will be able to tell if they need cooking a bit longer because there will be a little resistance.*

Baked Jacket Potatoes Energy 182kcal/772kJ; Protein 3.8g; Carbohydrate 36.2g, of which sugars 2.9g; Fat 3.4g, of which saturates 0.6g; Cholesterol 0mg; Calcium 14mg; Fibre 2.3g; Sodium 25mg.
Roast Potatoes Energy 484kcal/2048kJ; Protein 9.4g; Carbohydrate 84.2g, of which sugars 2g; Fat 14.6g, of which saturates 5.9g; Cholesterol 13mg; Calcium 26mg; Fibre 5.9g; Sodium 29mg.
Chips Energy 403kcal/1689kJ; Protein 5.4g; Carbohydrate 51.5g, of which sugars 2.9g; Fat 14.5g, of which saturates 6.1g; Cholesterol 0mg; Calcium 19mg; Fibre 3.7g; Sodium 59mg.

Hasselback Potatoes

This dish is named after the Stockholm restaurant that created it, and is a method of cooking rather than a recipe. Choose similar-sized potatoes so that they cook uniformly, and the essential thing is to cut the potatoes most of the way, but not completely, through. It is a good idea to thread a skewer through the potato three-quarters of the way down before cutting, so that your knife travels just to the point you want it to reach and no farther.

Serves 4
4 large potatoes
75g/3oz/6 tbsp butter
45ml/3 tbsp olive oil
50g/2oz/1 cup fine fresh
    breadcrumbs
50g/2oz/2/3 cup grated
    Parmesan cheese
salt and ground black pepper

1 Preheat the oven to 200°C/400°F/Gas 6. Peel the potatoes, then – and this is the crucial part – cut them widthways, not lengthways, down to three-quarters of their depth at 3mm/1/8in intervals, preferably at a slight angle.

2 Wash the potatoes in cold water, then arrange, cut sides uppermost, in a deep, ovenproof dish.

3 Melt the butter in a small pan, then add the olive oil and mix together. Brush the mixture over the potatoes, then season well with salt and black pepper. Sprinkle over the breadcrumbs and the grated cheese.

4 Roast the potatoes in the preheated oven for about 1 hour, depending on their size, until golden brown and fanned apart along the cut lines. Serve hot.

> **Cook's Tip**
> *If the potatoes are to be served as an accompaniment to a roast joint of meat, you can use the cooking juices from the meat to baste them during cooking. Don't move them around while they roast, because they won't crisp up properly.*

Griddle Potatoes

This dish makes a tasty accompaniment to grilled meat or fish.

Serves 4–6
2 onions, peeled and chopped

450–675g/1lb–1 1/2lb whole
    cooked potatoes, boiled in
    their skins
a mixture of butter and oil, for
    shallow frying
salt and ground black pepper

1 Put the onions in a large pan and scald them briefly in boiling water. Refresh under cold water and drain well. Peel and slice the potatoes.

2 Put a mixture of butter and oil into a large, heavy frying pan and heat well. When the fat is hot, fry the onion until tender. Add the potato slices and brown them together, turning the potato slices to brown as evenly as possible on both sides. Transfer to a warmed serving dish and season with salt and pepper. Serve very hot.

Garlicky Roasties

Potatoes roasted in their skins retain a deep, earthy taste while the garlic mellows on cooking.

Serves 4
1kg/2 1/4lb small floury potatoes

60–75ml/4–5 tbsp sunflower oil
10ml/2 tsp walnut oil
2 whole garlic bulbs, unpeeled
salt

1 Preheat the oven to 240°C/475°F/Gas 9. Place the potatoes in a pan of cold water and bring to the boil. Drain.

2 Combine the oils in a roasting pan and place in the oven to get really hot. Add the potatoes and garlic and coat in oil.

3 Sprinkle with salt and roast for 10 minutes. Reduce the heat to 200°C/400°F/Gas 6. Continue roasting, basting occasionally, for 40 minutes. Serve with several cloves of garlic per portion.

Hasselback Potatoes Energy 380kcal/1593kJ; Protein 9.9g; Carbohydrate 42g, of which sugars 3.1g; Fat 20.4g, of which saturates 12.5g; Cholesterol 52mg; Calcium 182mg; Fibre 2.3g; Sodium 367mg.
Griddle Potatoes Energy 163kcal/681kJ; Protein 3.4g; Carbohydrate 26.4g, of which sugars 5g; Fat 5.5g, of which saturates 3.3g; Cholesterol 13mg; Calcium 26mg; Fibre 2.6g; Sodium 49mg.
Garlicky Roasties Energy 312kcal/1310kJ; Protein 6.2g; Carbohydrate 44.3g, of which sugars 3.7g; Fat 13.4g, of which saturates 1.7g; Cholesterol 0mg; Calcium 20mg; Fibre 3.5g; Sodium 29mg.

Biarritz Potatoes

A combination of classic mashed potatoes with finely diced ham and peppers.

Serves 4
900g/2lb floury potatoes, diced
50g/2oz/¼ cup butter

90ml/6 tbsp milk
50g/2oz cooked ham, finely diced
1 red (bell) pepper, seeded and finely diced
15ml/1 tbsp chopped fresh parsley
sea salt and ground black pepper

1 Boil the potatoes in lightly salted water for 20 minutes or until very tender. Drain and return the potatoes to the pan and allow the steam to dry off over a low heat.

2 Mash the potatoes or pass them through a potato ricer. Add the butter and milk and stir in the cooked ham, peppers and parsley. Season and serve.

Perfect Creamed Potatoes

These potatoes are the perfect comfort food and are easy to make.

Serves 4
900g/2lb firm but not waxy potatoes, diced
45ml/3 tbsp extra virgin olive oil

150ml/¼ pint/⅔ cup hot milk
freshly grated nutmeg
fresh basil leaves or parsley sprigs, chopped
salt and ground black pepper
basil leaves, to garnish
fried bacon, to serve

1 Cook the potatoes in boiling water until just tender but not too mushy. Drain thoroughly. Press the potatoes through a potato ricer (which looks like a large garlic press) or mash them with a potato masher. Beat in olive oil and enough hot milk to make a smooth, thick purée.

2 Flavour to taste with the nutmeg, salt and black pepper, then stir in the chopped fresh herbs. Spoon into a warm serving dish and serve immediately, garnished with basil leaves and pieces of fried bacon.

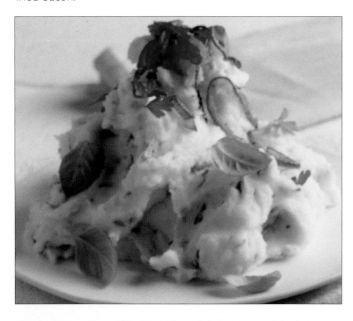

Root Vegetable Clapshot

This root vegetable dish is an excellent accompaniment to haggis or used on top of a shepherd's pie in place of simple mashed potato. Turnips give a delicious earthy flavour, and swede introduces a sweet accent. It is also slightly less heavy than mashed potato, which makes it good for a lighter meal or supper.

Serves 4
450g/1lb potatoes
450g/1lb turnips or swede (rutabaga)
50g/2oz/¼ cup butter
50ml/2fl oz/¼ cup milk
5ml/1 tsp freshly grated nutmeg
30ml/2 tbsp chopped fresh parsley
salt and ground black pepper

1 Peel the potatoes and turnips or swede, then cut them into small, even chunks. You will need a large sharp knife for the turnips.

2 Place the chopped vegetables in a pan and cover with cold water. Bring to the boil over a medium heat, then reduce the heat and simmer until both vegetables are cooked, which will take about 15–20 minutes. Test the vegetables by pushing the point of a sharp knife into one of the cubes; if it goes in easily and the cube begins to break apart, then it is cooked.

3 Drain the vegetables through a colander. Return to the pan and allow them to dry out for a few minutes over a low heat, stirring occasionally to prevent any from sticking to the base of the pan.

4 Place the butter and the milk in a small pan over a low heat. Gently heat until the butter has melted, stirring constantly to combine it with the milk.

5 Mash the dry potato and turnip or swede mixture with a potato masher, then add the milk mixture.

6 Grate in the nutmeg, add the chopped parsley, mix thoroughly and season to taste with salt and pepper. Serve immediately with roast meat or game.

Biarritz Potatoes Energy 289kcal/1214kJ; Protein 7.5g; Carbohydrate 40.4g, of which sugars 6.9g; Fat 11.9g, of which saturates 7.4g; Cholesterol 37mg; Calcium 54mg; Fibre 3.2g; Sodium 284mg.
Perfect Creamed Potatoes Energy 249kcal/1049kJ; Protein 5.1g; Carbohydrate 38.1g, of which sugars 4.8g; Fat 9.6g, of which saturates 1.8g; Cholesterol 2mg; Calcium 59mg; Fibre 2.3g; Sodium 46mg.
Clapshot Energy 204kcal/852kJ; Protein 3.4g; Carbohydrate 24.1g, of which sugars 7.2g; Fat 11.2g, of which saturates 6.8g; Cholesterol 27mg; Calcium 78mg; Fibre 3.8g; Sodium 111mg.

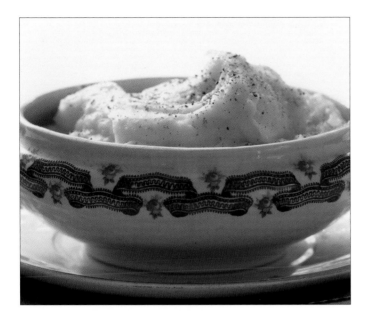

Spiced Potato Purée

A flavoursome and fragrant addition to a festive dining table, this delicately spiced potato purée, originating from Holland, is the perfect accompaniment to any roast dinner and is especially delicious when served alongside game.

Serves 4
750g/1lb 10oz peeled floury
  potatoes, cut into quarters
½ tsp salt
½ tsp paprika
½ tsp nutmeg
½ tsp black pepper
2 egg yolks
knob (pat) of butter
milk

1 Preheat the oven to 220°C/425°F/Gas 7. Grease an ovenproof dish with butter or line a baking sheet with baking parchment.

2 Put the potatoes in a pan, add water to cover, bring to the boil and cook for about 15 minutes, or until tender. Drain well.

3 While still warm, pass the potatoes through a potato ricer or alternatively, mash with a hand-held electric mixer, but take care as a mixer can produce a purée that is too sticky.

4 Stir in the salt, spices, egg yolks and butter. Add some milk if the purée seems too thick.

5 While still warm, pipe or spread the purée with a fork into the prepared dish. Alternatively, pipe rosettes on to the baking sheet lined with baking parchment.

6 Bake the purée in the oven for 20 minutes. When cooked, if unpiped, transfer the hot purée into a serving dish and place on the dining table. Allow people to serve themselves.

> **Variation**
> *This traditional side dish makes a warming and decadent meal in its own right if smothered in a rich cheese sauce and baked for around 20 minutes, until golden.*

Garlic Sweet Potato Mash

Delicious mashed with garlicky butter, orange-fleshed sweet potatoes not only look good, they're packed with vitamins.

40g/1½oz/3 tbsp unsalted butter
3 garlic cloves, crushed
salt and ground black pepper

Serves 4
4 large sweet potatoes, total
  weight about 900g/2lb, cubed

1 Put the sweet potatoes in a large pan. Add enough water to cover and bring to the boil. Add a little salt, then simmer for about 15 minutes, or until the potatoes are tender, but do not let them get too soft. Drain thoroughly in a colander and then return them to the pan.

2 Melt the butter in a heavy frying pan, then cook the garlic over a low to medium heat for about 1–2 minutes until it turns light golden. Stir the garlic frequently to prevent it from burning, otherwise it will taste bitter.

3 Pour the garlic butter over the sweet potatoes, season with salt and plenty of black pepper, and mash thoroughly until smooth and creamy. Serve immediately.

> **Variation**
> *Add some chopped fresh herbs, such as parsley or coriander, if you wish.*

> **Cook's Tips**
> • *If the sweet potatoes seem to be on the dry side when you are mashing them, add a little milk.*
> • *Orange-fleshed sweet potatoes are rich in beta carotene and vitamins C and E, which are believed to be linked with lowering the risk of cancer, heart disease and strokes.*

Potato Purée Energy 174kcal/732kJ; Protein 4.5g; Carbohydrate 28.4g, of which sugars 2.3g; Fat 5.4g, of which saturates 2.3g; Cholesterol 106mg; Calcium 24mg; Fibre 1.8g; Sodium 236mg.
Sweet Potato Mash Energy 586kcal/2477kJ; Protein 16.3g; Carbohydrate 101.4g, of which sugars 52.1g; Fat 15.8g, of which saturates 7.1g; Cholesterol 240mg; Calcium 182mg; Fibre 2.8g; Sodium 968mg.

Grated Potato Dumplings

These dumplings contain a mixture of mashed and grated potato, which gives them an interesting texture. They make an ideal accompaniment to many casseroled or braised dishes and are tasty served with fried cubes of pork fat.

Serves 4

1kg/2¼ lb potatoes, peeled
2 eggs, beaten
pinch of salt
115g/4oz plain (all-purpose) flour, plus extra for dusting
15ml/1 tbsp potato flour
150g/5oz pork fat, cut into 1cm/½ in cubes

1 Chop half the potatoes into chunks, then add to a pan of lightly salted, boiling water. Cook for 10 minutes, or until soft. Drain the potatoes, then mash in a large bowl.

2 Grate the remaining potatoes and squeeze in a sieve (strainer) to remove the excess liquid. Add to the mashed potato.

3 Add the eggs, a pinch of salt and both the flours to the bowl, and knead thoroughly to form a dough. Using floured hands, roll spoonfuls of the dough into balls.

4 Bring a large pan of lightly salted water to the boil, then add the dumplings. Cook for 4–5 minutes, or until the dumplings float on the surface of the water.

5 Meanwhile, fry the cubes of pork fat for about 4 minutes, or until golden brown all over.

6 Transfer the cooked dumplings to a serving plate and spoon over the fried pork fat cubes.

Variation
Delicious served as a quick snack or floating in a robust casserole, these dumplings can also be transformed into a substantial and delicious meal in their own right. Try smothering with a rich cheese sauce and baking at 200°C/400°F/Gas 6 for 20–25 minutes until beautifully golden and bubbling.

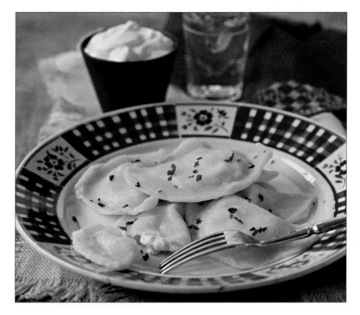

Potato and Cheese Pierogi

These traditional Polish dumplings, stuffed with potato and curd cheese, are made from simple, cheap ingredients and are deceptively easy to make. They are a wonderful side dish or, by being creative with the stuffing, a substantial meal in their own right.

Serves 4-6

500g/1¼lb plain (all-purpose) flour, plus extra for dusting

2.5ml/½tsp salt
2 eggs, beaten
45ml/3 tbsp vegetable oil
250ml/8fl oz/1 cup warm water
chopped fresh parsley, to garnish
thick sour cream, to serve

For the filling
15g/½oz/1 tbsp butter
½ large onion, finely chopped
250g/9oz peeled, cooked potatoes
250g/9oz/1¼ cups curd cheese
1 egg, beaten
salt and black pepper, to taste

1 For the filling, heat the butter in a small pan, add the onion and cook for about 5 minutes. Push the cooked potatoes through a ricer, add the cheese and stir thoroughly. Add the egg, onion and seasoning to the potato mixture and mix well.

2 For the dough, sift the flour into a bowl, then add the salt and eggs. Pour in the oil and water, and mix to form a loose dough.

3 Turn out on to a floured surface and knead well for about 10 minutes, or until the dough is pliant and does not stick to the work surface. Divide the dough into four pieces, then roll each one out thinly with a floured rolling pin. Cut the dough into 5–6cm/2–2½in circles using a pastry (cookie) cutter.

4 Place a heaped teaspoonful of the potato filling mixture in the centre of each of the circles of dough, then fold over the dough and press to seal the edges. The dumplings should be neat and well filled, but not bursting.

5 Bring a large pan of lightly salted water to the boil, add the dumplings and cook for about 4–5 minutes, or until they rise up to float on the surface. Cook for a further two minutes once they have risen, then remove to a serving dish. Garnish with chopped parsley and serve with thick sour cream.

Potato Dumplings Energy 658kcal/2746kJ; Protein 10.3g; Carbohydrate 65.6g, of which sugars 3.7g; Fat 41.1g, of which saturates 16.2g; Cholesterol 130mg; Calcium 71mg; Fibre 3.5g; Sodium 64mg.
Pierogi Energy 419kcal/1768kJ; Protein 11.7g; Carbohydrate 71.6g, of which sugars 2.3g; Fat 11.5g, of which saturates 2.9g; Cholesterol 100mg; Calcium 136mg; Fibre 3.1g; Sodium 57mg.

Marquis Potatoes

These crispy potato treats are finished with a deliciously tangy tomato mixture set in the centre of the potato nest.

Serves 6

900g/2lb floury potatoes

450g/1lb ripe tomatoes
15ml/1tbsp olive oil
2 shallots, finely chopped
25g/1oz/2 tbsp butter
3 egg yolks
60ml/4 tbsp milk
chopped fresh parsley, to garnish
sea salt and ground black pepper

1 Peel and cut the potatoes into small chunks, then boil in a pan of lightly salted water for about 15–20 minutes or until they are very tender.

2 Meanwhile, cut a small cross into each tomato, blanch them in boiling water and then plunge into a bowl of cold water. Peel the skins and scoop the seeds out. Chop the tomato flesh.

3 Heat the olive oil in a large frying pan and fry the shallots for 2 minutes, stirring constantly.

4 Add the chopped tomatoes to the pan and fry for a further 10 minutes until the moisture has evaporated. Set aside.

5 Drain the potatoes through a colander, return them to the pan and allow the steam to dry them off. Set the potatoes aside to cool slightly.

6 Mash the potatoes thoroughly with the butter and two of the egg yolks and the milk. Season with plenty of salt and ground black pepper.

7 Grease a baking sheet. Spoon the potato into a piping (pastry) bag fitted with a medium star nozzle. Pipe six oval nests on to the baking sheet. Beat the remaining egg with a little water and carefully brush over the potato. Grill for 5 minutes or until golden.

8 Spoon the tomato mixture inside the nests and top with a little parsley. Serve them immediately.

Swiss Soufflé Potatoes

A fabulous combination of rich and satisfying ingredients – cheese, eggs, cream, butter and potatoes. This is perfect for cold-weather eating.

Serves 4

4 floury baking potatoes

115g/4oz/1 cup Gruyère
  cheese, grated
115g/4oz/8 tbsp
  herb-flavoured butter
60ml/4 tbsp double
  (heavy) cream
2 eggs, separated
salt and ground black pepper

1 Preheat the oven to 220°C/425°F/Gas 7. Prick the potatoes all over with a fork. Bake in the oven for 1–1½ hours until tender. Remove them from the oven and reduce the temperature to 180°C/350°F/Gas 4.

2 Cut each potato in half and scoop out the flesh into a bowl. Return the shells to the oven to crisp them up while making the filling.

3 Mash the potato flesh using a fork, then add the Gruyère, herb-flavoured butter, cream, egg yolks and seasoning. Beat well until smooth.

4 Whisk the egg whites in a separate bowl until they hold stiff but not dry peaks, then carefully fold into the potato mixture.

5 Pile the mixture back into the potato shells and place on a baking sheet. Bake in the oven for 20–25 minutes until risen and golden brown.

6 Serve the potatoes hot, sprinkled with fresh, chopped chives, if wished, and a bowl of mayonnaise on the side.

> **Variation**
> Use other cheeses, if you like. Mature (sharp) Cheddar would work well, or go for another blue cheese such as Stilton or Dolcelatte, if you prefer.

Marquis Potatoes Energy 136kcal/571kJ; Protein 3.3g; Carbohydrate 18.5g, of which sugars 3.6g; Fat 5.9g, of which saturates 2.4g; Cholesterol 74mg; Calcium 27mg; Fibre 1.6g; Sodium 43mg.
Swiss Potatoes Energy 576kcal/2394kJ; Protein 14.2g; Carbohydrate 32.6g, of which sugars 3g; Fat 44.3g, of which saturates 27.2g; Cholesterol 209mg; Calcium 251mg; Fibre 2g; Sodium 486mg.

Grilled Potatoes with Chive Flower Dressing

There is something very enjoyable about using edible plants and herbs from the garden. Chive flowers and champagne vinegar are used here as a dressing to grilled potatoes, and the result is a truly special dish. This is ideal served with simple grilled fish or meat, and also makes a sophisticated potato salad at a barbecue.

Serves 4–6

900g/2lb salad potatoes, such as
    Charlottes, Jersey royals or
    French ratte
15ml/1 tbsp champagne
    vinegar
105ml/7 tbsp olive oil
45ml/3 tbsp chopped chives
about 10 chive flowers
4–6 small bunches yellow cherry
    tomatoes on the vine
salt and ground black pepper

1 Light the barbecue and leave until the flames have died down. Boil the potatoes in a large pan of lightly salted water for about 10 minutes, or until just tender.

2 Meanwhile, make the dressing by whisking the vinegar with 75ml/5 tbsp of the oil, then stirring in the chives and flowers. Drain the potatoes and cut them in half horizontally. Season to taste with salt and pepper.

3 Once the barbecue flames have died down, position a grill rack directly over the coals to heat. When the coals are medium-hot, or with a moderate coating of ash, toss the potatoes in the remaining oil and lay them on the grill rack, with the cut side facing down. Leave over the heat for about 5 minutes, then press down a little so that they are imprinted with the marks of the grill.

4 Turn the potatoes over and cook the second side for about 3 minutes. Place the potatoes in a bowl, pour over the dressing and toss lightly to mix.

5 Grill the tomatoes for 3 minutes, or until they are just beginning to blister. Serve with the potatoes, which can be hot, warm or cold.

Crispy Potato, Onion and Garlic Gratin

This is a simple but delicious way of cooking potatoes and onions together. Choose stock to complement the main dish that it is accompanying. Alternatively, use water and add some bacon to give flavour. This gratin also makes a good base on which to bake fish.

Serves 4–6

40g/1½oz/3 tbsp butter or bacon
    fat or 45ml/3 tbsp olive oil
2–4 garlic cloves, finely chopped
900g/2lb waxy potatoes,
    thinly sliced
450g/1lb onions, thinly sliced
450ml/¾ pint/scant 2 cups fish,
    chicken, beef or lamb stock
salt and ground black pepper

1 Use half the butter, fat or oil to grease a 1.5 litre/2½ pint/ 6¼ cup gratin dish. Preheat the oven to 180°C/350°F/Gas 4. Sprinkle a little of the chopped garlic over the base of the dish and then layer the potatoes and onions in the dish, seasoning each layer with a little salt and pepper and adding the remaining garlic. Finish with a layer of overlapping potato slices on top.

2 Bring the stock to the boil in a pan and pour it over the gratin. Dot the top with the remaining butter or bacon fat cut into small pieces, or drizzle over the reserved oil. Cover tightly with foil and bake for 1½ hours.

3 Increase the oven temperature to 200°C/400°F/Gas 6. Uncover the gratin and then cook for a further 35–50 minutes, until the potatoes are completely cooked and the top layer is browned and crusty. Serve immediately.

> **Variation**
> Layer 175g/6oz thinly sliced cheese with the potatoes.
> About 15–20 minutes before the end of cooking time, sprinkle
> the gratin with another 50g/2oz/½ cup grated cheese, dot
> with more butter and finish baking. This version is also good
> made with leeks.

Grilled Potatoes Energy 232kcal/970kJ; Protein 3g; Carbohydrate 26.2g, of which sugars 4g; Fat 13.5g, of which saturates 2.1g; Cholesterol 0mg; Calcium 14mg; Fibre 2.2g; Sodium 23mg.
Potato Gratin Energy 181kcal/762kJ; Protein 3.5g; Carbohydrate 30.1g, of which sugars 6.2g; Fat 6.1g, of which saturates 3.8g; Cholesterol 15mg; Calcium 29mg; Fibre 2.6g; Sodium 69mg.

Summer Squash and Baby New Potatoes in Warm Dill Sour Cream

Fresh vegetables and fragrant dill are delicious tossed in a simple sour cream or yogurt sauce. Choose small squash with bright skins that are free from blemishes and bruises. To make a simpler potato salad, pour the dill sour cream over warm cooked potatoes. Serve either version of the potato salad with poached salmon or chargrilled chicken.

Serves 4
400g/14oz mixed squash, such as yellow and green courgettes (zucchini), and pale green patty pan
400g/14oz tiny baby new potatoes
1 large handful mixed fresh dill and chives, finely chopped
300ml/½ pint/1¼ cups sour cream or Greek (US strained plain) yogurt

1 Cut the squash into pieces about the same size as the potatoes. Put the potatoes in a pan and add water to cover and a pinch of salt. Bring to the boil, then simmer for about 10 minutes, until almost tender.

2 Add the squash to the pan with the potatoes. Bring back to the boil and then reduce the heat and continue to simmer gently until the vegetables are just tender, then drain.

3 Transfer the vegetables into a wide, shallow pan and gently stir in the finely chopped fresh dill and chives.

4 Remove the pan from the heat and stir in the sour cream or yogurt. Return to the heat and heat gently until warm. Season with salt and pepper and serve.

> **Cook's Tip**
> *This dish is equally delicious if served cold. If you chill it in the refrigerator, allow it to come to room temperature and stir well before serving.*

Glazed Sweet Potatoes with Smoked Bacon

Smoky bacon is the perfect addition to these melt-in-the-mouth, sugar-topped potatoes. They taste great as a change from roast potatoes, with roast duck or chicken.

Serves 4–6
butter, for greasing
900g/2lb sweet potatoes
115g/4oz/½ cup soft light brown sugar
30ml/2 tbsp lemon juice
45ml/3 tbsp butter
4 rashers (strips) smoked lean bacon, cut into matchsticks
salt and ground black pepper
1 flat leaf parsley sprig, chopped, to garnish

1 Preheat the oven to 190°C/375°F/Gas 5 and lightly butter a shallow ovenproof dish. Cut each unpeeled sweet potato crossways into three and cook in boiling water, covered, for about 25 minutes until just tender.

2 Drain thoroughly in a colander and leave to cool. When cool enough to handle, peel and slice thickly. Arrange in a single layer, overlapping the slices, in the prepared dish.

3 Sprinkle the sugar and lemon juice on the potato slices and dot the surface with butter.

4 Top with the bacon and season well with salt and black pepper. Bake in the oven, uncovered, for about 35–40 minutes, basting once or twice.

5 The potatoes are ready once they are tender – test them with a knife or metal skewer to make sure. Remove from the oven once they are cooked.

6 Preheat the grill (broiler) to a high heat. Sprinkle the potatoes with the chopped flat leaf parsley. Place the pan under the grill for about 2–3 minutes until the sweet potatoes are evenly browned and the pieces of bacon have turned crispy. Serve immediately.

Summer Squash Energy 317kcal/1317kJ; Protein 5.8g; Carbohydrate 21g, of which sugars 6.1g; Fat 23.9g, of which saturates 14.8g; Cholesterol 66mg; Calcium 105mg; Fibre 2g; Sodium 104mg.
Glazed Potatoes Energy 387kcal/1627kJ; Protein 7.2g; Carbohydrate 49.5g, of which sugars 26.1g; Fat 19.3g, of which saturates 9.8g; Cholesterol 50mg; Calcium 49mg; Fibre 3.6g; Sodium 562mg.

Sweet Potatoes, Onions and Beetroot in Coconut and Ginger Paste

Sweet potatoes and beetroot take on a wonderful sweetness when roasted.

Serves 4

30ml/2 tbsp groundnut (peanut) oil or mild olive oil

450g/1lb sweet potatoes, peeled and cut into thick strips or chunks

4 beetroot (beets), cooked, peeled and cut into wedges

450g/1lb small red or yellow onions, halved

5ml/1 tsp coriander seeds, lightly crushed

3–4 small whole fresh red chillies

salt and ground black pepper

chopped fresh coriander (cilantro), to garnish

For the paste

2 large garlic cloves, chopped

1–2 green chillies, seeded and chopped

15ml/1 tbsp chopped fresh root ginger

45ml/3 tbsp chopped fresh coriander (cilantro)

75ml/5 tbsp coconut milk

30ml/2 tbsp groundnut oil or mild olive oil

grated rind of 1/2 lime

2.5ml/1/2 tsp light muscovado (brown) sugar

1 First make the paste. Process the garlic, chillies, ginger, coriander and coconut milk in a food processor, blender or coffee grinder.

2 Turn the paste into a small bowl and beat in the oil, lime rind and muscovado sugar. Preheat the oven to 200°C/400°F/Gas 6.

3 Heat the oil in a roasting tin (pan) in the oven for 5 minutes. Add the sweet potatoes, beetroot, onions and coriander seeds, tossing them in the hot oil. Roast for 10 minutes.

4 Stir in the paste and the whole red chillies. Season well and toss the vegetables to coat them thoroughly with the paste.

5 Roast the vegetables for a further 25–35 minutes, or until the sweet potatoes and onions are fully cooked and tender. Stir two or three times to prevent the paste from sticking to the pan. Serve immediately, sprinkled with chopped coriander.

Bombay Potatoes

This authentic dish is most closely linked to the Gujarati, a totally vegetarian people and the largest population group in the city of Mumbai.

Serves 4–6

2 onions

2 fresh green chillies

50g/2oz/2 cups fresh coriander (cilantro)

450g/1lb new potatoes

5ml/1 tsp turmeric

60ml/4 tbsp vegetable oil

2 dried red chillies

6–8 curry leaves

1.5ml/1/4 tsp asafoetida

2.5ml/1/2 tsp each cumin, mustard, onion, fennel and nigella seeds

lemon juice, to taste

salt

1 Chop the onions and chillies finely, and coarsely chop the coriander.

2 Scrub the potatoes under cold running water and cut them into small pieces.

3 Boil the potatoes in water with a little salt and 2.5ml/1/2 tsp of the turmeric for 10–15 minutes, or until tender. Drain the potatoes well, then mash them and set aside.

4 Heat the oil in a frying pan and fry the dried chillies and curry leaves until the chillies are nearly burnt.

5 Add the sliced onions, green chillies, fresh coriander and remaining turmeric to the pan and fry for two minutes, until the onions are starting to soften.

6 Add the asafoetida, cumin, mustard, onion, fennel and nigella seeds. Cook, stirring occasionally, until the onions are soft.

7 Fold in the potatoes and add a few drops of water. Cook over a low heat for about 10 minutes, stirring well to ensure the spices are evenly mixed.

8 Stir the lemon juice to taste into the potatoes, and serve immediately.

Sweet Potato Energy 272kcal/1143kJ; Protein 4.4g; Carbohydrate 39.8g, of which sugars 19.2g; Fat 11.8g, of which saturates 1.7g; Cholesterol 0mg; Calcium 98mg; Fibre 6.3g; Sodium 122mg.
Bombay Potatoes Energy 143kcal/595kJ; Protein 2.1g; Carbohydrate 17.4g, of which sugars 4.7g; Fat 7.7g, of which saturates 0.9g; Cholesterol 0mg; Calcium 21mg; Fibre 1.7g; Sodium 10mg.

Patatas Bravas

The name of this Spanish tapas dish, patatas bravas, means fiercely hot potatoes, but luckily tapas are usually only eaten in small quantities.

Serves 4
900g/2lb small new or
  salad potatoes
60ml/4 tbsp olive oil
1 onion, finely chopped
2 garlic cloves, crushed

15ml/1 tbsp tomato purée (paste)
200g/7oz can chopped tomatoes
15ml/1 tbsp red wine vinegar
2–3 small dried red chillies,
  seeded and finely chopped, or
  5–10ml/1–2 tsp hot
  chilli powder
5ml/1 tsp paprika
salt and ground black pepper
1 flat leaf parsley sprig, to garnish
chopped fresh red chillies,
  to garnish (optional)

1 Put the potatoes in a large pan. Add water to cover and bring to the boil. Add salt, then simmer for about 15 minutes, or until the potatoes are tender, but do not let them get too soft. Drain thoroughly and leave to cool slightly, then cut in half and set aside.

2 Heat the oil in a large pan and add the onion and garlic. Fry them gently for 5–6 minutes until just softened. Stir in the tomato purée, tomatoes, vinegar, chillies or chilli powder and paprika and simmer for about 5 minutes.

3 Stir the potatoes into the sauce mixture until they are well coated. Cover and simmer gently for 8–10 minutes until the potatoes are tender.

4 Season the potatoes well and transfer to a warmed serving dish. Serve immediately, garnished with a sprig of flat leaf parsley. To make the dish even hotter, add a garnish of chopped fresh red chillies.

> **Cook's Tip**
> *If you don't like your potatoes to be too fiery, simply reduce the amount of chilli to taste. Conversely, if you prefer a little more heat then increase the quantity used.*

Fiery Spanish-style Chilli and Potatoes with Peppers

The most important thing with this potato dish is the spicing, which is made hotter still by adding vinegar. This version is made with fresh tomato sauce flavoured with garlic and chilli, and is a variation of traditional patatas bravas. The name implies that the potatoes are so hot that it is manly to eat them. Patatas bravas often appear on tapas menus and are good with drinks.

Serves 4
675g/1½lb small new potatoes
75ml/5 tbsp olive oil
2 garlic cloves, sliced
3 dried chillies, seeded
  and chopped
2.5ml/½ tsp ground cumin
10ml/2 tsp paprika
30ml/2 tbsp red or white
  wine vinegar
1 red or green (bell) pepper,
  seeded and sliced
coarse sea salt, for sprinkling
  (optional)

1 Scrub the potatoes and put them into a pan of lightly salted water. Bring to the boil and cook for 10 minutes, or until almost tender. Drain and leave to cool slightly. Peel, if you like, then cut the potatoes in half.

2 Heat the oil in a large frying or sauté pan and fry the potatoes, turning them frequently, until golden.

3 Meanwhile, crush together the garlic, chillies and cumin using a mortar and pestle. Mix the paste with the paprika and red or white wine vinegar, then add to the potatoes with the sliced pepper and cook, stirring, for 2 minutes. Scatter with salt, if using, then serve hot as a tapas dish or cold as a side dish.

> **Variation**
> *Patatas bravas means fierce potatoes. They are meant to be fiery but the flavour can be moderated by reducing the amount of chilli. Although classically vegetarian, they are often served with chorizo or with chunks of roast pork. Try making them with sweet potatoes for a tasty change.*

Patatas Bravas Energy 384kcal/1605kJ; Protein 5g; Carbohydrate 45g, of which sugars 7.3g; Fat 21.6g, of which saturates 3.3g; Cholesterol 0mg; Calcium 21mg; Fibre 3.6g; Sodium 31mg.
Spanish Potatoes Energy 256kcal/1070kJ; Protein 3.3g; Carbohydrate 30g, of which sugars 4.9g; Fat 14.4g, of which saturates 2.2g; Cholesterol 0mg; Calcium 14mg; Fibre 2.4g; Sodium 20mg.

Cumin and Fennel Spiced Potatoes

If you like chillies, you'll love these potatoes. However, if you're not a fan of very fiery flavours, simply leave out the chilli seeds, from both the dried and fresh chillies, and use the flesh by itself.

Serves 4

12–14 small new or salad
  potatoes, halved
30ml/2 tbsp vegetable oil
2.5ml/½ tsp dried red
  chillies, crushed
2.5ml/½ tsp white cumin seeds
2.5ml/½ tsp fennel seeds
2.5ml/½ tsp crushed
  coriander seeds
5ml/1 tsp salt
1 onion, sliced
1–4 fresh red chillies, chopped
15ml/1 tbsp chopped fresh
  coriander (cilantro), plus extra
  to garnish

1 Cook the potatoes in boiling salted water until tender but still firm. Remove from the heat and drain off the water. Set aside until needed.

2 In a deep frying pan, heat the oil over a medium-high heat, then reduce the heat to medium. Add the crushed chillies, cumin, fennel and coriander seeds and salt and fry, stirring, for 30–40 seconds.

3 Add the sliced onion and fry until softened and golden brown. Then add the potatoes, red chillies and chopped fresh coriander and stir well.

4 Reduce the heat to very low, then cover and cook for 5–7 minutes. Serve the potatoes hot, garnished with more fresh coriander.

Cook's Tips
• *To prepare fresh chillies, trim the stalk end, slit down one side and scrape out the seeds, unless you want a really hot dish. Finely slice or chop the flesh.*
• *Wear rubber gloves if you have very sensitive skin and wash your hands thoroughly after handling chillies. Avoid touching your eyes if you have any trace of chilli on your fingers.*

New Potatoes in Dashi Stock

As the stock evaporates in this delicious dish, the onion becomes meltingly soft and caramelized, making a wonderful sauce that coats the potatoes.

Serves 4

15ml/1 tbsp vegetable oil
15ml/1 tbsp toasted sesame oil
1 small onion, thinly sliced
1kg/2¼lb baby new or salad
  potatoes, unpeeled
200ml/7fl oz/scant 1 cup water
  with 5ml/1 tsp instant
  dashi powder
45ml/3 tbsp shoyu, dark soy
  sauce or kecap manis

1 Heat the vegetable and sesame oils in a wok or large frying pan until very hot. Add the onion slices and stir-fry for about 30 seconds, then add the potatoes. Stir constantly, until all the potatoes are well coated in the sesame oil, and have begun to sizzle.

2 Pour on the dashi stock and shoyu, dark soy sauce or kecap manis, and reduce the heat to the lowest setting. Cover the wok or pan and cook for 15 minutes, using a slotted spoon to turn the potatoes every 5 minutes to prevent sticking and to ensure that they cook evenly.

3 Uncover the wok or pan for a further 5 minutes to reduce the liquid. If there is already very little liquid remaining, remove the wok or pan from the heat, cover and leave to stand for 5 minutes. Check that the potatoes are cooked, then remove from the heat.

4 Transfer the potatoes and onions to a deep, warmed serving bowl. Pour the sauce over the top and serve immediately.

Cook's Tip
Toasted sesame oil is recommended because of its distinctive aroma, but mixing it with vegetable oil not only moderates the flavour, it also lessens the likelihood of the oil burning when heated in the pan.

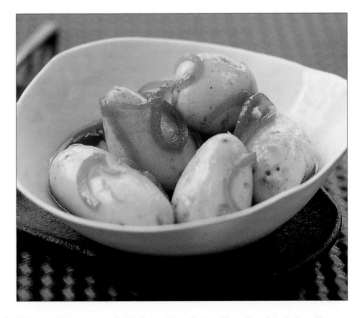

Cumin Potatoes Energy 260kcal/1091kJ; Protein 4.8g; Carbohydrate 35.2g, of which sugars 2.8g; Fat 12.1g, of which saturates 1.5g; Cholesterol 0mg; Calcium 39mg; Fibre 3.4g; Sodium 40mg.
Potatoes in Dashi Stock Energy 210kcal/890kJ; Protein 4.8g; Carbohydrate 42.4g, of which sugars 4.9g; Fat 3.5g, of which saturates 0.7g; Cholesterol 0mg; Calcium 21mg; Fibre 2.7g; Sodium 829mg.

Spicy Potato Cakes

Quick and easy to make, these piquant potato cakes are very popular. Try serving them with salsa as a light meal, or as an accompaniment to roasted or pan-fried meats.

Makes 10
600g/1lb 6oz potatoes
115g/4oz/1 cup grated
   Cheddar cheese

2.5ml/½ tsp salt
50g/2oz/⅓ cup drained pickled
   jalapeño chilli slices, finely
   chopped (optional)
1 egg, beaten
small bunch of fresh coriander
   (cilantro), finely chopped
plain (all-purpose) flour,
   for shaping
oil, for shallow frying
fresh citrus salsa, to serve

1 Peel the potatoes and halve them if large. Put them in a large pan. Add water to cover and bring to the boil. Add salt, then simmer for about 15 minutes, or until the potatoes are tender, but do not let them get too soft.

2 Drain the potatoes thoroughly and return to the pan and mash. Don't overdo this step as the mashed potato should not be too smooth.

3 Scrape the potato into a bowl and stir in the grated cheese, with the salt and the chopped jalapeños, if using. Stir in the beaten egg and most of the chopped fresh coriander and mix to a dough.

4 When the dough is cool enough to handle, put it on to a lightly floured board. With floured hands, divide it into ten pieces of equal size. Shape each piece into a ball, then flatten to a cake.

5 Heat the oil in a large frying pan. Fry the potato cakes, in batches if necessary, for about 2–3 minutes over a moderate heat until golden brown on the underside.

6 Turn them over and cook until both sides are evenly golden. Pile on a platter, sprinkle with salt and the remaining chopped coriander and serve with salsa.

Potatoes in Chilli Tamarind Sauce

In this favourite potato dish from India, the combination of chilli and tamarind awakens the taste buds immediately. This version adapts the traditional recipe slightly, to reduce the customary pungency and enhance the fiery appearance of this delicious combination.

Serves 4–6
450g/1lb small new potatoes,
   washed and dried

25g/1oz whole dried red chillies,
   preferably Kashmiri
7.5ml/1½ tsp cumin seeds
4 garlic cloves, chopped
90ml/6 tbsp vegetable oil
60ml/4 tbsp thick tamarind juice
30ml/2 tbsp tomato
   purée (paste)
4 curry leaves
5ml/1 tsp sugar
1.5ml/¼ tsp asafoetida
salt
coriander (cilantro) sprigs and
   lemon wedges, to garnish

1 Boil the new potatoes until they are fully cooked, ensuring they do not break. To test, insert a thin sharp knife into the potatoes. It should come out clean when they are fully cooked. Drain and cool the potatoes in iced water to prevent them from cooking further.

2 Soak the chillies for 5 minutes in warm water. Drain and grind with the cumin seeds and garlic to a coarse paste, either using a mortar and pestle or in a food processor.

3 Heat the oil and fry the paste, tamarind juice, tomato purée, curry leaves, sugar, asafoetida and salt until the oil can be seen to have separated from the spice paste.

4 Add the potatoes and stir to coat thoroughly in the sauce. Reduce the heat, cover the pan and simmer for 5 minutes. Garnish and serve immediately.

Variation
Chunks of large potatoes can be used as an alternative to new potatoes. Alternatively, try this dish with sweet potatoes. The spicy sweet-and-sour taste works very well in this variation.

Potato Cakes Energy 149kcal/621kJ; Protein 4.8g; Carbohydrate 9.8g; of which sugars 0.9g; Fat 10.1g; of which saturates 3.4g; Cholesterol 30mg; Calcium 101mg; Fibre 0.8g; Sodium 197mg.
Potatoes in Chilli Sauce Energy 90kcal/379kJ; Protein 2.7g; Carbohydrate 19.5g, of which sugars 5.7g; Fat 0.7g, of which saturates 0.1g; Cholesterol 0mg; Calcium 30mg; Fibre 1.9g; Sodium 12mg.

Indonesian Potatoes with Onions and Chilli Sauce

This dish gives another dimension to potato chips, with the addition of crisp onions and a spicy chilli dressing. Eat these hot, warm or cold, as a tasty snack.

Serves 6

3 large potatoes, about 225g/8oz each, peeled and cut into chips (French fries)

sunflower or groundnut (peanut) oil for deep-frying
2 onions, finely sliced
salt

For the dressing

1–2 fresh red chillies, seeded and ground, or 2.5ml/½ tsp chilli sambal
45ml/3 tbsp dark soy sauce

1 Rinse the potato chips and then pat dry very well with kitchen paper.

2 Heat the oil in a large pan. Deep-fry the chips, until they are golden brown in colour and evenly crisp.

3 Drain the chips on kitchen paper and then transfer to a dish, sprinkle with salt and keep warm.

4 Fry the onion slices in the hot oil until they are similarly crisp and golden brown. Drain well on kitchen paper and then add to the potato chips.

5 Mix the ground chillies or chilli sambal with the soy sauce and heat gently.

6 Pour over the potato and onion mixture and serve immediately if you want them hot or leave to cool before serving.

Variation
Alternatively, you could boil the potatoes in their skins. Drain, cool and slice them and then shallow-fry until golden. Cook the onions and pour over the dressing, as above.

Curried Spinach and Potatoes

Traditional Indian spices – mustard seed, ginger and chilli – give a really good kick to potatoes and spinach in this delicious and authentic curry.

Serves 4

450g/1lb spinach
30ml/2 tbsp vegetable oil

5ml/1 tsp black mustard seeds
1 onion, thinly sliced
2 garlic cloves, crushed
2.5cm/1 in piece root ginger, finely chopped
675g/1½lb firm potatoes, cut into 2.5cm/1 in chunks
5ml/1 tsp chilli powder
5ml/1 tsp salt
120ml/4fl oz/½ cup water

1 Wash the spinach in several changes of water, then blanch it in a little boiling water for 3–4 minutes.

2 Drain the spinach thoroughly and leave to cool. When it is cool enough to handle, use your hands to squeeze out any remaining liquid.

3 Heat the oil in a large pan and fry the mustard seeds for 2 minutes, stirring, until they begin to splutter.

4 Add the onion, garlic and ginger to the pan and fry for 5 minutes, stirring.

5 Stir in the potatoes, chilli powder, salt and water and cook for about 8 minutes, stirring occasionally.

6 Finally, add the spinach to the pan. Cover and simmer for 10–15 minutes until the spinach is very soft and the potatoes are tender. Serve hot.

Cook's Tip
To make certain that the spinach is dry before adding it to the potatoes, put it in a clean dish towel, roll up tightly and squeeze gently to remove any excess liquid. Choose a firm waxy variety of potato or a salad potato so the pieces do not break up during cooking.

Indonesian Potatoes Energy 194kcal/815kJ; Protein 2.9g; Carbohydrate 25.6g, of which sugars 3.1g; Fat 9.6g, of which saturates 1.3g; Cholesterol 0mg; Calcium 13mg; Fibre 1.6g; Sodium 551mg.
Curried Spinach Energy 201kcal/845kJ; Protein 6.2g; Carbohydrate 30.2g, of which sugars 4.7g; Fat 6.9g, of which saturates 0.9g; Cholesterol 0mg; Calcium 205mg; Fibre 4.3g; Sodium 668mg.

Potatoes with Chorizo and Green Chillies

Mexicans make their own chorizo sausage, sometimes using it fresh, but also putting it into casings to dry, when it resembles the Spanish version which is now popular the world over. This recipe makes a delicious brunch dish. Typical of peasant food, it is based on the combination of plenty of potato mixed with strongly flavoured meat to help it go further.

Serves 4–6

900g/2lb potatoes, peeled
  and diced
30ml/2 tbsp vegetable oil
2 garlic cloves, crushed
4 spring onions
  (scallions), chopped
2 fresh jalapeño chillies, seeded
  and diced
300g/11oz chorizo
  sausage, skinned
150g/5oz/1¼ cups grated
  Monterey Jack or
  Cheddar cheese
salt (optional)

1 Bring a large pan of water to the boil and add the potatoes. When the water returns to the boil, lower the heat and simmer the potatoes gently for about 5 minutes. Transfer the potatoes into a colander and drain thoroughly.

2 Heat the oil in a large frying pan, add the garlic, spring onions and chillies and cook for 3–4 minutes. Add the diced potato and cook until the cubes begin to brown a little.

3 Cut the chorizo into small cubes and add these to the pan. Cook the mixture for 5 minutes more, until the sausage has heated through. Season with salt if necessary, then add the cheese. Mix carefully, trying not to break up the cubes of potato. Serve immediately, while the cheese is still melting.

> **Cook's Tip**
> Use firm-textured potatoes such as Desirée, Pentland Dell and Estima for this dish. If you can't locate Monterey Jack, look out for a mature Gouda, or use a medium mature Cheddar.

Potatoes in Spicy Yogurt Sauce

Tiny potatoes cooked with their skins on are delicious in this fairly spicy yet tangy yogurt sauce. Serve with any meat or fish dish or just with hot chapatis.

Serves 4

12 small new or salad
  potatoes, halved
275g/10oz/1¼ cups natural
  (plain) low-fat yogurt
300ml/½ pint/1¼ cups water

1.5ml/¼ tsp turmeric
5ml/1 tsp chilli powder
5ml/1 tsp ground coriander
2.5ml/½ tsp ground cumin
5ml/1 tsp salt
5ml/1 tsp soft brown sugar
30ml/2 tbsp vegetable oil
5ml/1 tsp white cumin seeds
15ml/1 tbsp chopped fresh
  coriander (cilantro)
2 fresh green chillies, sliced
1 coriander (cilantro) sprig, to
  garnish (optional)

1 Cook the potatoes in their skins in boiling salted water until just tender, then drain and set aside.

2 Mix together the yogurt, water, turmeric, chilli powder, ground coriander, ground cumin, salt and sugar in a bowl. Set aside.

3 Heat the oil in a medium pan over a medium-high heat and stir in the white cumin seeds.

4 Reduce the heat to medium, and stir in the yogurt mixture. Cook the sauce, stirring constantly, for about 3 minutes.

5 Add the fresh coriander, green chillies and potatoes to the sauce. Mix well and cook for 5–7 minutes, stirring occasionally.

6 Transfer to a serving dish, garnish with the coriander sprig, if you like, and serve hot.

> **Cook's Tip**
> If new potatoes are unavailable, use 450g/1lb large potatoes instead, but choose a waxy not a floury variety. Peel them and cut into large chunks, then cook as described above.

Potatoes with Chorizo Energy 443kcal/1847kJ; Protein 16g; Carbohydrate 32.4g, of which sugars 3.6g; Fat 28.1g, of which saturates 12.3g; Cholesterol 49mg; Calcium 226mg; Fibre 1.9g; Sodium 728mg.
Potatoes in Yogurt Sauce Energy 161kcal/677kJ; Protein 5.9g; Carbohydrate 24.7g, of which sugars 7g; Fat 5.1g, of which saturates 1g; Cholesterol 1mg; Calcium 154mg; Fibre 1.1g; Sodium 73mg.

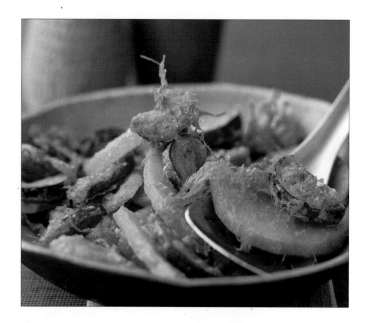

Crisp Deep-fried Vegetables

Stir-fried, steamed or deep-fried vegetables served with a dipping sauce are common fare throughout Asia, and often appear among the delightful 'no-name' dishes popular in Thai tourist fare.

Serves 4–6

6 eggs
1 long aubergine (eggplant), peeled, halved lengthways and sliced into half moons
1 long sweet potato, peeled and sliced into rounds
1 small butternut squash, peeled, seeded, halved lengthways and sliced into half moons
salt and ground black pepper
vegetable oil, for deep-frying
chilli sambal or hot chilli sauce for dipping

1 Beat the eggs in a wide bowl. Season with salt and pepper. Toss the vegetables in the egg to coat thoroughly.

2 Heat enough oil for deep-frying in a large wok. Cook the vegetables in small batches, making sure there is plenty of egg coating each piece.

3 When they turn golden, lift them out of the oil with a slotted spoon and drain on kitchen paper.

4 Keep the vegetables hot while successive batches are being fried. Serve warm with chilli sambal, hot chilli sauce or a dipping sauce of your choice.

Cook's Tips
• To encourage the beaten egg coating to adhere to the pieces of aubergine (eggplant), sweet potatoes and butternut squash, toss them in flour or cornflour (cornstarch) before coating with the egg.
• Courgettes (zucchini), angled loofah, taro root or pumpkin could also be used.

Balti Baby Vegetables

There is a wide and wonderful selection of baby vegetables available in supermarkets these days, and this simple recipe does full justice to their delicate flavour and attractive appearance. Serve as part of a main meal or even as a light appetizer.

Serves 4–6

10 new potatoes, halved
12–14 baby carrots
12–14 baby courgettes (zucchini)
30ml/2 tbsp corn oil
15 baby onions
30ml/2 tbsp chilli sauce
5ml/1 tsp crushed garlic
5ml/1 tsp grated fresh root ginger
5ml/1 tsp salt
400g/14oz/scant 3 cups drained canned chickpeas
10 cherry tomatoes
5ml/1 tsp crushed dried red chillies
30ml/2 tbsp sesame seeds

1 Bring a medium pan of salted water to the boil and add the new potatoes and baby carrots. Cook for 12–15 minutes, then add the courgettes, and boil for a further 5 minutes or until all the vegetables are just tender. Take care not to overcook them, as they will be given a brief additional cooking time later.

2 Drain the vegetables well and put them in a bowl. Set aside.

3 Heat the oil in a karahi, wok or deep pan and add the baby onions. Fry until the onions turn golden brown. Lower the heat and add the chilli sauce, garlic, ginger and salt to the pan, taking care not to burn the mixture.

4 Stir in the chickpeas and stir-fry over a medium heat until the moisture has been absorbed.

5 Add the cooked vegetables and cherry tomatoes, and stir constantly over the heat with a slotted spoon for about 2 minutes until everything is heated through.

6 Sprinkle the crushed red chillies and sesame seeds evenly over the vegetable mixture and serve.

Deep-fried Vegetables Energy 280kcal/1164kJ; Protein 8; Carbohydrate 11.9g, of which sugars 5.7g; Fat 23g, of which saturates 4g; Cholesterol 190mg; Calcium 90mg; Fibre 3.5g; Sodium 84mg.
Balti Baby Vegetables Energy 311kcal/1306kJ; Protein 12.3g; Carbohydrate 48.7g, of which sugars 15.2g; Fat 8.5g, of which saturates 1.3g; Cholesterol 0mg; Fibre 8.4g; Sodium 230mg.

Spiced Potatoes & Carrots Parisienne

Ready-prepared 'parisienne' vegetables have recently become available in many supermarkets. These are simply root vegetables that have been peeled and cut into perfectly spherical shapes. This dish looks very fresh and appetizing and is delicious. If you can't locate 'parisienne' vegetables, you can simply dice the potatoes and carrots yourself, or cut them into batons.

Serves 4

175g/6oz carrots parisienne
175g/6oz potatoes parisienne
115g/4oz green
   beans, sliced
75g/3oz/6 tbsp butter
15ml/1 tbsp vegetable oil
1.5ml/¼ tsp onion seeds
1.5ml/¼ tsp fenugreek seeds
4 dried red chillies
2.5ml/½ tsp mustard seeds
6 curry leaves
1 medium onion, sliced
5ml/1 tsp salt
4 garlic cloves, sliced
4 fresh red chillies
15ml/1 tbsp chopped fresh
   coriander (cilantro)
15ml/1 tbsp chopped fresh
   mint, plus 1 mint sprig
   to garnish

1 Drop the carrots, potatoes and green beans into a pan of boiling water, and cook for about 7 minutes, or until they are just tender but not overcooked. Drain in a colander, then refresh under cold water to arrest the cooking process. Drain again and set to one side.

2 Heat the butter and oil in a deep frying pan or a large karahi and add the onion seeds, fenugreek seeds, dried red chillies, mustard seeds and curry leaves.

3 When the seeds have sizzled for a few seconds and are starting to pop, add the onion and fry for 3–5 minutes, until the onion is soft, stirring the mixture occasionally.

4 Add the salt, sliced garlic cloves and fresh chillies, followed by the cooked vegetables, and stir gently and constantly for around 5 minutes, over a medium heat.

5 Add the fresh coriander and mint, and serve hot, garnished with a sprig of mint.

Roasted Vegetables and Spicy Sauce

Served as a vegetable side dish or as a main course, a selection of roasted vegetables in a peanut sauce, enhanced by chillies and soy sauce, is a favourite throughout South-east Asia.

Serves 4

1 aubergine (eggplant), partially
   peeled and cut into long strips
2 courgettes (zucchini), partially
   peeled and cut into long strips
1 thick, long sweet potato, cut into
   long strips
2 leeks, trimmed, halved
   and sliced
2 garlic cloves, chopped
25g/1oz fresh root ginger, peeled
   and chopped
60ml/4 tbsp vegetable or oil
salt
45ml/3 tbsp roasted peanuts,
   ground, to garnish
fresh crusty bread, to serve

For the sauce

4 garlic cloves, chopped
2–3 red chillies, seeded
   and chopped
5ml/1 tsp shrimp paste
115g/4oz/1 cup roasted
   peanuts, crushed
15–30ml/1–2 tbsp dark soy sauce
juice of 1 lime
5–10ml/1–2 tsp Chinese
   rice vinegar
10ml/2 tsp palm sugar (jaggery)
   or honey
salt and ground black pepper

1 Preheat the oven to 200°C/400°F/Gas 6. Arrange the vegetables in a roasting pan. Using a mortar and pestle or food processor, grind the garlic and ginger to a paste, and smear it over the vegetables. Sprinkle with salt and pour over the oil.

2 Place the pan in the oven for about 45 minutes, until the vegetables are lightly browned, tossing halfway through cooking.

3 Meanwhile, make the sauce. Using a mortar and pestle or a food processor, grind the garlic and chillies to a paste. Beat in the shrimp paste and peanuts. Stir in the soy sauce, lime juice, vinegar and sugar or honey, and blend with a little water so that the sauce is the consistency of pouring cream. Season with salt and pepper and adjust the balance of sweet and sour to taste.

4 Arrange the roasted vegetables on a plate. Drizzle the sauce over them, or serve it separately in a bowl. Sprinkle over the ground peanuts and serve with bread.

Spiced Potatoes Energy 186kcal/790kJ; Protein 7.4g; Carbohydrate 37.2g, of which sugars 5.9g; Fat 2g, of which saturates 0.9g; Cholesterol 5mg; Calcium 121mg; Fibre 2.9g; Sodium 51mg.
Roasted Vegetables Energy 361kcal/1502kJ; Protein 11.9g; Carbohydrate 22.7g, of which sugars 11.1g; Fat 25.4g, of which saturates 4.1g; Cholesterol 0mg; Calcium 76mg; Fibre 6.9g; Sodium 292mg.

Pumpkin, Sweet Potato and Banana in Coconut Milk

This dish of sweet potato and pumpkin cooked with bananas in coconut milk is a Malaysian favourite. Traditionally served as a sweet snack, or for breakfast, it is both nourishing and warming. The recipe can be adapted by alternating the sweet vegetable; try gourds such as yam, butternut squash and winter melon.

Serves 4–6

900ml/1 1/2 pints/3 3/4 cups coconut milk

1/2 small pumpkin, seeded and cut into bitesize cubes

2 sweet potatoes, cut into bitesize pieces

1 pandanus (screwpine) leaf

150g/5oz/3/4 cup palm sugar (jaggery)

2.5ml/1/2 tsp salt

3 bananas, cut into thick diagonal slices

1 Pour the coconut milk into a heavy pan and slowly bring it to the boil, taking care not to scald the bottom of the pan.

2 Stir the pumpkin, sweet potatoes and pandanus leaf into the pan of coconut milk. Continue to boil for 1 minute, then reduce the heat and simmer for about 15 minutes, until the pumpkin and sweet potato are tender but not too soft.

3 Using a slotted spoon, lift the pumpkin and sweet potato pieces out of the coconut milk and put them on a plate.

4 Add the sugar and salt to the coconut milk and stir until the sugar has dissolved.

5 Return the pan to the heat and bring the sweetened coconut milk to the boil, then reduce the heat and simmer for 5 minutes.

6 Add the bananas to the sweetened coconut milk and simmer for 4 minutes.

7 Put the pumpkin and sweet potato back into the pan and gently mix all the ingredients together. Remove the pandanus leaf and serve warm.

Pratie Potato and Apple Cake

This farmhouse classic is the perfect indulgent recipe for high tea, especially when using home-grown apples in autumn. The mashed potato dough is filled with deliciously sweet apples dredged in sugar, butter and lemon juice. A truly comforting tea-time treat.

Makes 2 farls; Serves 4–6

450g/1lb cooked potatoes in their skins, preferably still warm

pinch of salt

25g/1oz/2 tbsp butter, melted

about 115g/4oz/1 cup plain (all-purpose) flour

For the filling

3 large or 4 small cooking apples, such as Bramley's Seedlings

a little lemon juice (optional)

about 50g/2oz/1/4 cup butter in thin slices

50–115g/2–4oz/1/4 – generous 1/2 cup caster (superfine) sugar, or to taste

1 Preheat the oven to 200°C/400°F/Gas 6. Peel the potatoes and mash them in a large heavy pan until very smooth. Season to taste with the salt, and drizzle the melted butter over. Knead in as much plain flour as necessary to make a pliable dough. The dough should be elastic enough to roll out, but do not knead more than necessary.

2 Roll the potato mixture out on a lightly floured surface into a large circle and cut into four farls (triangular pieces).

3 To make the filling, peel, core and slice the apples and pile slices of the raw apple on to two of the farls. Sprinkle the apple with a little lemon juice, if you like. Dampen the edges of the farls with water or melted butter, place the other two on top, and press with your fingers around the edges to seal them together. For a less rustic finish, press round the edges, with a fork. Cook the farls in the preheated oven for about 15–20 minutes until browned.

4 Slit each cake around the side and turn the top back. Lay thin slices of butter over the apples, until they are almost covered, and then sweeten with sugar. Replace the top and return to the oven until the butter and sugar have melted to make a sauce. Cut each farl into pieces and serve.

Pumpkin in Coconut Energy 249kcal/1063kJ; Protein 2.6g; Carbohydrate 61.4g, of which sugars 51.7g; Fat 1g, of which saturates 0.5g; Cholesterol 0mg; Calcium 97mg; Fibre 2.8g; Sodium 187mg.
Pratie Apple Cake Energy 786kcal/3307kJ; Protein 9.5g; Carbohydrate 121.9g, of which sugars 40.5g; Fat 32.4g, of which saturates 19.9g; Cholesterol 80mg; Calcium 117mg; Fibre 6.1g; Sodium 253mg.

Chocolate Potato Cake

Mashed potato makes this cake moist and delicious.

Makes one 23cm/9in cake

200g/7oz/1 cup sugar
250g/9oz/1 cup and 2 tbsp butter
4 eggs, separated
275g/10oz dark
  (bittersweet) chocolate
75g/3oz/³⁄₄ cup ground almonds
165g/5¹⁄₂oz mashed potato
225g/8oz/2 cups self-raising
  (self-rising) flour
5ml/1 tsp cinnamon
45ml/3 tbsp milk
white and dark (bittersweet)
  chocolate shavings, to garnish
whipped cream, to serve

1 Preheat the oven to 180°C/350°F/Gas 4. Grease and line a 23cm/9in round cake tin (pan) with baking parchment.

2 In a bowl, cream together the sugar and 225g/8oz/1 cup of the butter until light and fluffy. Then beat the egg yolks into the creamed mixture one at a time until it is smooth and creamy.

3 Finely chop or grate 175g/6oz of the chocolate and stir it into the creamed mixture with the ground almonds. Pass the mashed potato through a sieve (strainer) or ricer and stir it into the creamed chocolate mixture. Sift together the flour and cinnamon and fold into the mixture with the milk.

4 Whisk the egg whites until they hold stiff but not dry peaks, and fold into the cake mixture.

5 Spoon into the tin (pan) and smooth the top, but make a slight hollow in the middle to keep the surface of the cake level while cooking. Bake in the oven for 1¼ hours, until a skewer inserted in the centre comes out clean. Allow the cake to cool slightly in the tin, then turn out and cool on a wire rack.

6 Break up the remaining chocolate into a heatproof bowl over a pan of hot water. Add the remaining butter in small pieces and stir until the mixture is smooth and glossy.

7 Peel off the lining paper and trim the top of the cake so it is level. Smooth over the chocolate icing. When set, decorate with the chocolate shavings and serve with whipped cream.

Steamed Cake with Sweet Potatoes

This soft steamed cake, known as mushi-kasutera in Japan, is not too sweet, and can be eaten almost like bread. The secret is a little miso, which adds a delicious and subtle saltiness to the cake.

Serves 4

200g/7oz/scant 2 cups plain
  (all-purpose) flour
140g/4³⁄₄oz/scant ³⁄₄ cup caster
  (superfine) sugar
45ml/3 tbsp sweetened
  condensed milk
4 eggs, beaten
40g/1¹⁄₂oz shiro miso
150g/5oz sweet potatoes
10ml/2 tsp cream of tartar
2.5ml/¹⁄₂ tsp bicarbonate of soda
  (baking soda)
30ml/2 tbsp melted butter

1 Sift the flour and the sugar together into a large mixing bowl. In a separate bowl, beat the condensed milk, eggs and shiro miso together to make a smooth cream.

2 Add the cream mixture to the flour and mix until well combined. Cover the bowl with clear film (plastic wrap) and leave to rest for 1 hour.

3 Trim the hard end of the sweet potatoes and thinly peel, then cut into 2cm/³⁄₄in dice. Cover with water to prevent discolouring. Drain just before using. Preheat the steamer, and line with muslin (cheesecloth).

4 In a bowl, mix the cream of tartar and bicarbonate of soda with 15ml/1 tbsp water. Add the mixture to the cake mixture along with the melted butter and two-thirds of the diced sweet potato.

5 Carefully pour the cake mixture into the steamer, then push the rest of the sweet potato on to the surface of the cake.

6 Steam the cake for 30 minutes, or until risen to a dome shape. Remove from the heat and cool a little. Serve warm or cold, cut into wedges.

Chocolate Cake Energy 5749kcal/24,034kJ; Protein 87.1g; Carbohydrate 590.9g, of which sugars 391.8g; Fat 354.8g, of which saturates 188.1g; Cholesterol 1465mg; Calcium 1408mg; Fibre 21.5g; Sodium 2731mg.
Steamed Cake Energy 512kcal/2165kJ; Protein 12.9g; Carbohydrate 90.5g, of which sugars 46.5g; Fat 13.6g, of which saturates 6.3g; Cholesterol 210mg; Calcium 162mg; Fibre 2.5g; Sodium 862mg.

Savoury Potato Drop Scones

A light scone with a mild mustard and cheese flavour, these make a delicious breakfast dish served with scrambled eggs and juicy grilled tomatoes.

Makes 16

175g/6oz floury potatoes, diced
5ml/1 tsp mustard powder
115g/4oz/1 cup self-raising (self-rising) flour
1 egg, beaten
25g/1oz/¼ cup Cheddar cheese, grated
150ml/¼ pint/⅔ cup milk
oil, for frying and greasing
salt and ground black pepper
butter, to serve

1 Put the potato in a large pan. Add water to cover and bring to the boil, then simmer for about 15 minutes, or until the potatoes are tender, but do not let them get too soft.

2 Drain the potatoes thoroughly and then return to the pan. Mash with a potato masher or pass through a potato ricer or food mill into the pan.

3 Spoon the mashed potato from the pan into a large mixing bowl and then add the mustard powder, flour, egg, grated cheese and milk.

4 Beat well until the mixture comes together. Season with salt and ground black pepper.

5 Heat a griddle pan and brush lightly with oil. Drop generous tablespoonfuls of the mixture on to the griddle and cook for 1–2 minutes until browned on the underside. Flip the scones over and cook the second side. Repeat to make 16 scones. Serve warm with butter.

Cook's Tip
It is best to use a flat griddle rather than one with ridges for this recipe as the scones are quite small and thin. If you don't have a griddle, then a frying pan with a heavy base will work just as well.

Dill and Potato Scones

Potato scones flavoured with dill are quite scrumptious and can be served warm just with butter. Or if you want to make them substantial enough for a light supper, serve them topped with flaked salmon, kipper or mackerel.

oil, for greasing
225g/8oz/2 cups self-raising (self-rising) flour
40g/1½oz/3 tbsp butter, softened
pinch of salt
15ml/1 tbsp finely chopped fresh dill
30–45ml/2–3 tbsp milk

Makes about 10

175g/6oz potato, peeled and cut into chunks

1 Put the potato in a large pan. Add water to cover and bring to the boil, then simmer for about 15 minutes, or until the potatoes are tender, but do not let them get too soft. Drain thoroughly and then mash with a potato masher or pass through a potato ricer and set aside.

2 Preheat the oven to 230°C/450°F/Gas 8. Grease a baking sheet. Sift the flour into a bowl, and rub in the butter with your fingertips. Add the salt and dill and stir.

3 Add the mashed potato to the mixture and enough milk to make a soft, pliable dough.

4 Turn out the dough on to a well-floured surface and roll out until it is fairly thin. Cut into rounds using a 7.5cm/3in cutter.

5 Place the scones on the prepared baking sheet, leaving space between each one, and bake for 20–25 minutes until risen and golden. Serve warm.

Cook's Tip
If you don't have any dill you can replace it with the herb of your choice. Try fresh parsley or basil as an alternative.

Potato Drop Scones Energy 59kcal/249kJ; Protein 1.9g; Carbohydrate 7.7g, of which sugars 0.7g; Fat 2.5g, of which saturates 0.7g; Cholesterol 14mg; Calcium 50mg; Fibre 0.3g; Sodium 48mg.
Dill and Potato Scones Energy 118kcal/499kJ; Protein 2.5g; Carbohydrate 20.1g, of which sugars 0.8g; Fat 3.7g, of which saturates 2.3g; Cholesterol 9mg; Calcium 86mg; Fibre 0.9g; Sodium 115mg.

Irish Griddle Potato Scones

These are also called potato cakes or griddle cakes, but whatever you call them they are delicious served hot with butter and jam, or with bacon for a hearty and sustaining breakfast.

Makes 6

225g/8oz floury potatoes, cut into
   uniform chunks
115g/4oz/1 cup plain
   (all-purpose) flour
2.5ml/½ tsp salt
2.5ml/½ tsp baking powder
50g/2oz/4 tbsp butter, diced
25ml/1½ tbsp milk
bacon rashers (strips), to serve
butter, for greasing

1 Cook the potatoes in a pan of boiling water until tender.

2 Drain the potatoes and return them to the pan over a high heat. Using a wooden spoon, stir the potatoes for 1 minute until all traces of moisture have evaporated. Remove from the heat. Mash well, making sure there are no lumps.

3 Sift together the flour, salt and baking powder into a bowl. Rub in the butter with your fingertips until it has the consistency of fine breadcrumbs.

4 Add the mashed potatoes and mix thoroughly with a fork. Make a well in the centre and pour in the milk. Mix to form a smooth dough.

5 Turn out on to a lightly floured surface and knead gently for about 5 minutes until soft and pliable. Roll out to a round about 5mm/¼in thick. Cut in half, then cut each half into three wedges.

6 Before you cook the scones, fry a batch of bacon rashers to serve with them. Keep warm in a low oven, until the scones are ready.

7 Grease a griddle or frying pan with a little butter and heat until very hot. Add the cakes and fry for 3–4 minutes until golden brown on both sides, turning once. Serve hot with the bacon rashers.

Chive and Potato Scones

These little potato scones should be fairly thin, soft and crisp on the outside. Serve them for breakfast.

Makes 20

450g/1lb potatoes
115g/4oz/1 cup plain
   (all-purpose) flour, sifted
30ml/2 tbsp olive oil
30ml/2 tbsp chopped chives
salt and freshly ground black pepper
low fat spread, for
   topping (optional)

1 Put the potatoes in a large pan. Add water to cover and bring to the boil. Add salt, then simmer for about 15 minutes, or until the potatoes are tender. Drain the potatoes thoroughly in a colander.

2 Return the potatoes to the clean pan and mash them with a masher or pass through a potato ricer. Preheat a griddle or heavy frying pan.

3 Add the flour, olive oil and chopped chives with a little salt and black pepper to the hot mashed potato in the pan. Mix to a soft dough.

4 Roll out the dough on a well-floured surface to a thickness of 5 mm/¼ in and stamp out rounds with a 5cm/2in plain pastry (cookie) cutter. Lightly grease the griddle or frying pan with a little oil.

5 Cook the scones, in batches, on the hot griddle or frying pan for about 10 minutes, turning once, until they are golden brown on both sides. Keep the heat low.

6 Top the scones with a little low-fat spread, if you like, and serve immediately.

> **Cook's Tip**
> Cooking the scones over a low heat ensures that the outsides do not become burnt before the insides of the scones are cooked through.

Irish Griddle Scones Energy 155kcal/650kJ; Protein 2.6g; Carbohydrate 21.1g, of which sugars 1g; Fat 7.2g, of which saturates 4.6g; Cholesterol 19mg; Calcium 35mg; Fibre 1g; Sodium 70mg.
Chive and Potato Scones Energy 45kcal/191kJ; Protein 0.9g; Carbohydrate 8.1g, of which sugars 0.4g; Fat 1.2g, of which saturates 0.2g; Cholesterol 0mg; Calcium 9mg; Fibre 0.4g; Sodium 3mg.

Savoury Cranberry and Potato Bread Slice

An interesting combination of cranberries with bacon and potatoes.

Makes a 450g/1lb loaf

450g/1lb/4 cups strong white bread flour
5ml/1 tsp easy-blend (rapid-rise) dried yeast
5ml/1 tsp salt
25g/1oz/2 tbsp butter, diced

325ml/11fl oz/1⅓ cups lukewarm water
75g/3oz/¾ cup fresh or frozen cranberries, thawed
oil, for greasing
225g/8oz floury potatoes, halved
6 rashers (strips) rindless streaky (fatty) bacon, chopped
30ml/2 tbsp runny honey
salt and ground black pepper

1 Sift the flour into a bowl, stir in the yeast and 5ml/1 tsp salt. Rub in the butter to form breadcrumbs. Make a well in the centre and stir in the water.

2 Bring the mixture together with a round-bladed knife and then turn out on to a floured surface. Knead for 5 minutes. Place the dough in a bowl and cover with a damp cloth. Leave to rise for 1 hour or until doubled in size.

3 Turn the dough out and knock back (punch down) to remove the air bubbles. Knead for a few minutes. Carefully knead the cranberries into the bread. Roll the dough out to a rectangle and place in an oiled 23 × 23cm/9 × 9in flan tin (pan). Push the dough into the corners and cover with a damp cloth. Leave to rise in a warm place for 30 minutes.

4 Preheat the oven to 220°C/425°F/Gas 7. Meanwhile, boil the potatoes in plenty of salted water for 15 minutes or until just tender. Drain and when cool enough to handle, slice thinly.

5 Sprinkle the potatoes and bacon over the risen bread dough, season, then drizzle with the honey and bake for 25 minutes, covering the bread loosely with foil after 20 minutes to prevent burning. Remove the bread from the oven, transfer to a wire rack and leave to cool.

Russian Potato Bread

This lovely, moist potato loaf is delicious just served with butter. This easy-to-make bread also keeps really well.

Makes 1 loaf

butter, for greasing
225g/8oz floury potatoes, diced
6g/¼oz sachet easy-blend (rapid-rise) dried yeast

350g/12oz/3 cups unbleached white bread flour
115g/4oz/1 cup wholemeal (whole-wheat) bread flour, plus extra for sprinkling
2.5ml/½ tsp caraway seeds, crushed
10ml/2 tsp salt
25g/1oz/2 tbsp butter, diced

1 Lightly grease a baking sheet. Cook the potatoes in boiling water until tender. Drain well, reserving 150ml/¼ pint/⅔ cup of the cooking water. Mash the potatoes and leave to cool.

2 Mix together the yeast, white bread flour, wholemeal bread flour, caraway seeds and salt in a large bowl. Add the butter, cut into small pieces and rub in to form a breadcrumb consistency.

3 Mix together the reserved potato water and sieved potatoes. Gradually work this mixture into the flour mixture to form a soft dough. Turn out on to a lightly floured surface and knead for 8–10 minutes until smooth and elastic.

4 Place the dough in a large, lightly oiled bowl, cover with lightly oiled clear film (plastic wrap) and leave to rise, in a warm place, for about 1 hour, or until it has doubled in size.

5 Turn out on to a floured surface and knead gently. Shape into a plump oval loaf about 18cm/7in long. Place on the prepared baking sheet and sprinkle with a little wholemeal flour. Cover with lightly oiled clear film and leave to rise, in a warm place, for 30 minutes, or until doubled in size.

6 Meanwhile, preheat the oven to 200°C/400°F/Gas 6. Using a sharp knife, slash the top with 3–4 diagonal cuts to make a criss-cross effect. Bake for 30–35 minutes until golden and hollow sounding when tapped on the base. Transfer to a wire rack to cool.

Cranberry Bread Energy 2196kcal/9292kJ; Protein 58.4g; Carbohydrate 415.5g, of which sugars 39.3g; Fat 44.7g, of which saturates 20.8g; Cholesterol 106mg; Calcium 657mg; Fibre 17.4g; Sodium 3141mg.
Russian Bread Energy 1893kcal/8026kJ; Protein 51.5g; Carbohydrate 381.8g, of which sugars 10.7g; Fat 28.3g, of which saturates 14.3g; Cholesterol 53mg; Calcium 553mg; Fibre 23.4g; Sodium 4120mg.

Sweet Potato Bread with Cinnamon and Walnuts

A wonderful sweet potato brunch dish, completely delicious served with crispy bacon for a hearty breakfast.

Makes a 900g/2lb loaf
1 medium sweet potato
5ml/1 tsp ground cinnamon
450g/1lb/4 cups strong white
   bread flour
5ml/1 tsp easy-blend (rapid-rise)
   dried yeast
50g/2oz/³⁄₂ cup walnut pieces
300ml/½ pint/1¼ cups
   warmed milk
salt and ground black pepper
oil, for greasing

1 Boil the whole potato in its skin in a pan of lightly salted water for 20–30 minutes or until tender.

2 Meanwhile, sift the cinnamon and flour together into a large bowl. Stir in the dried yeast.

3 Drain the potato and cool in cold water, then peel the skin. Mash the potato with a fork and mix into the dry ingredients with the nuts. Make a well in the centre and pour in the milk. Bring the mixture together with a round-bladed knife, place on a floured surface and knead for 5 minutes.

4 Return the dough to a bowl and cover with a damp cloth. Leave to rise for 1 hour or until doubled in size.

5 Turn the dough out and knock back (punch down) to remove any air bubbles. Knead again for a few minutes. If the dough feels sticky, add more flour to the mixture.

6 Shape the dough into a ball and place the bread in an oiled and lined 900g/2lb loaf tin (pan). Cover with a damp cloth and leave to rise in a warm place for 1 hour or until doubled in size.

7 Preheat the oven to 200°C/400°F/Gas 6. Bake on the middle shelf of the oven for 25 minutes. Turn out and tap the base; if it sounds hollow the bread is cooked. Cool on a wire rack.

Cheese and Onion Potato Bread

A braided potato and olive loaf with a crisp cheese and onion topping.

Makes a 900g/2lb loaf
225g/8oz floury potatoes
350g/12oz/3 cups strong white
   bread flour
7.5ml/1½ tsp easy-blend
   (rapid-rise) dried yeast
25g/1oz/2 tbsp butter, diced
50g/2oz/½ cup pitted green or
   black olives

For the topping
30ml/2 tbsp olive oil
1 onion, sliced into rings
50g/2oz/½ cup mature (sharp)
   Cheddar cheese, grated
salt and ground black pepper

1 Chop the potatoes and cook in a large pan with plenty of salted boiling water for 15–20 minutes or until tender.

2 Meanwhile, sift the flour into a bowl, add the yeast and a little salt. Rub in the butter to form fine crumbs. Drain the potatoes and mash well. Add to the dry ingredients with 300ml/½ pint/1¼ cups lukewarm water.

3 Bring the mixture together with a round-bladed knife and then turn out on to a floured surface. Knead for about 5 minutes. Return the dough to the bowl and cover with a damp cloth. Leave to rise for 1 hour or until doubled in size. Turn the dough out on to a floured surface and knock back (punch down) to remove any air bubbles. Carefully knead in the olives. Cut the dough into three even pieces.

4 Roll each piece out to a long thick sausage. Twist the sausages over each other to form a plait. Lift on to a greased baking sheet. Cover with a damp cloth and leave to rise for 30 minutes or until doubled in size.

5 Preheat the oven to 220°C/425°F/Gas 7. Heat the oil in a pan and fry the onions for 10 minutes, stirring occasionally, until golden. Remove the onions from the pan and drain well on kitchen paper.

6 Sprinkle the onions and grated cheese over the bread and bake for 20 minutes until golden. Serve warm or cold.

Sweet Potato Bread Energy 87kcal/372kJ; Protein 2.5g; Carbohydrate 19.3g, of which sugars 2.4g; Fat 0.6g, of which saturates 0.2g; Cholesterol 1mg; Calcium 50mg; Fibre 1g; Sodium 16mg.
Cheese Potato Bread Energy 231kcal/971kJ; Protein 8.7g; Carbohydrate 26.4g, of which sugars 0.8g; Fat 10.4g, of which saturates 5.2g; Cholesterol 21mg; Calcium 203mg; Fibre 1.2g; Sodium 162mg.

Index